"Colin Cooper's book is a splendid synthesis of the theory, statistics and applications of psychometrics. We are taken on a journey through this 'measurement of the human spirit', spanning basic concepts (reliability/validity), workhorse statistics (factor analyses), more recent techniques (item response theory), how to interpret test scores and, even, how to develop scales. But there is more: this is a hands-on book – each chapter comes with a datasheet on which to practice newly-acquired knowledge of psychometrics. Students, lecturers, test developers and practitioners will delight in this charming book." Professor Philip J Corr, City, University of London, UK

"What a gem of a book this is! I am delighted to recommend Colin Cooper's Psychological Testing: Theory and Practice to students, researchers, clinicians, and educators. While the book eschews unnecessary diversions into mathematical and statistical obscurities, it also steers clear of the superficial, homespun presentations that sacrifice rigour in the altar of unrewarding readability. Without a doubt, this is one of the most accessible, effective, and comprehensive introductions to psychological testing in the market today." Professor K. V. Petrides, London Psychometric Laboratory, University College London, UK

"Colin Cooper has written the 'down-to-earth' book that many of us have been waiting for on the very complex and often misunderstood field of psychology tests and assessment. It is grounded in both the established cornerstones of psychological testing and contemporary developments necessary to understand how tests are made, evaluated, and used in research and clinical assessment. This book will be of particular relevance for undergraduate and graduate university courses in psychological tests and measurement." Dr. Don Saklofske, Western University, Canada

PSYCHOLOGICAL TESTING

Psychological tests are everywhere. They are widely used by practitioners, researchers, clinicians and educators – anyone, in fact, who needs to measure various aspects of personality, cognitive abilities, mood and suchlike. Psychometrics is the science of psychological assessment. It covers the construction, use and interpretation of psychological tests of all kinds – from simple questionnaires measuring personality, moods and attitudes, through to specialised tests measuring IQ and other mental abilities.

Psychological Testing: Theory and Practice provides students, test users, test developers, practitioners and researchers from the social sciences, education and health with an evaluative guide to choosing, using, interpreting and developing tests. Its aim is to give readers a thorough grasp of the principles and limitations of testing, together with the necessary methodological detail. Unusually for an introductory text, it includes coverage of several cutting-edge techniques. If you find mathematics frightening and statistics dull, this engaging text will help you to understand the fundamental principles of psychometrics that underpin the measurement of any human characteristic using any psychological test.

The book is accompanied by additional resources, including a set of spreadsheets which use simulated data and other techniques to illustrate important issues, and allow users to understand how various statistical procedures work, without getting bogged down in mathematical detail. These are fully integrated into the text.

This is an essential introduction for all students of psychology and related disciplines, as well as a useful resource for practitioners and those seeking accreditation in psychological testing.

Dr Colin Cooper has researched and taught psychometrics and individual differences at Queen's University, Belfast for 20 years. He has published widely in these fields and has been extensively involved in test design and consultancy.

Psychological Testing

THEORY AND PRACTICE

COLIN COOPER

Routledge
Taylor & Francis Group

LONDON AND NEW YORK

First published 2019
by Routledge
2 Park Square, Milton Park, Abingdon, Oxon OX14 4RN

and by Routledge
711 Third Avenue, New York, NY 10017

Routledge is an imprint of the Taylor & Francis Group, an informa business

British Library Cataloguing-in-Publication Data
A catalogue record for this book is available from the British Library

Library of Congress Cataloging-in-Publication Data
A catalog record for this book has been requested

ISBN: 978-1-138-22888-7 (hbk)
ISBN: 978-1-138-22889-4 (pbk)
ISBN: 978-1-315-39134-2 (ebk)

Typeset in Avenir, Bell and Bembo
by Swales & Willis Ltd, Exeter, Devon, UK
Printed in Great Britain
by Bell & Bain Ltd, Glasgow

Visit the eResources: www.routledge.com/9781138228894

DEDICATION
To Wesley

CONTENTS

FIGURES

TABLES

EXERCISES AND SPREADSHEETS

Spreadsheets available at www.routledge.com/9781138228894

PREFACE

Psychological tests are everywhere. Job applicants complete personality tests and have their cognitive abilities or leadership skills assessed. Health professionals use them to assess dementia and other clinical conditions. Children may be assessed for dyslexia, developmental difficulties or behavioural problems. Researchers in psychology, medicine, education and other disciplines routinely measure self-esteem, personality, cognitive abilities, attitudes, moods, emotional states and a whole host of other characteristics. And we even complete them in our spare time to try to learn more about ourselves. But how confident can we be that the scores on such tests really tell us anything useful? How are tests constructed and used? How should test scores be used to draw inferences about people? How can we decide which tests say something meaningful and which are no more useful than reading tea leaves?

My interest in psychological assessment began in the 1970s in Exeter, when Paul Kline (the UK's first professor of psychometrics) introduced this most challenging of subjects. For psychometrics is a brave attempt to quantify all that is essentially human – our personality, mental abilities, moods and motives. What could be more important for the science and practice of psychology than that?

There are two types of psychometrics books. Some are aimed at those who plan to develop, administer and use tests, scales, questionnaires and other assessments; they may not be interested in the statistical minutiae but do need a conceptual grasp of the theory which underpins psychological tests so that they can locate, evaluate, administer, score and interpret them properly. Other books are far more technical. They are written for mathematicians rather than psychologists, are often highly specialised, bristle with fierce equations – and say little or nothing about how tests are actually used.

This book falls firmly into the first category. It is designed to give anyone who uses or develops tests a sound, fairly detailed and up-to-date grasp of the principles of psychological assessment – together with suggestions of how tests may be developed and used in real life and how techniques such as factor analysis may be used to build hierarchical models of ability and personality, how it can be used to develop mood scales and so on. Although some of the basic theory underlying test use was developed half a century ago, new developments are continually being made. As well as covering the basics, this book also considers new developments, such as item response theory, alternatives to coefficient alpha for calculating reliability, and parallel analysis. It also considers (and attempts to evaluate) some devastating criticisms of the whole rationale of psychological assessment from Joel Michell.

What makes this book unique is its 'hands on' approach. Rather than showing equations (which experience tells me 9/10 students will ignore) most chapters are accompanied by some simple-to-use spreadsheets which are available for Open Office and Microsoft Excel. They have three purposes. Some of them show how commonly used techniques work; the spreadsheet which performs factor rotation in factor analysis, for example. Some use simulated data to demonstrate an important point – for example, to show how test length influences reliability. And some of the spreadsheets are utilities; they compute statistics and perform analyses which most statistical packages ignore. Thus one spreadsheet computes a whole range of different types of correlations between dichotomous (two-valued) variables. Another scores questionnaires. A third performs item analysis to identify and remove under-performing items; there are others, too. All the spreadsheets are integrated into the text in the form of exercises with clear instructions and learning outcomes.

My aim in writing this book was to encourage test users and test developers to

- think carefully about what to measure and why;
- appreciate how to locate, evaluate, use score and interpret appropriate tests;
- be able to use factor analyses to inter-relate results from several studies;
- see how test scores may be used as part of a personnel selection procedure;
- appreciate that at the end of the day, psychometric tests are fairly crude (albeit useful) devices whose scores are rather different from proper scientific measurements;
- recognise that even well-regarded tests used to assess individuals are quite capable of producing misleading results.

Thanks are due to several people. Several generations of undergraduate and graduate students at Queen's University, Belfast, taught me how to teach psychometrics, whilst I was trying to teach them psychometrics. Ceri McLardy and Sophie Crowe at Routledge were enormously helpful, supportive and tolerant of missed deadlines. And of course, special thanks to Wesley – for his unflagging support, love and help.

EXERCISES AND SPREADSHEETS

The spreadsheets which accompany this book use either Open Office or Microsoft Excel. Open Office is free to download and use, and runs on most platforms including MacOS, Windows and Linux. It may be downloaded from https://www.openoffice. org/. The spreadsheets and links to other software referenced in the text may be downloaded from www.routledge.com/9781138228894. The spreadsheets do not use macros, Active-X or other extensions and so should run in most environments. Some run perfectly well on mobile devices, whilst those which involve heavy computation or interactive graphics will need a laptop or desktop machine.

CHAPTER 1
INTRODUCTION TO
PSYCHOMETRICS

Psychometrics translates as 'the measurement of the human spirit', and it is hard to think of any more ambitious project than this in psychology – nor one which is of more practical use. For, as we shall see, psychological tests are widely used by practitioners, researchers, clinicians, educators and others – anyone, in fact, who needs to measure various aspects of personality, cognitive abilities, interests, motivation, mood and suchlike, using questionnaires, tests or measures of human or animal performance. Despite the wide range of characteristics being measured by tests, most test users need to know the same basic things.

- What do tests measure?
- What types of tests are there?
- How can I find a test?
- How should tests be administered and scored?
- How should these scores be interpreted? For example, how can I tell whether a score of 20 on a particular test is low, average or above-average?
- How confident can I be that the test measures what it *claims* to measure? For example, do people's scores on a test of anxiety accurately reflect their true levels of anxiety and not something else?
- How much measurement error is associated with people's scores on the test? If a test tells me that someone has an IQ of 110, could their IQ really be as high as 130? Or as low as 95?
- Are the scores on this test influenced by other things? For example, if a personality test is given to job applicants, will they try to distort their scores in order to get the job? Will anxiety affect performance on a test used for academic selection?
- When searching for a test, how can I evaluate whether a particular test has been well developed?
- How can I develop a test myself?

- Are there any useful statistical tips and tricks which will help me interpret and use test scores?
- What is factor analysis and how is it used?
- How can I use test scores in order to predict behaviour?
- How is it possible to give people different items yet still be able to compare their scores?
- Is it reasonable to add up people's scores on various test items and interpret this total score?
- Can anyone just think of a concept ('egocentric optimism', for example) and develop a test for it? Should we develop tests which measure the important ways in which people really *do* differ, rather than inventing more and more?

This book is written to help students, test administrators, test users, practitioners and researchers to gain a conceptual understanding of all of these issues. It will also be useful for those seeking to obtain professional qualifications in test use. It introduces fundamental concepts and techniques such as test design, test administration, test scoring, reliability, validity, item-writing, item analysis, factor analysis and item response theory, the aim being that readers will be able to identify and/or develop a test or other measurement instrument appropriate for their needs, evaluate its technical merits, administer and score it. It also suggests how tests of personality, abilities, mood and motivation may be developed and validated. Finally, readers will then be guided in how the test scores may be used for a number of practical applications.

Unusually, perhaps, this book also alerts readers to Michell's (1997a) devastating critique of psychological assessment, which argues that test construction (by any method) has no sound scientific basis and that test scores are essentially meaningless; they have the mere pretence of being a science. It also considers Cattell's (1973) comments regarding 'source traits', and whether it is possible to identify traits which correspond to real individual differences in the way in which people function (perhaps caused by differences in development, biological makeup or social experiences) rather than personality traits which are social constructions and are *assumed* to exist without any real evidence.

Having taught the principles of psychological assessment to students, graduate students and professionals for 30 years, two things stand out in my memory.

First, psychologists and other test users generally do not love mathematics or statistics. This is unfortunate, as psychometrics is essentially a rather specialised branch of statistics: journals such as *Psychometrika* and *Applied Psychological Measurement* contain cutting-edge papers which require considerable mathematical sophistication, and most psychometric texts also contain enough formulae to thoroughly frighten most psychologists and test users. This book therefore contains as few formulae as possible and is emphatically not a statistics text. It instead aims to give readers a conceptual grasp of the main issues. Whilst it does assume that readers have at some stage been exposed to correlations, t-tests and so on, it does not require a detailed knowledge of these techniques.

Second, it often seemed to me that students only really understood psychometric concepts when they rolled up their sleeves, got their hands dirty and actually analysed some data. I have tried to follow the same approach when writing this book. For this reason, the book should be read in conjunction with the specially prepared spreadsheets. Rather than showing formulae in the text, it is far more interesting to allow readers to see for themselves how numbers behave. My feeling is that this will give a deeper level of understanding than most of us could acquire from examining (or more probably, ignoring) a printed formula. Some of these spreadsheets may also be useful for everyday analyses – although no guarantee is given as to their freedom from error.

WHO NEEDS TESTS?

Psychological tests and assessments are widely used by practitioners – professionals such as clinical, educational, occupational, sport and forensic psychologists. They are also widely used by researchers and students in psychology and other disciplines, and by organisations seeking to select the most promising applicants or candidates for promotion.

Different types of test users face different issues when selecting, administering, scoring and interpreting the results from tests, and the following pages outline a little about how tests are used in the real world – along with some mention of the pitfalls which test users will encounter.

PRACTITIONERS

Tests may be used for the guidance and assessment of individuals, often in medical, clinical or educational settings. An educational psychologist may use a test to help them determine whether a child's verbal skills are substantially weaker than their other reasoning skills, which may suggest a diagnosis of dyslexia. A clinical psychologist may ask the carers of children with behavioural problems to rate their behaviour using a standard checklist in order to determine the areas of concern and their severity. Or the psychologist may give a screening test to help them determine whether a child shows signs of autism. A physician may use a screening test to help them evaluate whether an elderly patient shows signs of cognitive decline, or symptoms of depression. And (controversially) a teacher may try to assess the preferred learning styles of children in their class in an attempt to identify which children are 'linguistic', which are 'spatial', which are 'kinaesthetic' and so on, so that the style of teaching to which each child is exposed is chosen to match their learning style. Sports psychologists try to assess motivation, mental toughness, self-efficacy (self belief) and so on. Health psychologists may need to measure how much pain a person experiences or how well they understand the information given them by a medical practitioner – and there are many other examples of test use, too.

Occupational psychologists (sometimes called 'industrial psychologists', or 'organisational psychologists' in the USA) will often use tests as part of a screening process to help them select which job applicants to invite for interview. Tests tend to be used when selecting the wrong person for the job would have major financial or other consequences. Senior executives may be hauled away to an assessment centre where occupational psychologists will assess their leadership styles, creativity and a host of other characteristics which may help to determine whether they become the next chief executive officer or president of a company.

Forensic psychologists may also use tests, for example, in order to determine whether someone who is accused of a crime is able to distinguish between right and wrong or whether they are likely to be able to understand the court proceedings, give instructions to their legal representative and so on – 'fitness to plead' in English law. They may also try to use tests to help them make difficult decisions about individuals, such as whether a dangerous prisoner has reformed enough to be freed. This is problematical, as one of the main characteristics of psychopaths is their tendency to lie!

The key point is that all of these practitioners will seek to make accurate assessments of individuals using data which they have probably collected themselves. They will almost invariably compare an individual's scores with 'norms' to determine (for example) whether a person's score on a test measuring depression is so high that they may wish to discuss therapy or some other intervention or whether an individual's profile of cognitive and psychomotor skills suggests that they are likely to be able to learn to fly an aircraft. The practitioners will probably use only widely known, well-constructed tests whose content, foibles, limitations and properties are well documented. They will also follow guidelines as to which instruments are suitable for the person being assessed (in terms of age, language skills, freedom from bias, acceptability etc.) and will usually assess individuals face to face, one-to-one – an expensive and often time-consuming process.

These test users will probably need to attend courses approved by the test publisher and/or undergo a period of supervision to train them in the administration, scoring and interpretation of the tests which they plan to use; evidence of such training is normally required before test materials will be sold to an individual. There are good reasons for this requirement. For example, if part of a test times how long it takes a child to assemble a four-piece jigsaw, it is obvious that the four pieces need to be presented to every child in the same initial positions, otherwise the test will be easier for some children than for others: test users will need to be trained so that children's scores may be compared, no matter by whom they are tested. Or suppose that vocabulary is assessed using an item such as 'What is a kitten?' It might seem obvious that the correct answer is 'a young cat' – but what should the test administrator do if the child says, 'a sort of cat' or 'a cat'? If some administrators treat 'a sort of cat' as being correct, whilst others treat it as incorrect, or if some administrators encourage the child to elaborate on their answer whereas others do not, then it should be obvious that the scores on the test will not be accurate for all children. So, tests such as these require specific training.

However, these practitioners will need a general understanding of the logic of how psychological assessments work, with particular focus on issues such as scaling (converting scores into an 'IQ', for example), the accuracy of assessments and issues such as cultural sensitivity, which is why they have an interest in this book. All of these test users will want to know something about 'reliability', 'validity' and 'bias', principles for selecting and using, administering and scoring a test, and the merits and limitations of psychometric assessment.

A note of caution is needed, however, as just looking at a test cannot always reveal whether it measures anything useful. During my consultancy work, I have seen several tests that have been sold to government departments and private businesses which are slickly presented (and *very* expensive) but which lack evidence to suggest that they actually measure anything of worth. Well-designed tests, on the other hand, can be enormously useful to organisations. Kanfer et al. (1995) suggest that

> Companies have unarguably saved billions of dollars by using ability tests to assure a merit-based selection process . . . Overall, tests of intellectual abilities are the single most predictive element in employee selection . . . and certainly more valid than the use of personal interviews . . . in predicting training and on-the-job success.
>
> (597)

Nevertheless, some degree of technical knowledge, coupled with a healthy scepticism is essential. Caveat emptor – let the buyer beware!

RESEARCHERS AND STUDENTS WHO RELATE TEST SCORES TO BEHAVIOUR

The second group of test users are students or researchers who do not claim to be experts in the psychology of individual differences. Their prime interest might be in social psychology – for example, studying whether being a member of a minority group affects feelings of self-worth. They will therefore need to find some way of measuring 'self-worth'. They might be geneticists, health or medical researchers, perhaps linking variations in DNA (at the molecular level) to individual differences in depression, aggression or perfectionism. Or they could be developmental psychologists keen to determine whether a programme of environmental enrichment improves scores on some trait (intelligence or anxiety, perhaps) relative to the scores of a control group. Another researcher may wish to test whether stimulating an area of the brain with a substantial magnetic field (transcranial magnetic stimulation) has an effect on some aspect of cognitive performance and so will need to be able to measure the appropriate cognitive abilities as accurately as possible. Even behaviourists sometimes use tests; personality scales have been developed which supposedly measure how quickly a person will condition, following positive and negative reinforcement. Others may want to determine whether stand-up comedians differ from the rest of us in terms of several personality traits, whether romantic partners tend to have similar personalities, whether children who are bullied in childhood lack self-confidence as adults or whether caffeine improves working memory. Tests may also be used to measure transient moods or emotions – 'states' rather than traits. For example, tests measuring the main moods may be administered on multiple occasions to determine whether the extent to which a person's moods vary over time is related to their personality, to examine how various classes of life events affect stress levels, and so on. The key point is that almost all psychological research involves some kind of psychological questionnaire, test or assessment. If these measurements are not accurate, then either the research will fail to show anything or the conclusions may be misleading.

Researchers who link test scores to behaviour are not interested in assessing or understanding individuals. The primary interest of these researchers is not the prediction of individuals' scores for practical purposes. They instead want to determine whether scores on some psychological test differ significantly between groups of people – for example, whether the environmental enrichment programme improves children's levels of intelligence relative to a control group of children who do not receive the intervention.

Such researchers are in a more difficult position than the practitioners. Practitioners need to use top-quality commercial tests which are widely used and are capable of providing accurate assessments when properly administered to appropriate individuals. However, many of the tests which are available to measure other individual differences will not have not gone through much in the way of quality control. The test items will often be printed as appendices to journal articles, and it is up to the individual researcher to evaluate the quality of the test before using it. How can one know whether a test which seemed to be marginally acceptable when it was developed with 15-year-old inner-city students in Chicago 20 years ago will give sensible results if it is administered to British job applicants? No one can know for sure, and so the researcher will need to perform some analyses on the data to check whether all (or at least some) of the test items seem to perform satisfactorily.

All too often it seems that the main reason for using a particular test is because other researchers do so, which can lead to the continued and uncritical use of some really rather suspect measures, particularly in social psychology. Readers who are in this position will want to use this book to help them identify for themselves whether a particular test is likely to measure what it claims to, whether it is likely to be useful for a particular application with a particular sample of people, how to check whether it performs properly when used in a different context and how the scores should be interpreted.

RESEARCHERS WHO RELATE TEST SCORES TO OTHER TEST SCORES

Members of the third group are psychologists, often personality psychologists or social psychologists, who are mainly interested in the inter-relationship between two or more traits, each of which is measured by some scale. Rather than relating test scores to things such as variations in DNA, school achievement or age, these test users relate scores on one test to scores on other tests. For example, they might study the link between self-concept and cheerfulness (both measured by questionnaires) or whether high levels of creativity are found in people who show slight signs of schizophrenia ('schizotypy'). Sometimes the concepts are rather less clear, and several variables may be involved. For example, a researcher might study whether 'sense of self-empowerment' influences 'feelings of self-esteem' and whether depression influences both of these.

The tests used by these researchers are generally not administered one-to-one. Instead they often involve questionnaires which may be administered online, on sheets of paper to a group of students in a lecture or by post. There is always a trade-off between the amount of time taken to assess a variable and the accuracy of assessment, as will be shown in Chapter 6.

In this type of research:

- The test scores are not being used to make potentially life-changing decisions about individuals but will be related to the scores of other people using correlations, structural equation modelling or other techniques.
- Participants usually volunteer to take part in such research or are coerced into doing so for some form of course credit and will often complete the questionnaires anonymously. They thus have little to lose by not fully engaging with the process.
- The researcher is often not present to answer any queries, suggest a rest-break, encourage the participant to perform their best or otherwise do their best to ensure that the questionnaires or tests are being answered carefully and honestly.
- It is not uncommon for participants to be given a whole sheaf of questionnaires (or their electronic equivalent) to complete in one session, which can be a grisly experience. It has been found that participants may start to respond randomly towards the end of a long testing session (Weirich et al., 2017), so it may be better to use shorter, potentially less-accurate assessments rather than involving participants in a long assessment session. How short can they become?

Because these researchers relate test scores to other test scores (rather than to behaviour) they encounter a rather different set of problems to those who relate scores on a test to some aspect of behaviour. First, by definition, they need to assess more than one variable – which means that the assessment session will generally be longer, which can lead to the problems with concentration, co-operation etc. noted above. Second, it is quite possible that something other than the trait that the test is supposed to measure might influence scores on both tests. For example, suppose that a researcher administers tests measuring social independence and verbal ability to a sample of teenagers and finds that there is a positive correlation. This could lead them to develop a complex theory about why verbal skills can help adolescents to develop individual identities through deeper interactions with others, or it could just be because the researcher used adolescents with a wide range of ages (say 12–18). The younger children will have lower levels of verbal skills and will also still be more dependent on their families. So the only reason that the correlation appears might be that the participants in the study differ widely with respect to age. If the researcher had tested a narrower age group (or somehow corrected statistically for the effects of age, using techniques such as partial correlation, path analysis or structural equation modelling) then they might well have found that in reality there is zero correlation between social independence and verbal ability.

It is very, very easy to fool yourself (and others) when relating scores on one test to scores on other tests – either through correlations or more complex statistical techniques. When interpreting the results from studies which involve correlating different questionnaires, one needs to be alert for problems such as these.

In the previous example, it was quite straightforward to identify that there may be a problem. The 'method' section of the journal article will report the age range of the participants, and an alert reader could realise that there might be an alternative (and simpler) explanation for the results. However, sometimes there is little or no evidence that something is amiss, because the variable which influences scores on both tests is psychological rather than physical. Suppose, for example, that a researcher examines the correlation between scores on a test measuring how highly people rate their own sense of humour and scores on a test measuring a personality trait known as Psychoticism – which basically involves enjoying hurting others, callousness etc. Suppose too that there is a significant correlation; people high on Psychoticism may tend to be humourless. What can one make of this?

The problem here might be that some people in the sample may try to give a good impression of themselves whereas others will not (this is discussed in Chapter 7). This former group will probably both report having an excellent sense of humour and claim not to have violent fantasies or hallucinations, to enjoy teasing animals etc., and so they will have low scores on the Psychoticism scale. A person's tendency to give socially desirable answers may very well affect the way they respond to the items on both of these scales. So it *might* be the case that the correlation between sense of humour and Psychoticism is found only because both are influenced by social desirability. If (as is likely) the researcher has not chosen to measure social desirability as part of the study, there is little chance that this problem will ever be detected.

My point is that a large number of personality psychologists and social psychologists build up ever more complex models, using ever more complex statistical tools, but without always being alert to the possibility that they are building these theories on a foundation of straw. For this reason, I would personally pay much more attention to studies which relate scores on a questionnaire to some aspect of behaviour rather than to scores on other questionnaires.

There is yet another problem which is widespread in the social psychology literature when researchers correlate (or perform more fancy analyses) on several scales. What if two scales contain items that are very similar? The Rosenberg self-esteem scale (Rosenberg, 1965) is a very widely used test in social psychology. So too are the Harter scales (Harter, 1988). One of the 10 items from the Rosenberg scale reads 'On the whole, I am satisfied with myself', and respondents are asked to rate how much they agree with that statement. One of the five items in the global-self-worth scale of the Harter scale (adolescent form) is '[some] teenagers are pretty pleased with themselves'; respondents are asked to rate how true that statement is for them.

As far as I can see, these items essentially ask the same question. How could someone who agreed with the question from the Rosenberg scale possibly disagree with the question from the Harter scale? Yet they are supposed to measure quite different things, and several researchers blindly correlate the scales together and interpret the correlation as if it measured something interesting. One does not need to be a psychometrician to appreciate that this is patent nonsense. If the same item appears in two different questionnaires, then this will almost certainly result in the two scales being correlated (assuming that the two scales have high reliability, a term which will be discussed in Chapter 6). Scales measuring depression also contain items that are very similar to the two mentioned above (the 10-item Beck Depression Inventory contains the item 'I do not feel like a failure', for example) – and so any research linking scores on *this* questionnaire to the Rosenberg and Harter scales must surely also be flawed.

Surely no one would be misguided enough to perform a study such as this, and surely journal editors would reject any such papers which were submitted to them? Unfortunately, this is not the case, as can be seen by performing a literature search using Web of Science or some other tool for searching the psychology literature. In order to make this point I have chosen just one item from each of three widely used questionnaires. The literature is full of studies using other scales where scores on questionnaires are correlated and interpreted without considering what items are asked. More surprisingly still this problem is little recognised. It is time to shout that the emperor wears no clothes!

But how big an issue is item overlap in practice? If one has two tests which measure quite different things (and should therefore correlate 0.0), how large does the correlation between them become if they share one or more items? Now might be as good a time as any to introduce a spreadsheet to help explore what sort of effect having one (or more) items in common can have on the correlation between two tests.

EXERCISE 1.1: CORRELATIONS CAUSED BY SHARED ITEMS

Resources required: Spreadsheet 1.1: Correlations caused by shared items. This and the other resources referenced in this book are held in a zip file, which may be downloaded from www.routledge.com/9781138228894. Versions are available for Open Office and Microsoft Excel.

Purpose: To explore how large the correlation between two tests can become if they contain one or more items which mean the same thing

Contents of spreadsheet: Simulated data from 110 people, with a normal distribution of scores on two uncorrelated scales

Suggested activity:

- Decide how many 'items' there should be in Test 1 and Test 2, and enter these values in the green cells.
- Check that the total score, shown to the right of each blue area, is calculated correctly.
- Set the number of shared items to zero.

- The yellow box shows the correlation between the total scores on Test 1 and Test 2, based on 110 simulated people.
- To generate a new set of simulated data, press f9 (Windows or Linux) or fn/f9 or CTRL/SHIFT/f9 (MacOS). Repeat 10 or so times and note the typical value for the correlation.
- Change the number of shared items – e.g., to 1 or 2. Generate another 10 or so sets of random data, and note the correlation.
- Explore how changing the length of the tests influences the size of the correlation between two tests which share 1 or more items.
- Answer the question posed in Chapter 1: how large would the correlation between two tests (one containing 5 items, the other 10 items) typically be if they have one item in common?

Points to note:

- Experiment by changing entries in the GREEN areas. Results are in the YELLOW areas.
- Simply download another copy if you accidentally change formulae.
- The simulated data representing these items appears in the blue shaded areas.
- The spreadsheet always generates data from 110 'people'.
- Correlations which are less than −0.19 or greater than 0.19 are statistically significant (P<0.05).
- The spreadsheets are not sophisticated or user-proof. For example, strange things will happen if the number of shared items is set to be larger than the number of items in a test.
- Readers who are familiar with the concept of 'reliability' may wish to experiment by changing the value of this parameter in the 'calculations' tab. Otherwise it is safe to leave it at the default value of 0.7.
- Readers who want to explore how the spreadsheet operates can click the 'calculations' tab at the bottom of the spreadsheet.

Learning outcomes:

Readers should now be able to
- appreciate how scales which share items can appear to be spuriously correlated;
- recognise that the problem can be very severe with short scales or several overlapping items.

PSYCHOMETRICIANS

The fourth group of people with an interest in testing are not psychology practitioners or researchers at all. Theoretical psychometricians typically have one or more mathematics or statistics degrees and will be keen on developing new methods of analysing data. Their work fills journals such as *Psychometrika* and *Applied Psychological Measurement* and will be of interest to those implementing new software packages – for adaptive testing for example. This is a computerised technique of test administration where each participant is given a set of items whose difficulty is carefully matched to their apparent ability; some clever mathematics allows people's scores to be compared, even though they have been given quite different sets of items. We introduce this technique in Chapter 12. Although the psychometrics literature up until the 1990s was often fairly accessible to those without mathematics degrees, test users without a strong mathematical background are likely to find modern contributions challenging, if not incomprehensible.

This book does not set out to be a detailed up-to-the-minute account of sophisticated techniques for constructing, developing, administering, scoring or evaluating tests. But, whilst it covers the old, simple, tried-and-tested methodology which has a proven track record in helping practitioners and researchers measure abilities, personality, mood and so on, it also serves as an introduction to newer developments which seem to me to be important – such as alternatives to 'coefficient alpha' for measuring reliability, Mokken scaling and item response theory. However, this is not a book on the formal, mathematical basis of psychometric theory. Although this underpins much of the content and spreadsheets, statistical formulae are kept to a bare minimum. The book also deals with topics (such as how to write good test items, and how to use test scores in practice) which psychometricians generally eschew. It seems to me that whilst it is all very well developing wonderful new ways of analysing responses to test items, if the raw data are meaningless because of poorly written items, the whole exercise is rather pointless. It will, however, give psychologists and others a basic understanding of the main issues in psychological assessment, which will allow the more mathematically sophisticated reader to explore modern developments in psychometric theory.

THOSE SEEKING SELF-KNOWLEDGE

The final group of test users will probably not read this book, though I mention them for the sake of completeness. Many books, newspapers, magazines and websites contain personality tests, quizzes and tests, and whilst some of these are obviously frivolous ('Which type of dog do you most resemble?'), others claim to assess personality, intelligence and so on. Whilst some such tests can probably give accurate results when taken under appropriate conditions (e.g., Eysenck and Wilson, 1976) the technical details which allow most such tests to be evaluated are simply not available, and so they should be treated with extreme caution. Online intelligence (IQ) tests are a particular problem, as large random samples of the population need to be tested in order to interpret the scores – and it is difficult to see how a free-to-use online site could possibly gather such data. We did so when developing the BBC's *Test the Nation* IQ tests, but that was a long, expensive process. Unless the provenance of a test is well known, it is best to be very sceptical of claims such as 'this pop star has an IQ of 180', for reasons which will be explained in Chapter 3, and to be wary of tests which claim to analyse personality through investigating which colours you prefer, your name or suchlike. Are these tests properly designed and so potentially capable of giving some accurate insights? Or are they written by a journalist without any proper development at all – which begs the question of why we bother taking them. It is possible that these assessments could actually prove harmful; if a vulnerable person or a child were to take one of these tests and feel upset about their results or be teased by others, the consequences could be tragic.

PSYCHOLOGY AND PSYCHOMETRICS

All decent tests should be linked to some kind of theory of individual differences in psychology, biology, developmental psychology, neuroscience, sociology or some other area. For example, the researcher who studies state-dependent memory (whether recall is easier if the person is in the same mood state that they were when they learned the material) needs to know what the main mood states are before they can try to measure them. They also need to know what type of memory process they should measure. For this, it is necessary to turn to previous research; just devising a test off the top of one's head is unlikely to be well received by one's peers or by reviewers of papers submitted to journals. Likewise, if we want to assess leadership styles to help us select an executive or measure a child's cognitive performance to help us decide if they are dyslexic, we need to know the number and nature of leadership styles and be able to demonstrate that they are relevant to job performance. We need to know something about how many distinct cognitive abilities there are and which patterns of cognitive abilities reflect dyslexia and which do not, in order to draw any valid conclusions about the child.

There is a two-way relationship between psychological theory and psychometrics. Sometimes psychological concepts arise from speculation, personal experience, clinical observation or some other process which is not based on the careful analyses of data. The now-popular notion of emotional intelligence originated from a 'theoretical and philosophical framework' developed in Wayne Payne's PhD thesis (Payne, 1983), rather than hard data. Likewise, Howard Gardner's (1983) model of multiple intelligences is based on a literature review which sought to identify groups of cognitive skills which appeared to resemble each other in terms of their developmental history, all being affected by damage to a particular area of the brain, and so on. And there are numerous theories of personality which have their roots in clinical observation rather than any statistical analysis; Carl Jung's 'analytical psychology' (a form of psychoanalysis) led him to suppose that people can be classified as introverts or extroverts, for example. Whilst psychometrics did not help to develop these theories, it can be used to devise measurement instruments. For example, the techniques outlined in this book have been used to develop questionnaires to measure emotional intelligence, depression, extraversion, anxiety and a huge range of other important characteristics.

Can we perform the same trick backwards? Can we use psychometric techniques to analyse a wide range of behaviours and develop a theory from this? The answer is 'perhaps'. Some psychometric techniques (notably factor analysis) have been used to develop theories about personality and mental abilities. For example, the analysis of the relationships between various tests have led Spearman, Thurstone, Cattell and Horn, and Carroll (amongst others) to develop theories about the number and nature of human cognitive abilities.

Few psychologists claim that psychometric analyses alone are enough to develop a 'model' of human behaviour. Take general intelligence as an example. It has been known for over a century that performance on all tasks which involve thought tend to correlate together positively, even if they seem to involve quite different cognitive processes. Why *is* it that people who have above-average short-term memory (for example) are also generally better than average at visualising shapes, coming up with creative solutions to problems, solving puzzles requiring logic, identifying whether two briefly presented shapes are the same or different? Psychometric analysis tells us that this is the case; it does not give us any understanding of why this happens, and this is what is needed for any proper science of psychology. In much the same way that psychologists discovered general intelligence, our prehistoric ancestors living away from the equator no doubt noticed that at some times of the year days seemed longer than others, which coincided with warmer weather etc. However, they did not have any understanding of why this happened; for this they had to wait for Copernicus and Kepler.

In order to gain a proper scientific understanding of the variables identified by psychometric techniques it is necessary to perform laboratory studies to try to build up a picture of what social, developmental, genetic, cognitive and physiological processes cause people to behave in this way. Using psychometric techniques really is just the very first step in understanding what is going on. Psychometric analyses can help psychologists identify that something interesting is there which merits study; they cannot tell us what causes it.

Although there is considerable interplay between psychometrics and theories of cognitive ability, personality, mood and motivation, this book does not attempt to cover these theories; it is not a textbook on individual differences, though some readers might wish to read it alongside a book such as Cooper (2010, 2015) which does explore these issues. Nor is it necessary to know anything about psychological theory in order to grasp the principles laid out in this book, for, although I will occasionally refer to some characteristic such as 'anxiety', 'depression' or 'intelligence' when giving examples of how a psychometric technique might be used, the examples I use are those with which every reader of this book is likely to be familiar. Thus readers from disciplines other than psychology should find few problems following the principles laid out in the following chapters.

WHAT DO TESTS MEASURE?

Tests have been developed to measure a wide range of variables – from aesthetic taste to pain sensitivity, attitudes, personality, cognitive abilities, interpersonal skills, emotional sensitivity . . . The list is almost endless. Fortunately, it is possible to categorise them and use similar techniques to develop and evaluate them.

TRAITS

Traits are an important concept in psychology. The idea of a trait is simply a disposition – a characteristic which is fairly stable over time and fairly stable from situation to situation. For example, it has been found through research that some people are more anxious than others. If we took 20 people and ranked them in order of anxiety from 1 (least anxious) to 20 (most anxious), the idea of a trait suggests that were we to go back and test these people in the same situation a few weeks or a few years later, the person ranked twentieth should still have a ranking of 20 (or nearby); they certainly should not be ranked 1 or 2. Note that this does *not* imply that situations do not affect how a person acts or feels. When put in a stressful situation, everyone's level of anxiety will rise; when relaxing at home, everyone's anxiety levels will fall. But what the idea of a trait does imply is that, within each situation, the rank ordering of people will stay roughly constant.

There are two types of traits. Personality traits, such as anxiety, refer to the manner in which people behave; their personal style, if you like. Thus someone with high anxiety is likely to sweat more than someone with low anxiety, talk faster, be more wary of snakes, spiders etc. and generally be more alert to signs of danger in the environment. Personality traits describe the way in which a person behaves, not the level of performance which they can achieve; asking if a person 'is good at anxiety' makes no sense.

Ability traits instead reflect level of performance on unfamiliar tasks or those which have not involved training. For example, solving an anagram or reading the emotion in a stranger's face would be abilities. Psychologists are usually interested in *cognitive* abilities and so focus on abilities which require thinking for their successful performance. The key thing about all ability traits is that the quality of performance can be assessed, in principle, at any rate. It should be possible to determine how quickly people can solve anagrams or how accurately they can recognise which emotions a person is experiencing from studying a video of their face. So, asking if a person 'is good at solving anagrams' is a perfectly sensible question.

It is also possible to measure attainments. These measure performance on some familiar task and are influenced by knowledge, experience or performance as well as abilities, personality, moods etc. Sales performance may reflect ability (being able to engage would-be customers in conversation) and training or experience (knowing what information or how much of a discount might clinch a sale) together with motivation ('Do I want to make this sale?'). The child's performance on their history test will be influenced by their exposure to the information, plus their ability to learn and recall, and their motivation to study. Performance on attainment tasks is therefore a mixture of several different things – which is why psychologists tend not to focus on them, though they are clearly of enormous practical use.

Fortunately, however, these distinctions are largely irrelevant as far as this book is concerned. Whilst users of tests need to decide whether they need to measure personality, an ability or an attainment, the tests that are designed to measure them are all constructed quite similarly. However, there is one important point to bear in mind. Abilities and attainments are usually measured directly; that is, participants are shown test items and asked to produce the correct answer. It is only possible to obtain a high score on such a test if one has a high level of ability (or if one cheats!). Personality tests and the ability tests used by Howard Gardner and his followers (Armstrong, 1994; Shearer, 2007) rely on self-report. Typical items would be 'I panic easily' (which measures Neuroticism), 'I am skilled at handling social situations' (Extraversion), 'Can you easily remember a tune which you have heard once?' (Musical Intelligence) and so on. Participants are usually asked to rate themselves (or are rated by parents, friends, teachers etc.) by choosing a phrase such as 'very true of me', 'somewhat true of me' etc. for each item in the test, as will be described in Chapter 2. However, there are obvious problems with this approach. People may simply lie. They may want to portray themselves (or the person whom they are rating) in a particular way. They may make erroneous judgements; I have known people who are quite alone in thinking that they are musically gifted! Or they may be confused about how the rating scale works; does everyone apply the same criterion when deciding that a statement is 'somewhat true', for example? What do 'usually' and 'often' mean? All of these issues are well known but pose a mighty problem for rating scales. This might be part of the reason that ability tests tend to have rather stronger links to behaviour than personality tests or ability tests based on rating scales.

STATES

Unlike traits, states are short-lived and vary over time; they may also depend greatly on life events, thoughts or physiological effects. For example, I may experience great fear when a driver nearly kills me when driving on the highway; a few minutes later my fear will have returned to its normal (trait) level, and in a few hours I will probably have forgotten about the whole event. I am writing this late in the afternoon and feel hungry (a state) and so will need to prepare dinner sooner rather than later; after dinner I will have no interest in food for a few hours. Thus states may be altered by external events and/or internal (physiological) states; cognitions may also be important in determining motivation (e.g., the realisation that one is not providing for one's family).

As you will have gathered from these examples, psychologists normally identify two types of states: mood (or emotion) states and motivational states. One might expect a person's average state to correspond to their level of their trait, as proposed by Cattell (1973) – and indeed it does (Hepburn and Eysenck, 1989).

There are several ways of measuring states. Most psychologists simply use self-report questionnaires; items measuring traits ask, 'How do you usually behave?' (or 'feel') or 'How well does this phrase describe you?' However, scales measuring moods instead ask people to reflect on how they feel 'right now' (in which case being asked to answer these silly questions will have altered their mood state) or at some other time, such as when they arrived at work this morning (in which case their memory might be faulty). Readers may detect a certain cynicism here. But regardless of the questions asked, it is necessary to ensure that items such as these really do measure states (and not traits), as discussed in Chapter 10.

ATTITUDES

Attitude measurement has a long history in psychology. It is possible to assess attitudes by behavioural techniques, for example, counting the number of times a person nods or shakes their head when listening to a statement; this might be taken as a measure of their strength of feeling – positive or negative – towards the topic being expounded. Physiological measures might also be used, as when measuring paedophiles' degree of pupil dilation when viewing images of young children.

It is also possible to measure attitudes by indirect methods. For example, if a reasoned argument produces a conclusion with which a person disagrees, they are likely to be more critical and more aware of the assumptions made and flaws of logic than if they agree with the end conclusion. If we were to ask people whether they agreed with the conclusion reached here:

> People who are smart succeed in life.
>
> People who are smart do not need to work hard.
>
> Therefore, if people want to succeed in life, they do not need to work hard.

Those who do not have a particularly positive attitude to work might be more likely to agree with the conclusion than someone who believes that hard work produces results.

There are other indirect methods too; people tend to like others who share similar attitudes, so one approach to measuring someone's attitudes would be to present them with descriptions of several people and ask them which person they would like to meet. There are also several tasks which use reaction times to assess attitudes (e.g., Roddy et al., 2010).

However, the easiest way to measure attitudes is via rating scales – and as these are similar to personality scales (presenting several statements and asking participants to choose the one which best describes how they feel) and suffer from the same problems such as social desirability effects, much of what is said about personality tests in the following chapters also applies to the assessment of attitudes.

ASSUMPTIONS MADE WHEN MEASURING TRAITS OR STATES

Unfortunately, it is all too easy to overlook the sorts of assumptions that are being made when using or devising a test.

ASSUMPTION 1: THE CHARACTERISTIC MIGHT NOT EXIST

Psychiatrists used to use terms such as 'Degree of Oedipal fixation' to differentiate between people, but most would now agree that this is meaningless. It is all too easy to invent a term which we *think* describes an important way in which people differ but which has little or no basis in reality. However, it is very easy for psychologists and others to construct tests which do not measure what they expect. The Repression-Sensitisation scale developed by Byrne (1961) supposedly measures how people deal with threat – repressors avoid or deny it whilst sensitisers are alert to signs of danger, which they confront. This sounded perfectly plausible, reputations were formed, and the scale was widely used until it was discovered that scores on this scale correlated over 0.9 with anxiety – showing that Repression-Sensitisation was not a new concept at all (Slough et al., 1984). We return to issues such as this when discussing the validity of tests in Chapter 7.

ASSUMPTION 2: SITUATIONS, NOT PERSONALITY, ABILITY ETC. MIGHT DETERMINE HOW PEOPLE BEHAVE

It obviously makes no sense to categorise people as anxious versus relaxed (for example) without considering the situation in which anxiety is measured. In some settings – such as just before an examination or sitting in a dentist's waiting room – almost everyone will feel anxious, whilst very few people would feel anxious whilst meditating or taking a long, hot bath. Sternberg has taken much the same view with regard to intelligence; he points out that children may be able to solve problems in situations where the outcomes matter to them, yet may perform dismally when exactly the same problem is presented in a different context in school (Sternberg, 2004).

This has led some social psychologists such as Mischel (1968) to suggest that situations determine how people behave; we may be fooling ourselves entirely whenever we think that people behave consistently. Traits may not exist, and so we should not bother trying to measure them. However, three types of evidence seem to suggest that this argument is not entirely correct. First, if traits do not exist, scores on questionnaires measuring them could not predict how people behave. Authors such as Herriott (1989) however show that scores on tests measuring traits can predict many real-life behaviours. Second, scores on traits measured by questionnaires correlate (sometimes substantially) with biological markers. For example, traits such as general intelligence are highly heritable, indicating that they reflect individual differences in people's biological makeup. This simply could not be true if the test scores were substantially influenced by situational factors. Third, studies such as Conley (1984) show that scores on personality tests are extremely consistent over time, which is unlikely to be the case if responses were situationally determined.

ASSUMPTION 3: TEST SCORES ALLOW US TO MEASURE TRAITS OR STATES

What do we mean by 'measurement' – and just because we generate numbers by calculating people's scores on tests, can we then be confident that we have measured their behaviour? This potentially damning problem has been raised by several philosophers of science (Maraun, 1998; Michell, 1997a) who point out that the numbers which arise from scoring psychological tests are very different from the numbers which arise from physical (or other proper scientific) measurements and cannot be presumed to behave in the same way. Psychological characteristics simply may not be quantifiable – or at least there may be no *evidence* that they are quantifiable. Assigning numbers to people's responses to test items is therefore not measurement, as such. We can *count* the number of problems which people solve correctly when taking an ability test. But this does not mean that we can measure ability – in the same way that counting the number of houses in your street does not mean that you can measure the length of your street. (You cannot say that my street of 60 houses is twice as long as your street which has 30 houses – the size of the plots will probably be different.) It may well not be legitimate to talk about 'measuring' anything at all using psychological scales, and it would certainly be quite wrong to manipulate or interpret these numbers in the same sort of way that we manipulate numbers from rulers, thermometers or other devices. These problems are serious, so serious that they suggest that all forms of questionnaires, ability tests and surveys produce data which must not be interpreted in the way that psychologists normally use. We return to these issues in Chapter 4.

SUMMARY

This chapter has outlined the aims and objectives of this book and has made the point that psychological tests and assessments are very widely used by practitioners (e.g., in clinical, forensic, health and sport psychology), by researchers in areas other than cognitive psychology who need to relate behaviour to some form of psychological measure and by individual-difference and social psychologists who explore the relationships between the scores which people obtain on two or more psychological tests. It is argued that this last form of research is potentially problematic, and it is demonstrated that several commonly used tests may share the same item or may be influenced by the same response style (such as portraying oneself in a good light). This can create huge (though largely unrecognised) problems for the interpretation of such analyses. The chapter also introduced a spreadsheet so that readers can explore the effect of overlapping items on the correlation between tests of various lengths.

The chapter then mentioned the interplay between psychological assessment/psychometrics and psychological theory, noting that it can work two ways. Tests can be constructed to measure characteristics which have been identified through medical research etc. In addition, psychometric analyses of behaviour can show how we might usefully describe the way in which people behave, feel and act – but not why they do so. To gain a proper scientific understanding of this requires laboratory studies.

The chapter introduced two important concepts: traits, which are rather stable aspects of personality or ability, and mood and motivational states, which are short-lived and often influenced by internal events (e.g., physiological changes, thoughts) or the environment. The concept of attitude was also briefly introduced.

Finally, we considered some rather fundamental assumptions made whenever attempting to use any scale to measure anything. One of these suggests that assigning numbers to people's responses to test items involves counting, not measurement as such.

CHAPTER 2
TESTS, SCALES AND TESTING

So far we have used terms like 'test', 'scale' and 'item' without really specifying what they mean. This chapter will clarify these terms, outline the general logic of testing and give some general information about the principles of testing and test administration together with some practical guidance about how to locate tests.

The phrase 'psychometric test' strikes terror into the heart of many job applicants who, like so many others, think that tests offer some deep insights into the soul which cannot be obtained by any other means. Reality is very different. A test, of any sort, is simply a standardised way of gathering information about a person. By 'standardised' we mean that any person, anywhere in the world has exactly the same experience when taking the test – no matter who administers it, when or where. *Everything* should be standardised: the instructions, the environment (as far as possible), the amount of time given to answer the items, the way the test booklet is printed, the wording of the items, the format of any answer sheet . . . It is possible that altering any of these may affect the test's ability to measure the trait or state which it is supposed to assess.

Each test also comes with instructions for scoring it using a standardised method, which in practice usually means turning the participant's responses into some type of numerical scores. These scores can be compared with the scores obtained by other persons, correlated with other variables or correlated with other scores. It turns out that the rationale for scoring tests is more complex than it may seem, and so this will be considered in Chapter 3; the present chapter provides a general introduction to test items, testing procedures and introduces the distinction between scales and tests.

ITEMS

Let us start off with a very simple example. Suppose that a teacher wants to measure how many historical dates her pupils can remember after a year of instruction. The pupils have been given a book containing 400 dates and should have memorised them all. (I sincerely hope that history is no longer taught like this – but this example is easy to visualise.) The range of possible items which could be measured is called the 'domain' – an important term in psychometrics. The teacher wants to test their knowledge of this domain of 400 items. How should she do it?

One approach would be to prepare a test in which students were tested on all 400 of the dates that were mentioned in the book, using items such as 'What year did . . . happen?' In theory this is both the simplest and best approach: it allows the extent of each child's knowledge of dates on the day of the test to be determined exactly. There is no estimation involved: their score on all of the items in the domain (all the items which could possibly have been asked) is their 'true score'. This is another important term to bear in mind.

But testing all 400 items would take a long time and be tedious for everyone involved. It would also probably be necessary to split the testing over several occasions to prevent the children becoming bored or fatigued, and hence answering carelessly towards the end of the test. So in practice it might be better to measure performance on a smaller number of questions and hope that the children's scores on the short test will give a good estimate of how they would have performed on the 400-item test.

How should the teacher sample items from the textbook? What she should most certainly *not* do is select the items from the same part of the book: if all of the items were selected from the very last pages, this would underestimate the ability of those children who had not quite read the entire book but who knew the earlier pages well. Likewise drawing all of the questions from the first page would not be a good idea, as this would overestimate the scores of students who never read any further! Selecting the items by topic would not be a good idea either, as some children may be interested in (say) medieval history but nothing earlier and nothing later. If the test were to consist of items which covered the medieval period only, then these children's knowledge would be overestimated. Conversely if the teacher asked *no* questions from this period, then the ability of these children would be underestimated. So it would be sensible to draw a proper random or stratified sample of items (without replacement so that each item appears only once) from the book. This will ensure that the items which are to be given to the children are representative of all 400 items in the domain: they will not all be on the same topic or from the same part of the textbook, and so they should give an unbiased estimate of each child's knowledge.

I have used the example of a history test because it is easy to specify what the domain of knowledge is and because it is easy to visualise how the teacher might select items from the domain. Other types of item (those measuring personality, mood, motivation, cognitive abilities etc.) are much more common, and these will be introduced later in this chapter. However, the key thing to remember is that all items which form a scale are assumed to represent some domain of interest. This domain can sometimes be very broad in nature – for example, the domain of all types of puzzles which require thought for their successful solution. These might include anagrams, identifying which shape might come next in a series, visualising what an object would look like from another position, assembling a jigsaw within a particular time limit; the list of possible puzzles is almost endless.

SINGLE-ITEM SCALES

It is possible, though unusual, to measure personality, attainment, ability, mood or any other characteristic using just one item. See, for example, Table 2.1.

The first problem with doing so is that by using a single question, it is possible that momentary loss of attention, problems understanding the meaning of some of the words in the question or some other transient problem may affect the way in which a person responds to that single question. For example, suppose that a respondent has a completely unrealistic view of how depressed other people are: they may feel that everyone else in the world is completely happy and they alone feel miserable. Or they might take offence and choose not to label themselves as 'depressed' even though they probably are. Either or both of these will distort the way in which this individual responds to the single item shown above. At least asking multiple questions may avoid the problem of momentary lapsed attention (it is unlikely that a person will be distracted or take issue with the wording of *all* questions and averaging the scores on several questions should therefore produce more accurate estimates of a person's level of the trait). Thus it seems likely that multi–item scales might lead to more accurate assessments than single-item measures. That said, several psychologists propose using single items to measure traits (e.g., Konstabel et al., 2012) particularly when administration time is short.

There is another reason for avoiding single-item tests, too. We have seen that psychologists often measure quite broad traits such as depression. If a trait such as this has several different symptoms, or facets, then asking just one question ('Do you feel depressed?', for example) ignores all the other pieces of evidence which may point to depression. It is quite possible that a person may not wish to admit to feeling depressed but might freely say that they had sleep problems, weight fluctuations etc. By measuring the whole range of indicators, the scale is much more likely to give an accurate measurement of a person's level of depression.

Table 2.1 A single item measuring depression

	Extremely	Quite	Average	Not very	Not at all
How depressed are you?					

Third, when a multi-item scale is administered, it is possible to test whether or not all of the items measure the same characteristic within a sample of people. It will show whether respondents answer items at random, for example, as doing so will reduce the correlations between items. It might be worthwhile knowing this if a questionnaire is included towards the end of a long session (fatigue), if participants are completing an experiment for money or course credit (low motivation to answer honestly) or if a questionnaire is likely to be used in a setting where participants might be tempted to give socially desirable answers, such as when applying for a job.

Fourth, the more items in a scale, the larger the range of potential scores. This is perhaps most obvious in the case of ability items: a single ability item can yield a score of 0 or 1, which is not particularly useful for making fine distinctions between people; increasing the number of items to 20 obviously gives a range of possible scores between 0 and 20. Thus a scale made up of many items has the potential to draw finer distinctions between people than do short scales or those which are scored as correct/incorrect.

Thus, although it may sometimes be expedient to try to measure a trait using just one item, this cannot really be recommended – largely because it is impossible to tell how accurately that item measures the trait other than by measuring the consistency of scores over time, as discussed in Chapter 6.

That said, there is lively literature about personality assessment using single items, though these seem to work best when the scale is so narrow in content that it merely consists of several paraphrases of the same item. As Robins et al. (2001) observe, 'In our experience, even when the . . . items are interspersed with items from other scales, participants frequently write comments such as, "I have already answered this question!"'. So perhaps it is not surprising that if the domain of items is extremely narrow, asking a question once is almost as effective as asking (almost) the same question ten times! Thus single-item scales may be useful when measuring something as narrow in scope as self-esteem or happiness. On the other hand, measuring broader traits using single items seems to be less effective (Gosling et al., 2003), as might perhaps be expected.

MULTIPLE-ITEM SCALES

A scale consists of group of items whose scores are combined. It should be obvious that all of the items which form a scale should measure the same trait or state; for example, a scale measuring depression could usefully consist of an item measuring low mood, another about weight changes, another about sleeping patterns and so on (see Table 2.2).

Table 2.2 Four items measuring depression

1	Do you often feel down for no good reason?	Yes	No
2	Do you sleep well?	Yes	No
3	Has your weight gone up or down by more than 5 kg in the last six months?	Yes	No
4	Do you have much energy?	Yes	No

In Table 2.2 the answers indicating depression are shaded: they would not be in a real questionnaire, of course. So if each 'depressed' answer is awarded one point, and the other answer zero points, it is obvious that each person's score on this scale must be between 0 and 4, with a larger score indicating a greater level of depression.

However, this approach only makes sense if we somehow know that all of these items measure the same thing: that they are all indicators of depression, in other words. In the case of depression this is easy because the clinical symptoms are well-documented. It would be much less obvious if someone wanted to measure creativity. Is the ability to think of novel uses for objects (for example, 'What useful object could you make from two pencils, a rubber band and some paper?') related to the ease with which people can think of new ideas ('How many different uses can you think of for a brick?'), for example? Should ability to write a poem be included? Or inventing a novel game involving playing cards? It is important to know this because it would make little sense to put items together in the same scale if they measured different things.

For example, suppose that we added another four items to the depression scale – only these items all measured Extraversion/Introversion (how sociable and outgoing someone is). We could tell that someone who scored 8/8 on this scale must be both depressed and extraverted: someone who scored 0/8 likewise has to be an introvert who is low on depression. But what of someone who scores 4/8? They could be depressed and introverted. Or not depressed and extraverted. Or have moderate degrees of both introversion and depression. These are clearly very different people, yet they would all obtain the same score (4) on the questionnaire, which makes little sense. It is for this reason that psychologists and others take great care to ensure that the items which form scales all measure the same thing, often using a technique known as factor analysis (discussed in Chapters 8–11) for this purpose. That way it would be possible to develop one scale measuring depression and another measuring extraversion. Each of these would be interpreted separately.

A scale is therefore a collection of items which all measure the same trait, state, ability or area of knowledge – some domain, in other words. The number of items in the domain can vary. Only 169 items can measure children's knowledge of their 12-times table (assuming they know about the concept of zero). On the other hand, the domain of items is sometimes so large that it could be considered infinite. For example, a near-infinite number of items could be written to measure how depressed a person is or how well they can solve any problem which requires reasoning.

It is vital, absolutely vital, for anyone who designs or uses a scale to have a very clear idea in their mind what domain the scale sets out to measure. It is otherwise all too easy to write items which fail to represent the breadth of the trait or state which the scale is supposed to measure.

HOW LONG SHOULD A SCALE BE?

The fun starts when we try to ascertain how many items are needed in a scale. In our history scale, would 100 items give a good-enough approximation of people's true scores? Perhaps 50 items might suffice? Or even 10? It is probably intuitively obvious that long scales are likely to be more accurate than short ones. For example, finding the percentage of items answered correctly on a 50-item scale will give a better estimate of each child's knowledge than finding the percentage answered correctly using a 10-item scale. How do we know this? Suppose a particular child knows the answers to half of the questions in the book. If the scale was just 10 items long, it *could* be that all of the dates in the scale just happened to be ones which they knew. However, it is far less likely that all the items in the 50-item scale just happened to be the ones that this student knew: they would have to be lucky much more often to obtain full marks in a longer test than in a shorter one. So longer scales are generally more accurate than short ones, though if a scale is *too* long, participants might feel fatigued or bored, and so start to answer randomly – and this will reduce the accuracy of the assessment.

The aim of any scale is to estimate a person's true score, the score which they would obtain if they answered all possible items in the domain. It turns out to be surprisingly easy to estimate how well scores on a particular scale will correlate with the true score. This may sound like an impossibility. As a domain could contain a near-infinite number of items (all the important dates in history, for example – not just the 400 listed in the book), it would clearly be impossible to test anyone's knowledge of all of them. But suppose that we have two scales, both built from the same number of items from the same near-infinitely large domain – two 50-item scales measuring performance on randomly chosen historical facts, perhaps. We do not know the correlation of either scale with the true score. However, we can easily find out the correlation between the two scales simply by giving both scales to a large sample of children. If each scale consists of a random selection of items, carefully sampled to cover the whole domain, and the scales are the same length, each scale should have the same correlation with the true score. And if both of the scales are long, then the correlation between them will be fairly similar, no matter which particular items are put into each scale. (Take this on trust, for now.) As will be shown in Chapter 6, it is quite easy to estimate the size of the correlation between each scale and the true score from the knowledge of the correlation between the two scales.

The length that a scale should be therefore depends on the purpose for which it is to be used. A scale which is used to help a practitioner make a potentially life-changing decision about an individual will need to be extremely accurate and therefore probably quite long; in other settings it may be more cost-effective to use a short scale and accept that the scores will not be extremely accurate. The length of a scale also depends crucially on the quality of the items. Some scales contain items which correlate quite substantially with the true score, and so a few items will be able to estimate the true score quite accurately. However, in real life it is quite common for the correlation between each item and the true score to be as low as 0.3 or so. As will be seen in Chapter 6, if the quality of the items is poor, more of them need to be added together in order to measure a trait with the desired degree of precision.

TYPES OF ITEMS MEASURING ABILITY OR ATTAINMENT

Several types of items have been devised to measure abilities and attainment. In each case the participant is given a problem to solve or a question to answer. This problem/question is sometimes known as the 'stem'. There are several different ways in which participants can indicate their response.

FREE-RESPONSE ITEMS

With these items, participants give their answer in their own words (writing, speaking or typing the response) or by making any other type of response which does not involve choosing between alternatives. For example, a vocabulary test for a young child might involve a child being asked 'What is a kitten?' and speaking their response. They might be given a set of coloured blocks and be asked to arrange them so as to replicate a design shown in a booklet. Essays such as 'What were the causes of World War I?' can be regarded as free-response items – albeit ones which involve long responses which will be challenging to score accurately. A respondent might be asked to type the answer to a problem such as 'How far is Winnipeg from Montreal?', 'Draw the shape which comes next in the series \ | /', or asked to 'Sing the tune which I just played you', 'Tell me who is the prime minister', 'Draw a picture of a bicycle' . . . The number of possible formats is huge.

Free-response items have several advantages over other types of items discussed below. First, they cannot 'lead' the participant towards the right answer; as soon as one presents a person with several different answers and asks them to choose between them, there is the possibility that someone who does not know the answer might be able to eliminate all but one and so work out what must be the correct answer without actually *knowing* the correct answer at all. For example, if someone was asked 'How many sides does a pentangle have?' and were given the alternatives (a) 3 (b) 4 (c) 5, they might have absolutely no idea what the correct answer was. However, if they know that a three-sided figure is called a triangle and a four-sided figure is a quadrilateral, it is unlikely that either of these can be the correct answer. Thus they will arrive at the correct answer by a process of elimination – which is presumably not what the person who set the test intended. Free-response items – asking each person to simply write what they think the answer is – overcomes this problem.

Second, free-response items can be given verbally, which may be particularly useful when testing young children or those with limited reading or writing skills (e.g., many prisoners, those with eyesight problems or Parkinson's disease).

Third, free-response items sometimes seem to be the only possible choice – e.g., when assessing how accurately a person can draw a familiar object from memory. Anagrams are another form of item which is difficult to assess by any other means. If a person was asked to rearrange the letters in 'rat heel' to form a single word and given four choices: 'athlete', 'reheats', 'leather' and 'armhole', the astute individual would simply check to see which of the four alternatives contained all of the letters in 'rat heel'. Comparing letters is a different (and probably much easier) task than solving the anagram – and so if one wants to assess how well people can solve the anagram rather than comparing letters, a free-response format would seem to be the best option.

They also have several disadvantages.

First, answers can be ambiguous and therefore hard to score. For example, if someone writes that a kitten 'is a type of cat', it can be hard to know whether to mark this as correct or incorrect.

Second, the practicalities of scoring free-response items are appreciable. A human eye and brain is almost always needed, and these are both slow and expensive. Furthermore, execrable handwriting, spelling etc. may cause problems for the person who reads the answer; a correct answer may be misinterpreted and vice versa. Even the responses that are not handwritten, oral etc. may need some human judgement. If someone uses a keyboard, which sounds as if it should be a fairly safe way of recording their response, it is possible that someone will insert a comma after the 'thousand' when typing a large number or use an 'O' instead of a zero. Or they may just make a random typing error which a human would spot but a machine probably would not. If the answers are written on sheets of paper which are then scanned and run through a handwriting-recognition program, there are still more opportunities for errors to creep in.

Poor handwriting, crossings-out and so on might lead to inaccurate interpretations of what has been written. So, scoring free-response items really requires human input.

MULTIPLE-CHOICE ITEMS

Most ability or attainment tests involve multiple-choice items, purely for ease of scoring. Here the respondent is shown both the stem and a list of options, only one of which is correct. For example, 'World War I started in (a) 1066 (b) 1812 (c) 1914 (d) 1939'. The respondent then chooses one of the options – normally by clicking a mouse or ticking a box on an answer sheet.

There are several issues arising from such items.

- Respondents who do not know the correct answer will sometimes choose the correct answer by luck alone if they guess an answer at random. This causes problems for some techniques used to estimate people's abilities – notably Rasch scaling, which is discussed in Chapter 12.
- Inventing plausible but incorrect answers (known as 'distracters') is difficult, as discussed in Chapter 13. It requires some insight as to what might confuse respondents and/or how they might go about eliminating incorrect answers to arrive at the correct one. Guessing (and the use of strategies to eliminate obviously incorrect answers) means that the response to the item does not *just* reflect ability; it also reflects luck to some extent, along with the ability to identify an efficient strategy for eliminating some distracters. If someone is unsure of the answer, multiple-choice items involve knowledge and cognitive processes which are very different from those involved in writing the answer in a free-response format.
- How many distracters should there be? I cannot offhand think of any commercial test which offers respondents more than eight choices of answer, and four is probably the most common number. The reason for this is rarely articulated, but having just two alternatives would obviously mean that each person has a 50% chance of guessing correctly if they choose an answer at random. Thus the scale would need to be longer than if there were more distracters, to compensate for the effects of lucky guessing. On the other hand, showing a person a large number of distracters will make each item much longer to solve, and the extra reading involved will slow down the assessment process. In addition, Miller's (1956) work suggests that if there are more than about five alternatives, some respondents might find it difficult to keep them all in mind and will need to keep checking the page or screen – again slowing some (but not all) respondents and introducing random error into the scores on the item.
- The number and choice of distracters determines how easy the item is – and once again, this is an arbitrary choice made as the item is being constructed.

For example, it is probable that had we chosen the years 1915, 1916 and 1917 as distracters, the item would be harder than using the widely spread dates shown above because some people will have known that World War I took place early in the twentieth century.

- Many multiple-choice tests have time limits. This is more or less essential when groups of people are being tested, otherwise an obsessional respondent would take many hours over what was meant to be a short assessment, to the annoyance of all the others in the room. However, if some respondents do not finish all the items in time, should they guess the answers to those that remain, just before time is called? The problem is that if some people do so and others do not, then the scores of the latter group will be underestimates (they will have no 'lucky guesses' to boost their score).

- Next, and perhaps most seriously, it can be difficult to measure some higher-order problem-solving and reasoning skills using multiple-choice tests. For example, suppose that an organisation wanted to assess how well an applicant for a senior position could draw up a development plan to move a company forward from some (hypothetical) financial calamity. It is not really obvious how one could measure this sort of skill using multiple-choice items.

- A respondent who is not fully engaged with the assessment process will sometimes just tick boxes randomly in order to end the assessment as quickly as possible. It is much harder to spot that this has occurred with a multiple-choice test than with a free-response test, where the respondent would need to leave each item unanswered or (perhaps) write some word which has no connection with the question.

- Finally, what should participants be told about guessing or omitting answers? Many multiple-choice ability tests urge participants to guess if they are unsure of the correct answer – so what should be done with those who do not guess but leave an answer blank? The safest plan is to make a random guess or statistically estimate how many of the unanswered items the respondent would probably have answered correctly, considering their performance on the items which they *did* attempt. A few tests ask participants *not* to guess and warn them that incorrect answers will be penalised. However, this introduces a whole new problem. What if participants use different criteria for deciding whether they think that their answer is correct? One person might be terrified of being penalised for an incorrect answer and so will leave an item blank if they are not 100% positive that their answer is correct, whilst someone else might take a chance and only leave the item blank if they cannot eliminate any of the distracters. These different strategies will influence the scores which the participants obtain and will probably make them less accurate. It is probably best to ask participants to guess if unsure, but, in any case, it is vital that participants should be told precisely what to do if they do not know the answer to a question – even though the way in which they define 'know' will probably vary from person to person.

TYPES OF ITEMS MEASURING PERSONALITY, MOOD, MOTIVATION AND ATTITUDE

There are three main options for measuring personality, attitudes etc. By far the most popular is the rating scale, where respondents are shown a statement and are asked how much they agree with it, how well it applies to them or something similar. Historically several other methods have been tried, including projective tests (where participants make their own interpretation of some ambiguous stimulus, such as a picture or inkblot) and 'objective tests' – tests where the participant is either unable to modify their behaviour or where they do not know which aspect of their behaviour is being assessed. However, as these techniques are highly specialised (and frequently ineffective) they will not be considered further.

LIKERT SCALES

Rating scales are widely used for scales which measure states and traits. The main difference is that the stem for a personality item will ask how people normally behave, whilst scales measuring mood or motivation will ask how they feel right at this moment. Some are completed by the participant, who describes how they think, feel or behave. These are (unsurprisingly) known as self-report scales. Self-report scales rely on the participant being motivated to answer truthfully – and also having the self-knowledge to allow them to do so. Asking participants to complete research studies anonymously might be expected to improve the quality of the data. However, several studies (e.g., Butler, 1973; Francis, 1981) suggest that respondents often behave no differently under anonymous/named conditions. The only real problem with anonymous data is that it is difficult to assess people on more than one occasion where their answers on two or more measures will need to be matched up. However this *can* be overcome with a little ingenuity – for example, giving each person a code to memorise (or a set of stickers to put on the questionnaires) or asking them to generate the same code on each occasion using well-known information (e.g., the first initial of their first pet followed by the house number where they grew up, followed by the last two digits of the number plate of their first car). The context in which the data are gathered is clearly important. Using self-report scales as part of an employment selection process may well be problematical, as some respondents will probably deny having any characteristics which may be viewed negatively. Nevertheless, some organisations do so regularly.

Rather than rating oneself, it is also possible to obtain ratings from line managers, teachers, friends or others who know the individual well.

Choosing whether to use a self-report scale or a scale where the person is rated by someone else is not straightforward. It is advisable to consult the literature to determine which format seems to yield the best results in similar circumstances.

Both formats of rating scales are physically very similar and so will be considered together. The stem for each item consists of a question or statement. As there can be no correct or incorrect answers to these types of questions, participants are usually asked to rate how well each statement describes them (or the person being rated), how much they agree with a statement or something similar. For example, they might be asked to fill in one of the circles in order to answer each of the following items (see Table 2.3).

Table 2.3 Items using Likert scales

	Strongly agree	Agree	Neutral	Disagree	Strongly disagree
I am the life and soul of the party	O	O	O	O	O
Global warming will destroy the planet	O	O	O	O	O
The benefits of recreational drugs outweigh their risks	O	O	O	O	O

	Definitely	Probably	Neutral/ unsure	Probably not	Definitely not
My mother was smarter than me	O	O	O	O	O

	Very much	Somewhat	Unsure/ neutral	Not much	Not at all
How much do you enjoy travelling to new places?	O	O	O	O	O

	Very much better than other brands	Better than other brands	No better or worse than other brands	Worse than other brands	Much worse than other brands
GleemyChompers toothpaste cleans my teeth . . .	O	O	O	O	O

Items with responses such as these are known as Likert scales. It is normal for Likert scales to have five or seven alternative answers – probably because Miller's (1956) work suggests that many people would find it hard to make more than about seven meaningful distinctions. However, there are some personality scales with as many as nine alternatives and some (Eysenck's EPQ and Cattell's 16PF questionnaires) use only two or three: Yes/No or Yes/?/No.

The key thing about the labels attached to the various alternative answers for the Likert scales is that they are arranged in order (very much, somewhat, unsure, not much, not at all) forming *ordered categories*. So someone who marks the 'strongly agree' option is assumed to agree with the statement more than someone who marks the 'agree' option. However, this is an assumption; it is quite possible that two individuals will use different criteria when using the scale. In the toothpaste example, suppose that two users of the product found that it was awful. One person might decide that this merits a rating of 'very much worse than other brands', whereas the other person might feel that this makes the product only 'worse than other brands'. And indeed, there is absolutely no guarantee that the characteristic which is being assessed is quantitative in the first place; it is possible that psychologists waste their time trying to measure something that is qualitative. This is a serious problem, and we return to it when discussing the scoring of tests in Chapter 3.

The number of alternatives is normally an odd number, so that respondents have a 'neutral' choice in the middle, which may be a particular issue when measuring attitudes. Here some respondents may genuinely have no view about an item – those who have never used GleemyChompers toothpaste, for example – and so will resent being forced to say that it is either more or less effective than its competitors.

Issues with self-report questionnaires

One of the problems with items such as these is that people will happily rate almost anything. An old personality questionnaire contained the item 'I see things or animals or people around me that others do not see'. But how could anyone *know for certain* that other people did not see what they saw? This brings us to an important issue: whether or not we should believe what people say when they answer questions like this. For, if someone strongly agrees that they see things or animals or people around them that others do not see, this could indicate either that they do, in fact, have visual hallucinations, or it could be the case that statistical analyses show that *saying* that one has visual hallucinations is one aspect of a particular personality disorder. In the first case, we believe what the respondent says. In the second, we do not – but rely on statistical analyses to help us determine what (if anything) responding this way indicates about a person. For example, it might be found that people who strongly agree with this statement might go on to develop symptoms of schizophrenia – so the fact that a person says that they experience hallucinations may have some useful diagnostic value.

It does not matter a jot whether the person really *does* experience hallucinations – all that matters is that they *say* that they do. This is an important point to bear in mind; it may not matter how stupid or irrelevant an item appears to be. All that really matters is whether the way people answer this and other items allows us to describe or predict their personality, attitudes etc. It may be naive to assume that the response says something useful about how the individual truly feels or behaves, though social psychologists regularly make this assumption when measuring attitudes etc.

Because of this Cattell (1946) suggested that two different terms should be used to describe data from questionnaires. He suggested that responses to questions which are treated as revealing some insight about the individual (such as attitude questionnaires) should be termed Q'-data, the Q being short for 'Questionnaire'. Data which are not taken at face value but which are simply used because they have been found empirically to predict behaviour or to show useful associations with other responses are known as Q-data. It is important to bear this distinction in mind when analysing responses from questionnaires. Treating responses as Q-data means that even bizarre items (how much do you agree with the statement 'I am the smartest person in town' – another genuine item) may be useful. If the statement were interpreted as Q'-data it would imply that the person was intelligent; if interpreted as Q-data it might, perhaps, indicate hubris – but this would need to be determined empirically. Throughout the rest of this book we treat all responses to items as being Q-data, for the statistical analyses which allow us to check how accurately items and scales measure what they claim to assess do not require us to take responses at face value.

The second problem with self-report questionnaires is that people might compare themselves to different groups. For example, an item whose stem is 'I am more intelligent than most people' is almost impossible to answer unless the person is told which reference group to use. Should a student rate their intelligence relative to the rest of their class at university? Given that the correlation between intelligence and academic performance is over 0.8 (Calvin et al., 2010), if students at a good university rated themselves relative to their classmates, they would seriously underestimate their scores because their classmates would almost all be of above-average intelligence. So, someone who correctly perceived that they were appreciably less intelligent than their classmates could be well above average intelligence when compared to the population as a whole. It would, in theory, be possible to specify the norm group: 'Thinking about all the people in your school, would you say that you are more intelligent than most people?' might work if participants had gone through an education system which did not rely on academic selection. But this makes the stem rather long, and most psychologists do not think about such issues carefully enough when writing items.

The third problem is self-knowledge. Most people think they have an above-average sense of humour, intelligence and are more popular than they really are; indeed psychologists and sociologists study this as the 'Lake Wobegon Effect' or 'Illusory

Superiority' which is the tendency to overestimate one's capabilities or knowledge. This is not the place to explore the literature in detail but suffice to say that people do seem to exaggerate their strengths without meaning to. Once again, this would not matter in the slightest if everyone exaggerated their strengths to the same extent, but it seems that they do not.

Fourth, there may be individual differences in the way in which people use the rating scales. For example, there is also a well-researched tendency for some people to tend to agree with personality items, whatever they are. Others try to give a good impression of themselves. Yet others see complex issues as clear-cut and strongly agree or strongly disagree with everything. We return to these issues in Chapter 5.

Fifth, there is the problem of random responding. It is common to find that some respondents tick the same alternative (often the centre, 'neutral' answer) for many items in succession, suggesting that they may be responding randomly – however it is hard to be certain of this. If respondents just tick a different box each time without reading the item, this would be difficult to detect by eye. However, it is possible to find pairs of items which correlate very substantially; if a person gives very different responses to each of these pairs of items, this may indicate that they are responding randomly, and some questionnaires incorporate scales which allow such random responding to be detected.

Finally, In the case of personality questionnaires, it is normal to ask participants to answer each question, and this is normally stressed during the instructions for these scales. However, what should be done if someone leaves blanks?

Issues with ratings of behaviour

There are several advantages and drawbacks to using ratings of other people, rather than self-report.

- One advantage is that if each rater assesses several people whom they know it is possible to correct for any bias that the raters may show – for example, rating everyone favourably (or unfavourably) – by standardising each rater's scores.
- It is possible that rating others may yield more objective results than rating oneself; it eliminates the problem of self-delusion.
- Of course, it is possible that the raters will not be objective. They may want a colleague, a student or a friend to get a job or just appear in a good light.
- There are also areas of each person's life which the rater may not be qualified to judge; a work-colleague may have only observed someone in a very restricted range of settings, and it is quite possible that they may view a colleague as supremely confident whereas the ratee might acknowledge that this is just an act and they truly feel insecure much of the time.

- There may also be a 'halo effect'. If the rater rates someone highly on some desirable trait, they may also tend to rate them highly on all other desirable traits.
- Finally, it is possible that the raters use the questionnaire to show which characteristics they *think* go together – not how the individuals actually behave. For example, the rater may believe that religious people are tolerant, so having rated a colleague as being strongly religious, they may then rate them as tolerant, completely ignoring all the evidence which suggests the exact opposite.

FORCED-ALTERNATIVE ITEMS

In these items, respondents are given two or more alternatives and are asked which of them best describes them, which one they are most likely to adopt etc. See, for example, Table 2.4.

Unlike Likert scales, each of the possible responses to a forced–alternative item represents a *different* scale. The number of alternative answers for each item is thus usually equal to the number of scales in the test. The two items in Table 2.4 were designed to measure three scales: Neuroticism, Extraversion and Openness to Experience (three important personality factors). Each stem is therefore followed by three options – one indicating Neuroticism, one indicating Extraversion and one Openness to Experience. Someone who chose the third alternative to both stems would value cultural activities and would therefore have a high score on Openness to Experience; someone who chose the second alternative would be extraverted, and so on. In practice, of course, the order of the answers is randomised so that it is less obvious to the respondent that the choices reflect the same three scales.

One obvious problem with this approach is that it is only appropriate for tests which measure more than one scale.

A second difficulty is that if one option is hugely more attractive than the others, then almost everyone will choose it, regardless of their personality. Thus, when these

Table 2.4 Examples of forced-choice items measuring Neuroticism, Extraversion and Openness to Experience

In each scenario, choose the ONE phrase which best describes how you would behave.			
If I won the lottery I would	move house in case my family was held to ransom	host a huge party for my family and friends	travel to better understand other cultures
When travelling, my priority is to	always ensure I know where my passport is	make lots of new friends	tour art galleries and museums

tests are being developed, the items are normally given to a large sample of people who are asked to rate each alternative for its level of social desirability. Three items from different scales having similar social desirability are then used as the alternative answers for each stem. Unfortunately, however, social desirability is likely to vary from sample to sample as well as over time; what was socially desirable for a group of elderly churchgoers in the 1990s might not be the same as what is socially desirable for psychology students in the twenty-first century! Thus there is a danger that tests which are designed in this way may lose their effectiveness over time or when used with groups different from the ones used to develop it.

Finally, as will be shown in Chapter 3, interpreting the scores from these tests is very difficult indeed; standard statistical techniques for evaluating tests and scales (factor analysis etc.) are inappropriate, and so those who select or use these tests need to be very cautious.

TESTS

A test is simply a collection of one or more scales. For example, a personality test may set out to measure Extraversion, Neuroticism, Openness to Experience, Conscientiousness and Agreeableness. These are five different scales, each containing several items. However, it is normal to mix up the order of the items within the personality test. If a person was presented with all of the Extraversion items first ('Do you like lively parties?', 'Do you make friends easily?', 'Can you easily persuade other people to do what you want?' etc.) followed by a block of Neuroticism items ('Do you worry a lot?', 'Do you sometimes feel unhappy for no obvious reason?', 'Are you afraid of any harmless animals, such as birds or moths?') some people taking the test will probably realise what it is intended to measure. If they say that they like lively parties, they may then feel that they *have* to agree with the next two items (which also measure extraversion) just to appear consistent. For this reason, tests which consist of several different scales usually have the items presented in a random order. In the above example, a Neuroticism item might be followed by an Extraversion item, then a Conscientiousness item, an Openness item, perhaps another Conscientiousness item, an Agreeableness item and so on. This makes it harder for participants to guess what the items measure, and which form scales.

Ability tests, on the other hand, tend to present blocks of similar items; perhaps 20 items measuring visualisation followed by another block of items measuring creativity and so on. This is probably because the items in each scale often need to be preceded by detailed instructions, practice items and so on. Thus it would often not be possible to mix the items up, although a few tests whose items are quite straightforward do so (e.g., Heim, 1967). Also, unlike personality items, it does not really matter if the person taking the scale knows what it measures.

SPEED TESTS VERSUS POWER TESTS

A speed test is one where participants need to work quickly – for example, to solve as many anagrams as possible in two minutes, where the list of anagrams is so long that virtually no one would be able to solve them all in the time allowed. The items will need to be easy – the key question is how quickly they can be solved. To determine whether something is a speed test, ask whether almost everyone could get 100% correct if they were given as long as they wanted to tackle every item. It seems likely that strategies, motivation etc. will have a large influence on performance on speed tests; for example, how long should one spend on an item before giving up and moving on to the next? How much error checking should be carried out?

A power test imposes few (if any) time limits. The difficulty of the items is what allows power tests to differentiate between people. A power test based on anagrams would involve anagrams which varied considerably in difficulty level; participants would be asked to solve the list of anagrams, taking as long as they wanted to do so.[1] The items in power tests are usually ordered in terms of difficulty, with the easiest at the start and the hardest at the end. This ensures that almost every participant will be able to solve some of the early items, which should motivate them to do well. It also means that most participants will only encounter items which are beyond their ability after they have completed the items which are (for them) challenging but possible – and this too should stop participants becoming demotivated before they have solved all the problems which they can. It has been found that speed tests and power tests seem to measure rather different abilities (Davidson and Carroll, 1945) and techniques have been devised based on reaction times from a computer-administered ability test which allow power and ability to be estimated separately and correlated together (Partchev et al., 2013). Like the earlier work, the correlation between power and ability was small for a verbal analogy task.

TEST ADMINISTRATION

More detail about test administration is given in Chapter 13. The paramount consideration is that no one should be harmed by taking a test. Thus, all possible steps must be taken to ensure that answers (and scores on the test) remain confidential to each participant; other people participants must not be able to see which responses are made or even *whether* a response has been made, to avoid bullying, embarrassment, name-calling etc. If many people are being tested in the same room, this means keeping good separation between them, with no opportunity for answer sheets, screens etc. to be viewed by others.

A risk assessment should also be carried out – particularly in the case of assessments which might deal with sensitive issues. The use of anatomically detailed dolls in forensic examinations or an item asking about attitudes to abortion might trigger painful memories for some participants, and a proper evaluation of the risk/benefits (to the individual) of testing is needed. As well as signing a form which gives their informed consent to filling in the questionnaires or taking the test, participants should always be provided with contact details so that they may raise any queries or concerns with the researcher or professional at a later date.

The next important consideration is that the experience of taking the test should be exactly the same, no matter who in the world administers it to which person. This sounds straightforward, but in practice it may not be. Each commercial test normally comes with a manual, which specifies precisely what instructions the participants will be given; these need to be read verbatim, stilted though this sometimes appears, in order to ensure that everyone taking the test has the same experience. It would otherwise be impossible to compare people's scores. Some of the factors that need to be controlled are discussed in the subsections that follow.

THE ENVIRONMENT

The environment should be free from distractions, noise, talking etc. with no opportunity for collaboration, cheating or copying. This is fairly easy to arrange when questionnaires, ability tests or attainment tests are completed using pen and paper in a large room, such as a lecture hall. It is much harder to ensure that the environment is suitable when a test is administered via the internet. If anonymous participants complete an internet questionnaire or ability test, then there is obviously no guarantee that the testing conditions are optimal. The test could be taken on a mobile phone with a dirty cracked screen which cannot display high-resolution graphics over an internet connection which is so slow that pages take a long time to load. The items might be answered by a group of people working together, perhaps accessing other websites to help them find the correct answers. Or there might be loud music or conversations in the background, which would affect concentration. It is in any case extraordinarily difficult to ensure that the person actually taking the test or questionnaire is who they say they are, though a webcam may be of use here. And there is absolutely no way of ensuring that participants take the test seriously. Some participants may treat the whole thing as a joke, ticking boxes at random – particularly if they are being paid or coerced into taking part in order to obtain 'course credit' or something similar. Though internet testing of anonymous volunteers makes data collection very easy, the quality of that data is always going to be suspect. It makes far more sense to ensure that the testing happens under the eye of a trained test administrator.

THE INSTRUCTIONS

The instructions ensure that all participants understand what they are being asked to do when completing each scale of the test; examples are given in Chapter 13.

TIME LIMITS

Ability tests normally have strict time limits for each scale; computerised tests may automatically impose a time limit for each item or each scale. It goes without saying that these should be imposed strictly to ensure that scores are comparable from group to group.

INDIVIDUAL TESTING

Some tests are administered one-to-one rather than in groups. These tend to be high-quality ability tests used by clinical psychologists, educational psychologists and others to evaluate children's performance on a number of tasks involving thinking, reasoning, knowledge and memory. Because these tests involve an interaction between just two people, the items can be rather more varied than in the standard, group-administered ability or personality tests mentioned above. For example, participants can be given an assortment of cards and asked to rearrange them into a sequence which tells a logical story (e.g., 'boy playing football in street', 'football heading towards window of house', 'window broken, with angry man coming out of house', 'boy running away, man in garden with broken window visible'). Other tests might involve manipulating small objects using tweezers or using spanners and screwdrivers on nuts and bolts in a frame. Because it is essential that the difficulty of each item is the same for everyone, it is essential that the cards, jigsaw pieces, nuts and bolts etc. are placed in exactly the same position on the table for each participant – something which requires considerable skill from the test administrator! For this reason, these tests are normally only supplied to professionals who have undergone a period of supervised training in their use.

LOCATING TESTS

Identifying the 'best' test for a particular application is not straightforward. Researchers and practitioners will need to bear in mind the context in which the test is used (as a test which works with well-motivated students may not work when used as part of a job-selection procedure), the characteristics of the sample (age, cultural background, reading-skills etc.), as well as the psychometric qualities of the tests. Giving suggestions as to which tests might be appropriate for each ability, trait and state that has been studied in the last century would make the book both enormous and excruciatingly dull, and it would be out of date almost immediately. However, readers will need to locate tests from time to time, and so here are some suggestions which may be useful.

Some tests are well-known commercial products, and psychologists and others who need to find a test measuring anxiety, general intelligence or virtually any other trait or state should firstly turn to the Buros Organisation's 'Mental Measurements Yearbooks'. These books list commercially published tests by topic and (crucially) also review many of them in some detail. Few of us would buy a washing machine without reading an independent review by an expert, and the same principle applies to tests. Test reviews can also be purchased from the website http://www.buros.org. Independent reviews such as these really are essential for identifying good, well-constructed tests which may be worth the substantial price sometimes charged by test publishers.

Test publishers' catalogues are another option. However useful these may be for finding out what tests are available, it is important to remember that these are marketing tools and are unlikely to offer balanced evaluations of tests. It is essential to consult the literature to determine whether a particular test seems to measure what it claims to measure using a sample which is fairly similar to the one that you propose to use. Publishers are unlikely to mention that a particular test is technically flawed, so selecting a test from a publisher's catalogue alone is a courageous act. It is necessary to read the research literature to determine whether the test is likely to be useful; guidance about the desirable properties that a test should show is given later in this book.

Locating tests which are not published commercially can be harder. Lew Goldman has an excellent selection of personality scales known as the 'International Personality Item Pool' or IPIP, hosted at http://ipip.ori.org which are free to use for any purpose. This website also gives some information about their validity with various samples.

Many tests used in psychology appear as appendices to journal articles. A literature search using keywords such as 'anxiety', 'Mexic*' and 'child*' in a bibliographic database for locating journal articles (Web of Science, PsychINFO or the like – not a simple internet search) will identify journal articles that have studied anxiety in Mexican children, for example. It is then necessary to read these journal articles to find out which tests were used; they will be listed in the reference section. The paper will very often contain the test items.

If the author of a test is known and there is reason to believe that the test may be published in the back of a journal article, a citation search can be useful. Papers containing tests tend to be heavily cited by others and so are easy to find.

Members of the American Psychological Association (or those whose universities have purchased access to their databases) can access a database known as Psychtests. It is possible to search for tests using this and sometimes download tests and supporting documentation directly – for a fee.

The Educational Testing Service maintains a substantial database listing commercial and non-commercial tests, which anyone can search. It is called Test Link and its URL at the time of writing is https://www.ets.org/test_link. It allows keyword search (so that one can search for scales measuring anxiety, for example) together with author search etc. and gives details of where each test may be obtained; in the case of recent unpublished tests, this may include the email address of the author. This database includes details of some very old tests as well as up-to-date ones and is warmly recommended.

It is also vital to critically evaluate the test for oneself, in order to determine whether it was soundly constructed and is likely to be suitable for use for your application with your sample. All too often researchers seem to assume that, because others have used a particular test, it must be well constructed and measure what it claims to assess. If the test was developed in a different country or a long time ago, it will be necessary to check that it measures what it claims to measure (see Chapter 7) before it is used for any serious purpose. Above all, it is important to read through the items and convince yourself that (a) they are different in meaning from each other, (b) they completely cover the domain of interest, and (c) they are appropriate for the sample with whom they are to be used (language, difficulty, cultural assumptions etc.). It may also be necessary to check that the items behave as they should, as described in Chapters 6 and 13.

Finally, it is important to bear copyright considerations in mind when administering scales in *any* format. Whilst items from the IPIP are free to be used however one wishes, most commercial tests explicitly forbid the photocopying of test booklets or answer sheets and do not permit test items to be administered by other means (e.g., using survey software). There is something of a grey area when items are published as an appendix to articles in commercial scientific journals.

OVERVIEW

This chapter has introduced some key terms and introduced the basic logic of psychological assessment – that items in a scale must be selected so that they sample all the items that could possibly be written to measure some trait or state (the 'domain' of items). It then examined various types of items used in tests of ability, personality etc. and gave a critical evaluation of each format. This reveals that the commonly used Likert-scale format has a surprising number of problems. The chapter then outlined the importance of administering tests in a standardised way and outlined some advantages and pitfalls of various methods of test administration. The chapter concluded with some practical guidance on how to find a test for a particular application.

NOTE

1 This is not quite true. Many tests impose some sort of very generous time limit, otherwise some dedicated or obsessional participants will wrestle with the more difficult items until doomsday. However, these limits are usually set so that 90% or more of the participants normally complete all items in the time allowed.

CHAPTER 3
SCORING TESTS AND SCALES

Chapter 2 showed several different types of items and suggested that items measuring the same trait should be grouped together to form scales. However, it never considered how responses to test items should be turned into numbers. It is normal to do so for ability and personality tests and questionnaires; objective tests will probably already give numerical measurements (e.g., the number of fidgets per minute, the change in skin resistance in ohms or the change in the inter-beat-interval of the heart), whilst users of projective tests tend to prefer qualitative rather than quantitative interpretations of the participants' responses.

However, the vast majority of scales involve some form of scoring process. For example, the teacher scoring the attainment test which measured knowledge of historical dates (see Chapter 2) would probably give students one point for each answer that is correct. As this is a free-response test, guessing is unlikely to be much of an issue. Each child's score on the test would then be calculated by adding up the number of items correctly answered.

Ability tests are usually scored in a similar way, with one point being awarded for each correct answer. If the instructions specify that participants should not guess, incorrect answers would be penalised – normally by deducting one point. Matters become slightly more complex with multiple-choice tests. What if the instructions ask participants to guess if they are unsure, but some do not? This is a fairly common situation. Sometimes participants leave an item blank meaning to return to it later but forget to do so. Some tests have time limits which are so short that participants do not have time to attempt all of the questions. So what should happen if someone has not attempted all of the items despite having been asked to guess if unsure? The best solution is probably to randomly guess answers on behalf of the participant for those items which are left blank. The score of the participant would otherwise be underestimated, as some of the guesses to multiple-choice items will probably be correct.

Table 3.1 Three items measuring Extraversion, showing the answer sheet and marking key

		Strongly agree	Agree	Neutral	Disagree	Strongly disagree
1	I am the life and soul of the party	O	O	O	O	O
2	I would rather sit by myself than socialise	O	O	O	O	O
3	I have more friends than most people	O	O	O	O	O
	Marking key for Items 1–3					
		Strongly agree	Agree	Neutral	Disagree	Strongly disagree
1	I am the life and soul of the party	5	4	3	2	1
2	I would rather sit by myself than socialise	1	2	3	4	5
3	I have more friends than most people	5	4	3	2	1

Likert scales are commonly used to measure personality, attitudes etc. They award a high mark to a response at the end of the scale corresponding to a high level of the trait or state; the response indicating a low level of the trait or state is awarded a low score, and the other responses are spread evenly between these two.

For example, suppose that the three items shown in Table 3.1 were used to measure Extraversion, or sociability. The top half of the table shows the answer sheet, and the bottom of the table shows which marks would be awarded for the various answers. So, someone high on this trait would strongly agree with Item 1, strongly disagree with Item 2 and strongly agree with the Item 3.

It does not matter which numbers are used, as long as the difference between adjacent numbers (one, in the above example) is always the same.

One could even start each item at a different (arbitrary) value, though it is difficult to think of a rationale for why one would do so. Table 3.2 gives an example.

Table 3.2 Marking key where responses are equally spaced, although starting at different (arbitrary) numbers

		Strongly agree	Agree	Neutral	Disagree	Strongly disagree
1	I am the life and soul of the party	11	13	15	17	19
2	I would rather sit by myself than socialise	9	7	5	3	1
3	I have more friends than most people	2	4	6	8	10

However, the following example (Table 3.3) would not work for two reasons: first the difference between the marks awarded to adjacent statements is not constant (in Item 1), and second, the difference between adjacent cells is not the same for every item (scores for Item 2 increase by one from low to high; scores for Item 3 increase by two).

The rationale for all this is as follows. The scores from psychological scales are normally correlated with other things – for example, scores on *other* psychological scales, some aspect of behaviour such as simple reaction time. The important thing about correlations is that they are insensitive to the scale of measurement. So it does not matter whether the 'low' score for an item starts at 0, 1, 1199816 or anything else – the correlation between scores on the test and anything else will be exactly the same.

Table 3.3 Marking key where the difference between adjacent categories is not always identical and where there are also differences *between* items

		Strongly agree	Agree	Neutral	Disagree	Strongly disagree
1	I am the life and soul of the party	1	3	4	6	9
2	I would rather sit by myself than socialise	5	4	3	2	1
3	I have more friends than most people	1	3	5	7	9

EXERCISE 3.1: CORRELATIONS

Resources required: Spreadsheet 3.1: Correlations. From www.routledge.com/9781138228894

Purpose: To show that correlations are unaffected by the scale of measurement, or the starting value

Contents of spreadsheet:

- Section A shows the responses that five people make to the items in Table 3.1. Each person places an x in the box which best describes them.
- Section B shows the scoring key – the table which converts the 'x's into numbers. When freshly downloaded, this shows that for Item 1 anyone strongly agreeing with the statement is awarded 5 points, 4 points if they agree, and so on. For Item 2 (where strongly *disagreeing* with the items represents a high level of Extraversion), strongly agreeing is awarded 1 point, agreeing 2 points and so on.
- Section C shows the scores which each of the five people obtained on some other scale.
- It also shows the scored responses obtained by applying the scoring key to the responses in Section A, plus each person's total score on the three items.
- Section D shows the correlation between the total score and the score on the other scale.

Suggested activity:

- Check that you understand how the scoring key translates each person's response to each item into a number. Perhaps alter some of the responses (deleting one x and inserting another on the same line) to check.
- To convince yourself that the correlations in Section D are not influenced by whether the values in the scoring key start at 1, 0 or some other number, try adding a constant to all the numbers in the scoring key for one of the items; add 10 to each value of the scoring key for Item 1, perhaps. The correlation between the total score and the score on the other test does not change – though of course the total score increases.
- You might also like to change the interval between adjacent categories for all items. Perhaps use the values in Table 3.2. Again, the correlation does not change.
- However, if the interval between adjacent categories in the scoring key are not all the same, the correlation *will* change. Try the values in Table 3.3 or any other values which you choose.

Points to note:

- Experiment by changing entries in the GREEN areas. Results are in the YELLOW areas. Simply download another copy if you accidentally change formulae.

Learning outcomes:

Readers should now be able to

- show an understanding of how Likert scales are scored using a scoring key;
- appreciate that as long as the interval between adjacent categories is the same within and between items, the correlation between scores on a test and another variable remain the same;
- appreciate that it does not matter whether the interval between adjacent categories is large or small.

THE PRACTICALITIES OF SCORING TESTS

LIKERT-SCALED ITEMS MARKED ON A TEST BOOKLET OR ANSWER SHEET

It is still common practice to gather data using paper questionnaires (and sometimes separate answer sheets) similar to those shown below. Unlike the example in Table 3.1, the items in Figure 3.1 measure two different traits; Items 1 and 3 measure Extraversion (sociability and optimism) whilst Items 2 and 4 measure Neuroticism.

A scoring template would normally be printed on a transparent acetate sheet which is placed over the answer sheet (or question booklet) so that the marked response is visible.

There is one transparent acetate sheet for each scale. Each shows how many marks should be awarded for a particular response and which responses should be added together. In the example shown in Figures 3.1 and 3.2, when the Extraversion scoring template is placed over the answer sheet, this individual obtains a score of 4 points for Question 1 and 5 points for Question 3. Questions 2 and 4 do not contribute to the Extraversion score. If the Neuroticism scoring template is placed over the answer sheet, scores of 2 and 1 would be awarded for Questions 2 and 4. Thus this person would obtain a score of 9 for Extraversion and 3 for Anxiety.

MARKING BY HAND

There is plenty of scope for errors to creep in when scoring tests manually using templates – typically because the acetate scoring sheet is not correctly placed over the paper answer sheet or because the person scoring the test makes an arithmetic slip when adding together the scores for the individual items (which is normally done using mental arithmetic without writing down anything but the final score for a trait). Errors could also creep in if the respondent does something

Item	Practice items	Strongly agree	Agree	Neutral/ unsure	Disagree	Strongly disagree
P1	I understand how to mark my answers to the items in this questionnaire	●	O	O	O	O
P2	I will be try to be honest when giving my answers	O	O	O	O	O
Item	**Main test**	**Strongly agree**	**Agree**	**Neutral/ unsure**	**Disagree**	**Strongly disagree**
1	I find it easy to talk about myself	O	O	O	O	O
2	I rarely feel 'down'	O	O	O	O	O
3	I'm a pessimist at heart	O	O	O	O	O
4	I worry a lot	O	O	O	O	O
etc.						

Item	Strongly agree	Agree	Neutral/ unsure	Disagree	Strongly disagree
P1	●	O	O	O	O
P2	O	●	O	O	O
Item	**Strongly agree**	**Agree**	**Neutral/ unsure**	**Disagree**	**Strongly disagree**
1	O	●	O	O	O
2	O	●	O	O	O
3	O	O	O	O	●
4	O	O	O	O	●
etc.					

Figure 3.1 Typical format of personality test booklet and (optional) completed answer sheet

strange – for example, marking two answers for a question, one of which was correct, or crossing out a correct answer but not marking any other choice. In this sort of setting, it is quite possible that two scorers might sometimes reach different conclusions about whether or not an answer was correct. However the great advantages of scoring tests this way are

a) the ability to test large groups of people at once – either using test booklets or test items presented using a data projector – without having to set up large numbers of computers;

b) speed of setup – answer sheets and marking templates can be prepared in a few minutes;

c) costs are minimal whereas optical scanners are expensive, and the answer sheets used with them may need to be purchased or specially printed.

A scoring template for Extraversion

Item	Strongly agree	Agree	Neutral/ unsure	Disagree	Strongly disagree
P1					
P2					

Item	Strongly agree	Agree	Neutral/ unsure	Disagree	Strongly disagree
1	5	4	3	2	1
2					
3	1	2	3	4	5
4					

A scoring template for Neuroticism

Item	Strongly agree	Agree	Neutral/ unsure	Disagree	Strongly disagree
P1					
P2					

Item	Strongly agree	Agree	Neutral/ unsure	Disagree	Strongly disagree
1					
2	1	2	3	4	5
3					
4	5	4	3	2	1

Figure 3.2 Transparent scoring templates for Extraversion and Neuroticism scales, for use with the booklets or answer sheets shown in Figure 3.1

The main disadvantages are that

a) the whole process is slow and tedious to perform;
b) it requires mental arithmetic skills from the person scoring the test;
c) the only output is each person's total score on each scale of the test. It is surprising how often one needs a record of precisely which response was made to each item – for example to check the internal consistency of the test (see Chapter 6), identify which responses were most popular, perform a factor analysis to check that all of the items measure the same trait (see Chapter 8) or to identify items which were not attempted. My advice is always to record the responses to individual items even if scoring templates are available because it is extremely likely that these will be needed at some stage during the analysis.

MARKING BY SCANNER

What of optical scanners? These use specially designed answer sheets and commercial software. They scan responses to multiple-choice items, and the associated software also scores the items. This is probably much safer than relying on the mental arithmetic prowess of a human, who may have spent several hours sleepily scoring responses. Furthermore, if the system detects a problem with any items (for example, if two responses are marked for the same item or a coffee stain covers part of the answer sheet), it will normally flag that sheet as requiring human intervention to decide what should be done. Here the degree of accuracy is likely to be high, and it is quick and easy to check this by scanning and scoring sheets twice. The software provides an abundance of information, including the total scores for each person, scores for individual items and various statistical breakdowns.

MARKING BY SPREADSHEET

An alternative to using templates to score responses to multiple-choice tests answered on paper involves simply entering a code identifying which boxes were ticked into a spreadsheet and using this to score the items and test. For example, a mark in the 'strongly disagree' box could be coded as '1', 'disagree' as '2' and so on, using adjacent keys on a QWERTY keyboard which makes data entry much faster than if responses were coded a, b, c etc. It is then necessary to reverse the scores on some items. This solution is likely to be faster and more accurate than marking answer sheets manually using templates. Like the optical scanner it provides the full item-by-item breakdown of results.

Spreadsheet 3.2 scores Likert scales, produces some simple-item statistics and helps one decide which values to use for any missing data. If there are no missing data, it also calculates the total score for each person on each scale. It might be of some practical use, though as before, no guarantee can be given as to its accuracy.

EXERCISE 3.2: SIMPLE LIKERT SCORER

Resources required: Spreadsheet 3.2: Simple Likert scorer. From www.routledge.com/9781138228894

Purpose: To show Likert-scaled data may be scored using a spreadsheet

Contents of spreadsheet: Sample data from seven people on two scales, with one piece of missing data

Suggested activity:

- After entering some basic information in the 'Raw_data' tab, Section A specifies the names for the scales and how the items should be scored. A '1' indicates which scale each item measures; there should therefore only be one '1' in each column.
- Section B contains raw data – indicating which box each person ticked (1 for the leftmost box etc.). Each person *must* be given a name or code in Column A. Missing data should be left blank.
- The 'Scored_Items' tab holds the scored data, which can be copied and pasted into another program. If desired, it is also possible to sort these data in Open Office, so that all of the items in the same scale are next to each other. Missing data appear as blanks.
- The Scores tab shows the mean and standard deviation for each item *based just on those people who answered the item*. This can be useful when deciding which value to use for missing data.

- As the mean of the other participants is 4 for Item 3, it might be useful to go back to the Raw_data tab and replace the blank with 4.
- As there are now no missing data, the scores of each person on each scale are shown in the Scores tab.

Points to note:

- Experiment by changing entries in the GREEN areas. Results are in the YELLOW areas. Simply download another copy if you accidentally change formulae.

Learning outcomes:

Readers should now be able to

- score a Likert-scaled questionnaire.

OTHER METHODS OF RECORDING RESPONSES

When the test taker responds using a keyboard, joystick, mouse, touchscreen, mobile device or similar, there is obviously far less room for error. There are several free websites (e.g., SurveyMonkey www.surveymonkey.co.uk) which perform online surveys that are ideal for administering simple Likert-scaled personality questionnaires. Commercial software for presenting and scoring test items other than simple Likert scales can be eye-wateringly expensive, whilst designing one's own software to administer a test can be time consuming, particularly if it includes features such as the ability to modify one's answers. The cost of multiple machines may limit the number of people who can be tested simultaneously. In addition, care must be taken to ensure that familiarity with the hardware will not impact on performance, particularly when testing older people who may also have eyesight and coordination issues. The main advantages of computer administration are that

a) Timings for sections of the test or indeed for individual items can be imposed, whereas when answer sheets are used there is always the problem that some individuals may continue to try to solve ability items after being asked to stop.
b) It is possible to measure a wider range of responses. For example, it is possible to measure how long it takes for each person to answer each item, to measure mouse or joystick movements, to record what a person says . . .
c) It is possible to test remotely – for example, allowing someone to take an aptitude test at home rather than in an assessment centre. (That said, the obvious difficulties are ensuring that the person taking the test is who they say they are and that they do not have any help from other people or electronic devices when taking the test.)

d) It is possible to implement adaptive ability tests (see Chapter 12) where the difficulty of the items administered varies for each participant so that each participant is given items which are taxing but not impossible.

e) Scores may be obtained immediately, allowing feedback to be given.

IPSATISED SCALES

So far, each item in a scale has attempted to measure a person's position along a single trait. For example, each item correctly answered on a test of memory would normally increase a person's score by one point; strongly agreeing with a statement such as 'I suffer from "nerves"' will increase the individual's anxiety score. Ipsatised (or ipsative, or 'forced choice') scales are different. Instead of measuring the extent to which a person agrees with statements measuring various levels of one trait ('normative scales'), ipsative scales provide respondents with several different statements, *each measuring quite different traits*, and requires them to choose which statement best describes them and which is most untrue of how they feel, think or act.

These tests are usually scored by counting the number of times that a person says that a particular trait describes them well, minus the number of times that they say that the trait describes them badly.

An example may make this clearer.

Suppose that a researcher is interested in measuring four different traits: the extent to which they blame others when things go wrong, their level of depression, their belief in luck and their inability to focus their thoughts. It would be possible to devise several items such as those shown in Table 3.4.

In this example, the participant chose the 'neurotic' answer twice; they did not blame others, and they did not have problems focusing their thoughts. When this scale is scored, they would therefore have a score of 2 for Neuroticism, 0 for belief in luck, −1 for blaming others and −1 for inability to focus their thoughts.

This all looks very appealing, and several published tests use this sort of format (mostly in education and occupational/organisational psychology) including the Schwartz Value Survey, the Defense Mechanisms Inventory and the Occupational Personality Questionnaire. However, there are well-documented problems with this approach; those who defend the use of ipsative tests (Baron, 1996; Bartram, 1996) against their critics (Johnson et al., 1988; Meade, 2004) tend to have a vested interest in their use. I certainly have very major reservations about the techniques. The reasons for this are several.

Table 3.4 Examples of two ipsative items

Each item outlines a scenario and offers you four possible reactions. For each item, simply choose the ONE answer which best describes how you would think, feel or act, and put a mark in the 'Best answer' column. Please also identify the ONE answer which is unlike how you would think, feel or act, and mark the 'Worst answer' column.				
			Best answer	**Worst answer**
1	If I perform badly in a test, it is	because the test is unfair.		x
		my own fault for not studying hard enough.	x	
		just bad luck.		
		because I couldn't concentrate.		
2	If I lock myself out of my car,	it's because the locking system is badly designed.		
		I feel like crying.	x	
		it's because everyone makes mistakes sometimes!		
		it's probably because my mind wandered.		x
etc.				

a) They cannot say anything about how one person's *level* of a trait compares with another's.

Psychologists are usually interested in determining a person's level of a trait relative to others; for example, to determine whether a person is neurotic, extraverted or how intelligent they are, or to correlate their scores on some scale with other things. This is more or less essential in many applied settings; for example, to help a personnel manager decide whether a job applicant shows sufficient evidence of leadership ability to be appointable.

Unfortunately, ipsatised tests cannot provide any such information. All they can say is whether a person's (self-reported) level of one trait is lower or higher than their own self-reported score on another trait. But they cannot show whether any of that person's scores are low or high relative to those of other people. So, whilst they may perhaps be of some use when counselling individuals, it makes little sense to try to use ipsatised scales for anything else.

To see why, consider how two people might respond to one of the items from the example in Table 3.4.

Table 3.5 Two respondents with very different levels of agreement produce the same responses to an ipsative item

Item 1	Possible answers to Item 1	Person a			Person b		
			Best	Worst		Best	Worst
If I perform badly on a test, it is	because the test is unfair.	Agree		x	Very strongly disagree		x
	my own fault for not studying hard enough.	Very strongly agree	x		Disagree	x	
	just bad luck.	Strongly agree			Strongly disagree		
	because I couldn't concentrate.	Strongly agree			Strongly disagree		

Table 3.5 shows how two people feel about each possible answer. It can be seen that they have nothing much in common. Person a tends to think that all of the answers describe them quite well, whilst Person b feels that none of them do so. Yet based on their responses to that item, they both end up with exactly the same score on the four scales measured by the test. This is because this format ensures that each person's score on a scale (such as Neuroticism) *is relative to their scores on the other scales.* If all of the scales measure different things (i.e., are uncorrelated) this makes little sense conceptually. Why *should* a person's level of Extraversion affect their score on the Neuroticism scale? It is hard to justify this on any grounds.

b) All the scales are negatively correlated – even when people respond randomly.

Because each item awards one point to one scale and takes away one point from another scale, each person's total score (summed across all traits) will always be zero. So a person who has a high score on one trait (Neuroticism, say) *must* have low scores on the other traits. This means that all of the traits will be negatively correlated together.

EXERCISE 3.3: CORRELATIONS BETWEEN IPSATIVE SCALES FROM RANDOM DATA

Resources required: Spreadsheet 3.3: Correlations between ipsative scales from random data. From www.routledge.com/9781138228894

Purpose: To show that ipsative scales are negatively correlated. To explore how the number of scales, the number of items and the number of people in the sample influence these correlations

Contents of spreadsheet: This spreadsheet simulates data. It simulates how people would respond randomly to items such as those in Table 3.4 and shows the correlations between the scales.

Suggested activity:

- Start by setting the number of scales to 4, and the number of items to 2 in Section A. Set the number of simulated people to 250. This represents the scores of 250 people who respond entirely randomly to the two items in Table 3.4. In Section B, Note the correlations between scales (and the average correlation). Generate another set of random data by pressing f9 (Windows or Linux) or fn/f9 or CTRL/SHIFT/f9 (MacOS) and repeat several (10?) times, in order to establish what the correlations between the scales typically are.
- Try altering the number of scales (perhaps using 3, 5 and 8) and for each condition try altering the number of people (20 and 250?) and the number of items (perhaps 2, 10 and 20). What influences the size of the correlations between the scales? What influences the standard deviation – in other words the amount of variation between the correlations?
- Try to produce the largest correlation that you can between a pair of scales.
- Using a calculator, work out −1/(no. of scales −1). Does this resemble the correlation you find?

Points to note:

- Experiment by changing entries in the GREEN areas. Results are in the YELLOW areas. Simply download another copy if you accidentally change formulae.
- Pay particular attention to how small numbers of people result in correlations which vary considerably – though the average size of the correlation stays roughly the same. Note too that correlations between the scales get larger as the number of scales decreases. So a small sample with few scales will produce some very appreciable (negative) correlations between scales. It would be easy to interpret these as being of psychological interest, even though they mean nothing as they stem from random numbers.
- For those who wish to delve deeper, the simulated data are shown below the correlations. Each participant's data consists of two lines – the responses which they classify as 'like me' and the second row, those responses which they feel do not describe them. (The two entries are obviously different!) Each scale is scored by adding up the number of times an item is marked 'like me' minus the number of times it is marked 'unlike me'. These scores are shown to the right of the data. It is these scores which are correlated together.

Learning outcomes:

Readers should now be able to

- show some familiarity with the idea of using simulated data to understand statistical issues;
- appreciate that ipsative scales show substantial negative correlations – even when there is really no relationship between the scales at all (i.e., when the responses are completely random).

If participants filled in the answers to several Likert scales randomly, the correlations between the scales would be close to zero. This makes sense; a correlation of zero implies that there is no relationship between the scores on one scale and the scores on another scale, and when people respond at random then of course there *should* be no relationship between the scores on the various scales. That is what randomness implies.

It should be obvious that this is not the case for these ipsatised scales. The correlations suggest that the scales are negatively correlated – even when people respond at random. This poses several problems for the statistical analyses described in subsequent chapters. For example, techniques such as factor analysis and reliability analysis simply will not yield sensible results (Cornwell and Dunlap, 1994); although techniques have been developed to allow the factor analysis of ipsative data (e.g., Yu et al., 2005), these are complex and not implemented by any statistical package of which I am aware.

c)   The wording of an item can influence the scores obtained on all scales.

Suppose that an item was phrased in such a way that almost everyone would choose the answer which corresponded to that scale. For example, in Item 2 in Table 3.4, if the second alternative was changed from 'I feel like crying' to 'I feel a little upset', then almost everyone would choose that answer – which of course would increase everybody's Neuroticism score and decrease their scores on the other scales. So the way in which one item is worded can affect the scores obtained on different scales. To get round this, advocates of ipsative testing recommend ensuring that all alternatives are equally popular. This can be done as the test is being developed by asking people to rate themselves on Likert-scaled versions of the items; for example, 'On a scale of 1–5, if you lock yourself out of your car, how likely are you to feel like crying?' Only phrases measuring different traits which are rated similarly are put together as alternative answers for an item. However, this begs the question of how similar the scores need to be – and it involves a lot of extra work and ultimately produces a scale which is difficult or impossible to analyse.

CLEANING DATA

One problem which is frequently encountered is that of missing or corrupted data. If participants complete a questionnaire by hand, some individuals will inevitably leave some questions unanswered, mark two answers to the same item or something similar. In other cases, participants may decide to respond randomly – perhaps by ticking the same box for every item on the page.

When answering items in an ability or attainment test, some participants will mark more than one answer for an item or leave some items unanswered. This is a particular problem if the test instructions ask respondents to guess if they do not know the answer to a question. If a questionnaire or test is administered via computer then this may not be an issue, provided that the program or website requires that participants make a response before seeing the next item/problem or proceeding to the next page. Some websites (such as SurveyMonkey) can make this straightforward to implement – however it is necessary to ensure that the person who sets up the questionnaire actually does so. (The default for SurveyMonkey is to allow participants to skip questions if they wish.)

It is therefore unwise to simply take the scores from a questionnaire or test at face value until one has performed some quality control. Ideally, the research protocol should specify how missing data are to be treated before any data are collected. However, in practice, it is more likely that many researchers will not have thought this through and may be faced with a stack of questionnaires with missing values scattered through them. How should one proceed?

RANDOM RESPONDING ON LIKERT SCALES

If participants are not motivated to take the questionnaire or test seriously, it is possible that they may tick boxes at random or give the same response to all of the items on an answer sheet. It clearly makes sense to try to identify and eliminate such individuals before performing any statistical analyses on the data, as random responses will generally reduce the size of any correlations, t-tests or other statistical tests which are performed using the test scores. If test takers are more highly motivated (for example, if the scale is administered as part of a selection procedure) then this is less likely to be a problem. However, identifying random responding is not always straightforward.

First of all, it makes sense just to look at the answer sheets (or the coded responses) *before* the items are scored, in order to check whether each individual seems to have chosen the same response to many consecutive items; this may (perhaps) indicate that they are not answering the questions honestly. However, it will always be a matter of judgement; someone who ticks the 'neutral' or 'unsure' box to all the items on a Likert scale might genuinely have problems formulating an answer to the questions that are posed. However, if a person strongly agrees (or disagrees) with each item, or chooses the same alternative for every item in an ability test, then it might make sense to consider discarding their data.

Some questionnaires include a random responding scale. In Chapter 1, I bemoaned the fact that many scales in common use essentially paraphrase the same item many times. Whilst being deplorable for measuring personality traits, such items may be useful when checking for random responses. For, if someone strongly agrees that they feel anxious and also strongly agrees that they feel calm and relaxed, it seems probable that they have either misread a question or are ticking boxes at random. Some personality questionnaires contain a 'random-responding' scale to check whether individuals give discrepant responses like these, and it is not too arduous a job to construct one oneself if necessary by identifying pairs of items which have a very high positive or negative correlation (above 0.7 or below −0.7, say), and using these items to form a random-response scale. It does not matter at all if the pairs of items measure quite different traits or states.

For example, suppose that previous analyses had shown that Items 1 and 3 in the questionnaire shown in Table 3.6 correlated 0.8, whilst Items 2 and 4 correlated −0.7. It would be possible to construct a random-responding scale based on these items by using the scoring key shown in the table.

If someone is consistent, then their score on Item 1 should be the same as their score on Item 3. Likewise, their score on Item 2 should be the same as their score on Item 4 (which is reverse-scored, as the correlation between Item 2 and Item 4 is large and *negative*). So a random-responding scale could be constructed by adding together a person's scores on one item of each highly correlated pair and subtracting the scores

Table 3.6 Four items which may be useful for detecting random responding

		Strongly agree	Agree	Neutral	Disagree	Strongly disagree
1	I prefer my own company to being in large gatherings	1	2	3	4	5
2	I feel on top of the world	1	2	3	4	5
3	There's nothing worse than a large party	1	2	3	4	5
4	I feel sad	5	4	3	2	1

from the remaining items. In this case one could add together the scores from Items 1 and 2 (or 1 and 4, or 2 and 3) and subtract the scores from Items 3 and 4 (or 2 and 3, or 1 and 4). The closer this number is to zero, the more consistent a person is.

But what should one do if a person's score on a random-responding scale is high? This is a difficult decision. If the assessment is being made for the purpose of individual assessment (for clinical purposes, for example), then raising the issue with the participant might give some insight as to whether and why they intentionally responded in this way. If the data are being gathered as part of a norming exercise (see below) then it makes sense not to eliminate anyone, as other samples of people will probably also contain a similar proportion of people who respond randomly. However, if the data are being gathered for research purposes (for example, to correlate scores on a scale with some other variable(s)) then it might be acceptable to remove a small percentage of people from the sample if there is clear evidence of random responding – although this should obviously be done before performing any statistical analyses, otherwise it might be tempting to simply remove cases in order to increase the size of the correlation, improve model fit and so on.

MISSING DATA FROM LIKERT SCALES

What if some items are left unanswered? Several options are available. These include ignoring the missing data, dropping anyone with missing data from the sample and trying to estimate what the missing data might have been.

Ignoring missing data from a Likert scale is a very bad idea. Assuming that the items are scored 1–7 (or something similar), it is clear that simply ignoring missing items (essentially giving them a score of 0) will result in the individual having a lower score than they should for the scale. Dropping anyone with missing data from the analysis is much more defensible, but much depends on how much data is missing and how long the scales are. There are no hard-and-fast rules, but if someone omits just one item from a 50-item seven-point Likert scale, it should be fairly clear that estimating their score on that item might be a sensible option. With so many items in the scale, the standard deviation of scores within the sample is likely to be quite large, and, even if the estimate is terribly inaccurate, it will not greatly affect their score on the scale. However, if more than a few per cent of data are missing from any participant, it might be better to drop that participant from the sample and not use their scores on any of the other scales or measures either. This is sometimes called 'listwise deletion of data'. Unfortunately, listwise deletion of data is not a panacea. First, it might lead to biased samples. Suppose that some individuals chose not to answer an item asking about attitudes to abortion, for example. Might they have strong views which they chose not to disclose? If so, dropping them might make the sample less representative of the population than it would otherwise be. Second (and more pragmatically) listwise deletion of data can sometimes lead to a drastic decrease in the size of the sample.

The next option is to drop only the person's score on the scale which is affected by missing data. Thus if 100 people complete three scales (Scale A, Scale B and Scale C) suppose that five people omit one or more items from Scale A, and three different people omit one or more items from Scale B. Everybody answers every question in Scale C. The correlation between Scale A and Scale B would be based on 92 people, the correlation between Scales A and C would be based on 95 people, and the correlation between Scales B and C would be based on 97 people. The disadvantages of this approach are first that the correlations might, in extreme cases and in theory, be based on completely different samples of people. And it means that the correlations differ in their statistical power, which could complicate the interpretation of the results. However, if the sample size is large and only a few per cent of data are missing for any variable, this 'pairwise deletion' procedure can be the most practical.

Estimation of scores is another option – and this is where life can become needlessly complicated in my opinion. Suppose that an item has a seven-point Likert scale, giving scores between 1–7. If someone omits to answer this item, what score should they be given? One possibility would be to give them the mid-point score (4 in this case). Why this and not (say) 1 or 7? If we estimate their score as 4, then the worst-case scenario is that the person would have answered the item with a 1 or 7 had they attempted it – meaning that we have over- or underestimated their score by three. If we estimate their score to be 1, then the discrepancy could be as large as $7-1=6$. So it is safer to choose the mid-point.

But suppose that everyone else in the sample obtains a score of 1 or 2 on this item. It could ask people how much they agree with some extreme view – capital punishment for minor offences, for example. In this case estimating missing data as a '4' might not seem so sensible; it might be safer to look at the modal score (the most popular score) given by the people who *did* answer that question and use this as our estimate of the missing data. There is a lot to be said for this simple technique.

Finally, it is possible to estimate what a person's score on the scale (or missing item) might have been, based on their responses to those items which are not missing. This is fairly simple to accomplish using techniques such as multiple regression, and there is substantial literature on the topic. Newman (2014) gives some useful practical guidelines, and computer programs such as SPSS allow missing data to be estimated ('imputed') with ease. There are also a number of mathematical techniques which can be used to estimate missing data and substantial literature on the subject.

The reason I do not propose going into detail about such methods is that (a) they are potentially dangerous, and (b) if the amount of missing data is small, then it should not matter much how the missing data are estimated. So why are the techniques dangerous? Missing-data estimation techniques will always ensure that a person's estimates are broadly in line with their responses to other, similar, items. Suppose that a person strongly agrees with nine statements such as 'Immigrants should be repatriated', 'The courts are too lenient' and other items indicating a right-wing political attitude, but they fail to answer a tenth item. We will never know why, but any imputation method will assume that the person would have answered this item in line with the others. But suppose that the item was 'Homosexuality is against Bible teaching' and the person with missing data was themselves gay. They might well have disagreed with such a statement, and this might be why they left it unanswered. Second-guessing how an individual might have responded based on the responses made by different individuals will not always be accurate. It might also affect the results of other statistical analyses. For, given that any imputation method based on regression or similar techniques will assume that the response to a missing item is consistent with a person's other responses, the estimation of missing data will quite possibly overestimate the consistency of people's responses. This will make the correlations between items somewhat higher than they ought to be, and this in turn will affect important properties of the scale, such as its reliability and factor structure – terms which we explore in later chapters.

The bottom line is that if large amounts of data are estimated, there is a real risk that the scale will appear to show better psychometric properties than it really has. And as soon as we start to estimate values, we move away from reality. Whatever its faults and challenges, psychometrics is based upon hard data – the responses made by real people to a standard set of items. Once one starts estimating items, this is no longer the case, and this should be a cause for concern. Statisticians delight in the challenge of using ever-more-complex mathematical models to estimate missing values – but just because one can, should one do so? It is hard to have much faith in any results from a dataset which is riddled with missing data.

In terms of practical guidelines, I would be wary of estimating more than 5–10% of the items from a scale; for short scales this would mean no estimation at all. I would also seriously consider dropping participants who omit items from several scales. If the data have been gathered from a carefully constructed sample, rather than a convenience sample, it would be necessary to check their demographics against the remainder of the sample to ensure that the people who omit several items are not similar in terms of age, location, background, gender, scores on those scales which they *did* complete etc. If this analysis shows that the people who omitted items do not form a random subset of the original sample, there is a problem with no real solution, as removing these individuals will bias the sample. One possibility might be to remove the individuals with missing data and also remove *other* people to keep the sample balanced. So, if 20 men showed unacceptable levels of missing data, one approach might be to remove both them and 20 women (with similar age, locations, background, scores on the non-missing scales etc.) to ensure that the sample remains balanced.

MISSING SCORES ON MULTIPLE-CHOICE ABILITY AND ATTAINMENT SCALES

Ability scales usually impose some sort of time limit. As discussed in Chapter 2, speeded tests have short time limits. Virtually nobody will have time to complete all of the items, and the score on a scale will be the number of items correctly answered within the time limit. Unanswered items are simply ignored when scoring these tests. Power tests have more generous time limits, and the items generally start off by being easy and then become more difficult as the scale progresses. Thus each person progresses through the easy items to a set of items which they find taxing, whilst the later items in the scale will be difficult or impossible for almost everyone. But what should people do if they do not know the answer? The test instructions need to make this clear and also specify whether incorrect guesses are penalised. If the instructions do not specify whether participants should guess if they do not know the correct answer, there is a risk that scores on the test will be confounded by willingness to guess; those who do so would have a higher score than others of equal ability who did not guess because some of the guesses would turn out to be correct. What if the instructions specify that wrong answers will be penalised? This is hardly a panacea either, as some participants might risk a guess if they manage to eliminate a few of the alternative answers to a question, whilst others might be more risk averse. So once again there is a danger that the scores on the scale will be influenced by willingness to take a risk. Some tests urge participants to guess if they are unsure of the answer. This will inevitably add some random 'noise' to each person's score, and this will reduce the size of correlations between the items etc. Someone who knows the answers to only four answers of a 20-item scale will have to guess the answers to 16 items, whilst someone who knows the answers to 16 items will only have to guess the answers to four of them. Worryingly, it will mean that the scores of the lower-ability individuals are likely to be less accurate than the scores of higher-ability individuals, as they will have guessed more answers.

If this is not obvious, look at Spreadsheet 3.4.

EXERCISE 3.4: GUESSING IN ABILITY TESTS

Resources required: Spreadsheet 3.4: Guessing in ability tests. From www.routledge.com/9781138228894

Purpose: To show that asking participants to guess can increase the range of scores of low-ability participants

Contents of spreadsheet: Simulated data from low-ability and high-ability respondents to a 20-item ability test

Suggested activity:

- Scroll down to see the data in Section B: 40 high-ability participants score 16/20 correct and guess the remaining four answers at random. Low-ability participants score 4/20 and guess the rest.
- The graph shows the frequency distribution of the total scores obtained by all 80 participants. Generate several new sets of data (f9, fn/f9 or SHIFT/CTRL/f9) to show this is not a fluke.

Points to note:

- Note that the range of scores is larger for the low-ability participants, because they have guessed more answers.

Learning outcomes:

Readers should now be able to

- appreciate that guessing increases the standard deviation of test scores, as some people's luck is better than others when they guess.

This finding has some rather unpleasant implications for statistics (such as the Pearson correlation, analysis of variance and regression) that assume that the amount of scatter is roughly the same at each level of ability. It is fair to say that if most psychologists are aware of this problem, they ignore it.

That said, if a test requires participants to guess if they are unsure of an answer and, despite this, some items are left unanswered, it is necessary to guess on their behalf. Of course, if participants were to guess, it is probable that they would be able to eliminate some incorrect responses – but as we cannot know what strategies an individual would have used to answer an item which they did not attempt, it is normal to assume that they would have just guessed answers at random. This is less than ideal, but it is hard to think of a better solution without becoming bogged down with complex estimation procedures.

Missing data is a problem with no good solution, and it is advisable to make every attempt to ensure that each participant in a study follows the instructions and attempts all items of a Likert scale, and all items of a test where the instructions ask them to guess if unsure. One otherwise has to make difficult decisions as to whether to drop participants or enter the realms of fantasy-land by second-guessing why participants did not answer certain questions and deciding what to do about the situation. Although much has been written about the estimation of missing data, in my opinion, if one needs to worry about whether one estimation method is markedly better than another, then one has so much missing data that *any* analysis will be unsafe. Meade and Craig (2012) and Gallitto and Leth-Steenson (2015) provide useful guidelines for dealing with missing data *in extremis*.

MEASUREMENT IN PSYCHOLOGY

The guidelines for scoring tests given above are very straightforward; after all, how else *could* one sensibly score tests other than by giving one point for each correct answer? We have all been so accustomed to this procedure, used when assessing school performance, in game shows on television and in numerous other contexts, that it seems to be second nature. In fact, it makes some quite substantial assumptions about the relationship between performance on individual items and ability, though these are rarely considered or made explicit.

Consider an ability test whose items differ in difficulty. For example, ten items might ask participants to solve anagrams whose lengths vary from four to 12 letters. (We will assume that all of the words are equally common, so that the length of the word is what determines the difficulty of the item.) Suppose that two people get five of these correct within the allocated time period of three minutes.

If one point is awarded for each correct answer, these people have equal levels of ability. But what if one person correctly solved all of the easy items (4–8 letters long) whilst the other person got some of these wrong but correctly solved several of the harder items? Would it still be sensible to regard these people as having the same level of ability?

'Of course,' readers will exclaim at this point, 'this is highly unlikely, for it is obvious that anyone who solves a hard item will also be able to solve all items which are easier, too.' And this is quite possibly correct; my purpose in mentioning it is to point out that whenever scores on items are added together, there is an assumption that (almost) everyone who correctly solves a difficult ability item will be able to solve all (or almost all) of the easier ones. Otherwise it makes little sense to add together the scores on several items.

Louis Guttman suggested a very simple model linking people's abilities to item difficulties. He argues that it should be able to plot these on a graph as shown in Figure 3.3.

The vertical axis shows the probability of getting an item correct, which Guttman argued should be either 0 (assuming a free-response rather than a multiple-choice item) or 1.0. The horizontal axis represents the abilities of the people taking the items; the four arrows represent four people with various levels of ability. The lines

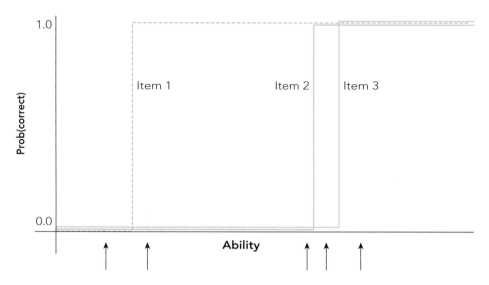

Figure 3.3 Item characteristic curves for three items forming a Guttman scale. Arrows represent people scoring 0, 1, 1, 2 and 3 on the scale

('item characteristic curves' or 'ICCs' – an important term) show the probability that someone with a particular level of ability will pass each of the items.

Someone with a very low level of ability (leftmost arrow) would have a zero probability of correctly answering any item. People with slightly higher ability (second and third arrows) would answer Item 1 correctly – but are bound to answer Item 2 incorrectly. The fourth person will answer the first two items correctly but will fail the third. The final person will answer all three items correctly. Guttman's model makes explicit the assumption that we make when adding together scores on items – that everyone who answers a difficult item correctly also answers all easier items correctly. If we do not make this assumption, then it makes little sense to treat the total score as a measure of a person's ability.

The good thing about Guttman's model is that it is empirically testable and needs nothing in the way of fancy statistics – although it does assume that people either agree/disagree with a statement or answer an ability item correctly or incorrectly.

Suppose that five people respond to three ability items as shown in Table 3.7; 1 represents a correct answer and 0 an incorrect answer. The total score for each person and for each item are also shown.

To determine whether the items form a Guttman scale, all that is necessary is to firstly sort the data by the total score per person so that the person with the lowest score appears in the first row, a person with the next highest total score appears in the second row and so on. This is shown in Table 3.8.

Table 3.7 Responses of five people to three ability items

	Item 1	Item 2	Item 3	Total
Person 1	0	0	0	0
Person 2	0	0	1	1
Person 3	1	1	1	3
Person 4	1	0	1	2
Person 5	0	0	1	1
Total for item	2	1	4	

Table 3.8 Guttman scaling: sorting rows by total score

	Item 1	Item 2	Item 3	Total for person
Person 1	0	0	0	0
Person 2	0	0	1	1
Person 5	0	0	1	1
Person 4	1	0	1	2
Person 3	1	1	1	3
Total for item	2	1	4	

Next, sort the *columns* by the total for each *item* – so that the first column of data shows an item which most people got correct, the second column shows the next most difficult item, and so on. This is shown in Table 3.9.

Just inspecting this Table 3.9 will show whether the items form a Guttman scale. Read across the rows for each person. It can be seen that a 0 is *never* followed by a 1. This means that a person who answers an item incorrectly *never* goes on to answer an easier item correctly. This indicates that the items form a Guttman scale.

Table 3.9 Guttman scaling: sorting columns by total correct

	Item 3	Item 1	Item 2	Total for person
Person 1	0	0	0	0
Person 2	1	0	0	1
Person 5	1	0	0	1
Person 4	1	1	0	2
Person 3	1	1	1	3
Total for item	4	2	1	

This all sounds very straightforward – but unfortunately like many good ideas it does not work well in practice. It does not really apply to Likert scales, although Likert items could be rephrased in order to undergo Guttman scaling. So the item 'Do you like large social gatherings? (a) Very much (b) Quite a lot (c) Not particularly (d) Not at all' could become four items: 'Do you very much enjoy social gatherings', 'Do you quite enjoy social gatherings' etc. for the purposes of Likert scaling. However, the obvious problem with this approach is that participants will check back to make sure they are acting consistently, and so it would be amazing if these items did not form a Guttman scale (unless, of course, the items are separated by other items asking quite different questions, which would make the checking process harder).

It is often claimed that social-distance measures form Guttman scales. These involve items such as

a) I would happily share a house with a person of a different ethnic background to my own.
b) I would not mind living next door to someone from a different ethnic background to my own.
c) I would not mind living in a town where there are significant numbers of people from a different ethnic background to my own.

The rationale for constructing these items is that if a person agrees with the first statement, then their lack of prejudice also suggests that they should agree with the other statements, too. Thus the items will form a Guttman scale.

This sounds very encouraging – but the problem really is that this 'scale' is more a psychometric exercise than anything else. As discussed in Chapter 1, the content of these items is terribly narrow in scope, and so a scale such as this is unlikely to reveal any unexpected insights about human personality, attitudes and so forth. Each item assesses whether or not a person would feel comfortable living at a certain level of proximity to members of other ethnic backgrounds, and one might as well measure this with a single item as this scale. In addition, there is no guarantee that the way in which people answer such questions predicts how they would actually behave, whilst it could be argued that the questions are silly anyway; it is quite possible that people might be prejudiced against some ethnic groups but not others. Implicit prejudice and other types of evidence for prejudice (see e.g., Pettigrew and Meertens, 1995) are not considered at all. So it is hard to see that scores on this scale can say much on their own. They would need to be combined with other evidence in order to be useful – see 'hierarchical models' in Chapter 11.

The good thing about Guttman scaling is that it can be related to how we measure objects in the physical world. Suppose that we want to measure the height of trees. Imagine that the horizontal axis measures height, and the items in the test are:

a) Is the tree more than 2 m high?
b) Is the tree more than 7 metres high?
c) Is the tree more than 9 metres high?

You wander through a wood, measuring a random sample of trees and giving each tree a score based on the answers to the questions shown above – where answering 'yes' to a question achieves a score of 1, and 'no' is scored as 0. Thus an 8-metre-high tree would be given a score of 2 on this scale.

These items form a Guttman scale as shown in Figure 3.3, as every object that is over 9 metres high is also over 7 metres and over 2 metres high. You might wonder why I chose these particular values of height. I chose them more or less at random, based only on the intuition that some of the trees might be quite small (under 2 metres) whilst others will be more than 9 metres high. But, within these limits, my choice of heights was arbitrary; I could have chosen 1, 3 and 8 metres if I wanted to. The appropriate values of height (item difficulty) depend on the objects (people) one wants to measure. The reason why I chose these random values (rather than, say, neatly spacing the distances at 3, 6 and 9 metres) is that when writing items for a psychological scale, one certainly cannot assume that they are equally spaced. In the prejudice example above, one cannot assume that the difference in prejudice between Item a and Item b is the same as the difference between Item b and Item c. We just write our items using our intuition (or results of previous research) to try to ensure that not everybody will answer all of the items the same way – in much the same way that when measuring trees we do not have items such as 'Is the tree more than 1 cm high?' (as they all will be) or 'Is the tree more than 100 m high?' (none will be).

It should be clear from all this that adding together scores on items from Guttman scales can only tell us which objects are taller than which other objects or which people are more able than which other people. It does not allow us to tell how *large* the differences between people are. A tree that scores '1' on the tree test (and is thus between 0 and 2 metres high) is not half the size of one which scores 2 (between 7 and 9 metres high). Likewise, though Figure 3.3 shows us that one person scores 0, two score 1, one scores 2 and one scores 3; it does not allow us to quantify the *size* of the difference between people. In other words, even if items can be found which fit the model, the Guttman scaling procedure only allows us to determine the rank order of objects (people), rather than putting them on a useful metric, such as height in metres.

Very few ability items actually do form Guttman scales – and those which do tend to vary so drastically in difficulty that they are unlikely to be of much practical use for making fine discriminations between people. For example, the following knowledge-based items would probably form a Guttman scale:

a) Item 1: What is a cat?
b) Item 2: When would you use an umbrella?
c) Item 3: Why isn't everybody given the same name?

But adding additional items of intermediate difficulty would, in practice, result in the data not fitting the model (Kline, 2000a). If a model does not fit the data, the obvious thing to do is to modify it slightly. Perhaps rather than showing a sudden increase from 0 to 1, the lines should show a gradual increase in probability over a range of abilities? And perhaps the steepness of the lines should be allowed to vary from item to item, rather, as shown in Figure 3.4.

Here the probability of answering an item correctly does not suddenly flip from 0 to 1. Instead, the probability of answering an item correctly gradually increases as people's ability increases. The responses to any ability items will reflect both the ability of the people to whom the item was administered plus some random 'noise', as some people who know the answer will press the wrong button on the computer keyboard or suffer a mental blank and therefore answer an easy item incorrectly, while some people who do not know the answer may make a lucky guess. This form of scaling turns out to be very useful, and we return to it in Chapter 12.

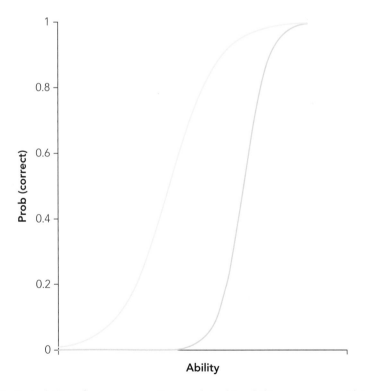

Figure 3.4 Probability of passing two items related to ability; compare with Figure 3.3

The key point to bear in mind is that when we write items for an ability test (or personality test) we have no guidelines for deciding how hard the items should be (or, in the case of Likert scales, how high or low the mean score should be). We just write items which look as if they will differentiate between people in the sort of sample with whom we plan to use them. This is hardly the most scientific approach, but it is difficult to think of a better one. So, if a test contains many items which are difficult but few which are easy for a sample of people, this will allow the test to make fine differentiations between people of high ability but will be less able to draw distinctions between people of low ability. This is because few of the item characteristic curves will move from 0 to 1 at the 'low' end of the ability scale, rather as shown in Figure 3.3. Whilst Item 2 and Item 3 have ICCs which are fairly close to each other, there is a large gap between the ICC for Item 1 and Item 2. Thus people whose ability falls in the range between Item 1 and Item 2 will all get the same score (1) on the test. ICCs that rise up close to each other are capable of making more precise discriminations between people than are ICCs which are far apart.

Thus there are two problems with adding up scores on items and using this total score as a measure of ability. First, doing so only makes sense if people who pass an item of a particular difficulty level also pass all easier items. Otherwise, two people with different levels of ability could have identical scores if one of them fails some easy items. The second problem is that item difficulty is always going to be arbitrary. It will depend on the cognitive demands of an ability problem and the extremity with which a personality item is phrased; for example, 'Do you sometimes feel nervous when . . . ?' as opposed to 'Do you always feel terrified when . . .?' Thus the ICCs will be random distances apart, and, as shown with the physical length example, this means that the total score can only ever show us that one person's score is higher or lower than another person's. It cannot tell us by how much, for in order to do so the ICCs would need to be evenly spaced. It is becoming clear that scores on psychological tests do not seem to measure things in the same way that rulers, weighing scales etc. operate – an issue which we consider in the next chapter.

OVERVIEW

This chapter has shown how responses to questionnaires may be translated into numbers, which is the usual precursor to interpreting what they mean and/or performing statistical analyses on them. Whilst it is straightforward to add up scores on Guttman scales and ability items, it is shown that scoring ipsatised scales poses major – perhaps insurmountable – problems. Finally, the idea of Guttman scales and item characteristic curves are introduced. This shows that adding together scores on test items requires some sort of model about the relationship between a person's level of the trait being assessed and the way in which they respond to items in the scale. These are important concepts which will be developed later.

CHAPTER 4
INTERPRETING SCORES

Whilst the previous chapters have shown how responses to items may be translated into numbers, we have not yet considered the assumptions made when doing so. Nor have we discussed how test scores can be interpreted. Whilst researchers normally just correlate scores on various scales with other things, as described in Chapter 1, practitioners need to determine what an individual's score on a scale implies about them. But before exploring how test scores should be interpreted and used, it is worthwhile considering what we mean by 'measurement' and whether it is ever possible to say that test scores 'measure' traits and states.

MICHELL

Joel Michell (1997a) provided a devastating critique of psychological measurement theory; his paper should be read by all test users. Michell's conclusion is simple; psychological assessments involving questionnaires and tests do not constitute proper scientific measurement. This may come as rather a surprise. After all, questionnaires generally produce numerical scores, and complicated statistical methods have been devised to develop and refine tests. Structural equation modelling, factor analysis and other sophisticated mathematical techniques are used to develop and refine theories based on test scores – it all certainly *looks* like science. Given the wealth of statistical theory that underpins psychological assessments and the objective statistical analyses that are used, how can anyone possibly claim that psychological tests are scientifically worthless?

Michell approaches the problem from the viewpoint of the philosophy of science. He argues that proper scientific measurement is only possible when the thing being measured (an 'attribute') has been *shown* to have 'quantitative structure'. This is an empirical issue. Length, time and temperature are examples of quantitative attributes. The specific instance of a quantity is known as its magnitude. Thus (for example) the number of seconds taken to read this chapter is a magnitude of the attribute 'time'.

So what is the problem? Why not define 'intelligence' as an attribute and 'score on Form 3 of the Cattell Culture Fair Test' as its magnitude? This is essentially what generations of psychologists have done – and the problem is that they have not demonstrated that the attribute (intelligence) is itself quantitative before rushing in and assigning numbers to behaviours (as described in the previous chapter) and performing mathematical operations on them. Wonderful though it is, mathematics only makes sense when the numbers that are being manipulated obey certain axioms which define a quantitative variable. Otherwise the numbers that are generated by any statistical procedure are meaningless.

The problem is basically that psychologists fail to distinguish between counting things and measuring things. Thus far we have done a lot of counting; we have counted the number of ability items which a person can solve correctly, for example. But this is not measurement. I can count the number of houses I pass before arriving home, but this does not mean that I have measured the length of my street. Telling a visitor that mine is the eighth house on the left after leaving the main street would not give them a good idea of how far they might have to walk; the houses might be small and close together, or we might be talking about farms strung out across a prairie . . .

The problem can be traced back to Stevens (1946). In *Through the Looking Glass*, Humpty Dumpty says 'when I use a word . . . it means just what I choose it to mean – neither more nor less'. This is precisely what Stevens did with numbers. One *can* assign numbers to ranks ('ordinal data'). One *can* use numbers to represent categories, and Stevens suggested that it was reasonable to do both of these things. The problem is that, when they are used like this, numbers do not behave the same way that we are accustomed to, and we cannot claim to have 'measured' something just because we have assigned a number (rather than a letter or a shape) to it. All we are doing is counting. So, whilst we can say that Jane solves twice as many problems as Karl, we cannot say that Jane is twice as intelligent as Karl – even if there is such a thing as intelligence, and it is quantitative.

The definition of what makes an attribute quantitative becomes somewhat technical; Hölder's seven rules for this are translated from German in Michell and Ernst (1997). But the bottom line is that if an attribute is quantitative, it is possible to calculate the ratio between any two magnitudes of that attribute, which expresses one magnitude in units of the other. For example, I can establish that my desk is 50 inches wide – a proper scientific measurement of the width of my desk, using an inch as marked on a tape measure as the standard unit of measurement. (Of course this choice is arbitrary – I could measure my desk in matchbox-widths, if I chose.) The key thing is that knowing that my desk is 50 inches wide and that the alcove in my office is 60 inches wide tells me that the desk will fit into the alcove with five inches to spare on either side. I could not perform this sort of operation using scores on psychological tests.

For the characteristics of people which are measured by psychological tests are (generally) inferred, not observable. They do not exist as physical objects which can be measured, such as length or weight. Of course, not all variables in the physical world can be measured either, and Michell gives the example of density which cannot itself be measured directly. This turns out to be a good analogy with psychological tests. For the only way in which we can determine the density of a solid directly is through determining whether it floats or sinks in a number of (arbitrarily selected) liquids. We could count the number of liquids in which it sinks, and this would give us a measure of its density. We could even construct tables of norms showing the number of solid substances which sink in our selection of liquids; this would allow us to discover that (for example) only 10% of the solids which we have tested are more dense than iron. This whole process is directly analogous to psychological assessment, where we give different people arbitrarily selected items to solve or answer. We count the number that they solve correctly (or their scores on Likert scales), and this is our measure of their ability or level of the trait. However, just as density is not a fundamental property of physical objects (it does not follow that an object which sinks in four of the liquids is twice as dense as one which sinks in two of them, for example), scores on psychological scales simply do not behave in the same way as the measurements with which we are familiar.

Suppose that you score 20 on a scale measuring Extraversion (sociability) whilst your partner scores 40. We *can* calculate the ratio, and he might tell all his friends that their score is twice yours. But what does that actually mean? For example, does it follow that someone who scores 80 on the test is four times as extraverted as you and twice as extraverted as your partner? If someone else scores 60 on the test, does it mean anything to say that the difference between their level of Extraversion and your partner's (20) is the same as the difference between your partner and you? The problem for psychology is that the numbers which are used to represent scores on psychological tests simply do not behave in the same sort of way as numbers which represent quantitative attributes. And although we can perform whatever fancy statistical operations that we choose on those numbers, the results from these analyses might well be meaningless. Michell (2000) called psychometrics 'a pathology of science' for this reason. It *looks* like science (involving what looks like quantification and complicated mathematical techniques being applied to what look like quantities), but in reality it can go nowhere. 'Garbage in, garbage out' as our computer science colleagues say. For it is certainly true that it is hard to imagine that laws such as Newton's laws of motion could emerge from relating scores on tests to other variables. The best that one can hope for seems to be a non-parametric correlation, under ideal conditions.

Most psychologists simply ignore these issues and argue that as scores on tests frequently correlate with other real-life behaviours that are unquestionably assessed using a proper unit of measurement (for example reaction time, inspection time, dopamine levels, genetic makeup, cerebral blood flow) then scores on such tests are (a) useful and (b) likely to be quantitative, given that they correlate appreciably with these physical measures. For although Hölder's axioms are used to demonstrate that an attribute must be quantitative, it is perhaps possible that some attributes might be quantitative, even though they cannot be shown to meet all of these criteria.

The first argument that tests are useful, even though they may not be proper scientific measurements, is a strong one. But it makes it hard to develop substantive theory. For example, mathematical techniques, such as factor analysis (discussed in Chapters 7–10), are widely used to build models of personality, ability and so on – and they assume that scores on tests are proper quantitative attributes. We have seen that this may well not be the case, and so a case could be made for rejecting every single theoretical model which is based on scores from tests. This would mean that the whole of social psychology, individual differences and much of health psychology, plus several other areas of the discipline are completely worthless. For without proper measurement, tests become mere technological tools, incapable of developing theories. It is hardly surprising that this suggestion has not proved popular with psychologists, and the most common approach has been to ignore the issue and carry on testing and using fancy statistical techniques as if Michell had never spoken. I have certainly not seen any convincing rebuttal of Michell's arguments in the literature.

I have some sympathy with the second argument posited above – that if the scores on some test can be shown to be *strongly* related to some attribute which is genuinely quantitative, then it is reasonable to use the scores on that test as a sort of proxy for the quantitative variable. The problem is that strong correlations between scores on tests and quantitative variables are few and far between. At the risk of ruffling the feathers of my colleagues, it is my experience that scores on personality questionnaires rarely correlate better than 0.3 with any genuinely quantitative attribute. (Their correlations with other personality questionnaires are obviously irrelevant, as these are not quantitative.) Ability tests fare better; inspection time (the amount of time that an individual needs to correctly recognise a simple shape) correlates about −0.5 with tests measuring intelligence (Grudnik and Kranzler, 2001), and scores on intelligence tests are also strongly related to individual differences in genetic makeup, with a heritability of up to 0.8 (Jacobs et al., 2001). So it might perhaps be appropriate to use these ability tests as rough-and-ready proxies for some biological aspect of brain functioning. This picks up on the point made in Chapter 2 where I argued that relating test scores to quantitative variables is likely to be far more useful than relating scores on questionnaires to scores on other questionnaires by increasingly complicated statistical methods.

There may be some light at the end of the tunnel. One approach to psychological measurement, known as additive conjoint analysis (Luce and Tukey, 1964), may make it possible to establish whether scores on some test actually possess an additive structure – i.e., whether or not they are quantitative – and a technique known as Rasch scaling, which is discussed in Chapter 12, may (Michell, 2014; Perline et al., 1979) or may not (Kyngdon, 2008) be an implementation of additive conjoint analysis. Although these issues are too advanced for consideration here, readers who are worried about the issues raised in this section will wish to explore them further.

Whilst it is undeniable that scores on psychological tests may sometimes be of practical use (e.g., in personnel selection), their lack of quantitative structure arguably makes them unsuitable for most of the complex analyses that are normally performed on them – and theories of human personality, abilities, prejudice, group dynamics, attraction, social cognition and the self are just a few of those which are therefore fatally flawed. Most readers of this book will be keen to learn how to use tests, whatever the rights and wrongs of the testing procedure, and so it would be wrong to end the book here. However, the concerns raised in this chapter are very real and will not go away, no matter how much we collectively choose to ignore them.

All of the rest of this book makes the unwarranted assumption that scores on psychological scales constitute proper scientific measurement. Doing so can sometimes produce something of practical value. However, it is now clear that scores on questionnaires, scales and tests do not constitute scientific measurement, which requires us to be able to compare scores against some standard.

INTERPRETING AN INDIVIDUAL'S SCORE ON A SCALE

This section explores how one might interpret one person's score on a particular test. This is the way that tests are usually used by clinical psychologists, educational psychologists and other professionals who administer a scale to one particular individual and seek to draw some inference about that person's intelligence, position on the autistic spectrum, level of dementia, suitability for employment or something similar. These psychologists use tests to help them understand individuals, and to do so it is necessary to use 'norms'. These are simply tables which show the frequency distribution of scores on a particular scale, as discussed below.

Of course, not everyone needs to interpret individual people's scores. If a researcher just wants to determine whether people's levels of anxiety (as measured by a questionnaire) are related to their performance at work, for example, then all they need to do is correlate the scores on the anxiety questionnaire with some measure of job performance. Because correlations are insensitive to the scale on which anxiety and job performance are measured (in other words, the mean and standard deviation of either set of scores do not influence the correlation) this correlation will show whether there is a linear relationship between anxiety and job performance. There is no need to use norms at all and, in fact, doing so might well make the distribution of scores rectangular, rather than bell-shaped, which might cause problems for the analysis. They can simply correlate scores together or use multiple regression, analysis of variance, factor analysis, structural equation modelling or other exotic techniques in order to establish how scores on tests are related to scores on other tests or to other things.

Whether or not norms are used, it is necessary to assume that adding together the scores on various items is able to tell us something sensible about an individual's level of a particular trait or state – which is a major problem, as shown in the previous section.

NORMS

Whilst calculating total scores on tests is simple and intuitive, the numbers that are generated by doing so will not behave in the same way as numbers in the physical world. Even if the items form a Guttman scale (which is unlikely, unless they differ drastically in difficulty), the total score on a test will only allow us to rank-order people, because the distances between the ICCs vary, rather than corresponding to a particular metric, such as length. So it is not possible to say that someone who scores 20 on a particular test measuring Extraversion is half as extraverted as someone who scores 40 on the same test. Nor can we tell whether a score of 20 represents a high, medium or low level of Extraversion; it all depends on how the questions are phrased. This is why one needs to use norms. Norms are simply tables which show the frequency distribution of scores on some scale within some group of people. If the sample is large and carefully constructed, it is then possible to extrapolate and claim that the table of norms is a good estimate of the distribution of scores within a particular population – for example, UK adults aged over 18.

It is obviously crucially important to use an appropriate normative sample to make sense of a person's scores. Using norms gathered from 18-year-old university students to interpret the score of an 8-year-old on an ability test would obviously be nonsensical, as levels of ability improve with age until late adolescence. So, in order to interpret the 8-year-old's score, it would be necessary to gather data from others of a similar age.

It follows that constructing tables of norms is a time-consuming and extremely expensive task. The norms for tests such as the Wechsler ability scales involve gathering data on a representative sample of people; the stratified sampling technique means that the sample resembles the population of the country in terms of age, geographical location, gender balance, educational qualifications, ethnic background etc. Some interesting dilemmas emerge when deciding who to exclude from the group. Should prisoners, hospital patients etc. be excluded when gathering normative data from adults? How about elderly patients with dementia, who will almost certainly obtain low scores on the test? Testing these individuals might prove taxing in the extreme, yet, if they are omitted from the normative group, this will lead to the scores of seniors being overestimated.

To give a concrete example to illustrate how norms are constructed and used, suppose that 2035 people were administered a 20-item ability test. Scores on this test can therefore range from 0 to 20. The number of people obtaining each score can be shown in a table such as Table 4.1.

Table 4.1 Norms from 2035 people on a 20-item test. The average score is 14.46, standard deviation 3.21

Score	Number of people with this score	Number of people with this score or lower	Percentile	Stanine	Quartile
0	3	3	$100 \times 3/2035 = 0.15$	1	1
1	2	3+2=5	$100 \times 5/2035 = 0.25$	1	1
2	6	3+2+6=11	0.54	1	1
3	8	19	0.93	1	1
4	8	27	1.33	1	1
5	13	40	1.97	1	1
6	17	57	2.80	1	1
7	23	80	3.93	1	1
8	25	105	5.16	2	1
9	33	138	6.78	2	1
10	57	195	9.58	2	1
11	87	282	13.86	3	1
12	133	415	20.39	3	1
13	201	616	30.27	4	2
14	293	909	44.67	5	2
15	357	1266	62.21	5	3
16	270	1536	75.48	6	3
17	198	1734	85.21	7	4
18	126	1860	91.40	8	4
19	100	1960	96.31	8	4
20	75	2035	100.00	9	4

The first column shows each possible score on the test. The second column shows the number of people who obtained each score. The third column shows the number of people who obtained each score *or less*. The fourth column converts Column 3 into a percentage – the percentage of people who obtain each score or less. This is known as the percentile – an important term. The remaining terms will be introduced later.

In order to interpret an individual's score, it is usual to use the percentile figure in the table of norms. In the above example, it can be seen that only about 20% of the normative group obtain a score of 12 or less. Assuming that the table of norms is appropriate for use with the individual and adequately represents the scores of the population, we can infer that someone who scores 12 on the test is in the bottom 20% or so of the population.

All commercial tests designed for use on individuals will have a table of norms; many will have separate tables for different nationalities, ages, and (perhaps) different clinical or occupational groups. However, care must be taken when choosing which norms to use, and selecting the wrong ones may result in legal challenges. For example, in many countries it may be illegal to use separate norms for males and females or (sometimes) for members of different minority groups. So, it might be proper to compare a man's scores against the scores obtained by the population as a whole – not just the scores from other men.

We have mentioned that scores on ability tests will increase from early childhood until (at least) late adolescence, and so separate norms need to be developed for each age band. Tests such as the Wechsler Intelligence Scales for Children report norms for each 3-month age band, so that children can be compared with others of very similar age. The width of these age bands will obviously depend on the degree to which scores on the scale change with age.

Gathering norms from thousands of children for 50 or more 3-month age bands would clearly be prohibitively expensive. So it is necessary to use smaller groups at each age band and/or test fewer age bands and perform some interpolation to estimate what the scores of intermediate age groups might look like. For example, if a score of 15 represents the 50 percentile for children aged between 8y0m–8y3m and the 40 percentile for children aged 8y6m–8y9m, if we assume that there is a gradual increase in test scores with age, then a score of 15 should be approximately the 45 percentile for children aged 8y3m–8y6m. If data have been gathered for a small sample of children of this age and suggest that a score of 15 should correspond to the 55 percentile, then there might be a case for moving this figure closer to 45 if the adjacent norms are based on larger samples. There are more sophisticated ways of performing such analyses too (fitting curves to represent how the mean scores change over a large range of ages and also estimating how the shape of the distribution changes smoothly over a large range of ages), but it is unlikely that many readers of this book will need to explore these issues in detail. All the hard work is done by the test publishers.

A perennial problem of norms is whether or not they transfer across cultures or from group to group. For example, suppose that a British university found despite offering a wide range of support options, some 25% of engineering students fail their course at the end of the first year because of a limited grasp of mathematics. The obvious solution would be to give applicants a test so that they could tell for themselves whether or not they are likely to encounter problems and perhaps reconsider applying (or possibly so that the university could decide to only admit those who scored above some criterion).

Suppose that such a test was available – but it had been developed using Australian technical-college students. Perhaps it showed that a score of 45 indicated that someone was at the 25 percentile (i.e., a score below 45 indicates that someone is in the lowest 25%). Is it possible to use these norms to help to make decisions about the British students? The Australians may have gone through a different system of mathematics education; the technical college may have different standards to the university; we may not be told much about how the sample was collected; the gender balance might be different . . . It is terribly hard to know whether or not norms collected in one setting will apply in another. Unless one uses a high-quality commercial test in the same country where the norms were developed, it will be necessary to norm the test oneself. In the case of the engineering applicants, this would involve gathering data from applicants, casting these data into a table such as Table 4.1, checking that the test scores do indeed predict which students have problems completing the course, then determining where the cut-off points might be so that students in subsequent years could be advised whether or not they have the necessary skills.

Ipsative scales cannot use norms (Closs, 1996) – which is a strong reason for not using them for individual assessment or guidance. This is because a person's score on one scale will also depend on how they score on other scales measured by the test.

AGE NORMS

When testing children, some tests still use 'age norms'. Here a child's score is compared with the average scores obtained by children of other ages. For example, if the average score of the large, representative normative sample of 9-year-olds on a scale is 20, and an 8-year-old child also scores 20, that child scores as well as the average 9-year-old. So, the child whose chronological age ('CA') is 8 has a 'mental age' ('MA') of 9 on that scale. Indeed, a child's intelligence quotient (IQ) used to be defined in this way. According to that outmoded definition

$$IQ = 100 \times \frac{MA}{CA}$$

which in this example would be 112.5.

However, there are several good reasons for not using this type of norm. First, it assumes that there is a steady increase in scores from year to year. Given that the difficulty of items in a test is essentially arbitrary, there can be no guarantee that this assumption is sensible. It might be the case that there is a huge jump in scores between the age of 8 and 9, but a much smaller increase in scores between 9 and 10. Second, it might be that the increase in performance with age is not linear (as the definition of IQ assumes) but follows a curve. Third, it is sometimes impossible to calculate age-related norms. Suppose that *no* group of younger or older children or adults ever scores an average as high as 10 on that difficult test. It is clearly impossible to interpret the scores of the child who scores 10. Age-related norms are best avoided.

PROBLEMS USING NORMS

Large, representative samples are necessary in order to construct tables of norms. 'Large' is generally taken to mean several hundred individuals, and we have already touched on the problem of ensuring that the normative group is appropriate. However, one issue which is rarely discussed is the relationship between the size of the normative group and the ability of the individual being assessed.

Suppose that a test is normed using a sample of 1000 people. This sounds as if it ought to be ample. For example, 200 people will have scores within a quarter of a standard deviation either side of the average, and so there are no problems using the table of norms with people of near-average ability. But consider what happens at the very end of the distribution. Suppose that Harry has a z-score of 2.32 – a very high score, and one which you would expect to find in only 1% of the population (as you may care to check, using a table showing the normal distribution). The problem is that if only 1% of the population obtain a score this large, only about 1% of the normative sample (10 people) will have a score this high. So really, when deciding whether Harry's score places him in the top 1% of the population, one is really only using a tiny sample of people to do so. We cannot be sure that the tiny sample of 10 people truly represents the distribution of scores in the population; when gathering the normative data we may have been unlucky and some of these 10 people may have been much more (or less) able than we assumed. As a result of this, one cannot expect estimates to be particularly accurate when interpreting very high or very low scores using norms.

Unfortunately, users of psychometric tests are generally more interested in scores near the extremes than at the middle of the distribution – for example, to determine whether a child shows significant problems with their verbal or non-verbal reasoning skills or to identify a genius or a psychopath. Thus, this issue is of great practical significance. The best advice that we can give is to ensure that the size of the normative sample is large and that it is sampled with exquisite care. Even then, users should be very careful when using norms to interpret extreme scores. There are plenty of urban myths out there – for example the pop singer whose IQ is supposedly 180 (five standard deviations above the mean). Is this likely to be true? Such a score would place her in the top 0.000005% of the population. However, it should be clear from what has been said here that even if the intelligence test is completely accurate, it is impossible to be sure whether a very high score places a person in the top 0.01%, 0.005% or 0.000005% of the population. To do so would require a set of norms comprising millions of people because only very large samples will provide enough people at the 'tails' of the distribution to allow us to draw inferences about the meaning of a score. Even if a sample of a million people were used, we would expect no one to obtain a score as large as our pop idol's. Without a sample large enough to provide (at least) tens of people with adjacent scores to those of our pop star, the best that one could sensibly say is that their score is high – and perhaps the size of the normative sample might allow one to say that they were likely to be in the top 1%. But inferring anything more extreme would be silly and impossible to justify.

SCALING SCORES

Different scales have different means and standard deviations – even if they supposedly measure the same thing. This is because scales contain different numbers of items that differ in their difficulty. For example, one scale measuring Extraversion might have scores which are normally distributed in the population (i.e., follow a bell-shaped curve) with an average of 20 and a standard deviation of 5. Another much longer test might have an average score of 40 and a standard deviation of 10. So it is impossible to tell what a score of (say) 30 on a particular test tells us about a person without knowing the mean and standard deviation of scores on the scale and performing a few mental mathematical gymnastics. It is therefore common practice to scale the scores so that they may be more easily interpreted. That way anyone looking at a person's score on any test will be able to see how it compares with their score on any other test and how it compares with the scores of other people.

Z-SCORES

Sometimes a psychologist may not have access to a table of norms such as those in Table 4.1. When a scale is published in a scientific journal, its authors usually only quote its mean and standard deviation, some information about the sample and a claim that the scores were normally distributed – in other words, that they follow a bell-shaped distribution rather as shown in Figure 4.1.

This is less than ideal. To start with, the sample may not resemble the sample whose data you have collected. The claim that the data are normally distributed may or may not be entirely accurate. But, in some cases, one may have no choice other than to try to interpret test scores by using the original researcher's norms – perhaps one has such a small or unrepresentative sample that it makes little sense to construct norms based on the data that one has collected oneself.

Suppose that the authors of a scale report that the average score is 14.46 and the standard deviation of the scores within that sample is 3.21 (the standard deviation shows how widely the data are spread either side of the average).

Figure 4.1 A normal distribution of scores on a psychological scale

By taking each score on that test, subtracting the average and dividing by the standard deviation, it is possible to convert the score on any normally distributed scale into a 'standardised score' or 'z-score'. These correspond to a normal distribution having a mean of 0 and a standard deviation of 1. So, for example, a score of 20 on the scale shown in Table 4.1, which has a mean of 14.46 and a standard deviation of 3.21, will correspond to a standardised score ('z-score') of $(20-14.46)/3.21$, or 1.72.

Why bother? The advantage of z-scores is that it is possible to interpret a person's score on any test quickly. For example, if someone has a z-score of 0, it follows that their score is average – no matter what the mean and the standard deviation of the original test scores happened to be. If someone has the same scores on two very different scales, their performance is equally good on each of the scales. Furthermore, it is possible to interpret the test scores by consulting a table showing the 'cumulative standard normal distribution', rather than having to consult a separate table of norms for each scale. This table of the cumulative normal distribution can be found in virtually any statistics text or online. Alternatively, you may wish to use Spreadsheet 4.1.

EXERCISE 4.1: Z-SCORES

Resources required: Spreadsheet 4.1: z-scores. From
www.routledge.com/9781138228894

Purpose: To calculate a person's z-score, and show what percentage of the
normative group are likely to have a lower score than this individual's score

Contents of spreadsheet:

- Section A calculates a z-score, assuming that the normative group follows a
  normal distribution.
- Section B uses that z-score to estimate what percentage of people will have a
  lower score than this individual.

Suggested activity:

- In section A, enter a score from Table 4.1, together with the mean and standard
  deviation shown at the bottom of that table. Note the value of z.
- In Section B, enter the value of z. Note the proportion of people estimated to
  have a score which is less than this.

Learning outcomes:

Readers should now be able to

- calculate and interpret a percentile score.

Whichever method is used, this technique will show what proportion (or percentage,
when multiplied by 100) of people obtain a particular z-score or less. So, for example,
you may wish to use the spreadsheet to check that 95.8% of people will obtain a z-score
which is less than or equal to the standardised score (1.72) of the person mentioned
above. Their score places them in the top 4% or so of the population.

However, this approach will only be accurate when the scores on the test really *do*
follow a normal distribution – and this may well not be the case. You may have noticed
that the mean and standard deviation shown above are those from Table 4.1. We have
seen from the fourth column of Table 4.1 that a score of 19 on this test corresponds
to a percentile score of 95.7; the person is in the top 4%. Yet when we estimate the
percentile using z-scores, a score of 20 (not 19) places a person in the top 4%. The
reason for this discrepancy is that the data shown in Figure 4.1 do not follow a perfect
normal distribution. Sometimes, making the assumption of normality may be the only
option available; however, interpreting performance using z-scores will only ever be a

rough approximation because one never really knows how closely the scores follow a normal distribution. Use it with caution for this reason – and for an important reason discussed in Chapter 14.

Converting test scores to z-scores merely alters the mean and standard deviation of the scores on the test; it is what is known as a 'linear transformation' because it involves subtracting the same number (the mean) from everyone's test score and then dividing everyone's score on this variable by the same number (the standard deviation of the scores). And as correlations are not influenced by either the mean or the standard deviation of the scores, it follows that the correlation between the raw scores and some other variable will be exactly the same as the correlation between the z-scores and that variable.

T-SCORES

The fact that z-scores are often negative confuses some simple-minded practitioners – particularly in education. To avoid this problem, they developed something called the T-score; note that this is nothing to do with the t-test in statistics or T-scaling (described below). Whereas z-scores have a mean of 0 and a standard deviation of 1, T-scores have a mean of 50 and a standard deviation of 10. To convert a z-score on a test to a T-score, one simply multiplies it by 10 and adds 50. This value is then rounded to the nearest integer. So a z-score of −1.39 (for example) corresponds to a T-score of −13.9+50=36. There is no good reason for using T-scores, other than because some non-specialists may be accustomed to them.

Once again, as T-scores merely change the mean and standard deviation of the scores, the correlation between the raw scores and some other variable will be exactly the same as the correlation between T-scores and that variable.

IQ

The 'intelligence quotient' is a widely used transformation for the interpretation of tests measuring intelligence or cognitive performance. Today, IQ scores are sometimes known as 'deviation IQs' to distinguish them from the obsolete ratio IQ discussed above. The definition of the deviation IQ is similar to that of T-scaling – but instead of producing scores with a mean of 50 and a standard deviation of 10, IQ scores have a mean of 100 and a standard deviation which is usually 15, though some tests use a standard deviation of 16 (e.g., the Stanford Binet series of intelligence tests) or even 24 (Cattell's 'culture free intelligence tests'). Thus, in order to interpret an IQ, great care must be taken to determine what standard deviation the test developer used. For a person's IQ of 115 on most tests would be equivalent to an IQ of 124 on the Cattell scales.

To convert a z-score to an IQ (with standard deviation of 15), all one does is multiply the z-score by 15 and add 100. Thus a z-score of 1.0 corresponds to an IQ of 115.

To interpret what a particular IQ score tells us about somebody, it is just necessary to perform the same trick backwards. Suppose someone has an IQ of 80. Their z-score is (80−100)/15 or −1.33. The cumulative standard normal distribution shows that about 91% of people perform better than this.

Once again, the correlation between IQ scores and some other variable will be the same as the correlation between the raw scores and that variable.

STANINES

Stanines are sometimes used in educational and occupational/organisational psychology as an alternative to z-scores. The term 'stanine' is a portmanteau word for 'standard nine', as stanines divide the population into nine groups, the width of each of which is half a standard deviation. This is shown in Figure 4.2. This figure shows the percentage of people who fall into each stanine (assuming that the data follow a normal distribution). To understand why they are convenient, knowing that a person falls in the first stanine tells you that they are in the lowest-scoring 4% of the population. If they are in the second stanine, they are in the lowest 4+7=11%. If in the third stanine, they are in the lowest-scoring 23%, and so on. It is easy to remember these figures, and so, rather than having to look up the cumulative standard normal distribution in order to interpret each individual's z-score, it is rather more straightforward to categorise people into groups (stanines) in order to interpret their scores.

So, someone with a stanine score of 5 has a score which is close to the average; someone with a stanine score of 3 is below average, and someone with a stanine score of 9 is well above average. In many practical situations this sort of crude categorisation is all one needs, for there is little point in obsessing about small distinctions between people in much applied work.

If one does not wish to assume that the test scores are normally distributed, it would also be possible to determine which test scores correspond to which stanine score simply by looking at the percentile scores in the table of norms. For we can see from Figure 4.2 that 4% of the scores should fall into the first stanine. Turning back to Table 4.1, it can be seen that 4% of the participants obtain scores of 7 or less on that scale. Hence a score of 7 or less on that scale corresponds to a stanine score of 1. Table 4.1 also shows the rest of the stanine scores calculated by this method.

As the stanine scores involve grouping people into categories (rather than using their raw scores), the correlations between stanine scores and some other variable will not be quite the same as the correlation between raw scores and that variable – though they should be very similar.

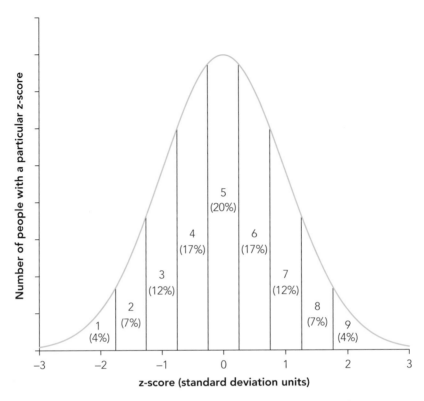

Figure 4.2 Stanines numbered 1–9. The numbers in brackets show the percentage of the population in each stanine, assuming that the data follow a normal distribution

STENS

The advantage of stanines is that the fifth stanine represents an average score, as shown above. Nevertheless, Raymond Cattell and his co-workers have developed a similar system based on 10 groups of people, called the sten ('standard ten'). Once again, each group is half a standard deviation wide, and so the first stanine represents z-scores of −2 or less, the second stanine corresponds to z-scores between −2 and −1.5 and so on. Not having a single central (average) category presents some problems for the use and interpretation of stens, which is probably why they are rarely used.

QUARTILES

Quartiles are sometimes used when one seeks to classify people into four groups; well below average, slightly below average, slightly above average or well above average. Unlike stanines or stens, there are roughly equal numbers of people in each group. Thus in Table 4.1, some 25% of people have scores between 0 and 12, another 25% have scores of 13 or 14, another 25% have scores of 15 or 16 and another 25% have scores of 17 or more. These quartile scores are shown in the final column of that table. The advantage of using quartiles is that one can easily see how a person's score compares with those of other people – a quartile score of 1 shows that someone is in the bottom 25% and so on. Beware of performing statistical analyses using quartile scores, though. As there are equal numbers of people in each group, the frequency distribution of quartile scores will follow what is known as a rectangular distribution – not a normal distribution. This can cause seriously misleading results if the quartile scores are correlated with other data which are normally distributed or are used as the dependent variable in t-tests etc.

T-SCALING

Sometimes one constructs a test and discovers that the scores are not normally distributed. After all, in the case of an ability test, merely including more easy items than difficult ones will lead to a skewed distribution of scores – and, when writing items, one does not know other than by intuition what difficulty level will be appropriate for a particular population. Likewise, when constructing a personality inventory, it is quite possible that more respondents will agree with items rather than disagreeing with them (or vice versa). This will lead to a skewed distribution of scores rather than a normal curve.

T-scaling (not to be confused with t-tests or T-scores) is a little-known technique due to McCall (1939) which attempts to make a non-normal distribution more normal in shape. It cannot achieve miracles. In particular, it will be unsuccessful if the distribution of scores on a test is J-shaped or very flat. But it can be useful if the distribution of scores is skewed – and this is perhaps the most common reason for non-normality.

For example, suppose that a group of people produce the following scores on a test (see Table 4.2).

When these are transformed into z-scores and plotted as a graph, as in Figure 4.3, it is clear that the distribution is a little skewed.

In Figure 4.3, all of the points are equally spaced along the x-axis; the intervals between the various scores on the test (0, 1, 2 etc.) are equal on the graph. T-scaling works by moving some of the data points to the left or right in order to produce a better approximation of the normal curve. In this case it moves the peak of the curve slightly to the right, as shown in Figure 4.4.

Table 4.2 Frequency distribution of test scores for T-scaling

Score	0	1	2	3	4	5	6	7	8
No. of people with score	3	5	10	19	17	13	10	6	4

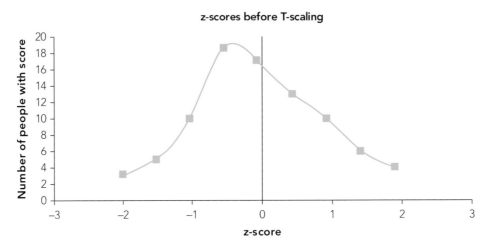

Figure 4.3 Frequency distribution of data from Table 4.2

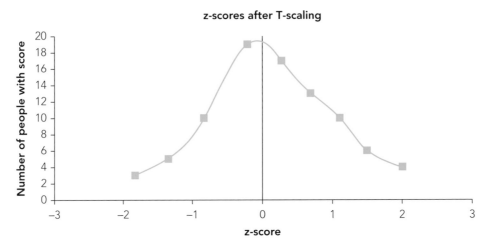

Figure 4.4 Data from Table 4.2 after performing T-scaling

If the technique is to be used in earnest on real data, it might make sense to smooth the frequency distribution before T-scaling – however, a discussion of these methods is beyond the scope of this book. See Kolen and Brennan (2014) if interested.

T-scaling may be useful where one needs to perform analyses which assume that the data are normally distributed (but where they manifestly are not) – although there is literature which suggests that many statistical procedures are not unduly influenced by breaking the assumption of normality. In any case, non-parametric methods are often available for even more advanced methods, and, as we argued earlier in this chapter, scores on psychological tests are probably better regarded as ordinal data than interval data – in other words, the scores might perhaps show which individuals score higher than which others but cannot show by how much, unless norms are used.

Because T-scaling moves some points a greater distance along the x-axis than others, it is not a linear transformation of the data. The correlation between T-scaled scores and another variable will not be the same as the correlation between the raw scores and that variable although they will almost certainly be very similar.

EXERCISE 4.2: T-SCALING

Resources required: Spreadsheet 4.2: T-scaling. From www.routledge.com/9781138228894

Purpose: To perform T-scaling on up to 60 variables

Contents of spreadsheet: Sample data showing how many people obtained each score on a 20-item scale

Suggested activity:

- Change the frequencies in Column B; these represent the number of people having each score on the scale. Perhaps use the data from Table 4.1.
- Note that T-scaling suggests that you should replace the original scores with those shown in the final column when performing further analyses: frequencies do not change.
- Try entering more values in Column B to discover which sorts of frequency distributions T-scaling can make more normal. For example, try one which is very 'peaked' in the middle, another which is very flat and one where the tail of the normal distribution goes down then up again. For example, 8, 3, 1, 5, 9, 14, 17, 25, 29, 36, 38, 42, 46, 47, 52, 50, 43, 35, 26, 11, 4.
- To use with a scale having more (or fewer) scores, simply add or remove values in Columns A and B.

Points to note:

- The first column shows the various scores of the test, and the second column shows the number of people with each score.
- The final column shows the rescaled scores. The scores in the final column should be used instead of the scores in the first column if the scaled scores are to be used for any statistical analyses.
- The scores in the final column have the same mean and standard deviation as the original data.

Learning outcomes:

Readers should now be able to

- perform T-scaling;
- appreciate which types of frequency distribution it can make more normal and which it cannot.

Because T-scaling alters the test scores, it follows that it should *not* be used when either developing tables of norms or interpreting scores using tables of norms. As these tables show the actual percentile scores, non-normality of the data distribution is not an issue. T-scaling is useful for making a distribution of scores look more normal, and this may facilitate the interpretation of these scores or make them better suited for parametric statistical analyses – but that is all.

OVERVIEW

This chapter began with a stern warning that scores on psychological scales cannot be used to quantify traits, which should be a major concern for all those who believe that psychometrics is akin to scientific measurement. Michell has argued that it is inappropriate to treat scores on tests as representing proper scientific measures – and so the potential of psychology to discover mathematically sound laws and principles based on test scores is limited. That said, it is possible that, despite their crudeness, scores on tests may have some practical value. The remainder of the chapter therefore examined how scores on scales may be transformed and interpreted and how the shape of the distribution of scores can be changed through various forms of scaling.

CHAPTER 5
CORRELATIONS

This book is not a statistics text; it focuses on how tests are devised and used, and how scores on tests may be used to help to draw inferences about personality, intelligence and so on. However, at this stage, it is necessary to digress slightly and consider how correlations can be used (and misused) when analysing responses to items. This is important because most of the techniques discussed in the following sections are based on correlations. There are many different types of correlations and many things which can affect their values, which means that there are plenty of traps for the unwary! This brief chapter therefore introduces the humble correlation coefficient and shows how it can be used and abused. I would strongly advise that readers should not skip this short chapter even if they are quite confident about their statistical skills, as it contains material which is not normally taught in statistics courses, as well as many useful techniques for dealing with issues encountered when analysing scores from psychological tests.

INTRODUCTION TO CORRELATIONS

Correlations are statistics which show the extent to which scores on one variable are proportional to scores on a second variable. For example, they may be used to show the extent to which people's height is related to their weight or whether scores on a questionnaire measuring anxiety are related to scores on a questionnaire measuring depression. The square of any correlation is particularly useful; it shows how much variance the two variables have in common. So a correlation of 0.7 between two tests indicates that about half ($0.7 \times 0.7 = 0.49$) of the person-to-person variability in the scores on one test can be predicted by knowing people's scores on the other test. This holds true no matter how large or small the sample may be.

Correlations are numbers which can be any value between -1.0 and $+1.0$. A positive correlation (i.e., one greater than zero) shows that if someone has an above-average score on one variable, their score on the other variable will also probably be above average. If one score is near average, the other will probably be near average too and so on. A negative correlation (one between -1 and 0) indicates that a high score on one variable tends to accompany a low score on the other. And, of course, a correlation of 0 implies that the two variables are completely unrelated.

It is also possible to test whether a correlation is significantly different from some other value (such as zero) or some other correlation. As this is a psychometrics text and not a statistical one, we shall not explore this much. However, a statistical 'teaser' might be in order here. Suppose that two researchers report correlations which, by some amazing coincidence, are significant at exactly the same probability level – p=0.000022. One of these results is based on a sample of 200 people. The other is based on a sample of 2000 people. Which is the more interesting finding?

The correlation which is based on the large sample will be smaller than the correlation which is based on the small sample. For the example in the previous paragraph, a correlation of 0.3 based on a sample size (N) of 200 is significant with P=0.000022. A correlation of 0.083 with N=2000 is significant with P=0.000022. The first correlation shows that the two variables share 9% of their variance; the second correlation shows that they are virtually unrelated. I make this point because (a) many researchers seem to believe that results from a huge sample are always more important than results from a moderate-sized sample, and (b) because researchers sometimes report correlations which are so tiny that they can have no relevance to any real-world behaviour. A propos this, I recently read a paper which attached great importance to a (statistically significant) correlation of 0.1. The fact that this is significant tells us that, with their huge sample, there is evidence that the true value of the correlation is unlikely to be zero. These authors believed that explaining 0.1×0.1=1% of the overlap between two variables was interesting; choosing to overlook that 99% of the person-to-person variation in scores was due to other things. There is much to be said for focusing on the size of the square of the correlation, as well as its statistical significance. That way one gets a feel for the size of the effect, as well as whether it is unlikely to have arisen by chance.

This brief chapter is highly selective, and there is a considerable amount of new research into how best to quantify the relations between variables. Choi et al. (2010) and Lalla (2017) give useful guidelines to those seeking a modern overview of the use of correlations to analyse interval-scaled data (which is, arguably, what scores on psychological scales represent) whilst Olkin and Finn (1995) provide a reasonably modern account of how differences between correlations may be calculated and contains a number of useful guides – for example, how to test whether two multiple correlations (from different samples) are different. Birnbaum (1973) is essential reading for those who worry about whether it is appropriate to assume a linear (i.e., straight-line) relationship between the variables – and the consequence of getting this decision wrong.

TYPES OF CORRELATIONS

Psychometricians correlate many different types of data (and use these correlations for many different purposes – e.g., reliability analysis, establishing the validity of tests, factor analysis and other techniques to be explored later in this book). The types of variables which are correlated also vary considerably. Everyone reading this will be familiar with the idea of correlating two continuous variables, such as the ratio of the length of the second and fourth fingers (thought by some to be related to the extent to which an individual was exposed to androgens in the womb) and simple reaction time. Some transformations may be necessary to make the distributions roughly normal, but at least these variables are proper quantities. More often than not, psychologists correlate responses to test items, scores on tests or ratings of behaviour. They may *choose* to treat these as being quantitative variables, but, as we demonstrated in Chapter 4, this is an act of faith which has little empirical or scientific basis. Sometimes psychologists correlate ordinal data – based on rankings. And in some cases, psychologists need to correlate variables which have only two values, such as whether or not an item was answered correctly. These all raise their own issues and will be considered in turn.

TWO CONTINUOUS VARIABLES

Two continuous variables, such as annual income and years spent in the education system, may be plotted against each other (a scatter diagram, or scatterplot) showing each person's data on the two variables as a dot. The correlation shows how closely the points cluster around a line running from bottom left to top right (for a positive correlation) or top left to bottom right (for a negative correlation). Inspecting this diagram can show whether the data are more or less normally distributed; if they are, there will be more data points towards the centre of the graph than at the extreme values. Looking at the graph can also show whether the variance (spread) of the data is proportional to one of the variables. It seems sensible to begin by simply looking at some correlations because most statistics textbooks include scatter diagrams showing a perfect correlation, a large positive correlation, a large negative correlation and a zero correlation – but nothing in between. Thus, researchers may become over-excited when interpreting the statistical significance of rather small correlations.

EXERCISE 5.1: PEARSON CORRELATIONS

Resources required: Spreadsheet 5.1: Pearson correlations. From www.routledge.com/9781138228894

Purpose: To show scatter diagrams of correlations

Contents of spreadsheet: Simulated scores on two normal variables, from between six and 200 people.

Suggested activity:

- Adjust the bottom slider to give a sample size of 100.
- Adjust the top slider to see what a correlation of (roughly) 0.2, 0.3 or 0.4 actually looks like.
- With sample sizes of (say) 20, 100 and 200, adjust the slider to see what a statistically significant correlation (P<0.05) looks like.

Points to note:

- It will be necessary to move the top slider to and fro in order to generate the appropriate correlation.
- As both variables are normally distributed, there are more data points towards the centre of the graph than at the periphery.
- Even though the correlation of 0.2 is statistically significant (i.e., we can be fairly sure that the data are not random), there is only 0.2×0.2=4% overlap between the two variables, and it is very hard to see any relationship between the two variables by eye – or even see whether the correlation is positive or negative.

Learning outcomes:

Readers should now be able to

- 'eyeball' data and roughly estimate correlations.

Correlations are not influenced by either the mean (the level of scores) or the standard deviation (the scale of measurement) of the variables being correlated. Thus, adding the same arbitrary number to each participant's score and/or multiplying each person's score by another arbitrary number will not change the correlation at all. In practical terms this is useful. It does not matter whether we measure reaction time in microseconds, milliseconds, seconds or years; it does not matter if the responses to a five-point Likert scale are coded 0/1/2/3/4, 5/7/9/11/13 or −37/−20/−3/14/31, the correlation will be unchanged.

If this is not obvious click on the 'scaling' tab at the bottom of Spreadsheet 5.1. This shows a scatter diagram based on two variables – Var1 and Var2 – along with the mean, standard deviation and the correlation between Var1 and Var2. It also allows you to rescale Var1 and/or Var2 by adding a constant (any number) to each person's score on either of these two variables and then multiplying the result by any constant. For example, one could add 47 to everyone's score on Var1 then multiply this total by 6. The spreadsheet shows the re-scaled scores, along with the scatter diagram, mean, standard deviation and correlation. It can be seen that the correlation does not change, no matter what number is added to the scores or what multiplier is used.

Textbooks usually stress that the correlation coefficient can be any number between −1 and +1. This is not quite true, even if the measurements which are being correlated are completely error free. The Pearson correlation can only be exactly 1.0 (or −1.0) if the two variables have the same frequency distribution. For example, the correlation can only be −1 or +1 if both variables follow a normal distribution or if both follow a rectangular distribution (where equal numbers of people obtain each score on a measure) or if both follow some other distribution. If one of the variables follows a normal distribution and the other follows a rectangular distribution or is skewed, the correlation cannot be 1.0. Most textbooks mention this; however, they do not consider how much of a problem this is likely to be in practice. Spreadsheet 5.2 allows this to be explored.

EXERCISE 5.2: PEARSON CORRELATIONS WITH SKEWED DATA

Resources required: Spreadsheet 5.2: Pearson correlations with skewed data. From www.routledge.com/9781138228894

Purpose: To show how skew affects the maximum possible correlation between two variables

Contents of spreadsheet: Simulated data from 1000 people forming skewed, normal and rectangular distributions

Suggested activity:

- Choose the same level of skew for both skewed distributions (e.g., means of 5). Scroll down to inspect the correlations between the two skewed distributions. Also note the correlation between the normal and skewed, the normal and rectangular, and the skewed and rectangular distributions.
- Generate several sets of data (f9 etc.) and note the typical values for these correlations.
- Change the skew on one of the distributions (e.g., to 15). Note the size of the correlations between the skewed distributions for several sets of data.
- Repeat for other, more extreme, differences in skew.

Points to note:

- The data in this simulation make the correlations as large as possible; the 'person' with the lowest score on one distribution also has the lowest score on all other distributions etc.
- This spreadsheet involves quite a lot of computation, so there may be a pause of a few seconds after pressing f9.

Learning outcomes:

Readers should now be able to

- appreciate that if two variables have equal skew, their correlation can be 1.0;
- appreciate that if distributions differ, correlations are marginally less than 1 but that this is unlikely to be a major problem unless variables are heavily skewed in opposite directions.

It can be seen that the maximum possible correlation is not *much* less than 1.0 unless the variables differ enormously in skew. So, when calculating correlations between two variables which have many possible values, one probably does not need to worry too much about the frequency distributions of variables being correlated unless they are severely skewed in opposite directions.

Outliers can cause major problems when calculating correlations. An outlier is a data point which lies well away from the 'swarm'; they may represent genuine scores, but more often than not they arise because a score has been wrongly entered (for example, typing 77 instead of 7 when entering data) or because missing data have not been treated sensibly. For example, unanswered items from Likert scales may have been given scores of zero rather than being estimated as outlined in Chapter 3. Sometimes missing data are coded as 9 or 99, with the intention of telling SPSS or whichever statistical package is being used to treat such data as being missing, but then forgetting to do so. It is essential to examine the frequency distributions of each variable to check for aberrant values before calculating correlations, for outliers can have a truly massive influence on the correlation. Just one outlier can easily turn a correlation of 0 into a correlation of 0.7, which will wreak havoc with any statistical procedure (reliability analysis, factor analysis etc.) which is based on correlations.

TWO TWO-VALUED (DICHOTOMOUS) VARIABLES

Psychologists often need to correlate scores which have only two values – the most obvious case being where responses to an ability test item are coded as correct or incorrect or when coding performance as pass/fail. In order to perform reliability analysis, factor analysis etc., as described in Chapters 6–11, these items need to be correlated together – and mathematically there is nothing wrong with doing so. When the usual (Pearson) correlation is calculated between two dichotomous (two-valued) variables, it is usually known as the phi coefficient.

However interpreting phi coefficients is difficult.

It is usual to summarise dichotomous variables using a table such as Table 5.1, simply because it is more convenient than showing many rows of data containing 0s and 1s (or whatever other codes are used – the correlation will be the same however the categories are coded).

Table 5.1 Datasets showing the number of people answering two ability items correctly (1) and incorrectly (0)

		Dataset A			Dataset B		
		Variable 1			Variable 1		
		0	1	Total	0	1	Total
Variable 2	0	20	10	30	48	48	96
	1	6	40	46	12	12	24
	Total	26	50	76	60	60	120

Dataset A simply shows that 20 people scored 0 on both Variable 1 and Variable 2, six scored 0 on Variable 1 and 1 on Variable 2, and so on. Phi simply shows the correlation that is obtained by calculating the Pearson correlation from a table of data containing 20 rows of '0 0', five rows of '0 1' etc. as shown in Table 5.1 Dataset A. Phi is 0.552 which looks sensible, as people tend to generally either score '1' for both items or score '0' for both, which should result in a positive correlation. But what if the items differ in their difficulty, as shown in Dataset B?

EXERCISE 5.3: CORRELATIONS FROM DICHOTOMOUS DATA

Resources required: Spreadsheet 5.3: Correlations from dichotomous data. From www.routledge.com/9781138228894

Purpose: A utility to compute several different correlations from dichotomous (two-valued) data

Contents of spreadsheet: Data from Table 5.1 Dataset A

Suggested activity:

- Enter the numbers from Dataset B from Table 5.1 into the spreadsheet. 50% of people score 1 on Variable 1, and 20% score 1 on Variable 2. Spend no more than a minute or two entering any numbers you like in the green cells trying to obtain a correlation of +1 *whilst keeping the proportion who score 1 on Variable 1 at 0.5, and the proportion who score 1 on Variable 2 as anything other than 0.5.*

Points to note:

- It is impossible to achieve a correlation of 1.0 unless the same proportion of people scoring 1 is the same for both items.
- It is possible to calculate many other different statistics from dichotomous data, each of which is another form of correlation coefficient. Several of these will be referenced in later chapters.

> **Learning outcomes:**
>
> Readers should now be able to
>
> - appreciate that dichotomous variables can only correlate perfectly if the same proportion of people score '1' on each variable;
> - use the spreadsheet to calculate a range of different correlation coefficients.

It turns out that it is mathematically possible to obtain a correlation of +1 (or −1) only if both of the items happen to have the same level of difficulty (the same proportion of people scoring '1'– otherwise known as the p-value[1]). Figure 5.1 shows what the maximum possible value of phi is if one variable has a p-value of 0.5 and the other has a different p-value. It can be seen from this graph that if the difficulty value of the second item is 0.2 (as with Dataset B) then it is mathematically impossible for phi to be any larger than 0.5 (Ferguson, 1941). The spreadsheet shows the maximum value of phi (phimax) which is possible for any pair of variables.

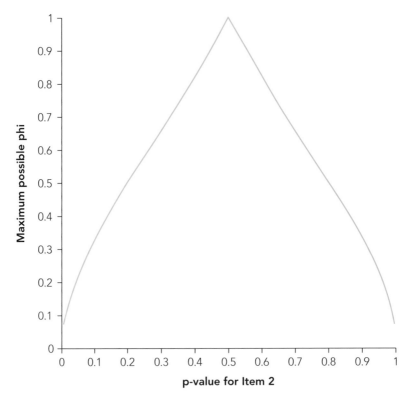

Figure 5.1 Maximum possible correlation between an item having a difficulty of 0.5 and other items of varying difficulty

This creates a major problem. The p–values of the variables cannot (usually) be changed to make them equal. For example, some ability test items will invariably be harder than others. Thus the correlation between two items generally can never equal 1.0, which poses some interesting questions about how one should interpret it. For how *does* one interpret a correlation of 0.5 between two items? It could (as in Dataset A) mean that there is a moderate relationship between variables of similar difficulty. Or it could (as in Dataset B) suggest a relationship which is as strong as it can be, given that the items have different p-values. The problem is that statistical techniques which use correlations (such as factor analysis) do not 'know' where the correlations have come from and so cannot intuit that sometimes the correlation is bound to be less than 1.0. It will cause major problems for such techniques.

One (old) solution suggested dividing a correlation by its maximum possible value. This ensures that every correlation lies between −1 and 1. However it introduces a host of other problems, too (Davenport and Elsanhurry, 1991) so cannot be recommended. It is therefore very dangerous to calculate the usual Pearson correlation ('phi') from two-valued data, unless the two variables have very similar difficulty levels.

Before leaving phi, we should note in passing that it is related to the chi-square statistic with which many readers will be familiar; details are given on Spreadsheet 5.3. Indeed, phi is calculated twice there – once using the Pearson formula and once from chi-square.

Rather than using phi, it is possible to calculate other types of correlation from this sort of data. Several have been proposed; the spreadsheet computes Goodman-Kruskal gamma (also known as Yule's Q), the contingency coefficient, the G-index and Kappa, just for information. (The computational formulae are quite simple and may be deduced from the spreadsheet.) Readers may find it interesting to explore how/whether these differ from phi, especially when the p-values of the items are both similar and different. All of these coefficients seek to get around the problems of the phi coefficient and are sometimes used when checking whether two people can rate behaviour similarly. However, they are rarely (if ever) used as the basis for reliability analysis or for factor analysis etc. although it is possible to use some of these for factor analysis using the R statistical package. The exception is the G-index, which can be used to correlate people together and as the basis for Q-factor analysis, discussed in Chapter 10 (Holley, 1973; Vegelius, 1973).

In some cases, we can imagine that the variables which are being analysed represent arbitrary 'cutting points' of some normally distributed continuous variable. For example, an item measuring whether or not a person understands the meaning of the word 'chair' presumably measures some underlying variable of verbal comprehension. So, in correlating the responses to that item with an item measuring mathematical ability (for example, 'What is 463×3?'), we really want to know what the correlation between the two underlying, continuous traits is. If it can be assumed that both of the two-valued variables represent points along some normally distributed trait (such as verbal comprehension or numerical ability), then it is possible to estimate what this correlation might be, using something called the tetrachoric correlation. It is *not* sensible to calculate this when one or both of the variables represents a genuine categorical variable, such as gender.

The tetrachoric correlation is difficult to calculate exactly (Olsson, 1979) and several approximations have been developed – the spreadsheet shows two of them. Matrices of tetrachoric correlations can be calculated using the Factor program introduced in Chapter 9 (Lorenzo-Seva and Ferrando, 2006) by specifying the 'polychoric' option or from within the R statistical environment (R Core Team, 2013). They may be used for factor analysis, as discussed in Chapter 8, and (controversially) for reliability calculations, as discussed in Chapter 6. Tetrachoric correlations are generally larger than phi correlations and so produce larger estimates of reliability, larger factor loadings and so on. This probably accounts for their popularity. However, they should *only* be used if both of the variables represent some continuous trait which just happens to have been coded as 0/1.

For example, an applied psychologist might calculate the tetrachoric correlation between whether or not trainee pilots have passed a test measuring visualisation skills and whether or not they successfully qualify as pilots. Both could be reasonably supposed to represent normally distributed variables – but it would be far safer to correlate scores on the visualisation test with some outcome score on the piloting variable rather than risk introducing error by calculating the tetrachoric correlation.

Should it be necessary to find the statistical significance of a tetrachoric correlation, see Guilford and Lyons (1942).

ONE CONTINUOUS AND ONE DICHOTOMOUS VARIABLE

It is sometimes necessary to calculate the correlation between one dichotomous variable and one continuous variable. For example, it is possible that in the previous example there *is* no detailed information available about why individuals passed or failed the piloting course, whereas scores on the visualisation test are a continuous variable. What happens when a Pearson correlation is calculated between a two-valued (dichotomous) variable and a continuous variable?

For historical reasons this is known as the 'point-biserial' correlation – and it suffers from the same problem as the phi coefficient. The point-biserial correlation can never ever be 1.0. At best, it can be about 0.8, as shown in Figure 5.2. However, the good news is that the maximum correlation is between 0.6 and 0.8 as long as the p-value of the dichotomous variable is between about −0.2 and 0.2 – that is, as long as the dichotomous variable is neither very easy nor very difficult.

Figure 5.2 Maximum possible correlation when a two-valued (dichotomous) variable is correlated with a normally distributed continuous variable

It is also possible to calculate a statistic known as the biserial correlation which adjusts for the problem that the point-biserial correlation can never equal 1.0. It assumes that the dichotomous variable follows a normal distribution (although some later developments have relaxed this assumption) and boosts the point-biserial to give a correlation which can range from −1 to 1. It is simply necessary to know the point-biserial correlation (or the Pearson correlation, which is the same thing) and the difficulty of the dichotomous item (the proportion of people who answer it in a particular direction). For example, if the point-biserial correlation is 0.4 and 20% of people pass an item (making its p-value 0.2), Spreadsheet 5.4 shows that the biserial correlation is 0.57.

EXERCISE 5.4: BISERIAL CORRELATION

Resources required: Spreadsheet 5.4: Biserial correlation. From www.routledge.com/9781138228894

Purpose: To calculate a biserial correlation

Contents of spreadsheet: A point-biserial correlation and a p-value for the dichotomous variable

Suggested activity:

• This is a utility, as biserial correlations are rarely calculated by statistical packages.

Points to note:

• The biserial correlation can be *appreciably* larger than the point-biserial.

Learning outcomes:

Readers should now be able to

• compute a biserial correlation.

The same caveats apply as with the tetrachoric correlation. Computing the biserial correlation if the dichotomous variable is categorical (e.g., gender) is nonsensical. And it is far better to try to measure both variables on a continuous scale than to use a dichotomised variable. However, if there genuinely is no alternative, the biserial correlation can be useful. Note that estimates which result from calculating a biserial correlation (or tetrachoric, for that matter) cannot be tested for statistical significance using the same formulae as for the Pearson correlation unless the sample size is large (Alf and Abrahams, 1971).

TWO ORDINAL VARIABLES

Readers will be familiar with Spearman's rho and Kendall's tau as non-parametric measures of correlation. Spearman's rho is often presented using a rather arcane formula – however, the same result may be obtained by simply ranking both variables from smallest to largest, and calculating a Pearson correlation on the two sets of ranks. As Spearman's correlation can be calculated using the usual formula for a Pearson correlation (only performed on ranks, not the original numbers), there can be little doubt as to its suitability for use in factor analysis etc. Given the concerns with the nature of psychological variables outlined in Chapter 2, it is surprising that this is not more common; this might just be because SPSS does not present it as an option.

There is another statistic known as the polychoric correlation which resembles the tetrachoric correlation – only with two *or more* levels of each variable. Again, it is necessary to assume that the numbers being correlated come from some underlying normally distributed continuous variable, but, unlike the Pearson correlation, the polychoric correlation does not assume that the distance between a rating of '1' and '3' (for example) is the same as the distance between '4' and '6' on the underlying variable.

This makes the polychoric correlation a sort of compromise between the ordinal Spearman correlation and the more stringent assumptions of the Pearson correlation. It is thus quite widely used – particularly in areas such as factor analysis. Calculating the polychoric correlation and its statistical significance is even more unpleasant than the tetrachoric correlation, and so there is no spreadsheet available to do so. The Factor program (Lorenzo-Seva and Ferrando, 2006) or Bill Revelle's Psych package in the R environment (Revelle, 2017c) will allow them to be calculated.

CORRELATIONS AND GROUP DIFFERENCES

Most psychologists ignore the possibility that their data may contain subgroups of individuals who respond differently to test items or other measures. The temptation is simply to plough ahead and calculate correlations. However, this can be dangerous. Consider the data in Table 5.2 and try to estimate (by eye) what the correlation between the two variables might be.

Few readers would have much of a problem correlating these two variables together. The correlation between Variable 1 and Variable 2 is 0.34, so most people would infer that this represents some sort of positive relationship – albeit one which is not statistically significant.

However, look again at these data. For in this fictitious example there is a huge *negative* correlation between the two variables for the men (r=−0.82) and a huge *negative* correlation between the variables for the women (r=−0.85), as you might care to verify. The only reason that there appears to be a positive correlation when the entire sample is used to calculate the correlation is because there is a substantial difference

Table 5.2 Sample data to be correlated

	Gender	Variable 1	Variable 2
Jack	M	7	9
Oliver	M	8	7
Ben	M	8	8
Gabriel	M	6	9
Nora	F	7	4
Violet	F	5	5
Emma	F	6	5
Susan	F	5	6

in the average scores of the men and women. This is not uncommon in psychology. For example, men score about 0.7 of a standard deviation higher than women on the personality trait of Psychoticism (Eysenck et al., 1985). So the presence of group differences can have a massive effect on correlations, and it makes great sense to explore them thoroughly before performing any more detailed analysis – factor analysis or reliability analysis, for example. The results can otherwise be meaningless.

This issue is obvious if one simply plots the scores of the men and women separately for all pairs of variables, as some computer packages allow. A quick glance will reveal gross group differences. Alternatively, t-tests, analysis of variance etc. can be used to check that none of the group differences are appreciable (*appreciable* rather than statistically significant).

If group differences *are* found on some variables, there are several options available. If the sample is large, it is safest to analyse data for each group separately. However, if the sample contains several different types of group (e.g., male/female, young/middle-aged/elderly, addicts/non-addicts) this is clearly unlikely to be feasible unless the sample is *very* large. Other options include standardising the data in order to eliminate any group differences or using partial correlation to control for the effects of differences between groups.

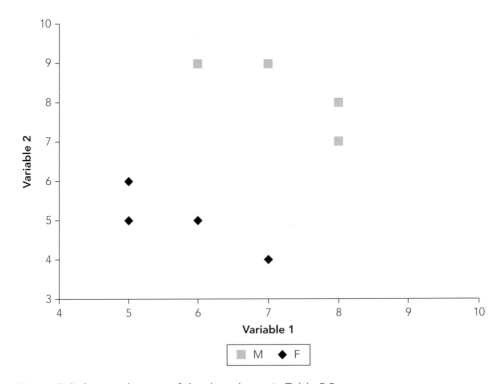

Figure 5.3 Scatter diagram of the data shown in Table 5.2

However, this is statistics, not psychometrics, so it would be inappropriate to explore the issue further. The important point is to recognise that group differences can wreak havoc with correlations. When researching variables which might show group differences, these *must* be explored before computing them – though research papers which do so are the exception rather than the rule.

CORRECTING CORRELATIONS FOR UNRELIABILITY

We can never measure anything accurately, and the effect of measurement error will be to reduce the correlation between two variables (i.e., bring it closer to zero). It is tempting to ask what the correlation might be had the variables been measured with greater accuracy. As will be shown in Chapter 6, a scale's 'reliability' is a statistic which estimates how accurate its scores are. For example, Chapter 6 shows that the square root of a statistic called 'coefficient alpha' estimates the correlation between people's scores on a test and their true score. So it should be possible to derive a formula to estimate what the correlation between two tests would be if both were measured completely accurately.

This can obviously be dangerous. If the best-available tests have been used to measure some trait (and if not, why not?), it would never be possible to measure the trait with greater accuracy. So correcting for reliability leads us away from real data into the fantasy land of latent traits; we look at the relationship between theoretical concepts and ignore the inconvenient problem that our statistics can never reflect what correlations between real tests can ever look like.

Spreadsheet 5.5 performs this analysis. One simply enters the correlation which has been found, the reliability of each of the variables (e.g., coefficient alpha or test-retest reliability) and it estimates what the correlation between the variables *would* be if both of them were completely free from measurement error.

CORRECTING CORRELATIONS FOR RESTRICTION OF RANGE

A common problem arises when using tests or other criteria for selection purposes. How can these tests be validated in order to check that they work properly? For example, suppose that a university selects students entirely on the basis of their grade-point-average, A-level grades or some other measure of achievement in school. Do these measures of school achievement predict how well the students will perform at university? Or, if a firm uses some form of ability test to screen potential employees, how well do scores on that test relate to job performance? The problem with both of these scenarios is that because the people who are accepted into the organisation must all have passed the selection procedure, the range of scores on the selection test (or the range of GPAs, A-level grades or whatever) will be smaller than in the population from which the people were selected. This implies that the standard deviation of the scores in the 'selected' group will be smaller than in the population.

A consequence of this is that the correlation between scores on the selection test and any other variable will be smaller than it would be if the correlation had been based on a random sample of people from the population. The validity of the selection measure (its correlation with performance) will be underestimated.

There are three ways round this problem.

a) One can administer the test to applicants – but not use it (or anything similar) to select people. Thus the people who are selected will form a random sample of the population with respect to their scores on the test; the correlation between the test and the outcome measure will not need to be corrected. However, this is unlikely to be feasible in practice if the organisation believes that the existing test has any merit whatsoever for selecting people.

b) The usual solution is to correct for 'restriction of range'. If one knows the standard deviation of scores in the population (from the test scores of a pool of job applicants or the national average of school performance indicators) and the standard deviation of the scores in the selected group, it is possible to correct the correlation by estimating what it would be if the standard deviation of the selected group were the same as that of the applicants. Spreadsheet 5.5 does this. For example, if the correlation between test scores and job performance is 0.3, the standard deviation of test scores in the sample is 10 and the standard deviation of test scores in the population is 20, then the 'corrected' estimate for the correlation is 0.53. This formula may also be used to reduce the correlation if a sample standard deviation is larger than in the population – for example, if a researcher puts together a sample which consists of more university students and people with special educational needs than would be found in the population, when performing research on intelligence. This will overestimate the correlation between an intelligence test and anything else.

c) A much better solution was put forward by Dobson (1988), though unfortunately it is rarely cited. It is unrealistic to correct the correlation by making the standard deviations of the sample equivalent to the standard deviation of the population in the scenarios mentioned above because the reason why people are not selected is because they scored below the cut-off on the selection test. The test scores of the selection test will therefore probably follow a 'truncated normal distribution' as shown in Figure 5.4 rather than a normal distribution which is narrower than in the population. Spreadsheet 5.5 performs this correction too.

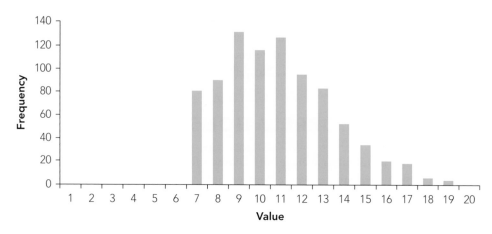

Figure 5.4 A truncated normal distribution of test scores from a sample where people are only selected if they have a score greater than 6

All that is needed is to enter the observed correlation between (for example) school performance and university performance, and the proportion of people selected from the population based on their school performance. For example, if a university department selected the best 200 of 2000 applicants, this figure (the 'selection ratio') would be 200/2000 or 0.1. If the correlation between school performance and university performance for this group was found to be 0.2, correcting it gives a figure of 0.44, as you might care to verify.

A more detailed discussion of these issues is given by Sackett and Yang (2000).

SIGNIFICANCE TESTING

Is a correlation different from zero? Is a correlation different from some other value? Is a correlation different from another correlation? The first question is, of course, just a test of the statistical significance of the correlation; it will be shown by any statistical package. The second and third questions should perhaps be addressed more often than they are. For example, if one researcher discovers that the correlation between two traits is 0.3 and someone else finds that it is 0.2, is there reason to believe that this difference is real, or might it have occurred by chance?

What one *cannot* do is infer that, because the correlation of 0.3 is statistically significant (i.e., likely to be different from 0) whilst the correlation of 0.2 is *not* statistically significant, the two correlations are different. For it might be the case that one correlation is significant with $P=0.049$ and the other just fails to reach significance ($P=0.051$) – even though the correlations are virtually the same size. (I assume that the sample sizes are equal.) It is instead necessary to test the significance of the *difference* between the correlations from two different samples. Spreadsheet 5.5 does so. It is very occasionally necessary to calculate the difference between correlations when the same sample is tested twice; see for example, Howell (2012).

AVERAGING CORRELATIONS

Sometimes it may be useful to average correlations – for example, when drawing some conclusion about several studies where the raw data are not available to be re-analysed. Strictly speaking, one should not simply average correlation coefficients, as the average one obtains will be a biased estimate – however, if the correlations are between −0.7 and +0.7, it probably does not matter too much, other than to obsessional journal referees. If the correlations are larger, it is necessary to perform what is known as a 'Fisher transformation' before averaging. This converts the correlation into a variable having a roughly normal distribution. After averaging these Fisher transformations, the result is converted back into a correlation. Spreadsheet 5.5 performs this analysis, averaging up to six correlations.

> ### EXERCISE 5.5: CORRELATION UTILITIES
>
> **Resources required:** Spreadsheet 5.5: Correlation utilities. From www.routledge.com/9781138228894
>
> **Purpose:** To correct correlations for unreliability and restriction of range, to average correlations, to test whether two correlations differ
>
> **Contents of spreadsheet:** Various sample data
>
> **Suggested activity:**
>
> * Reliabilities of 0.7–0.8 are quite common. Enter a correlation and then note how much it increases when corrected for unreliability. Try several different values of correlation and several different values for reliability (between 0 and 1).
> * Check how changing the proportion of people selected alters the correlation that is corrected for attenuation using Dobson's method.
> * Convince yourself that if the sample standard deviation is smaller than the standard deviation in the population, the correction for restriction of range increases the size of the correlation. What happens if the standard deviation in the sample is *larger* than in the population?
> * Try averaging some correlations. Note that the Fisher method (used here) gives similar results to a simple average unless the correlations are larger than about 0.8.

Points to note:

- These utilities are hard to find and are brought together for convenience. However, readers are reminded that although they are believed to be accurate, these formulae are intended for educational (rather than research) purposes and may contain errors.

Learning outcomes:

Readers should now be able to

- perform a range of corrections and significance tests.

OVERVIEW

Many psychometric analyses are based on correlations. If these are inappropriate for the data being analysed (e.g., if dichotomous data are simply treated as if they are continuous) or if care is not taken to check for group differences or outliers, the sophisticated analyses described in the following chapters are meaningless as well as scientifically and practically worthless. The issue of group differences is the one that I would single out for special attention. It is all too easy to rush ahead and calculate correlations for a diverse group of people without recognising that if the sample consists of two or more subgroups of people with different mean scores, the size and sign of the correlation can be massively influenced by such differences. Few psychologists appreciate this point. It can also be difficult to track down techniques for correcting correlations for the effects of restriction of range and unreliability, and so the spreadsheets may be of use to practitioners who need to perform such corrections.

NOTE

1 This has nothing to do with the use of the term 'p-value' in statistical significance testing.

CHAPTER 6
RANDOM AND SYSTEMATIC
ERRORS OF MEASUREMENT

No measurement is ever perfectly accurate. If I measure the length of a piece of paper using rulers, it is probable that I will over- or underestimate its length by a millimetre or two just because of problems aligning the end of the ruler with the end of the paper and reading the length corresponding to the other end of the piece of paper, plus possible problems with the rulers themselves; my selection of cheap, dollar-store rulers might be inaccurate. But if I measure the same piece of paper using the same ruler on many occasions or assume that a cheap ruler is as likely to underestimate as overestimate a length, it should be intuitively obvious that the average of all these measurements is likely to be close to the true length of the piece of paper. By taking multiple measurements the errors should cancel each other out.

For example, if I measured the same piece of paper on 15 occasions, the lengths (in millimetres) might be as shown in Table 6.1.

We can plot these lengths as a bar chart (see Figure 6.1), and both experiment and statistical theory (something called the central limit theorem) tell us that the distribution of these scores follows a normal distribution. In other words, (a) we are as likely to overestimate as underestimate a measurement, and (b) we are more likely to under or overestimate the measurement by a small amount than a large amount.

Table 6.1 Fifteen measurements of a piece of paper

Occasion	1	2	3	4	5	6	7	8	9	10	11	12	13	14	15
Measurement	92	93	91	90	92	92	92	93	92	94	91	92	91	92	93
Error	0	1	−1	−2	0	0	0	1	0	2	−1	0	−1	0	1

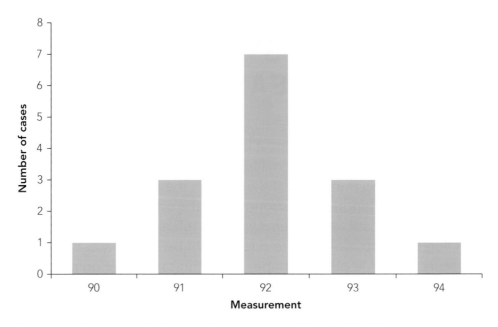

Figure 6.1 Frequency distribution of measurements from Table 6.1

Taken together (a) and (b) imply that the average error will be zero – as we are likely to overestimate the length as often as we underestimate it, and by a similar amount. If the average error is zero, it follows that we can average all the measurements to obtain an estimate of the true score: 92.0. This is the best estimate that we have of the true length of the piece of paper. In order to estimate this true score accurately we need to make a very large number of measurements – otherwise we might be unlucky and make some measurements which all just happen to be too large or too small. It should be obvious that as the number of measurements increases our estimate of the true score, obtained by averaging repeated observations, is likely to be more accurate.

WHY PSYCHOLOGICAL MEASURES ARE DIFFERENT FROM PHYSICAL MEASURES

Comparing psychological measurements with physical measurements like this has some appeal, but it falls down in four main respects.

First, as we noted in Chapter 4, there is no guarantee that the trait or state which the test is designed to measure is quantitative at all – in which case all attempts to measure it using numbers, adding together scores on items etc., will not constitute proper scientific measurement although they may have some practical utility in some circumstances. And as items vary in their difficulty (or for Likert-scaled items, how extreme a level of the trait they represent), it is not reasonable to treat sums of responses to these items as anything better than interval-scaled data. This suggests that the best that any test can do under ideal circumstances is rank-order people.

Second, in psychology we cannot ask the same question over and over again when trying to measure some trait, as respondents will simply remember their previous answer and repeat it. So it is necessary to devise different items, each of which measures the same trait but by different means. For example, if a scale is designed to measure vocabulary, one might assemble a selection of words of appropriate difficulty (perhaps by randomly sampling words which occur in the written language within a certain band of frequency). Or, if we try to measure a trait such as depression, we could ask questions each of which relates to a different aspect of depression, such as weight change, feelings of hopelessness, inability to concentrate etc. But the basic principle still holds: if we assume that the measurement errors are random, our best estimate of the true score is a person's total score on the scale.

Third, the instruments used to measure physical quantities are generally fairly accurate. The reading on the ruler is influenced by the length of the object being measured, not time of day, atmospheric pressure, distance from the equator or anything else, and so only a very few readings are needed to achieve an accurate measurement. On the other hand, items in psychological scales are almost invariably affected by many different traits, and so the correlation between responses to an item and the 'true score' (a person's level of the trait being assessed) is usually feeble. It is possible to estimate this in several different ways, but a correlation of 0.3 to 0.4 would be normal, whilst a correlation of 0.5 would be surprisingly large. In other words, most test items are only feebly related to the trait which they purport to measure; bear in mind that even a correlation of 0.5 implies that only 25% of the variance in the responses to the item is due to the influence of the trait being assessed!

Why is this? 'Do you enjoy lively parties?' is an item which has been shown to measure Extraversion. But think about what else might affect how a person responds to this item. Age might affect it – I certainly enjoy parties less than I used to. Even if I hate parties, I might *say* I enjoy them because I think it is expected of me. I might have decided to focus on my work instead of partying. Even a highly extraverted person might disagree with this item if they do not enjoy interacting with drunken people, if they have been to so many parties recently that they abhor the thought of yet another one . . . The list is almost endless. As well as measuring the trait which the scale is designed to measure, a person's response to an item will be influenced by a lot of other things, and there will probably be plenty of random error too as people's view may change from minute to minute for no obvious reason. And some people will just happen to like parties – even though they are not extraverted – an issue which will be picked up in Chapter 8.

If each of the items in a scale is affected by a different set of these nuisance variables, or if the nuisance variables which increase a person's score on one item decrease their score on another item, then there is no problem. Just as measuring the length of the sheet of paper several times increased the accuracy of the assessment, adding together several items *each of which is affected by a different set of nuisance variables* will produce a test score which is likely to be more accurate than the score on any single item. And the more items which are added together, the more accurate the test score will be. For now, we treat all of the nuisance variables (the things which influence the way in which people answer the item but which are not the trait we are trying to measure) as being random errors. This means that they will vary from item to item and from person to person.

Each person's answer to an item will thus be influenced by the level of the trait which the scale is designed to measure (their 'true score') together with some random errors of measurement. Spreadsheet 6.1 allows us to vary the extent to which the true score and random error influence people's responses to five items which form a scale. For example, one item might consist of equal amounts of true score and random error. Another (worse) item might consist of three parts true score and seven parts random error, and so on. Because this is a simulation, we actually know each person's true score – so the first important thing which this spreadsheet does is show the correlation between responses to an item and people's true scores.

The second thing which this spreadsheet does is add together the responses on several items. We argued above that computing a total score for each person by adding together scores on several items should show a large correlation with the true score because all of the random errors will tend to cancel out. So the spreadsheet shows the correlation between scores on the five-item scale and the true score.

Finally, we argued above that the more times we measure something, the more accurate the (total) score is likely to be. So the spreadsheet also adds another five items, of equal quality to the original five, to see whether this shows a still-better correlation with the total score.

EXERCISE 6.1: SUMMING ITEM SCORES

Resources required: Spreadsheet 6.1: Summing item scores. From www.routledge.com/9781138228894

Purpose:

- To show how the reliability of a test reflects the amount of measurement error.
- To determine whether test length influences reliability.

Contents of spreadsheet: Data on 10 items from 390 simulated people. Each person's score on each item is influenced by their true score and random error to an extent which can be varied.

Suggested activity:

- Enter some numbers between 0 and 10 in each green cell. 0 indicates that the true score does not influence the item score at all; 10 indicates that the true score completely determines the score on the item. The number underneath each green cell shows the extent to which random error influences each item. Re-calculate several times using f9 etc.
- Note the correlation between each item and the true score in Section B.
- Check that entering '0' produces a correlation of about zero, and that '10' produces a correlation of 1.0. Re-calculate several times.
- Set the influence of the true score to a fairly low value (say 2 or 3) for each item. This is typical of those found in real scales. Is the correlation between the sum of scores on Items 1–5 larger than the correlation between any individual item and the true score?
- The spreadsheet also generates Items 6–10, with identical characteristics to Items 1–5. This means that it is possible to see whether using a 10-item test, with the same quality of items as a five-item test, produces better correlation with the total score.
- Find out whether it is possible for a single-item scale to perform better than a five-item scale using items of varying quality. Perhaps use one item with a value of 6 or 7 and others with 2 or 3. Examine the correlation between the 'good' item and the total score and compare this with the correlation between the five-item scale and the total score.

Points to note:

- Note that the correlation between the score on the sum of Items 1–5 and the true score is much higher than the correlation between any single item and the true score when all items are of equal quality.
- The 10-item test is invariably a better measure of the true score than is the five-item test.
- If the scale consists of one good item and several mediocre ones, it may be better to use just the one good item. See Chapter 13.

Learning outcomes:

Readers should now be able to

- appreciate that the total score on a scale consisting of several equal-quality items is a better estimate of people's true scores than a single item;
- realise that longer scales provide better estimates of true scores than do shorter scales – assuming that Items 6–10 are of the same quality as the items in the five-item scale.

Although we can never know a person's true score, we can estimate it by using their total score on the items in the scale. So we could correlate each person's score on each item with the total score, as this is the best estimate which we have of the person's true score. This is a classic method of developing scales, described in Chapter 13. The best items are those having the largest correlation with the total score on the scale.

We could also look at the quality of the items by examining the correlations between them. An item which has a lot of random error associated with it will show a low correlation with all other items in the scale. An item which is little influenced by random error will show much higher correlations with the other items. So 'good' items will show large correlations between them; items which largely consist of random error will intercorrelate feebly. Reliability theory (described below) draws extensively on this idea.

The above is a statistical fact. However, there is a major problem with its implementation, for it is not completely obvious how we should define 'random error'. Most psychologists simply assume that anything other than the trait which one tries to measure is random error (or one of the forms of systematic bias considered at the end of this chapter). I believe that this is incorrect, and this is why I was so scathing in Chapter 2 about scales where the same item is paraphrased several times. For such items, the correlation between the items is not determined just by the trait which the item is designed to measure – but by all of the other 'nuisance variables' as well, since a person's level of all of these will be the same, too. If the item 'Do you agree that a good party is the best way to spend the evening?' appears in the same questionnaire as the item 'Do you enjoy lively parties?' it is obvious that the nuisance factors which affect the first item will also affect the second item *in the same way*. They are not random error at all. So the correlation between these two items will not show how much people's responses to the two items measure the trait of Extraversion. Because the items are so similar in content, all the 'nuisance factors' will influence each person's response to both items in the same way, and thereby boost the correlation rather than cancelling it out. Thus the correlation between the items reflects a whole bunch of traits – not just the one of interest. The correlation between items will be larger than it would be if it reflected Extraversion alone. This will make the psychometric properties of the scale appear much better than they would be if better questions had been asked.

MEASURING RELIABILITY

The reliability of a test is defined as the proportion of variance of test scores which is due to the influence of people's true scores. It is usually expressed as a number between 0 and 1, with 0 indicating that the score on the scale is nothing but measurement error (i.e., no more useful than picking a random number) whilst a reliability of 1 indicates that there is no measurement error associated with people's scores on the scale; they reflect people's true scores with perfect accuracy. The square root of the reliability coefficient estimates the correlation between people's scores on the tests and their true scores, and so the reliability coefficient estimates the proportion of variation in test scores which is due to the influence of people's true scores on their test scores. A reliability of 0.7 implies that about 70% of the variation in people's scores on the scale is caused by their true score; the rest is due to other things.

The reliability coefficient is one of the most useful concepts in psychometrics. There are several ways of estimating the reliability of a scale; it has to be estimated rather than measured exactly because in real life we never know a person's true score.

However, it is vital to remember than when estimating the reliability of a scale, that estimate will change if the scale is administered to a different population of people or for different purposes. A scale which shows high reliability when university students volunteer to take it as part of a research study may show dismal reliability when those same students take it as part of a job-selection procedure. All too often, researchers seem to believe that reliability is a fundamental property of a scale, which it is not. The whole point of studying reliability is to estimate how much measurement error is associated with people's scores on a scale, and it is almost certain that different testing settings will cause people to behave differently – for example, trying harder to do well at an ability scale or trying to create a favourable impression when applying for a job. And the makeup of the sample will also affect reliability; if 6-year-olds find many of the items of an ability test too hard for them (and so guess more of the answers), there will obviously be much more measurement error associated with their scores than if the test were given to 8-year-olds.

The range of scores in the sample will also affect the reliability of a scale, in exactly the same way that Spreadsheet 5.5 showed that the range of scores affects the size of a correlation; a scale measuring intelligence will show higher reliability when administered to a sample of the general population than when it is administered to a sample of people identified by their teachers as being of above-average intelligence. Whenever anyone justifies using a scale because some other researcher has found that its reliability is some impressive-sounding number, it is vital to check that the context of the assessment is similar and that the demographics of the sample are similar – otherwise the claim is meaningless. One should always be very suspicious. It is also necessary to estimate the reliability of the scale using one's own sample, although we will see below that such estimates are surprisingly inaccurate unless the sample size is astoundingly large.

TEST-RETEST RELIABILITY

One of the most obvious ways of assessing reliability is to give people the same scale on two or more occasions, and, by making the (major) assumption that people will forget their previous answers, it is possible to test whether the scores which people obtain on the two occasions are similar. This measures reliability because if people were just responding randomly to items in the test, the correlation between the scores on the two (or more) occasions would be close to zero. On the other hand, if the items are working perfectly, then each person should obtain the same score on each occasion and so the correlation should be 1.0.

This form of reliability is known as 'test-retest reliability'. There are various rules of thumb for the interval which should lapse between the testing sessions, as it is necessary to choose an interval which is long enough to minimise memory effects whilst not being so long that people's levels of the trait or ability will change. Kline (2000b) suggests 3 months, and this fits in with empirical studies of ability tests, such as Catron and Thompson (1979). For personality tests it should be possible to use a shorter interval, and the manuals for many such tests suggest that a period of 2–3 weeks is common; however, there appears to be little systematic evidence to support this practice.

There are four obvious problems with this approach to assessing reliability – over and above the logistical nightmare of gathering data from the same group of people on two occasions.

MEMORY

The problem is likely to be more severe for ability tests than for personality tests. If one laboriously works out an answer to some problem, it is likely that this will be remembered (along with the strategies which were used) if the test is readministered within a short time period. If this speeds up the amount of time taken to solve the test the second time it is administered, it might also free up some time to attempt other problems, which will lead to an increase in scores. This is the so-called 'practice effect'. It is therefore dangerous to administer the same cognitive test more than once, because the processes which are involved may well be different on the second occasion; participants may well remember the answers which they gave before, rather than solving them anew. And indeed this is what has been found. Collie et al. (2003) administered the same computerised ability test four times in one day and found a marked difference in performance between the first and second administrations – presumably because the participants remembered their previous answers – but not between the second and third, or third and fourth. This is exactly what one would expect if the cognitive demands of the task are different on the first administration to subsequent occasions.

Memory may also be a problem for personality scales and is particularly likely if the test content is interesting or unusual and is thus processed deeply on the first administration. I would guess that if a participant was asked, 'Do you like the feeling of soft wool slippers?' (which is an item from a genuine personality test), this item would stick in most people's minds because of its sheer bizarreness. It would not be obvious why this question was asked. Participants might make a mental note of it so that they can marvel at it with their friends afterwards – and many of us who do not possess a pair of soft woolly slippers would need to think carefully about what answer to give! All of these factors would tend to make the item (and one's answer) memorable. Compared to this, an item such as 'Do you like meeting new people?' is quite mundane, and one's answer might be more easily forgotten.

Thus although tests may show high test-retest reliability, it is not completely obvious what this means. Whilst high test-retest reliability *could* imply that the test measures the same trait on two occasions and these scores are commendably free of measurement error, it could also imply that the test measures the intended cognitive ability on the first occasion and memory (for the chosen answers, strategies for solving the problems etc.) on the second. There is no easy way to be certain which. Thus although low test-retest reliability indicates that the test is flawed because it produces inconsistent scores, high test-retest reliability does not necessarily imply that the test scores are free of measurement error. Polit (2014) provides a useful discussion of these issues from the perspective of a health researcher.

PEOPLE'S LEVELS OF THE TRAIT MAY CHANGE

Problems arise if people's levels of a trait change between two administrations of a scale. This will reduce the test-retest reliability, wrongly suggesting that there is something wrong with the test. This is a particular problem if the interval between test administrations is very long or the test is given to children or to adults during a period of transition (e.g., before and after therapy). Here it is quite possible that some people's scores will increase, other people's might decrease whilst some might stay the same. This will lead to a low estimate of reliability. That said, the test-retest reliability of a scale measuring general intelligence is above 0.7 over a 66-year period (Deary et al., 2000), showing that this trait, at any rate, stays remarkably stable.

HIGH TEST-RETEST RELIABILITY DOES NOT MEAN THAT THE ITEMS MEASURE A SINGLE TRAIT

It would be possible to devise a scale containing items measuring completely different things – for example, one item measuring Extraversion, another measuring Neuroticism. If they answer the items in the same way on each occasion, each person should achieve the same score on each occasion leading to a correlation of 1.0 between the two sets of scores. However, the correlation between the items will be close to zero, and the scale score would be meaningless. Test-retest reliability cannot show whether the items are sampled from some well-defined domain.

STATES

The technique only really works for traits. In order to measure states (which vary over time and from situation to situation), other methods would need to be devised, as the test–retest reliability of a state should be close to zero. (If it is not, it is probably measuring a trait.)

THE SAMPLE

Like any other form of reliability, test–retest reliability will vary depending on who is being assessed and why. If student participants are asked to take the test on two occasions they may feel bored or resentful when presented with the same items a second time and may start to answer randomly in order to get the loathsome process finished as soon as possible. This will obviously reduce the test–retest reliability. On the other hand, applicants for a job which they really want might be expected to try their best on both occasions. Problems may also arise when administering tests to children. It is possible that some young children may not understand all of the words in a personality test, for example, and so may choose an answer at random each time they take the test, which will reduce the test–retest reliability.

The size of the sample also matters. Like any statistic, the intraclass correlation (which is commonly used to assess test–retest reliability) has a certain 'standard error of measurement' – which basically shows us how closely the intraclass correlation which we have calculated from the sample of people we have available is likely to resemble its 'true' value – the value which we would obtain if we were to test everyone in the population. The larger the sample, the better this estimate is likely to be – but the literature here is surprisingly unpleasant (Donner and Wells, 1986).

GROUP DIFFERENCES CAN INFLATE TEST-RETEST RELIABILITY

We showed earlier that group differences can influence correlations. As test–retest reliability simply involves correlating scores on two occasions, it follows that if the sample contains two groups of people whose mean scores on the scale are appreciably different, this can lead to the overestimation of test–retest reliability.

MEASURING TEST-RETEST RELIABILITY

There are two commonly used options – the usual Pearson correlation coefficient, with which readers of this book will be familiar, and the intraclass correlation coefficient, which is probably less familiar. It is important to appreciate that they measure rather different things and which one is used will depend on the purpose of testing.

A researcher might not be too concerned whether people who are assessed twice perform better on the second occasion. They might just be interested in the extent to which scores on the second occasion are proportional to the scores which people obtain on the first occasion. According to this definition of test-retest reliability, the researcher would not care in the slightest if everyone's score on a scale of reasoning ability went up by (say) 10 marks or if everyone's level of Neuroticism went up by 15% the second time that they took the test. If the researcher is happy to ignore the possibility that scores might all go up (or down) on the second occasion that people are assessed or that the standard deviation might change, then the usual Pearson correlation may be used as an index of test-retest reliability. It shows the extent to which the scores that people obtain the first time they are assessed are proportional to the scores that they obtain on the second occasion. These researchers look at the test-retest reliability to convince themselves that scores on the test are not random; they are happy to accept that any change in the test scores between the two occasions might be attributed to some environmental influence which affects everyone similarly.

However, suppose that an educational or clinical psychologist wants to assess people on two occasions – perhaps to check whether their reading skills or level of self-reported pain has improved after some intervention. Or a researcher might wish to determine whether some intervention influences scores on a scale which is administered on multiple occasions. They would analyse differences in the mean scores on each occasion using analysis of variance or something similar, and they too would need to be confident that, in the absence of any intervention, people's scores would be the same on each occasion.

These researchers obviously need to use a different definition of test-retest reliability to the one described in the previous paragraph when selecting a test, for they need to identify a test where each person obtains the same score on each occasion when there is no intervention. This allows the person's first score to be compared with their second score. To assess how well a particular scale provides replicable scores, the intraclass correlation would be used, following the advice of Shrout and Fleiss (1979). Other possibilities exist too, and Vaz et al. (2013) explore some of them.

EXERCISE 6.2: PEARSON AND INTRACLASS CORRELATIONS FOR TEST-RETEST RELIABILITY

Resources required: Spreadsheet 6.2: Pearson and intraclass correlations for test-retest reliability. From www.routledge.com/9781138228894

Purpose: To show how Pearson and intraclass correlations behave differently when scores increase or decrease on retesting

Contents of spreadsheet: Data from 18 people, each administered the same scale on two occasions

Suggested activity:

- With 'multiply by'=1, add various values (e.g., −0.5, +0.5, 1, 5) to each person's score on the second occasion, using the setting in Section A. Compare the Pearson and intraclass correlations (right of Section B) to their original values (left of Section B).
- With 'add'=0, try multiplying everyone's Time 2 score by a constant – e.g., 2 or 0.5 and note what happens to both correlations.

Points to note:

- Experiment by changing entries in the GREEN areas. Results are in the YELLOW areas. Simply download another copy if you accidentally change formulae.

Learning outcomes:

Readers should now be able to

- demonstrate an understanding of how a positive intraclass correlation becomes closer to zero or negative if the mean score on the first occasion differs from the mean on retesting.

Unlike the Pearson correlation, the intraclass correlation decreases if there is any change in the average level of scores on the second occasion or if the variance of these scores changes. This is why it is widely used to assess test-retest reliability. If a test manual or journal article instead only gives a value for the Pearson correlation, it is necessary to check that there is no change in mean score (or variance) between the first and second administration – for example using a paired-sample t-test or the Levene test for equality of variance (Levene, 1960).

ALTERNATIVE-FORMS RELIABILITY

One occasionally finds scales which have two (or more) 'alternative forms'. In other words, there are two versions of a test that are the same length but have different items, both measuring the same trait or state, and designed to be used in the same population. These can be useful in practice – for example, if it is necessary to measure the same ability trait on several occasions and one wants to ensure that participants do not simply remember the answers previously given. People are normally given just one version of the scale. However, if people are given *both* versions, it is possible to correlate them together to draw some inferences about the amount of measurement error associated with each test score. When correlating the two scores together, each person's score on each scale is assumed to be determined by their true score (the score that they would obtain if they were administered all possible items) plus measurement error, which is exactly the same scenario as for test–retest reliability. So, once again, the correlation between the two forms estimates the reliability of either form.

SPLIT-HALF RELIABILITY

What if a scale does not have alternative forms, and is administered just once? One way of estimating the amount of measurement error in such a scale would be to divide the items into two halves. For example, if a scale consists of 20 items, one could work out each person's score on just the first 10 items and correlate this with their score on the final 10 items. This seems as if it ought to tell us something useful about the amount of measurement error in the test scores, but there are three obvious problems with this approach.

- It is possible that people respond differently to the later items in a questionnaire than they do to the earlier ones; they may get bored or careless. And if the test has time limits, it is possible that some people might not reach the end of the test – and so when the test is scored their score on the second half would be lower or more 'error-ful' than their score for the first half, depending on how missing data are treated when the test is scored. For this reason, it is normal to calculate each person's score on the odd-numbered items and correlate this with their score on the even-numbered items.
- If a test consists of n items, we correlate the score based on half the test items with another score based on half the test items. If the formula for estimating test-retest reliability were used, it would tell us what the reliability of the scale comprising n/2 items is – whereas we need to know the reliability of a scale which consists of n items. Something called the 'Spearman-Brown formula' may be used to achieve this. To estimate the reliability of a scale based on the correlation between two 'half-length scales', simply double the correlation and divide this by 1 plus the correlation. If the correlation between two 'half-length scales' is 0.7, the reliability of the full scale is

$$\frac{2 \times 0.7}{1 + 0.7}$$

or 0.82.
- Correlating the odd items with the even-numbered items is arbitrary. One would obtain a different answer if one correlated the sum of Items 1 and 2, 5 and 6 etc. with the sum of Items 3 and 4, 7 and 8 etc. As we are trying to establish the property of the test, we should not really base this on the arbitrary decision of how to divide the items into two groups. One solution might be to calculate all possible split-half reliabilities and average them – and fortunately there is a statistic (coefficient alpha) which does just this.

INTERNAL CONSISTENCY

Thus far we have just looked at the relationship between scale scores. Measures of internal consistency instead look at the behaviour of individual items within the scale. In what follows, we assume that the test items are independent – that is, the only thing which influences the way in which a person responds to each item is the single trait which all of the items are supposed to measure. For example, items such as 'Do you enjoy teasing animals?' and 'Are insurance schemes a good idea?' (Eysenck et al., 1985) are fine, whilst items such as 'On the whole, I am satisfied with myself' and 'I take a positive attitude toward myself' (Rosenberg, 1965) are not, because the way in which a person answers the first question determines how they must answer the second one.

The phrase 'internal consistency' is a misnomer, however. Its name seems to suggest that it measures the extent to which a set of items all measure the same thing (i.e., whether a set of items all measure a single trait). It does not; factor analysis is needed for this. Instead, if it *assumed* that all of the items measure the same trait, internal-consistency reliability tries to estimate the extent to which scores on the test reflect people's true scores; the scores which they would obtain if they completed an infinitely long test.

Suppose that we have four test items, each of which measures the same trait with complete accuracy. The average correlation between different items will be 1.0. This is the best-case scenario – a test with no measurement error at all. How about a ghastly test where none of the items has any relationship at all to the trait? Here all of the correlations between different items will be zero. One *could* simply look at the average correlation between different items in the test and infer from this how much measurement error there is. However, the more items we add together when calculating a person's score on a test, the more likely that test score is to be accurate, as was seen in Spreadsheet 6.1. There is some good statistical theory underlying this claim (and we have also acknowledged this when estimating split-half reliability from the correlation between two 'half-scales' using the Spearman-Brown formula). It should also be intuitively obvious from the example of measuring the page using a ruler with which we began this chapter. It is possible that the first measurement might overestimate the true length of the paper. But if we take 15 measurements, it is highly unlikely that they will *all* overestimate the length. So, given that we are trying to estimate the amount of measurement error in test scores, it makes sense to devise a statistic which

a) is influenced by the number of items in the scale (more items implying higher accuracy);
b) is influenced by the average correlation between the items.

The overwhelmingly popular choice for this measure is known as 'alpha', 'coefficient alpha' or 'Cronbach's alpha'. Note that this is nothing to do with the use of alpha in statistical significance testing. Coefficient alpha can be computed from people's responses to a set of items, and under certain conditions it can give some indication of how closely people's scores on a particular scale reflect their true scores – the scores which they would have obtained had all the items that could possibly be constructed to measure the trait been administered to them. This is possible *even though we never know what their true scores are.*

There are several formulae available for calculating coefficient alpha. The following equation

$$\text{Coefficient alpha} = \frac{\text{number of items}^2 \times \text{average correlation between different items}}{\text{sum of all correlations in the correlation matrix}\left(\text{including 1s}\right)} \qquad \text{Equation 6.1}$$

ties in well with the approach developed above. It is obvious from this formula that both the number of items (squared) and the average correlation influence alpha; the term at the bottom of the equation just ensures that the value usually stays between 0 and 1. (On rare occasions alpha can be less than 0, indicating that the test items are truly awful.)

The equation which is more often used is shown below.[1]

$$\text{Coefficient alpha} = \frac{\text{number of items}}{\text{number of items} - 1} \times \left(1 - \frac{\text{sum of variances of items}}{\text{variance of total score}}\right)$$

$$\text{Equation 6.2}$$

This is rather easier to calculate because there is no need to compute the correlation matrix.

Like any statistic, the value of coefficient alpha which one calculates will never be entirely accurate; it all depends on the number of people in the sample, and the number of items in the scale. So there is little point in quoting a value of coefficient alpha unless one also includes 'confidence intervals'. These indicate that we can be 90% (or some other percentage) certain that the value of alpha lies between two values. That said, I have yet to see a paper in which anyone actually does report confidence intervals. Feldt et al. (1987) show how this can be achieved, and also show how it is possible to test whether coeficients alpha from two different samples are significantly different.

EXERCISE 6.3: CONFIDENCE INTERVALS FOR
COEFFICIENT ALPHA

Resources required: Spreadsheet 6.3: Confidence intervals for coefficient alpha.
From www.routledge.com/9781138228894

Purpose: To compute confidence intervals for coefficient alpha

Contents of spreadsheet: Example data

Suggested activity:

- Explore entering some values of alpha (e.g., 0.5, 0.7, 0.9) and, for each, adjust
  the sample size (e.g., 50, 10, 1000) and note what happens to the confidence
  intervals.
- Perhaps also adjust the length of the scale – e.g., five or 20 items.

Points to note:

- The confidence interval for alpha is much wider than most people expect, unless
  the sample size is large (several hundred).
- The length of the scale has a fairly small effect on the size of the confidence
  interval.

Learning outcomes:

Readers should now be able to

- appreciate the need to cite confidence intervals when reporting alpha and have
  the means to do so.

There are several issues to consider when calculating and interpreting coefficient alpha.

First, there are common rules of thumb for determining 'acceptable' values of
coefficient alpha. These usually suggest that values of alpha lower than 0.7 are
unacceptable (e.g., Kline, 2000a) whilst values of 0.9 or above are necessary for using
tests for individual assessments. To my mind, these are not very helpful, given that
alpha combines two very different types of information: the number of items in a test,
and the average correlation between these items. As Cortina (1993: 101) observes,
'For a 3-item scale with alpha = .80, the average inter-item correlation is .57. For a
10-item scale with alpha = .80, the average inter-item correlation is only .28'. So,
when an author quotes 'alpha is 0.7', it is hard to know what to conclude! It could
be from a long test where each item is only feebly related to the trait it is designed to

measure or a short test where the trait being measured has a huge influence on the way in which people respond to each of the items. Cortina's paper is not technical and can be warmly recommended.

Second, extremely high levels of alpha can indicate that there are real problems with a test. If some test items are so similar in content so that they basically mean the same thing, a person who answers one question in a particular way is *bound* to answer another item similarly. This finding is not an interesting empirical discovery, and indeed has nothing to do with psychology. It is a pure consequence of the meaning of the words in the items. The items are thus not independent. They will correlate very substantially indeed, and this will lead to a huge alpha. So, whilst a large coefficient alpha is desirable, I would be wary of a short scale (under about 10 items) with a very high coefficient alpha (above 0.8, say). In such a case, the large alpha might well mean that the scale contains items that are virtual paraphrases of each other. This can only be detected by reading the items and reflecting on their meaning. Blindly performing psychometric analyses of such items is a waste of everyone's time.

Next, as mentioned earlier, large coefficient alpha does *not* imply that all of the items in a scale measure a single trait. Because it is based on the average correlation between items, a large alpha can arise when some of the correlations are large and others are near zero – as would be the case if the items which formed the 'scale' actually measured several different traits. Factor analysis is needed to determine whether the items all measure the same trait. The same average correlation would be found if half of the correlations between items were 0.8 and the rest were 0.2, or if all the items correlated 0.5. And it is the average correlation which determines coefficient alpha. Thus it makes little sense to compute coefficient alpha without first performing a factor analysis to check that all of the items have large loadings on a single factor.

Finally, coefficient alpha makes the usual assumptions that the variable being measured is quantifiable and that the numbers produced by Likert scales, or similar, behave much like numbers in the physical world, meaning that they can be added, multiplied and so on. We pointed out in Chapter 4 that these are very worrying and important assumptions that cannot be tested and that are very likely to be incorrect.

THE RELATIONSHIP BETWEEN COEFFICIENT ALPHA AND TRUE SCORES

We argued earlier that coefficient alpha is important because it can show how accurately test scores can reflect people's true scores on traits. Now is the time to explore these relationships in a little more detail – but unfortunately it is necessary to start by defining some terms which psychometricians sometimes use.

Parallel, tau-equivalent and congeneric scales

The idea of alternative forms of a test was introduced above; parallel tests take this idea to its extreme form. When the same sample of people take both versions of two scales, those scales are 'parallel' if each form of the scale produces the same score for each person (which is an estimate of the person's true score), where the true score has the same amount of influence on each of the items in the test for each person and where the standard deviations of all of the items are the same. This also implies (as we shall see) that all of the correlations between the items are identical. I have never seen a pair of tests where this held true.

'Tau-equivalent' scales are similar to parallel scales. Here two scales measure the same trait on the same scale with the same degree of precision – but the items may have different amounts of measurement error associated with them. Because the total score is measured on the same scale, the same norms etc. may still be used. The standard deviations of the items are different. (This should be obvious, if you think about it, for if people's scores on a particular item are greatly influenced by random error, the more variable they will be and hence the standard deviation will be larger.) The correlations between items may also be different, as will be seen later.

Congeneric measures do away with the assumption that a person's true score on a trait influences every item to an equal extent. This is far more like the sorts of tests that are encountered in real life; it might well be possible to devise two scales both of which measure the same trait but where the standard deviations of the items are different and where some items are better measures of the trait than are others.

Assessing the reliability of a parallel or tau-equivalent test is straightforward, which is why these are of interest to psychometricians.

Spreadsheet 6.4 demonstrates this. This spreadsheet simulates people's responses to four test items – and allows us to construct parallel, tau-equivalent and congeneric scales. It also calculates coefficient alpha for each type of scale by the two formulae given above.

The purpose of using this spreadsheet is to demonstrate what happens to coefficient alpha when it is calculated from items that are parallel, tau-equivalent or conjoint; how to recognise a set of items which are (nearly) tau-equivalent when one sees them; and why doing so aids the interpretation of coefficient alpha.

It is necessary to explain a little about how this spreadsheet generates data. It generates a normally distributed 'true score' for each person. It also generates an 'error term' for each person's score on each item; these too are normally distributed. The model assumes that a person's score on a test item is influenced in part by that person's true score and in part by that person's random error. The influence of the true score and the influence of the random error can be set separately for each of the four items at the top of the spreadsheet.

The first person's score is different; rather than being random it shows some simple numbers so that it is easy to check how the item scores etc. are being calculated. The rest of the 5000 'people' are simulated.

EXERCISE 6.4: COEFFICIENT ALPHA

Resources required: Spreadsheet 6.4: Coefficient alpha. From www.routledge.com/9781138228894

Purpose:

- To generate scores on parallel, tau-equivalent and congeneric items.
- To calculate coefficient alpha using Equations 6.1 and 6.2 and show that coefficient alpha can underestimate the correlation between the test score and the true score.

Contents of spreadsheet: Simulated data on four items from over 5000 people whose true scores are known.

Suggested activity:

a) Generate a set of parallel items by setting the influence of the true score to be the same for all items (e.g., 5) and the influence of the error to be the same for all items (e.g., 4) in Section A.

- ○ Note that all of the item standard deviations in Section B are the same (apart from some possible sampling error).
- ○ Note that all of the correlations between the items in Section C are identical (again, there may be some sampling error).
- ○ Note the value of coefficient alpha in Section D.
- ○ Note the value of the standardised coefficient alpha in Section C. This was computed by averaging the correlations in Section C, using Formula 16.1.
- ○ Because the data were generated, Section F shows the correlation between the true scores and the scores on the test. This is not normally known in real life, as we never know people's true scores. Note the square of this value. It should resemble coefficient alpha.
- ○ Generate some more samples of data (press f9, Ctrl/Shift/f9) to convince yourself that in every case coefficient alpha closely resembles the square of the correlation between the test score and the true score.
- ○ Change the influence of the true score and/or error on the items – keeping the values identical for all items. Note what happens to the correlations between items. I suggest you use values of 4/4/4/4 and 4/4/4/4, 10/10/10/10 and 4/4/4/4, 2/2/2/2 and 4/4/4/4 amongst others.

b) Generate a set of tau-equivalent items by setting the influence of the true score on each item to be the same but introduce a different amount of random error on each item.

- o Note that the standard deviations of the items are different. So are the correlations between the items.
- o Note that the more error variance added to an item, the lower its correlation with other items.
- o Note that the squared correlation between the total score and the true score is still close to coefficient alpha in Section D (there may be a little sampling error).
- o Note that the standardised alpha (Section C) is different because the standard deviations of the items are different; Equation 6.1 only works for parallel items.
- o Repeat a few times with different values to check this.

c) Generate a set of congeneric items by allowing each item to be affected by the true score to different extents and have different amounts of error influencing them (e.g., 4/1/5/3 and 5/4/2/1).

- o Note that coefficient alpha (Section D) is now lower than the true reliability of the test (see Section F) which is the squared correlation with the true score.
- o Repeat with different values to convince yourself that this happens consistently.
- o Just for enthusiasts: Section E shows the 'variance-covariance' matrix which is calculated by multiplying each of the correlations between the items by the standard deviation of the two variables, as can be easily checked. Variances go in the diagonal. When Formula 6.1 is applied to covariances (rather than correlations) we obtain the same alpha as in Section D. This is because we no longer make the assumption that the items have equal standard deviations.

Learning outcomes:

Readers should now be able to

- recognise that coefficient alpha is related to the average correlation between items (*perfectly* related in the case of parallel and tau-equivalent items);
- appreciate the difference between parallel, tau-equivalent and congeneric items;
- recognise that coefficient alpha equals the square of the correlation between the test score and the true score for parallel and tau-equivalent items;
- recognise that coefficient alpha underestimates the true reliability of a scale (the correlation between the test score and the true score) for congeneric items.

This exercise shows something rather important which is not generally appreciated. For most real-life datasets (which are congeneric), coefficient alpha will underestimate the true reliability of a scale. That is, it will be less than the square of the correlation between the test scores and the true scores. How much it underestimates the reliability is unknown, for in real life we never know the correlation between the test score and the true score. However, what you saw from this exercise is that coefficient alpha resembles the true reliability of the test only when the items are parallel or tau-equivalent; that is, when all of the items are equally influenced by the true score. So before interpreting coefficient alpha, it is sensible to test whether the items can be assumed to form a tau-equivalent scale. Graham (2006) suggests how this may be done.

When looking at the table of covariances computed in Section E of Spreadsheet 6.4 (the covariance between items a and b is simply the correlation between items a and b multiplied by the standard deviation of both items), it seems that these covariances are similar if the data are tau-equivalent. But whether or not it is possible to develop this into some technique for easily identifying tau-equivalent data I leave to interested readers to pursue.

A CONTRARIAN VIEW OF RELIABILITY

The previous sections argued that reliability indicates how much measurement error is associated with scores on a scale. Coefficient alpha resembles (or equals) the amount of measurement error. Coefficient alpha is also influenced by the average correlation between the items. Therefore, large correlations between items lead to accurate scales.

Suppose, however, that a clinician decides to develop yet another scale to measure depression. The relationship between depression and the test items might be as shown in Figure 6.2. The circle labelled 'depression' corresponds to all of the characteristics measuring depression – change in mood, feelings of hopelessness, changes in eating and sexual behaviour etc. Each of the items measures a slightly different aspect of depression; the correlation between each item and depression is indicated by the amount of overlap between an item and depression; the correlation between items is indicated by the amount of overlap between items.

Clearly, the scale *should* measure all aspects of depression if at all possible. In other words, the area of the 'depression' circle covered by the items should be as large as possible to ensure that the correlation between the true score and the sum of the items is as large as possible. It can be seen that whilst Item 1 does tap some aspect of depression, Item 2 does nothing extra – it overlaps substantially (correlates appreciably) with Item 1. It overlaps appreciably with depression. But it does not explain any more of the variance of depression than Item 1 does. Item 3 makes a very modest additional contribution. Here is an example of three items that correlate substantially together

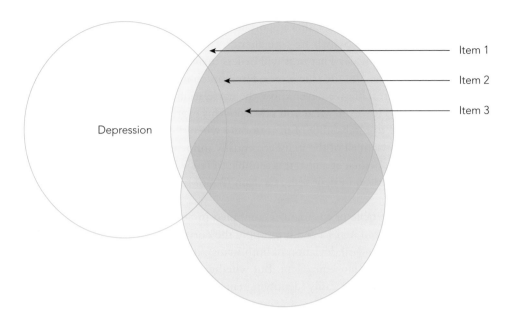

Figure 6.2 Three highly correlated items measuring a small aspect of depression

but that fail to measure the full breadth of the construct that they are designed to assess. They will have a very substantial coefficient alpha, each item will correlate with depression, and from a psychometric point of view they look ideal. Yet they manifestly fail to measure the full breadth of the construct – and Item 2 is clearly useless, as it does nothing more than duplicate Item 1.

Cattell (1973) argues that it would be much better if the correlations between the items were small – but that each measured a different aspect of the trait that they are designed to assess. In other words, it would be much better if the items measuring depression resembled those shown in Figure 6.3.

Here each item measures a different (and substantial) chunk of the variance of depression – but there is zero correlation between the items. It is clear that these three items do a better job of assessing depression than the items in Figure 6.2; the total score on these three items will correlate better with depression, which is, after all, the whole purpose of designing a scale. However, as all the correlations between the items are zero, coefficient alpha will be zero!

This is a powerful argument and reminds us of the importance of ensuring that the items in a scale are carefully chosen to represent the full breadth of the construct being measured. Having several highly correlated items in a scale may not be desirable. The problem is, as Kline (2000a) observes, that items such as those in Figure 6.3 prove to be almost impossible to find in practice.

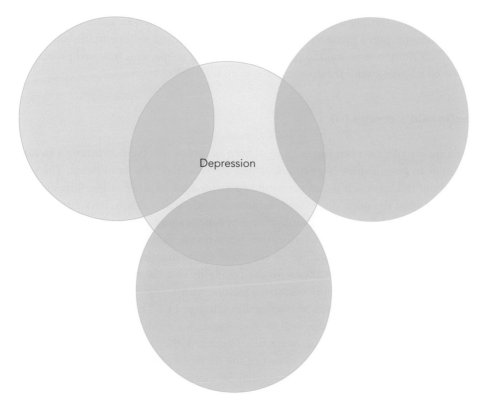

Figure 6.3 Three uncorrelated items, each measuring a different aspect of depression

OTHER MEASURES OF INTERNAL-CONSISTENCY RELIABILITY

Almost everyone reports coefficient alpha, but other measures have been devised too.

ORDINAL ALPHA

One of the more obvious alternatives is to compute something like alpha, but, rather than using Pearson correlations (which Michell's (1997a) work reminds us is unsafe), it is based on polychoric correlations. If their underlying assumptions are met, this allows us to assume that the numbers being analysed form an ordinal – rather than a ratio – scale. Zumbo et al. (2007) developed an ordinal coefficient alpha which appears not to underestimate the relationship between the test score and the true score for congeneric items. The problem is, however, that it says nothing about how well one's scale actually behaves. It instead estimates what the internal consistency of a scale probably would have been had a different type of test format been used to measure the trait.

This is therefore terribly hypothetical and divorced from reality. In addition, a paper by Chalmers (in press) points out several misconceptions and issues with the simulated data which Zumbo et al. used to justify the use of this coefficient. It would probably be unwise to rely on it until these issues have been resolved.

MacDonald's omega (ω)

There are actually two versions of omega, both of which involve performing a factor analysis as an intermediary stage to calculating the reliability of a set of items. The good thing about this approach is that performing a factor analysis more or less forces one to check that all of the items do, indeed, measure a single trait – that is, have large loadings on a single general factor. The simplest form of omega simply determines how well the first principal component describes the data – that is, how much of the variation between the items can be described by the single factor that the scale is designed to measure. The second version allows for the possibility that the items form not just one factor but a set of three or more correlated factors, with a single second-order factor above them. (Such models will be discussed in Chapter 11.) Those familiar with the Five Factor Model of personality will be aware of such a model. If all of the items from the NEO Extraversion scale were factor analysed, they should form six correlated factors, each factor corresponding to one of the six facets of Extraversion. Because these six factors are correlated, a general factor may be extracted – see the Schmid Leiman procedure in Chapter 11.

Raykov's composite reliability, rho (ρ)

Raykov (1997) developed a statistic that is identical to coefficient alpha when applied to tau-equivalent or parallel scales but that does not underestimate the size of the relationship between the scale score and the true score when applied to congeneric scales. There are also techniques available for calculating confidence intervals, comparing different coefficients for equality, and so on (Raykov, 2004). Like coefficient alpha, it shows how much of the variance in the item scores is due to variation in the true scores of various items. (It should not be confused with the other meanings of rho – the Spearman correlation or the population correlation.)

Raykov's technique requires some knowledge of structural equation modelling. For readers who have such skills, rho assumes that people's true score on the scale influences their true score on each of the items; the observed score on each item is also influenced by some error variance. The true score on the scale also influences the observed score on the scale (which is also affected by error variance). What makes this model interesting is the suggestion that it allows the sum of the observed scores on the items to be correlated with the true scale score; the value of this parameter (squared) is the composite reliability coefficient.

The technique seems sound, but in order for the reliability estimates to be accurate, large samples are needed – and each item needs to use as large a number of levels as possible. It is also important that the data fit the model – which can by no means be guaranteed. Raykov (1997) provides code for computing composite reliability using the EQS or LISREL packages for structural equation modelling.

SUMMARY

Coefficient alpha, and other coefficients based on it, are some of the most widely abused statistics in psychology.

- They do not show that all of the items in a scale measure just one trait.
- They are influenced by two quite different things – the number of items in the scale and the average correlation between these items. Thus a long scale whose items have small intercorrelations can have the same coefficient alpha as a shorter scale with high correlations between the items.
- Alpha only estimates the correlation between test score and the true score on the trait if some rather unlikely assumptions are made.
- There is a large margin of error associated with any estimate of coefficient alpha, unless the sample size is huge. So, if an author reports that coefficient alpha is 0.7, it could easily be 0.6 or 0.8.
- A very high value of alpha from a short scale (e.g., fewer than 10 items) might suggest that the items are *too* similar in content to measure anything of value; they may well be 'bloated specifics' or mere rephrasings of the same item.
- Rules of thumb such as 'alpha must be at least 0.7 for a test to be satisfactory' have little or no basis in theory or research and arise from misquoting Nunnally (1978).

There are far fewer problems with Raykov's composite reliability statistic, but it is seldom reported or used.

SYSTEMATIC ERRORS OF MEASUREMENT

Thus far we have considered random errors of measurement – where a person's true level of a trait is as likely to be underestimated as it is to be overestimated. However, it is possible for systematic errors of measurement to creep into any scale measuring personality, mood, emotion or attitudes. For example, it has been found that if people are asked to estimate their level of intelligence, men overestimate it whilst women underestimate it (Beloff, 1992), a finding which will be familiar to anyone who has conducted interviews for academic posts! There are several other types of systematic errors too. However, the good news is that it is sometimes possible to design scales so as to minimise their impact.

Systematic errors are only a problem if some people are more influenced by them than others. If *everyone* overestimated their level of intelligence by the same amount, then there would be no problem, as the correlation between estimated levels of intelligence and actual levels of intelligence would be unchanged. (Adding the same number to everyone's score does not affect the correlation between the test score and the criterion.)

ACQUIESCENCE

Some people tend to agree with whatever statement they are shown, whilst others do not. Known as 'acquiescent responding' or 'yea-saying', this is a problem for Likert scales where the items are all keyed in the same direction (e.g., so that agreeing with each statement or saying that it is an accurate description implies a high level of the trait). This means that a person's score on the scale will be a mixture of two things – their true score on the scale plus their tendency to agree. Thus, if all of the items are scored such that agreeing with an item corresponds to a high level of the trait, the scores of yea-sayers will be higher than they should be. If it is not measured or controlled acquiescence will lead to inaccurate test scores. Jackson and Messick's (1958) treatment of the issue is still a classic. They note that acquiescence is a particular problem where the questions in the scale appear irrelevant or silly, which is bad news for many personality scales. Fortunately, however, there is a straightforward solution. All one needs to do is rephrase half of the items so that agreeing implies a *low* level of the trait. For example, a scale measuring Neuroticism might ask people to rate themselves (using a Likert scale) as to how well items such as 'Do you worry a lot?' and 'Are you a calm person?' describe them. Agreeing with the first item and disagreeing with the second one indicates high Neuroticism. So an acquiescent person's score on the first item might be one point higher than it should be, whilst their score on the second item would be one point *lower* than it should be. When the scores on the two items are added together, the effects of acquiescence cancel out and the score is accurate. This is why most scales have about half of their items keyed in each direction – though sometimes it can be hard to write items which read naturally. 'How much do you dislike . . . ?' is clumsy, for example.

Acquiescence is considerably more common in some countries than others (Rammstedt et al., 2017) with differences between countries being surprisingly large – in the order of one standard deviation. It is more of a problem in Southern Europe than in the north. If individuals within countries have high levels of conservatism and/or lower educational qualifications, this makes it slightly more likely that they will agree with statements (Rammstedt et al., 2017; Narayan and Krosnick, 1996) although these effects are not large.

There is also excellent evidence that acquiescent responding can have a serious effect on the correlations between test scores and external criteria (Danner et al., 2015) and can also influence the correlations between test items. Items which should correlate together may not, and items from different scales may correlate because both are influenced by acquiescence (Bentler et al., 1971). Danner et al. (2015) additionally show that individual differences in acquiescence are comparable in different personality questionnaires; a person's level of acquiescence is very similar across a range of personality and attitude scales, though it is not hugely stable over time. This last finding ties in with research that shows that acquiescence seems to be influenced by situational variables (e.g., Trott and Jackson, 1967). Anyone using Likert scales to measure personality, attitudes or something similar should worry about the influence of acquiescence, particularly if a scale does not contain roughly equal numbers of positively and negatively keyed items. Suggestions as to how to measure and control for acquiescence and reduce its likelihood may be found in the references given above.

SOCIAL DESIRABILITY AND PERSONALITY ASSESSMENT

People often claim to have desirable characteristics (e.g., an above-average sense of humour, or honesty) and deny that they have common failings. This problem of social desirability arises when people rate themselves, their family and their friends, though not when rating 'people in general' (Pedregon et al., 2012; Edwards, 1959). It is thus likely to be a pervasive problem in questionnaire research. Like acquiescence, social desirability could cause items from different scales to correlate, it might cause scores from scales measuring different traits to appear to be correlated, and it can blur the factor structure of questionnaires. Unlike acquiescence, it is not straightforward to eliminate its effects.

If everyone behaved in the same way (for example, if everyone ticked the box one place to the left of the one that reflected their 'true' answer to a particular item), then there would not be much of a problem, for the answers given to the question would still be able to do a pretty good job at differentiating those who strongly agreed with the stem to those who disagreed with it. (The only real difficulty arises at the end of the scale; a person who 'strongly agreed' with the stem statement has already given the most extreme response possible, so they will be merged with the people who originally just 'agreed' with the stem.) However, people vary in the degree to which they seem to distort their responses, and this can create problems because it injects error into the measurement process. In theory, it should be possible to identify the extent to which each person distorts their responses and correct their scores for this tendency (or simply drop them from the analysis). However, in practice this turns out to be quite difficult and surprisingly ineffective, as discussed below.

Paulhus (1984) suggested that there are two aspects to socially desirable responding. Impression management involves deliberate deception. Sometimes the motivation for this might be obvious; an applicant for a post as an accountant or lawyer would probably deny being slapdash, using recreational drugs or experiencing hallucinations if they were asked to complete a personality scale as part of some selection process. A patient might perhaps want to portray themselves as being more distressed than they truly were. And a prisoner might wish to make it clear that they had truly reformed. But Paulhus also suggests that sometimes people may just have an unrealistic impression of themselves, and this he termed 'self-deceptive enhancement'. Someone may be convinced that they have a fine ready wit, even though they are in reality dull and morose.

Having established that socially desirable responding can be either deliberate or self-deceiving, Paulhus (e.g., 2002) argues that either form of it consists of two components. Egoistic bias is the tendency to exaggerate positive characteristics such as intelligence, fearlessness etc., whilst moralistic bias is the tendency to portray oneself as having high moral standards, being dependable and having few frailties or faults.

It may be useful to consider what might influence a person's decision to present a favourable impression of themselves when answering a self-report questionnaire, and their ability to do so effectively.

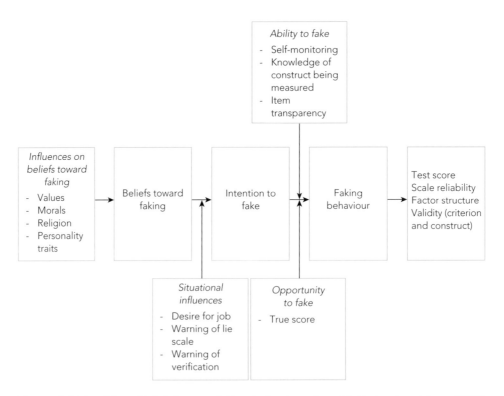

Figure 6.4 Variables which influence faking behaviour; from McFarland and Ryan (2000)

This model, from McFarland and Ryan (2000), suggests that, when a questionnaire is used in a particular situation, some people may believe that faking is acceptable whilst others do not. This will then interact with various situational influences (e.g., how much they want the job, what sort of image they want to portray to their professor, whether they have been warned that the questionnaire contains a 'Lie scale' which will detect faking) to determine whether or not they decide to fake their scores. But will they be *able* to fake their scores if they want to? Some studies (e.g., MacCann, 2013) suggest that intelligence may matter here; more intelligent individuals might better discern which responses will create the desired impression, though the 'transparency' of personality questions and knowledge of what traits are being measured by the test will also be important. Of course, if someone's true score on a trait is already high (in the desirable direction) they will not be able to improve it much, whereas if someone's score is low, they will have ample room to distort their measures. Hence a person's true score on the trait will also influence the extent to which they are able to fake their responses on a particular scale.

The most obvious way of eliminating socially desirable responses is to write items whose content is not socially desirable. However, this is easier said than done – especially if one is trying to write items for a scale measuring psychopathic traits, aggressive tendencies or anything else which is valued or frowned on by society or one's peer group.

The second method is to administer a scale designed to measure one or both forms of social desirability (e.g., Crowne and Marlowe, 1960; Paulhus, 1998) and use this to either drop people from the sample or perform some statistical corrections to their scores. The Paulhus scales measure both impression management and self-deception, and so should reveal the extent to which they are trying to portray themselves in a good light. Alternatively, some personality questionnaires such as the Eysenck Personality Questionnaire (Revised) (Eysenck et al., 1985) include items measuring social desirability (the 'Lie scale') that are scattered throughout the questionnaire rather than being administered as a separate scale. This might make them harder to spot. Eysenck recommends treating the personality scores of anyone with an extreme lie score as being untrustworthy and recommends dropping these individuals from any statistical analyses. However, there are three problems with this approach:

- The 'cut off score' above which one eliminates an individual is always going to be arbitrary.
- Removing people with high Lie-scale scores may bias the sample. The Lie scale correlates with personality traits such as Conscientiousness and low Neuroticism (McCrae and Costa, 1983); emotionally stable, conscientious people will tend to have high scores on social desirability indices, and so dropping individuals on the basis of their Lie-scale scores will eliminate some stable, conscientious people who just answer honestly.

- One sometimes has to make a decision about an individual even if one knows that they are probably lying, such as when using a questionnaire to help one decide whether a psychopath can safely be released from custody.

There is very extensive literature in this area; for an overview see Uziel (2010). Other researchers have examined the effects of statistically correcting scores for the effects of social desirability; doing so may not, however, improve the ability of the test to predict behaviour (McCrae and Costa, 1983; Ones et al., 1996) a finding backed up by Paunonen and LeBel's (2012) statistical simulation.

The third technique for controlling for impression management is a simple warning to participants that the questionnaire contains scales which are designed to detect deceptive responses. This is useful in contexts where questionnaires are administered for some purpose that is important to the individual (such as part of a selection process) as shown by McFarland (2003).

Next, it is worth considering abandoning self-rating scales and instead ask others to rate each individual, although this brings its own set of problems as noted in Chapter 3.

Finally, Edwards (1953) suggested that it should be possible to eliminate the effects of social desirability by using an ipsatised test. The Edwards Personal Preference Test was constructed by first asking people to rate the social desirability of each item. Pairs of items were identified that had the same level of social desirability but that measured different traits. For example, 'People would most often call me (a) unreliable or (b) neurotic'. Participants are then asked to choose which of the two items best describes them. However, the problems of ipsatised scales are so major that it is hard to recommend this approach (see Chapter 3).

Much research, however, suggests that correcting scores for impression management creates as many problems as it solves (Ellingson et al., 1999; McGrath et al., 2010; Ones et al., 1996). Nevertheless, Sjoberg (2015) does report considerable success in correcting scores in real-life situations, and this paper is well worth consulting if one uses a scale where social desirability may be a problem.

OTHER RESPONSE STYLES

There are several other response styles which have received less attention. For example, when scoring questionnaires by hand, it is obvious that some participants use the whole range of responses available from a Likert scale (plenty of 1s and 7s from a seven-point scale) whilst others rarely, if ever, use the extremes; most of their responses are 3, 4 or 5. This is reflected in individual differences in the standard deviation of a person's responses (calculated across all scales in a questionnaire). It has been found that authoritarian/conservative individuals tend to use the extremes of the response scale more than more moderate individuals – perhaps because they see issues as unrealistically clear-cut, whilst liberals try to see both points of view (Cooper et al., 1986). Thus conservatism may be a confounding variable which affects people's scores on any Likert scale.

Clinical scales cause particular problems, and there is substantial literature examining how susceptible these are to deliberate distortion – for example, from psychopaths who want to appear as if they have empathy or from people who want to exaggerate the effects of an illness (e.g., Fugett et al., 2014; Robinson and Rogers, 2015).

Finally, there is the issue of bias. This is where a scale *systematically* over- or underestimates the scores of particular groups of individuals. For example, an ability test might underestimate the IQ scores of participants whose first language is not English; a personality test might overestimate the prevalence of some psychiatric disorder in women but not in men (Kass et al., 1983). This is clearly an important issue, but we cover this in Chapter 7 when considering the validity of tests. It is well worth consulting a review by Podsakoff et al. (2003) which covers social desirability and other forms of bias.

CONCLUSIONS

Psychometricians love mathematics, and there is plenty of scope for interesting mathematics in reliability theory. This is probably why it is so well researched. However, it is clear that whilst almost all test users and developers grasp the importance of estimating the influence of random and systematic errors of measurement, it is less obvious that care is taken to ensure that the items in a scale capture the full breadth of whatever construct the scale is designed to measure. All too often, items in a scale are highly similar, which guarantees high internal-consistency reliability but breaks the assumption of local independence and also means that the scores on the scale fail to measure much of interest. This will not show up in the statistical analyses beloved of psychometricians.

It is also clear that coefficient alpha is much less useful than many researchers and test users believe. Unless it is estimated from a very large sample of people, any single estimate of coefficient alpha might be quite inaccurate. The true level of internal consistency is likely to be larger than coefficient alpha indicates, unless some rather unlikely criteria are met (tau equivalence). And, given that alpha is influenced by the size of the correlations between the items, the standard deviation of the item and the number of items in the scale, it is surely better to examine these independently; rather than developing a long, reliable scale where the average correlation between the items is paltry, it might be better to ensure that the correlations between items are fairly substantial and that the standard deviation of the items is appreciable. This will allow shorter scales to be used. And there are far more useful statistics available, such as Raykov's rho.

Systematic measurement errors, such as social desirability and acquiescence, can also add 'noise' to scores on psychological scales. Whilst it is straightforward to remove the influence of acquiescence, controlling for social desirability and other systematic errors is much more difficult – and the literature sometimes suggests that it is unsuccessful.

Despite all the research which focuses on reliability, it should be remembered that ultimately reliability is only a tool which may, perhaps, help develop and identify tests which adequately measure what they claim to assess. Cattell's claim that internal consistency of zero can be a good thing is perhaps an extreme example – but if a scale is clearly a good measure of what it claims, then debates about its psychometric properties are an irrelevance. Just because reliability theory produces numbers (and therefore has the appearance of scientific respectability), it is tempting to forget all of the issues raised by Michell, to ignore the problems inherent in adding together scores on items and to feign ignorance of the problems inherent in calculating correlations (revealed in Chapter 5). Establishing test reliability involves computing correlations (lots of them), and, as we have seen, each and every correlation can be affected by a whole range of different variables, most of which are ignored by researchers and test developers. Perhaps reliability theory has foundations of straw.

NOTE

1   These two formulae are not quite equivalent. The first one is based on the correlation matrix; it applies when standardised scores on the items are added together to give the total score on a scale and is known as 'standardised alpha'. The second formula does not make this assumption, as will be seen in Spreadsheet 6.4.

CHAPTER 7
VALIDITY

Earlier in this book we set out three criteria for adequate measurement. These are that scores on a scale should only reflect one property of the thing (person) being assessed (unidimensionality), that they should be free of measurement error (show high reliability) and that the scores on the measuring instrument should reflect the thing that the scale claims to measure; a scale purporting to measure anxiety should be directly influenced by anxiety and not anything else. The first two of these issues were dealt with in the previous chapters. The validity of a scale addresses the third issue, that of whether scores on a scale actually measure what they are supposed to. Unlike reliability theory, establishing the validity of a scale involves no particular statistical techniques – just common sense, critical evaluation and a healthy level of scepticism.

ESTABLISHING VALIDITY

Whilst most studies into test validity are correlational, this is dangerous, and I was careful to say 'directly influenced' in the previous paragraph. For, as with any correlation, it is possible that the scores on the scale and the scores on the criterion (which is used to establish the validity of the scale) are both influenced by some third variable. For example, if social desirability influences responses to both the anxiety scale that is validated and the standard scale measuring anxiety that is being used as the criterion, this will suggest that the novel anxiety scale is more valid than it really is.

We have seen that reliability theory can show how accurately a set of items can measure some underlying trait. What it cannot do is shed any light on the *nature* of that trait, for just because an investigator *thinks* that a set of items should measure a particular trait, there is no guarantee that they actually do so. We mentioned the 'Repression-Sensitisation scale' (R–S scale) in Chapter 1. The items formed a reasonably reliable scale, so everyone just assumed that this scale measured what it claimed to do – it generated a lot of research. Then Slough et al. (1984) found that scores on this scale correlated above 0.9 with a test of anxiety. The maximum correlation between two scales is limited by the size of their reliabilities, so *all* of the variance in the R–S scale could be accounted for by anxiety. It was not measuring anything new at all. This tale conveys an important message. Even if a set of items appears to form a scale, it is not possible to tell what that scale measures just by looking at the items. Instead, it is necessary to determine this empirically by a process known as validation.

The philosophical basis of test validation is actually a *lot* more complex than it might appear from this description (Borsboom et al., 2004). These authors provide an excellent discussion of the rationale of test validation of various kinds, and suggest that the notion of validation is very simple; is there good evidence that the scores on scales are directly influenced by some (psychological or other) attribute? If so, the test is valid, in exactly the same way that a voltmeter is valid if its readings reflect the difference in electric potential across its terminals.

Borsboom et al. argue that it is vitally important to understand the *processes* which lead to different levels of some attribute resulting in different test scores, rather than merely studying correlations (etc.) between scores on some scale and other variables. Gathering some empirical data and discovering relationships between variables is easy; all one needs to do is perform structural equation modelling. Developing a theory about why, precisely, some concept such as 'general intelligence' (assuming it exists) can *cause* some people to react faster than others, show better memory and so on is infinitely more challenging than discovering that scores on one scale correlate with scores on another scale yet fail to correlate with a third! Borsboom et al. (2004: 1068) remind us that science demands a grasp of the mechanisms involved: 'No table of correlations, no matter how big, can be a substitute for knowledge of the processes that lead to item responses'. The question that we need to address is what is it about the personality trait (or ability . . . or mood . . .) which makes people respond to an item in a particular way?

> It is disconcerting to find that a large proportion of test research is characterized by an almost complete absence of theories of response behavior and that so few researchers recognize that the problem of psychological measurement is not a matter of following the 'right' methodological rules but of tackling one of the most challenging problems in psychology; how do psychological characteristics relate to empirical observations?
>
> (Borsboom et al., 2004: 1068)

The issues raised in this paper are important, but although the work is widely cited, it is not clear that it has yet become mainstream – possibly because developing adequate theories is a lot more difficult than gathering data and developing scales! In addition, many test users are very pragmatic; if using a test of some sort saves them money or provides them with a number (such as a person's IQ) that is less likely to be challenged in court than a subjective opinion, then the niceties of philosophy and scientific measurement are seen as irrelevant. What follows is therefore a fairly conventional view of validity theory.

According to this, a scale is said to be valid if it does what it claims to do, either in terms of theory or in practical application. For example, a scale that is marketed as a measure of anxiety for use in the general UK population should measure anxiety and not social desirability, reading skill, sociability or any other unrelated traits. We can tell this by determining whether scores on this scale correlate with other measures that are also indicators of anxiety – for example, skin resistance or scores on some other questionnaire. We should also determine that it does not correlate substantially with scales measuring social desirability, reading skill, sociability etc.

The context is crucial; validity depends crucially on the purpose for which the scale is administered and the makeup of the sample being assessed. A scale may measure anxiety wonderfully well when it is administered to cooperative students. Use the same scale with a sample of job applicants, and the correlation will probably plummet because they will be less than truthful. So, rather than asking whether scores on a scale correlate with some other criterion (such as scores on another scale or some behaviour), it is necessary to consider the context in which the assessment is made, and the sample(s) used – together with all of their other individual differences (personality, abilities, hopes, fears, aspirations . . .) – before considering whether there is any evidence that scores on the scale are directly influenced by individual differences in the characteristic being measured.

The validity of a scale is related to its reliability. If a scale has low reliability, a lot of measurement error is associated with each person's score on the scale, and this will reduce its correlation with other variables. It follows that if a variable has low reliability, its correlations with other variables will be low, and so, if correlations are used to assess validity, its validity will also be low. On the other hand, if the reliability of a scale is high, there is no guarantee that the validity of the scale will be high; it may simply not be measuring what it claims to assess. High reliability is a necessary but not sufficient condition for validity when validity is measured using correlations.

Borsboom et al. (2004: 1061) remind us that 'a test is valid for measuring an attribute if (a) the attribute exists and (b) variations in the attribute causally produce variation in the measurement outcomes'. The key to studying its validity is to establish a causal relationship between the individual's level of some trait (or state) and scores on some scale. This is a challenge for psychology because it is difficult or impossible to be sure that a trait exists, let alone ascertain whether levels of that trait directly influence scores on some questionnaire or other measure.

Structural equation models (Kline, 2011; Loehlin, 2004) can indicate causal relationships between variables, rather than mere correlations and so may be well-suited for validating scales. These models consist of two parts. The 'measurement model' depicts the relationships between observed variables (scored responses to items or scales) and the hypothesised latent variables (traits). Less-than-perfect reliability is reflected in less-than-perfect relationships between levels of the latent variables and scores on the observed variables. The 'structural model' which would be important for validating the scales shows the relationships between the latent variables, unaffected by measurement error. A case can certainly be made for using these models (rather than simple correlations) when validating scales. However, it could well be the case that the structural model would show that the relationships between traits are consistent with some theoretical model, yet the measurement model shows that it is impossible to measure the factor with any accuracy. Pragmatically, it is all very well showing that various factors are interrelated, but if the measurement model shows that a scale cannot accurately assess a factor, what practical use can it possibly be?

The conventional literature suggests that there are six main ways of establishing whether a scale is valid.

FACE VALIDITY

Face validity merely checks that the scale looks as if it measures what it is supposed to. The R–S scale debacle described earlier shows that scrutinising the content of items is no guarantee that the scale will measure what it is intended to. Despite this, some widely used scales (particularly in social psychology) are constructed by writing a few items, ensuring that alpha is high (which is generally the case because the items are paraphrases of each other) and then piously assuming that the scale measures the concept that it was designed to assess. It is *vital* to ensure that a scale has better credentials than this before using it. It is necessary to establish that the scale has some predictive power and/or that it correlates as expected with other scales before one can conclude that the scale really does measure what it claims to.

Face validity is, however, necessary in order to encourage participants to take a questionnaire or test seriously and to work hard when attempting it. For example, Chan and Schmitt (1997) found that a video version of a judgement task was perceived as having higher face validity than a paper-and-pencil version of the same task. But, crucially, members of a minority group performed much better at the video version of the task, and this did not seem to be due to poor reading skills. Perceiving the task as being relevant may have motivated members of the minority group, and this reduced the adverse impact of the test. This seems to be a robust finding, and Ryan and Ployhart (2000) give a useful review of the older literature.

Low face validity can be a problem for some personality scales; in a previous incarnation, I was once asked to administer a scale to serving airforce officers which included items such as 'Do you enjoy the feeling of silk against your skin?' and suchlike. Their reaction was entirely predictable.

CONTENT VALIDITY

Very occasionally it is possible to construct a scale which *must* be valid, by definition. For example, suppose that one wanted to construct a scale to measure spelling ability. Since, by definition, the dictionary contains the whole domain of items, any procedure that produces a representative sample of words from this dictionary has to be a valid measure of spelling ability. This is what is meant by content validity. Content validity is (unsurprisingly, perhaps) most common in areas such as educational attainment, where learning outcomes are clearly defined, and teachers/students therefore know precisely what the assessment process will cover. For example, a student reading this chapter might be expected to describe and critically evaluate at least four types of test validity.

Occupational psychologists sometimes use 'work-basket' approaches in selecting staff, where applicants are presented with a sample of the activities that are typically performed as part of the job, and their performance on these tasks is in some way evaluated. Applicants for a customer-service role may each be given copies of letters of complaint to deal with. These exercises are not psychological tests in the strict sense, but the process can be seen to have some content validity. So too can many tests derived from clinical psychology. Although a clinical diagnosis clearly requires a skilled diagnostic interview from a professional, it might be possible to draw on the DSM-V criteria (which define which combinations of symptoms indicate various psychiatric diagnoses) to help one design a test to measure autism-like traits in the general population by ensuring that the items in such a questionnaire or rating scale cover all of the behaviours listed in DSM-V, and then argue that the test must have content validity. If the test over-represents some behaviours whilst omitting others, then it cannot have acceptable content validity.

Of course, content validity (like any form of validity) only applies to a particular group of people who are being assessed for a particular purpose; a test which is valid within one population for a particular purpose may well not be valid if it is used within another population or for a different purpose. It is also terribly atheoretical. If several quite different traits, attitudes etc. are required to solve a problem, the work-basket approach will measure them all simultaneously, and it will never be obvious what traits are being measured. We have zero understanding of why some people perform better than others at the task. What happens if the nature of the job changes over time or people move to different roles? Because we have no understanding of what the task measures, it is impossible to say whether people who performed well in their original role would excel if promoted to a different role. However, if job analyses were used to identify the traits that were important for each task, and these were each measured separately using standard scales, it should be possible to make better predictions. So, although tasks can be identified which have content validity, it may not always be prudent to use them.

It is possible to develop tests having content validity for selection purposes by performing some form of job analysis and ensuring that a selection test measures each of these skills and abilities. For example, it might be found that engineering apprentices frequently flounder because of their lack of mathematical skills. It would be possible to perform a detailed analysis of the tasks performed by these apprentices to identify a number of mathematical skills that are needed for the successful completion of the apprenticeship and to build a screening test to measure these skills. This screening test would then have content validity for that particular application when used with samples of applicants drawn from the same population (i.e., with the same mathematical backgrounds).

One of the problems with establishing content validity is that the behaviour which the scale is designed to assess may change over time. This may happen because of a better understanding of the concept (as when DSM-IV evolved into DSM-V, when the indicators for several clinical syndromes were altered) or organisational change (such as when changes in the apprentice training programme alter the list of mathematical requirements). Or a scale might lose its content validity just because of changes in the way in which words are used – the meaning of 'wicked' in a personality item, for example. Thus a scale that was content-valid a few years ago may not be content-valid today – a point which should be carefully kept in mind.

A second problem is that it is rarely possible to define the domain of potential test items with any accuracy. For example, how can one ever be sure that a scale measuring leadership covers all the possible ways in which leadership could manifest itself, given that it could cover crisis management, delegation, forward thinking and a whole host of other things? Whilst any test developer will often have *some* idea about what their scale is supposed to assess (but see Cattell, 1946) it is unlikely that this knowledge will be sufficiently detailed to allow them to claim that their items form a true random sample of all the items in the domain and thereby claim that the scale has content validity.

CONSTRUCT VALIDITY

One useful way of checking whether a test measures what it claims to assess is to perform thoughtful experiments. This is what is meant by construct validation. One simply asks the question, 'If this scale measures what it claims to measure, how should scores on the scale (or items) relate to other behaviours, measurements or test scores?' Then one performs a series of studies gathering as much data as possible, at the end of which a decision is made as to whether or not the evidence from these studies is sufficiently strong to support the claim that the test measures what it claims to measure.

Put like this, it sounds straightforward, but one also needs to consider the context in which the assessments are made and the nature of the sample used. Given that no one will have ever tested an identical sample under identical circumstances, it is necessary to use some rather creative thinking (before peeping at the results) to decide precisely which variables should correlate with scores on the scale that one is trying to assess. Should one expect the scale to correlate substantially with another scale that was developed in another culture or using a sample with different demographics? Will gender differences moderate the relationships between the variables? There is no way of telling for sure, but it is necessary to make a 'best guess' before analysing data and to be very aware of how easy it is to rationalise any contrary results after the analyses have been performed. It would be even better if one used structural equation modelling; it would be quite possible to draw up the diagram showing which variables are thought to link which other variables before performing any analyses to check model-fit or to estimate the various parameters, and a case could be made for journal editors to require such information to be submitted before a study is performed.

In practice, when validating a scale many authors will 'piggy-back' their scale on to a larger study which may not really allow it to be validated in the best possible way. Or, having found a few significant correlations (which is almost bound to happen if non-conservative statistical tests are performed) authors may then use considerable ingenuity to generate their 'hypotheses' to match what the results show – rather than doing so beforehand.

Psychologists are only human, and, having invested time and effort in developing a scale, it might be hard for them to admit that it is really not very good at measuring anything. Studies which did *not* support the validity of the scale might never be submitted for publication. Confirmation bias is also a matter of real concern; it is easy to pay more heed to evidence that confirms a test is valid than evidence that suggests it is not. For all of these reasons, when evaluating the construct validity of a scale, it is advisable to ensure that the hypotheses which are being tested are

- Highly appropriate. The scales that are used to test the construct validity of a novel scale must clearly be the most theoretically relevant ones that can be found. So a new scale measuring working memory needs to be tested against other measures of working memory – not (just) other tests of cognitive ability. There is no point in interpreting gender differences (for example) unless there is strong theoretical and/ or empirical literature suggesting that, without gender differences, the scale would be flawed. So, gender differences might be used in the construct validation of a scale measuring aggression but not when validating a scale measuring extraversion or working memory.
- Independent. Care should be taken to ensure that correlations between scales cannot arise because some of the items are highly similar in content. We have seen in Spreadsheet 1.1 that if the same (or similar) items appear in both scales, the validation exercise just indicates that participants behave consistently, which is not at all what is intended. Other possible confounds should be explored too, and consideration should be given to removing the influence of other moderating variables through the use of regression, partial correlation, structural equation modelling or other techniques. If scores on a questionnaire correlate substantially with non-questionnaire measures (for example, psychophysiological measures, developmental variables, measures of the family environment or performance on cognitive tasks), this provides particularly strong evidence for its validity. Here there will be little danger of the same 'nuisance factors' affecting performance on two questionnaires.
- Substantial. Small correlations (e.g., 0.2 or 0.3) may well be statistically significant. However, if the amount of overlap between the two variables is this small (4% to 9%) it is difficult to argue that the study provides strong evidence for the construct validation of a scale. Correcting for unreliability (as in Spreadsheet 5.5) may be useful here.
- Unambiguous. There is no point in performing any analysis where a positive, zero or negative relationship between the scale score and another variable could, with sufficient ingenuity, be taken as evidence for the validity of the scale. Every time

evidence is cited that supposedly supports the validity of the scale, one needs to ask oneself whether it is at all possible that a null result, or a result in the opposite direction, might also be taken as evidence for the validity of the scale. For example, finding that a scale which is designed to measure satisfaction with therapy actually correlates negatively with the therapist's rating of the effectiveness of the outcome could be explained away by the patient and therapist using different criteria, or by 'reaction formation' whereby the patient who is threatened by the depth of their therapeutic relationship turns hostile and denigrates the therapist . . . Any data which can be interpreted in many ways are not worth considering.

- Peer reviewed. Several authors are famous for presenting novel theories and/ or scales (together with 'evidence' for their validity) in books rather than in peer-reviewed papers in well-regarded journals. The peer-review process associated with journal articles is highly detailed, and so validation studies that are reported in a good journal should carry far more weight than studies reported in a book, which will not have been independently reviewed in depth.
- Impartially evaluated. All too often, a theory and associated scale are developed by a researcher and used (uncritically) by their graduate students or professionals who are not experts in test design. Eventually everyone assumes that the necessary validation has taken place because so many careers depend on it. Independent validation (ideally by a sceptic approaching the issue from a different theoretical perspective) is very important.

Suppose that a test is designed to measure anxiety in UK university students. How might its validity be checked through experiment?

The first approach (sometimes called 'convergent validation') is to check that the test scores relate to other things as expected. For example, if there are other widely used scales of anxiety on the market, a group of students could be given both tests, and the two sets of scores could be correlated together, after checking that none of the items in the two scales are similar in content. A large positive correlation would suggest that the new scale is valid. Alternatively, the scale could be administered to a group of students who claim to have a phobia about spiders, before and after showing them a tarantula. If their scores increase, then the scale might indeed measure anxiety. Scores on the scale could be correlated with measures of skin resistance, which have a known relationship to anxiety levels. Genetic variations linked to anxiety might be reflected in scores on the scale; the list of possible experiments is almost endless. The basic aim of these convergent validations is to determine whether the scale scores vary as would be expected on theoretical grounds. Unfortunately, a failure to find the expected relationships might be due to some problem either with the scale or with the other measures. For example, the *other* scale of anxiety may not be valid, or some of the individuals who say that they are phobic about spiders may not be. However, if scores on a scale do appear to vary in accordance with theory, it seems reasonable to conclude that the scale is valid.

The obvious problem with this approach is that, if the novel scale of anxiety correlates substantially with an existing one, why does the world need another scale? There may be several reasons. The new scale may be shorter. It might be freely available rather than a commercial product. It might claim to have better content validity. Or it might use a different format (e.g., be administered via a mobile device rather than a clinical interview). But if the new scale does not have any such merits, it is hard to see why it is needed.

Studies of 'divergent validity' check that the scale does not seem to measure any traits with which it should, in theory, be unrelated. For example, the literature claims that anxiety is unrelated to intelligence, socio-economic status, social desirability and so on. Thus, if a scale that purportedly measured anxiety actually showed a substantial correlation with any of these variables, doubt would be raised as to whether it is a good measure of anxiety.

PREDICTIVE VALIDITY

Psychological scales are all designed with some purpose in mind. They all set out to predict some form of behaviour, and their success in doing so is known as their predictive validity. For example, a scale might be given to adolescents in an attempt to predict which of them would suffer from schizophrenia later in life. Another might be used to select the most promising candidates for employment as a salesperson. These scales would have predictive validity if their scores were to be related to the later incidence of schizophrenia or if it could be shown that the people with the highest scores on the scale made the most sales. This method of validating a scale sounds remarkably straightforward but in practice tends not to be.

The first problem is the nature of the criterion against which the scale is to be evaluated. For, although noting a diagnosis of schizophrenia or the volume of sales achieved is quite straightforward, many occupations lack a single criterion. A university lecturer's job is a case in point. Mine involved teaching, research, applying for funding, curriculum design, managing colleagues, committee work, the supervision of postgraduate students, providing informal help with statistics and programming, supporting and encouraging undergraduates and so on – the list is a long one, and it is not obvious how most of these activities could be evaluated or their relative importance determined. So even if one's performance could be evaluated in each of these areas, how should these evaluations be combined to produce an overall score? In other cases (e.g., where employees are rated by their line manager) different assessors may apply quite different standards. When performance of employees is rated, it is highly advisable to obtain several independent assessments of each person's performance. This allows the reliability of these assessments to be calculated. The correlation between scale score and the (averaged) measure of performance can then be corrected for the effects of unreliability.

A second problem is restriction of range, as discussed in Chapter 5. Selection systems generally operate through several stages, e.g., initial psychometric testing to reduce the number of applicants to manageable proportions, followed by interviews and more detailed psychological assessments of individuals who get through the first stage. Applicants who are eventually appointed will all have similar (high) scores on all of the screening scales, otherwise they would have been rejected before the interview stage. Thus the range of scores in the group of individuals who are selected will be much smaller than that in the general population. This will create problems for any attempt to validate the screening test since this restricted range of abilities will tend to reduce the correlation between the scale and any criterion, as discussed in Chapter 5.

The third issue is deciding how large the predictive validity of a scale needs to be in order for it to be valuable. In many cases, this is determined by cost. For example, military flying training is a process which is extremely expensive and time-consuming. Here, even if a scale only has a very modest correlation with the criterion, it may be cost-effective to use it as part of the selection process – as a very small increase in one's ability to predict success at flying training might result in very substantial cost-savings. On the other hand, if training and attrition costs are minimal, it might only be cost-effective to use a scale as part of a selection battery if its predictive validity is very substantial.

Finally, it is not always reasonable to assume that there is a *linear* relationship between test score and job or school performance. This may make calculating correlations between test scores and performance of dubious value. For example, suppose that a job such as a delivery worker or a sales assistant requires a certain minimum level of numeracy and literacy. It seems unlikely that having a much higher level of numeracy or literacy – a PhD in mathematics or English, for example – would lead to a commensurate increase in job performance. So, when assessing the validity of a scale, it is vitally important to examine the scatter diagram between performance and test score, for it might well be the case that the relationship between test score and performance is non-linear. In such a case, it might be more appropriate to identify a simple pass mark, rather than using regression or similar techniques to combine the test scores with other information.

Establishing predictive validity

There are several designs that can be used to establish the predictive validity of scales. Most obviously, the scales may be administered and criterion data gathered later, such as when ability scales are used to predict who will eventually succeed in learning to pilot a military aircraft, or when an intelligence scale is administered to young children whose school performance is measured many years later. The advantage of this approach is that the psychological assessment is made a long time before performance is measured. This more or less guarantees that the psychological characteristic(s) measured by the assessment procedure influence performance, rather than vice versa.

The disadvantages of this approach are mainly practical. Administering scales and following people up over a period of years in order to obtain criterion data requires long-term funding, which may be hard to obtain. Sometimes there is simply no time to perform long-term studies; an organisation may need a selection process to be developed within a few months, which precludes any long-term follow-up to gather performance data. If a long-term study is undertaken, some participants will move house, decide that they no longer wish to take part in the study, change their name or otherwise become difficult to trace. Hence the administrative overheads of tracking people can be substantial, whilst attrition of the sample also raises statistical concerns. For, can it be assumed that the people who drop out of the study before the criterion data are obtained form a random sample of those who were initially tested? If not, the predictive validity of the scale might be inaccurate. For example, if intelligence truly does predict school performance and all the low-intelligence children dropped out of the study, the range of scores on both the ability scale and the measures of educational attainment would be reduced. This will make the correlation between the two variables smaller than it should be.

Concurrent validity

Sometimes the criterion data may be gathered at the same time as the scale is administered, such as when an ability scale is given to students at the same time that their school performance is appraised, or when a firm is considering using a new selection test and decides to see whether it can predict the effectiveness of workers who are already in the organisation. Designs where the test and performance measures (e.g., examination or other grades, supervisors' ratings, sales figures) are obtained at the same time that the test is administered are known as 'concurrent validity' studies. These studies have several clear merits. They are easy to perform, for one just needs to assess people and gather criterion data contemporaneously, and so there will be little or no dropout from the sample. It means that there is no delay in developing a selection test; if a scale shows a substantial correlation with job performance in an existing sample of employees, it would be possible to consider using it as part of a selection process without delay.

However, there are several problems with this approach, too. It is hard to be sure that the results from a concurrent validity study will accurately predict how effective a test would be if it were used at an earlier stage as part of a selection process. There are several reasons for this.

- Situational factors. As all the data are gathered at one time, when performing a concurrent validity study, it might be the case that some situational factor(s) might affect some people's scores on both the test and the measure of performance; these might include lack of sleep, depression, influenza etc. This will tend to inflate the correlation between the scale and the criterion by increasing the range of scores. If the scale were used for selection purposes at an earlier date, these situational factors would not influence both scores.

- Direction of causality. Perhaps going to school enhances intelligence, rather than intelligence boosting school performance? Perhaps working in an organisation enhances the abilities or develops the personality traits that are measured by the tests? If so there is clearly no causal relationship between test score and performance, and so the test would not work if it were used to select children or employees at an earlier date.

- Attrition. It might be the case that students who underperform at college or at work drop out or leave at an early stage and so are not part of the sample when the test and performance data are gathered. This reduced range of scores will tend to underestimate the correlation that the test would show if it were used for selection purposes at an earlier date.

- Motivation. Job applicants and college applicants will generally be highly motivated to perform well on the tests. However, there is no reason or incentive for students or employees who are already in post to answer questions honestly or put much effort into any test which is administered as part of a concurrent validation exercise; they have nothing to gain or lose by doing so. It seems reasonable to suggest that this might underestimate the potential that a test might have were it used for selection purposes.

Gathering data from concurrent validity studies is quick and easy, whereas true predictive validity studies involve tracking down individuals months or years later and are thus both time-consuming and expensive. However, concurrent validity studies simply cannot be expected to provide accurate estimates of how well a test would predict performance were it administered months or years beforehand.

Retrospective studies

One sometimes encounters studies where the criterion data precede the assessment. These are known as retrospective or 'postdiction' studies. For example, suppose that a researcher wants to determine whether the extent to which a child was breastfed is associated with IQ in adulthood, or whether the number of friends a child had between the ages of 4 and 6 is related to their adult levels of Extraversion. Rather than performing a proper predictive validation, measuring the breastfeeding experience of infants or monitoring their social behaviour and following them up into adulthood, a researcher might decide to simply measure intelligence and Extraversion in a sample of adults and then seek out (via their mothers) data about how long they were breastfed, how many friends they had during infancy and so on. Here the criterion data (length of breastfeeding, number of friendships) refer to activities which took place before the psychological assessments were made – a retrospective study.

The problem is that memories are fallible. Quite a lot is known about the accuracy of retrospective reports of traumatic childhood events, as a result of police and other investigations; it turns out that there are substantial amounts of error in such recollections (Hardt and Rutter, 2004), which is hardly surprising. Much less is known about how accurate the recall for 'normal' events is – and it would be difficult to estimate this with any precision. The fuzzier the behaviour being measured, the more inaccurate the measure might be. For how can anyone accurately gauge their number of childhood friends when the definition of 'friend' will vary from person to person?

It is also easy to infer a direct causal relationship where none exists when gathering data about parental behaviour during childhood. For example, it is known that more intelligent mothers choose to breastfeed (Der et al., 2006) and, as intelligence is highly heritable, breastfed children may grow up to be intelligent purely because they are related to their mothers. Breastfeeding per se may have zero direct influence on adult intelligence. There is similar literature on many other aspects of parent–child interaction (Plomin and Bergeman, 1991).

INCREMENTAL VALIDITY

Organisational psychologists may sometimes need to determine whether adding a new scale to an existing battery of selection tests will increase its ability to predict some criterion. Suppose that a retail organisation currently selects its graduate management trainees by means of an interview. It knows that the correlation between interview performance and subsequent job performance is only 0.2. It wonders whether it would be possible to better predict job performance by adding an additional test – for example a test of written English. If adding an additional scale to a test battery improves its performance, that scale provides incremental validity. It is normally established by using multiple regression, determining whether the multiple correlation increases significantly when a new predictor variable (test score) is added.

FACTORIAL VALIDITY

A final form of validity refers to the factor structure of the test items. If the odd-numbered items of a test are supposed to form one scale and the even-numbered items form another scale, performing a factor analysis (as described in Chapters 8–11) should produce two factors, with the odd-numbered items having large loadings on one factor and the even-numbered items all having large loadings on the other. The sign of these loadings should reflect whether or not an item is reverse-scored.

Running a factor analysis is quick and useful, and this approach is particularly useful when a test is used in a different culture or age group from the one in which it was designed. (Translating tests is a more difficult issue which we consider in Chapter 14.) However, it is difficult to know what to do if the expected factor structure does not appear cleanly. Should some items be dropped from the questionnaire? This is probably not advisable, as it will affect the content validity of the scale. Should the questionnaire be rescored as indicated by the factor analysis? This decision is difficult; my advice would be 'almost certainly not'. At a minimum, it would be necessary to repeat the analysis on another sample, use confirmatory factor analysis to make sure that any additional factors lead to a significant improvement in fit, ensure that any additional factors do not reflect some sort of response bias (e.g., all the negatively keyed items) and that they make great theoretical sense – which can only really be discovered by a thorough examination of the items, together with a detailed construct or predictive validation process.

Factorial validation is quick and easy to perform, but it should always be remembered that the correlations between items tend to be both small and prone to measurement error; failure to perfectly replicate a factor structure in one sample is quite common, but, unless the problems are really substantial, persuading a reviewer or sponsor that it is more appropriate to rescore a test than use the original method is unlikely to be successful.

DEVELOPING AND VALIDATING A BATTERY OF SELECTION TESTS

A common problem in applied psychology is knowing how to combine several different types of data in order to predict performance. In what follows, we assume that each of the variables we discuss predicts some criterion (e.g., ability to pass some training course); what we need to decide is how to arrange the selection process so as to gather this information in a cost-effective manner and produce a score based on all of the information available that best predicts performance.

For example, an organisation may use aptitude data, the results from an interview and a medical report in order to make a hiring decision. It *could* gather all this data from every applicant. However, aptitude testing is generally cheap (it can be performed in groups or over the internet) whilst medical examinations and interviews are expensive. It might thus make sense to divide the assessments into three blocks. Those who pass the aptitude tests might undergo the medical examination. Those who pass the medical examination might be invited for interview. Those who pass the interview would be hired. This is sometimes called the 'multiple-hurdle' approach, as applicants need to pass each stage of the selection process before moving on to the next.

But how to decide whether a person 'passes' a battery of different aptitude scales? There are two main possibilities. The multiple cut-off method involves the employer setting a minimum acceptable score for each scale. Under this model, applicants will only pass the aptitude test battery if they show a certain minimum level of aptitude on each scale – scoring above the mean, for example. Scoring below the mean on just one scale guarantees failure. Whilst this approach is commendably simple and guarantees that each person who passes on to the next stage of the process has a certain minimum competence in each area, it has several problems. The 'minimum acceptable score' which is set for each test is fairly arbitrary. Unless the tests that are used are highly reliable, measurement error alone makes it probable that some able candidates will fail one or more of the scales. And unless the cut-offs are kept low, this technique can reject a large proportion of applicants if the correlations between the measures are small or modest.

The second approach involves using multiple regression or logistic regression to weight the scores on the various tests. It assumes that both test and training data are available from a large sample of people (hundreds, at least), and uses regression to combine the scores on the different tests so as to predict how well each person will perform on the training course. Each scale is given a regression weight, and each person's score is multiplied by the regression weight for that test. These values are then summed to give an index score. The scales which best predict training performance will influence the overall aptitude index more than those which have a weaker relationship to this criterion. This aptitude index is then used to decide who should proceed to the next stage of the procedure; it is usual to simply work one's way down the list until all vacancies have been filled.

There are two main problems with this approach. It allows good performance in one area to compensate for poor performance in another. Thus someone with excellent mathematical skills but very weak verbal skills might end up moving to the next stage of the procedure, which might create problems for them later. Thus, in practice, organisations sometimes perform a two-stage analysis of the applicants' scores; a multiple cut-off with low cut-offs (e.g., a standard deviation below the mean) to ensure that applicants have some basic competency in each area, with those who pass this stage having their scores weighted according to the regression model. The second problem with regression is that statistical difficulties can arise when the scales are highly correlated (Wainer, 1978).

Under the regression model, it is possible to test whether adding a new scale to an existing battery of scales will result in enhanced prediction of the criterion. To do this, a multiple regression is performed using the existing variable to predict the criterion. Then the score from a novel scale is added and its effect on the multiple correlation coefficient is statistically tested. For example, it might be found that adding a new scale might increase R (the multiple correlation coefficient) from 0.4 to 0.45. It is possible to perform statistical significance tests to determine whether this increase is more than would be expected by chance; if adding a new variable does increase the predictive power of a battery of scales, it is said to have *incremental validity*. The organisation would need to perform some analyses to determine whether the overheads involved in administering the new scale are cost-effective, but this is a matter of econometrics and so will not be considered here.

TEST BIAS

Scales may sometimes systematically overestimate or underestimate the scores of groups of people. Suppose that a scale measuring general knowledge were given to random samples of people in different countries. If that scale contained plenty of items asking about cricket and soccer, it is probable that British respondents would outperform Americans and that men would outperform women. One obviously should not infer from this that British are more knowledgeable than Americans or that men are more knowledgeable than women; the differences between groups almost certainly arise because some of the items are easier for British men for cultural reasons. In other words, the same test score implies a different level of general knowledge, depending on whether one is male or female, British or American. This is precisely what is meant by test bias.

But what if there are genuine differences in scores between men and women, or between British and Americans? Can one infer that any test which shows differences between various groups is biased? The answer is a strong 'no'. It is always possible that differences between groups are real. Several psychological scales show large gender differences (scales measuring aggressiveness and those measuring psychopathic tendencies, for example), and this is mirrored in everyday life with men being more involved in violence and being more likely to be sadistic manipulators of others. Thus few would feel unhappy with the conclusion that the group differences detected by these psychological scales are genuine.

It is therefore impossible to conclude that a scale is biased merely by checking whether different groups obtain different average scores on it. A moment's thought will reveal why; it is quite possible that half the items in an ability scale could be much harder for men than women, whilst the other half could be much easier for women than men. When administered to a sample of men and women, there would be no difference in the mean score, despite the scale being riddled with biased items.

When group differences are found, determining whether these are genuine or whether they occur because the test is unfair to one or more groups of people becomes a major challenge. It is particularly important in the area of cognitive abilities. Here, differences in scores between white and black Americans have been consistently found, differences in the order of a standard deviation. The question is how much of this difference in performance is due to bias in the tests and how much is genuine? Readers who want to explore the psychological literature in this area might like to see Brown et al.'s (1999) still highly relevant review which discusses whether the evidence supports theories that social deprivation, differences in language etc. account for the black–white difference.

Eliminating bias from tests requires some sensitivity when writing items. For example, when writing ability tests, there is much to be said for using items which do not involve language – and several scales such as Raven's Matrices (Raven et al., 2003) follow this approach when measuring general intelligence. Using simple, clear language free of slang or concepts that are likely to be more familiar to members of some cultural or social groups than others will help guard against biased items, and guidelines for writing such items are given in Chapter 14. However, proper statistical analyses are required to determine whether a scale is biased.

EXTERNAL BIAS

By definition, if a test is biased, it will under- or overestimate the scores of a group of people. So, if criterion data are available, it should be able to test for bias by checking how the scores of a group of people – typically a minority group – relate to some criterion – such as how well children perform in school, job performance or something similar.

It is clear that there are four possibilities, as shown in Table 7.1.

If members of the minority group obtain lower scores on the test and this lower score is reflected in lower performance, it appears as if the group difference is genuine – as long as there is not some other variable (such as language skills) which influences both the score on the test and the measure of performance – a major assumption. But as long as this is true, the test does not seem to be biased against members of the minority group. It does not underestimate their performance. On the other hand, if a minority group has low scores on the test but their performance is higher than would be predicted by their test score, this is clear evidence that the test is biased. The test scores underestimate their potential performance.

It is also possible to think of this in terms of regression. If the regression line predicting performance from test score is the same for both groups, then there is no evidence that the test is biased, as long as there is no confounding variable affecting both test score and performance for members of the minority group. This is because the regression line shows that the relationship between the test score and the criterion is the same for both

Table 7.1 Relationship between test scores of a minority group and job performance

	Minority group has lower test score	Minority group has same test score
Minority group shows lower performance	Genuine group difference	Test shows bias in favour of minority group
Minority group shows same performance	Test shows bias against minority group	Genuine group difference

groups. If the two groups have regression lines which differ in slope or height, then this suggests that the test is biased.

Spreadsheet 7.1 allows this to be explored. It shows the relationship between test score and performance for two groups of people, identified by red and blue points on a scatter diagram. This scatter diagram also shows the regression lines for each group. Two sliders allow the difference in test score between the red and blue groups to be altered; if the top slider is completely to the left, the two groups perform at the same level on the test. If moved to the right, the red group outperforms the blue group. The bottom slider determines whether there is any difference in job performance. Moving it to the right makes the red group perform better than the blue group. It is also possible to alter the correlation between test score and performance for each group which is initially set at 0.7.

EXERCISE 7.1: BIAS

Resources required: Spreadsheet 7.1: Bias. From www.routledge.com/9781138228894

Purpose: To show how internal bias can be detected

Contents of spreadsheet: Simulated data from two groups of people

Suggested activity:

- Scenario 1: Put both sliders to the left and note that that the regression lines for the two groups are nearly identical. (As before, press f9 or equivalent to generate a different sample of data.)
- Scenario 2: Move the top slider to the right. Here, the blue group perform better on the test, but the work performance is the same for both groups. Note that the two regression lines are at different heights but parallel (press f9 etc. to confirm).
- Scenario 3: Move both sliders to the right. Now the blue group perform better at the test and also better at the job – a genuine group difference. Note that the two regression lines are almost identical.
- Scenario 4: Move the top slider to the left whilst keeping the bottom one to the right. Here both groups perform equally well on the test, but the blue group perform better at work.
- Try experimenting with changing the correlation between test score and performance for the two groups.

Points to note:

- Look upwards to see what a test score of (say) 120 would imply about job performance for members of each group in each of the four scenarios.

- Convince yourself that the first scenario (above) indicates no bias and that the second indicates bias against members of the red group (their performance is better than the regression line for the blue group would predict). The third scenario indicates a genuine group difference, where differences in test scores are reflected in differences in work performance. The fourth scenario shows bias against the blue group.
- Note that differences in the height of the regression lines imply bias for all members of a group.
- If the correlation between the test and performance is different for the two groups, note that the direction of bias changes depending on whether the test score is low or high.
- Therefore, differences in the height or slope of the regression line indicate external bias.
- Experiment by changing entries in the GREEN areas. Results are in the YELLOW areas. Simply download another copy if you accidentally change formulae.

Learning outcomes:

Readers should now be able to

- appreciate that regression can be useful in detecting external bias in test scores;
- recognise that differences in the slope and/or height of the regression lines can imply bias;
- appreciate that group differences do not necessarily indicate bias; a group difference may be accompanied by a difference in job performance, as in the third scenario.

Because this form of bias is inferred by looking at the relationship between scale scores and some external criterion, it is known as 'external bias'.

INTERNAL BIAS

Very often, however, there is no external criterion against which to test the scale. However, it may still be possible to check for biased items. If a test contains a few biased items, these will be much harder for members of a minority group than for members of the majority group. The assumption being made here is that, if all items favour one group rather than another, this probably indicates a genuine difference between the groups rather than bias. It could, of course, be the case that there are some 'outliers' in the data that cause this difference to occur; perhaps a few members of the minority group simply do not have sufficient language skills to understand what the scale involves and so guess answers randomly or leave many items unanswered. It would be prudent to screen the data for such cases before performing the analyses described below.

One very simple approach is simply to gather some data from members of two or more groups, and perform an analysis of variance,[1] where 'items' are the within-subjects variable and 'group' is the between-subjects variable, reflecting group membership. The output will show three things. The item effect will just show whether the mean scores for all of the items are the same. It is of no interest. The group effect will show whether the average score (computed across all items) is the same for each group. This may be of some interest. However, the item x group interaction is the really interesting term. This shows whether some items are appreciably more difficult for members of some groups than others. It is then possible to identify these items by analysing simple effects etc. and consider removing them from the scale. The whole process can then be repeated until the item x group interaction term is non-significant. The obvious problem with this approach is that the size of the sample will influence the significance of the interaction; a huge sample is able to identify tiny amounts of bias and so will end up removing almost all items. Rather than relying on significance tests, it might be more prudent to decide beforehand what effect-size indicates that items are biased and use this (rather than the significance level of the interaction) to decide whether to eliminate items. Osterlind (1983) identifies other problems with this technique, too – but the method is both quick and simple.

A second approach is simply to factor analyse the data from each group separately and check that the factor loadings are similar. If one item is so inappropriate for members of the group that it simply fails to measure its intended factor, this analysis will show it. However, it will *not* reveal whether an item is more difficult for members of one group rather than another. It is possible to check this using a form of structural equation modelling known as multiple group analysis, but this is beyond the scope of this book.

If there are just two groups, another straightforward method is to create a scatter diagram showing the difficulty of the item for each group. For statistical reasons (Angoff and Ford, 1973) it is usual to transform the item difficulties into z-scores, and then change these into a statistic called delta (Δ). These 'transformed item difficulties' (TIDs) follow a normal distribution with a mean of 13 and a standard deviation of 4. Possible values of delta thus range from about 0 to 26.

EXERCISE 7.2: TRANSFORMED ITEM DIFFICULTIES

Resources required: Spreadsheet 7.2: Transformed item difficulties. From www.routledge.com/9781138228894

Purpose: To plot transformed item difficulties in order to detect biased items

Contents of spreadsheet: Item difficulties (mean scores) from 16 items

Suggested activity:

- Notice that with the default dataset, items of middling difficulty, the difficulty (mean score) of the red group is lower than for the blue group.
- Change the difference in difficulty of one of the items and note that the graph shows that the item moves away from the line. The perpendicular distance of a point from the line is an estimate of its degree of bias.

Points to note:

- Note that the data points are items – not people.
- Note that the line is *not* a regression line as neither set of TIDs can be regarded as the independent variable.

Learning outcomes:

Readers should now be able to

- detect biased items by plotting transformed item difficulties;
- appreciate the difference between internal and external bias.

This approach to detecting bias is very straightforward and intuitive; it also works well in practice. However, problems can arise if the items vary in their discrimination power, and some critics may worry about how far from the line an item needs to be in order to be regarded as biased.

These days, the most popular method for detecting biased items is through the use of item response theory. Chapter 12 outlines how this technique may be used to assess bias. However, this requires large samples, makes some rather large assumptions about the relationship between test scores and ability and requires specialist software. Hence many practitioners will be content with the methods outlined here. For those who wish to read further, the definitive (older) text on detecting bias is Jensen (1980). Reynolds and Suzuki's (2013) chapter provides an excellent short summary of more recent research.

SUMMARY

Establishing whether a scale accurately reflects some underlying attribute of people is clearly of vital importance. Borsboom et al.'s (2004) suggestion that psychology needs to focus on understanding how, precisely, individual differences in the attribute influence the way in which people respond to items is surprisingly radical; most validation studies focus on relating scores on scales to behaviour or to scores on other scales. This is problematical. For a scale might predict behaviour even if it does not measure the trait which it is supposed to (the R–S scale mentioned at the start of this chapter would probably predict behaviour but because it measures anxiety rather than anything more esoteric). We also saw that if scales contain items that are similar in meaning, this can cause surprisingly large correlations between them – which could easily confuse those performing studies of construct validation. It is also important to check whether scales are equally valid for all groups, which is where the notion of test bias becomes important.

Whatever its form, validation is an incremental process – gathering data from a variety of sources to help one determine whether a trait or state actually exists, how the state or trait causes people to respond differently to items in a scale, and/or whether it is useful for anything. All too often, though, researchers act as if the existence of a trait is a given, just because they have developed a scale. A strong dose of scepticism is needed whenever any psychologist proposes a 'new' trait.

NOTE

1 Or, presumably, a multivariate analysis of variance.

CHAPTER 8
INTRODUCTION TO FACTOR ANALYSIS

Few techniques in psychometrics are as useful as factor analysis. It can be used to determine whether all of the items in a scale measure the same trait. It can be used to check whether the items in a test work properly – whether they all form scales as they are supposed to. It can help us check whether several different scales do, in fact measure the same thing – for example, whether scales supposedly measuring Anxiety, Emotional Instability, Depression and Defensiveness really do measure five distinct (but possibly correlated) traits, or whether some of these traits are identical to others. It can be used to generate theories of personality, cognitive abilities and suchlike. And (with a little ingenuity) it can be used to develop scales that measure mood and to develop hierarchical models of personality, ability, mood etc.

This chapter introduces the broad concepts of factor analysis. Details of how to perform and interpret factor analyses are covered in Chapter 9. Chapter 10 considers how factor analysis can be used for other purposes – e.g., to develop scales that measure moods, to identify groups of *people* (rather than items) and thus clinical syndromes etc. or to analyse longitudinal data. And Chapter 11 suggests how hierarchical models may be useful – particularly when analysing questionnaires that may contain items which are near synonyms.

INTRODUCTION TO FACTOR ANALYSIS

'Factor analysis' can refer to two very different statistical techniques. *Exploratory factor analysis* is the older (and simpler) technique and forms the basis of Chapters 8–10, and the first part of Chapter 11. *Confirmatory factor analysis* and its extensions (sometimes known as 'structural equation modelling', 'latent-variable analysis' or 'Lisrel models') are useful in many areas other than individual differences and are particularly popular in social psychology. A brief outline of *this* technique is given at the end of Chapter 11. Authors do not always make it clear whether exploratory or confirmatory factor analysis has been used. If the term 'factor analysis' is used in a journal, it normally refers to an exploratory factor analysis – so called because it explores the structure of the data. The great thing about exploratory factor analysis is that it does not try to test any preconceived model about the structure of a set of data. Instead, it lets the data speak for themselves.

Chapter 6 showed why it is important that the items in a scale all measure one (and only one) psychological variable and introduced coefficient alpha as a measure of the reliability of a scale. This technique *assumed* that all of the items in a test formed one scale, and the reliability coefficient essentially tests whether this assumption is reasonable.

The factor analytic approach does away with this assumption. It involves analysing people's responses to a sample of items and *discovering* how many distinct scales they contain and which items belong to which scale(s). Suppose that a psychologist administered 20 vocabulary items, 20 comprehension items and 20 anagram problems to a group of volunteers. Do they all measure a single 'verbal ability'? Or, because the anagram items involve thinking (rather than just knowing the meaning of words in and out of context), perhaps the items involving anagrams might measure one trait and the comprehension/vocabulary items might measure another? Or do the items form three quite distinct (but perhaps correlated) traits? Factor analysis can tell us this, and so it is a very useful technique for determining how many different constructs are measured by a set of variables. All one needs to do is make some assumptions about the data (for example, whether the responses to the items should be regarded as interval or ordinal measurements), gather some data from a fairly large sample (normally several hundred people) and find a computer program to perform the factor analysis. The computer program is necessary because factor analysis involves a lot of computation and most analyses would take weeks to perform by hand. However, several free pieces of software are available, as outlined below.

Rather than factor analysing responses to individual items, it is also possible to factor analyse scores on scales – although a major problem with this is that one has to assume that the scales were correctly constructed in the first place. Just because a scale has a large coefficient alpha, there is no guarantee that it measures a single trait, as discussed in Chapter 6. It may contain several clusters of highly correlated items, but with zero correlations between items from different clusters. We show a way round this ('hierarchical analyses') in Chapter 11. But if one is happy to make the assumption that a test measures the scales that it is supposed to in the context in which it is used, then factor analysis of the scale scores may be useful.

In factor analysis, the word 'factor' is usually used instead of the word 'construct', and we shall follow this convention from now on. Exploratory factor analysis essentially does two things:

- It shows how many distinct psychological constructs (factors) are measured by a set of variables. Do the 60 ability items measure one, two, three (or perhaps more) distinct abilities?
- It shows which variables measure which constructs. In the first example, it might show that the vocabulary items and the comprehension items all measure the same thing, whilst the anagram items measure something different. It can even show how well each of the items measure each construct. For example, it might be found that the first, fifth and sixteenth vocabulary items and the fourth and eleventh comprehension items do not really measure anything – perhaps because they are so easy that almost everyone gets them correct or so hard that everyone gets them wrong (or guesses randomly). Thus, factor analysis can also be a very useful tool for scale construction.

The technique is not restricted to test items or test scores. It would be possible to factor analyse reaction times from various types of cognitive test in order to determine which (if any) of these tasks were related. Alternatively, suppose that one took a group of schoolchildren who had no specific training or practice in sport and assessed their performance in 30 sports by any mixture of coaches' ratings, timings, mean length of throw, percentage of maiden overs obtained, goals scored or whatever performance measure is most appropriate for each sport. The only proviso is that each child must compete in each sport. Factor analysis could reveal whether individuals who were good at one ball game tended to be good at all of them, whether short-distance and long-distance track events formed two distinct groupings (and which events belonged to which group) and so on. Thus, instead of having to talk in terms of performance in 30 distinct areas, it would be possible to summarise this information by talking in terms of half a dozen basic sporting abilities (or however many abilities the factor analysis revealed). The technique is used outside psychology, too – for example in spectroscopy (chemistry) and genetic research. Basically, factor analysis is a powerful tool for data reduction; if we measure a large number of variables, it tells us whether and where there is appreciable overlap between them.

EXPLORATORY FACTOR ANALYSIS BY INSPECTION

The top section of Table 8.1 shows a six-item questionnaire. Six students were asked to answer each question, using a five-point rating scale as shown in the table, and their responses are shown towards the bottom of the table.

Eagle-eyed readers may notice some trends in these data. Individuals' responses to Questions 1, 2 and 3 tend to be similar. Stephen tends to agree with all three of them, Ann tends to disagree with them whilst the others feel more or less neutral about them. These are rough approximations, of course, but you can see that no one who rates themself as '1' or '2' on one of these three questions gives themselves a '4' or '5' on one of the others. This may suggest that enjoying socialising, acting on impulse and having a cheerful disposition correlate together, and so these three questions might be expected to form a scale. Much the same applies to Questions 4 to 6. Again, people such as Stephen or Ann who give themselves a low rating on one of these three questions also give themselves a low rating on the other two questions, whilst Christine gives herself high ratings on all three questions.

Table 8.1 Six-item personality questionnaire and responses of six students

Q1	I enjoy socialising	1	2	3	4	5
Q2	I often act on impulse	1	2	3	4	5
Q3	I am a cheerful sort of person	1	2	3	4	5
Q4	I often feel depressed	1	2	3	4	5
Q5	It is difficult for me to get to sleep at night	1	2	3	4	5
Q6	Large crowds make me feel anxious	1	2	3	4	5
For each question please circle ONE NUMBER which describes your reaction to each statement.						
Circle '5' if you strongly agree that a statement describes you very accurately						
Circle '4' if it describes you fairly accurately						
Circle '3' if you are neutral or unsure						
Circle '2' if you feel that the statement does not really describe you accurately						
Circle '1' if you feel strongly that the statement definitely does not describe you accurately						

	Q1	Q2	Q3	Q4	Q5	Q6
Stephen	5	5	4	1	1	2
Ann	1	2	1	1	1	2
Paul	3	4	3	4	5	4
Janette	4	4	3	1	2	1
Michael	3	3	4	1	2	2
Christine	3	3	3	5	4	5

Thus there seem to be two clusters of questions in this questionnaire. The first group consists of Questions 1, 2 and 3 and the second group consists of Questions 4, 5 and 6. However, spotting these relationships by eye is very difficult. Nor is it particularly scientific, as different people might come to different conclusions. Fortunately, some simple statistics can help.

If we make the common but probably unwarranted assumption that these numbers behave in much the same way as numbers corresponding to physical measurements (see Chapter 4), we might think it appropriate to calculate correlations between the six variables. These correlations are shown in Table 8.2. They confirm our suspicions about the relationships between the students' responses to Questions 1 to 3 and Questions 4 to 6. Questions 1 to 3 correlate strongly together (0.933, 0.824 and 0.696, respectively) but hardly at all with Questions 4 to 6 (−0.096 etc.). Similarly, Questions 4 to 6 correlate highly together (0.896, 0.965 and 0.808, respectively), but hardly at all with Questions 1 to 3. Thus it is possible to see from the table of correlations that Questions 1 to 3 form one natural group and Questions 4 to 6 form another – that is, the questionnaire actually measures two constructs or 'factors', one consisting of the first three questions and the other consisting of the final three questions.

Whilst it is easy to see this from the correlations in Table 8.2, it should be remembered that the correlations shown there are hardly typical.

- The data were constructed so that the correlations between the variables were either very large or very small. In real life, correlations between variables would rarely be larger than 0.5, with many in the range 0.2–0.3. This makes it difficult to identify patterns by eye.
- The questions were ordered so that the large correlations fell next to each other in Table 8.2. If the questions had been presented in a different order, it would not be so easy to identify clusters of large correlations.

Table 8.2 Correlations between the six items of Table 8.1

	Q1	Q2	Q3	Q4	Q5	Q6
Q1	1.000					
Q2	0.933	1.000				
Q3	0.824	0.696	1.000			
Q4	−0.096	−0.052	0.000	1.000		
Q5	−0.005	0.058	0.111	0.896	1.000	
Q6	−0.167	−0.127	0.000	0.965	0.808	1.000

- Only six questions were used, so there are only 15 correlations to consider. With 40 questions there would be

$$\frac{40 \times 39}{2} = 780$$

  correlations to consider, making it much more difficult to identify groups of intercorrelated items.

Well-known mathematical methods can be used to identify factors from groups of variables which tend to correlate together, and even the very largest factor analyses can now be performed on a desktop computer.

A GEOMETRIC APPROACH TO FACTOR ANALYSIS

It is possible to represent correlation matrices geometrically. Variables are represented by straight lines which are of equal length and which all start at the same point. These lines are positioned such that the correlation between the variables is represented by the cosine of the angle between them. Table 8.3 shows a few cosines to give you a general idea of the concept. When the angle between two lines is small, the cosine is large and positive. When two lines are at right angles, the correlation (cosine) is zero. When the two lines are pointing in opposite directions, the correlation (cosine) is negative.

It is sometimes possible to represent entire correlation matrices geometrically. A line is drawn anywhere on the page representing one of the variables – it does not matter which one. The other variables are represented by other lines of equal length, all of which fan out from one end of the first line. The angles between the variables are, by convention, measured in a clockwise direction. Variables which have large positive correlations between them will fall close to each other, because Table 8.3 shows that large correlations (or cosines) result in small angles between the lines. Highly correlated variables literally point in the same direction, variables with large negative correlations between them point in opposite directions and variables which are uncorrelated point in completely different directions. Figure 8.1 shows a simple example based on three variables. The correlation between V1 and V2 is 0.0; the correlation between V1 and V3 is 0.5 and the correlation between V2 and V3 is 0.867. The correlation between V1 and V2 is represented by a pair of lines of equal length joined at one end; as the correlation between these variables is 0.0 the angle between them corresponds to a cosine of 0.0; that is, 90°. The correlation between V1 and V3 is 0.5 corresponding to an angle of 60° and that between V2 and V3 is 0.867 (30°), so V2 and V3 are positioned as shown.

Table 8.3 Table of cosines for graphical representation of correlations between variables

Angle (in degrees)	Cosine of angle
0	1.000
15	0.966
30	0.867
45	0.707
60	0.500
75	0.259
90	0.000
120	−0.500
150	−0.867
180	−1.000
210	−0.867
240	−0.500
270	0.000
300	0.500
330	0.867

It is not always possible to represent correlations in two dimensions (i.e., on a flat sheet of paper). If the correlations represented in Figure 8.1 had not been chosen carefully, one of the lines would have to project outward from the page to some degree. This is no problem for the underlying mathematics of factor analysis, but it does mean that it is not possible to use this geometric technique to perform real-life factor analyses.

Figure 8.2 is a fairly good approximation of the data shown in Table 8.2. Ignoring lines F1 and F2 for the moment, the correlations between Variables 1, 2 and 3 shown in this figure are all very large and positive (that is, the angles between these lines are small). Similarly, the correlations between Variables 4 to 6 are also large and positive. As Variables 1 to 3 have near-zero correlations with Variables 4 to 6, Variables 1, 2 and 3 are at 90° to Variables 4, 5 and 6. Computer programs for factor analysis essentially try to 'explain' the correlations between the variables in terms of a smaller number of factors. It is good practice to talk about 'common

Figure 8.1 Geometric representation of the correlations between three variables

factors' rather than just 'factors' – later on we will encounter 'unique factors', and it is safest to avoid confusion. In this example, it is clear that there are two clusters of correlations, so the information in Table 8.2 can be approximated by two common factors, each of which passes through a group of large correlations. The common factors are indicated by long lines labelled F1 and F2 in Figure 8.2.

It should be clear that, from measuring the angle between each common factor and each variable, it is also possible to calculate the *correlations* between each variable and each common factor. Variables 1, 2 and 3 will all have very large correlations with Factor 1 (in fact Variable 2 will have a correlation of nearly 1.0 with Factor 1, as Factor 1 lies virtually on top of it). Variables 1, 2 and 3 will have correlations of about zero with Factor 2, as they are virtually at right angles to it. Similarly, Factor 2 is highly correlated with Variables 4 to 6 and is virtually uncorrelated with Variables 1 to 3 (because of the 90° angle between these variables and this factor). Do not worry for now where these factors come from or how they are positioned relative to the variables, as this will be covered in Chapter 9. It is possible to show all the correlations between every item and every common factor in a table, called the *factor structure matrix*. The correlations between items and common factors are

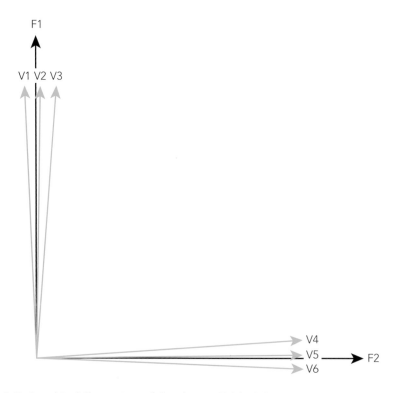

Figure 8.2 Graphical illustration of the data in Table 8.2

usually known as *factor loadings*. By convention, the common factors are shown as
the columns of this table and the variables as the rows. The values in Table 8.4 were
obtained by looking at the angles between each common factor and each variable in
Figure 8.2 and translating these (roughly) into correlations using Table 8.3.

Table 8.4 Orthogonal factors showing the correlations from Figure 8.2

Variable	Factor 1	Factor 2	Communality
V1 (Spelling)	0.90	0.10	0.82
V2 (Vocabulary)	0.98	0.00	0.96
V3 (Grammar)	0.90	−0.10	0.82
V4 (Geometry)	0.10	0.85	0.73
V5 (Calculus)	0.00	0.98	0.96
V6 (Arithmetic)	−0.10	0.85	0.73
Eigenvalue	2.60	2.42	

In the above example, the two groups of variables (and hence the common factors) are at right angles to each other – what is known technically as an *orthogonal solution* – an important term.

HOW TO NAME FACTORS

Factors can be tentatively named by noting which variables have loadings that are more extreme than some arbitrary value. By convention, the cut-off value is 0.4 or 0.3, which implies an angle of 60° to 75° between the variable and the common factor. The easiest way to see which variables 'belong' to a factor is thus to underline those that have loadings higher than 0.4 or less than −0.4. Table 8.4 shows that Factor 1 is a mixture of V1, V2 and V3 (but not V4, V5 or V6). Likewise, Factor 2 is a mixture of V4, V5 and V6. Thus the factor matrix can be used to give a tentative label to each common factor. Table 8.1 shows that V1–V3 ask about sociability, whilst V4–V6 relate to nervousness. Thus F1 and F2 could be tentatively labelled as "sociability" and "nervousness". There is no guarantee that labels given like this are necessarily correct. It is necessary to validate the factor exactly as described in Chapter 7 in order to ensure that this label is accurate.

It is important to appreciate that factor analysis has actually shown us that V1–V3 form a factor, as do V4–V6. We have not just looked at the names of the variables and decided to group them together. Factor analysis shows us what structure really exists in the data – without any need for us to specify any sort of theory.

EIGENVALUES AND COMMUNALITIES

For orthogonal solutions, the square of the correlation shows how much variance is shared by two variables – or, in simpler language, how much they overlap. Two variables which correlate 0.8 share 0.8^2 or 0.64 or 64% of their variance. As factor loadings are merely correlations between common factors and items, it follows that the square of each factor loading shows the amount of overlap between each variable and the common factor. This simple finding forms the basis of two other main uses of the factor matrix.

EIGENVALUES

It is possible to calculate how much of the variance each common factor accounts for. A common factor that accounts for 40% of the overlap between the variables in the original correlation matrix is clearly more important than another which explains only 20% of the variance. Once again it is necessary to assume that the common factors are orthogonal (at right angles to each other). The first step is to calculate what is known as an *eigenvalue* for each factor by squaring the factor loadings and summing down the columns. Using the data shown in Table 8.4, it can be seen that the eigenvalue of Factor 1 is $0.90^2+0.98^2+0.90^2+0.10^2+0.0^2+(-0.10)^2$ or 2.60. If the eigenvalue is divided by the number of variables (six in this instance), it shows what proportion of variance is explained by this common factor. Here Factor 1 explains 0.43 or 43% of the information in the original correlation matrix.

COMMUNALITIES

If the common factors are at right angles (an orthogonal solution), it is also simple to calculate how much of the variance of each variable is measured by all of the factors by merely summing the squared factor loadings across factors. It can be seen from Table 8.4 that $0.90^2+0.10^2(=0.82)$ of the variance of Test 1 is 'explained' by the two factors. This amount is called the *communality* of that variable.

A variable with a large communality has a large degree of overlap with one or more common factors. A low communality implies that all of the correlations between that variable and the common factors are small – that is, none of the common factors overlap much with that variable. This might mean that the variable measures something which is conceptually quite different from the other variables in the analysis. For example, one personality item in among 100 ability test items would have a communality close to zero. It might also mean that a particular item is heavily influenced by measurement error or extreme difficulty, e.g., an item which is so easy that everyone obtained the correct answer or which was ambiguously phrased so that no one could understand the question. Whatever the reason, a low communality implies that an item does not overlap with the common factors, either because it measures a different concept, because of excessive measurement error or because there are few individual differences in the way in which people respond to the item.

OBLIQUE FACTORS

Thus far we have assumed that the factors are at right angles to each other; however, this need not always be the case. Consider the correlations in Figure 8.3. Here it would clearly make sense to allow the factors to become correlated and to place one common factor through each cluster of variables; if the factors were kept at right angles, they would not pass through each cluster of variables.

Here the two factors are correlated with each other, and each factor is correlated with each variable. Factor analyses where the factors are themselves correlated (i.e., not at right angles)

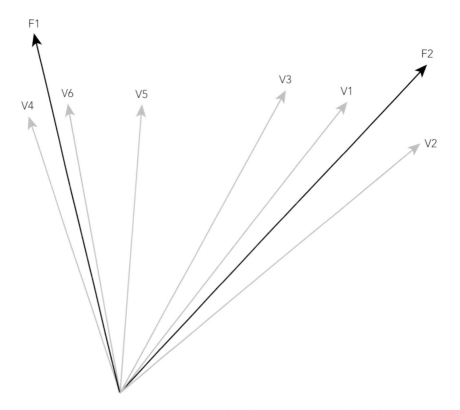

Figure 8.3 Correlations between six variables showing two correlated factors

are known as *oblique solutions*. The correlations between the factors form what is called a *factor correlation matrix*. In this example, the correlation between the two factors is about 60°, so (using Table 8.3) the correlation between them is approximately 0.5.

There is a problem when interpreting oblique rotations. It was easy to see which variables belonged with each of the factors when the variables and the factors were orthogonal (Table 8.4) because the correlations between each variable and each factor were either close to zero or quite large. When the factors are correlated, it is harder to see which variables belong to which factor. For example, as V1–V3 are appreciably correlated with Factor 2 (as well as having large correlations with Factor 1) the factor structure matrix will be as shown in Table 8.5. Variable 5, for example, is reasonably close to both factors and so has a fairly appreciable correlation with both of them in the factor structure matrix.

It is therefore usual to interpret a different table known as the *factor pattern matrix*. This too is shown in Table 8.5. The pattern matrix essentially corrects for the correlations between the factors and makes it easier to see which variables belong with each factor. The numbers in the pattern matrix are actually regression coefficients (not correlations) and they can, occasionally, be greater than 1.0.

Table 8.5 Approximate oblique factor matrices from Figure 8.3

	Factor structure matrix			Factor pattern matrix	
Variable	Factor 1	Factor 2		Factor 1	Factor 2
V1	0.56	0.31		0.52	0.12
V2	0.76	0.22		0.78	−0.06
V3	0.51	0.17		0.51	−0.02
V4	0.01	0.67		−0.16	0.73
V5	0.43	0.60		0.24	0.51
V6	0.35	0.58		0.16	0.52

FACTOR ANALYSIS AND PRINCIPAL-COMPONENTS ANALYSIS

In Table 8.4, we calculated that 82% of the variance of Test 1 was explained by the first two factors. What happened to the remaining 18%? It turns out that the answer depends on what sort of assumptions we want to make.

PRINCIPAL-COMPONENTS MODEL

It should be obvious that if we have three variables (V1–V3), then, whatever the correlations are between the variables, it is possible to represent them in three dimensions. (Imagine three pencils with the points all touching – whatever the angles between them are, they can be represented in three dimensions.) The number of dimensions used to represent a set of data corresponds to the number of factors. Thus a factor matrix showing as many factors as there are variables could look like Table 8.6.

Here all of the communalities (h^2) are 1.0. However, if we only considered the first two factors, the communality of each variable would obviously be less than 1 (it would be 0.85 in the case of V1). So one possible reason why the two factors did not explain all of the variance is simply because there were fewer factors than variables. Putting it another way, some of the lines in Figure 8.2 will not fit exactly onto the two dimensions defined

Table 8.6 Loadings of three variables (V1–V3) on three orthogonal factors (F1–F3) from a principal-components analysis

	F1	F2	F3	h2
V1	0.6	0.7	0.38	1
V2	0.7	0.7	0.14	1
V3	0.8	0.5	0.33	1

by these two factors; some of the lines will need to stick out of the page or go behind
the page to properly represent the correlations. Thus some of the lines are slightly shorter
than others when projected onto the two dimensions of Figure 8.2. If we had used six
factors rather than two, then all the communalities would be exactly 1.0.

So, according to this model, the reason why we lost 18% of the variance when calculating
communalities is because we were trying to squeeze the information which needs to
be represented in six dimensions into two dimensions; some information will be lost by
doing so. Of course, this trade-off is often worthwhile. Knowing that two traits do a very
good job of approximating six means that it is possible to shorten the time taken to make
assessments, and it may also be useful for theoretical purposes – for example, to debunk
the idea that the items in a newly devised scale really measure anything different from
those in older scales or to discover that ratings based on a sample of all the adjectives in the
English language typically produce five personality factors (McCrae and John, 1992).

This model is known as the *principal-components model*. The key thing to note is that
if as many factors are extracted as there are variables, then the communality of each
variable will be exactly 1.0. In other words, the principal-components model can
potentially explain all of the variance in a set of data – though by choosing fewer
factors than there are variables, we may sometimes decide that a smaller number of
factors will provide a good-enough approximation.

More formally, the principal-components model states that, for any variable being analysed

$$\text{total variance} = \text{common-factor variance} + \text{measurement error}.$$

Suppose we construct a test in which 10 items enquire about worries and negative
moods: 'My moods vary a lot', 'I feel agitated in confined spaces', 'I get embarrassed
easily' etc., with each item being answered on a five-point scale ranging from 'Very
like me' to 'Not at all like me'. Suppose that we know that all these items form a single
factor of 'Neuroticism'. The principal-components model therefore states that the way
a person answers an item depends only on their level of the traits that are measured by
all the items (here there is only one trait; Neuroticism) plus some measurement error.
It is the same assumption that was made in Chapter 5 when discussing reliability and
implies that when as many factors are extracted as there are variables, these common
factors can explain all of the information in the correlation matrix.

FACTOR ANALYSIS

The assumption that anything that is not measured by common factors must just be
measurement error is rather a strong one. Each test item may have some morsel of 'unique

variance' that is special to that item, but which cannot be shared with other items. Factor analysis suggests that each variable has a 'unique factor' associated with it, which describes variation in scores which is not measurement error but which is not shared with any other variables or factors. The extent to which people fear enclosed spaces may not be completely determined by their level of neuroticism; people may just vary somewhat in the extent to which they show fear of being shut in, perhaps as a result of childhood experiences. So to predict how a person would respond to the item, you would need to consider

- their level of neuroticism (common-factor loading);
- their level of this particular fear of being enclosed (unique factor loading);

and recognise that there will always be some random measurement error.

When performing a factor analysis (rather than a principal-components analysis) it is therefore necessary to estimate how much unique variance is associated with each variable before performing the factor analysis. We consider how to do this in Chapter 9.

Readers familiar with multiple regression might like to think of the issue in these terms. If we gather data on six variables and try to predict people's scores on one of the variables from their scores on the other five, then the multiple correlation could, in principle, be 1.0. On the other hand, the factor model suggests that there is something special about each variable which cannot be predicted by knowing people's scores on any other variables – and so the multiple correlation will be less than 1.

The *factor-analysis* model thus assumes that for any variable or item being factor analysed

total variance = common-factor variance + unique-factor variance + measurement error.

The amount of unique-factor variance in an item is reflected in its communality. The more variance an item shares with the other items in the test, the higher are its correlations with both them and the common factors. Therefore, the higher its communality will be. (Remind yourself how communality is calculated in order to check this.) Thus, whilst some of the 'missing 18%' of variance in the previous example will be due to extracting two factors instead of six, some of this 18% will also reflect the fact that the communalities are less than 1.0. An item with some unique factor variance will never have a communality as large as 1.0, even if the factor analysis extracts as many factors as there are variables. Some people are just more (or less) afraid of enclosed spaces than you would expect from knowing their level of neuroticism.

It follows that factor analysis is a more mathematically complicated process than principal-components analysis. Whereas principal-components analysis merely has to determine the number of factors to be extracted and how each variable should correlate with each factor, factor analysis also has to estimate how much of a variable's variance is 'common-factor' variance, and how much is unique to that particular variable and cannot be shared with any other variable.

In practice, it does not seem to matter too much whether one performs a principal-components analysis or a factor analysis, as both techniques generally lead to similar results. In fact, the authorities on factor analysis can be divided into three groups. Some believe that factor analysis should never be used. According to Stamm (1995, personal communication), Leyland Wilkinson fought to keep factor-analysis options out of his SYSTAT statistics package, although commercial pressures eventually won. On the other hand, some maintain that a form of factor analysis is the *only* justifiable technique (e.g., Carroll, 1993), and, finally, some pragmatists argue that, as both techniques generally produce highly similar solutions, it does not really matter which of them one uses (Tabachnick and Fidell, 2007).

One slightly worrying problem is that the loadings obtained from component analyses are always larger than those which result from factor analyses, as the former assume that each variable has a communality of 1.0, whereas the latter computes a value for the communality which is generally less than 1.0. Thus the results obtained from a principal-components analysis always look more impressive (i.e., have larger common-factor loadings) than the results of a factor analysis. This has clear implications for many rules of thumb, such as regarding factor loadings above 0.4 (or less than −0.4) as being 'salient' and disregarding those between −0.39 and +0.39. It is also vitally important that authors of papers should state clearly whether they have followed the factor-analysis or component-analysis model. Some authors mention 'factor analysis' in the text even though they have performed principal-components analysis.

USES OF FACTOR ANALYSIS

Factor analysis has three main uses in psychology.

TEST CONSTRUCTION

First, it may be used to construct tests. For example, 50 items might be written more or less at random; we do not have to assume that they all measure the same trait or state. The items would then be administered to a representative sample of several hundred individuals and scored (in the case of ability tests) so that a correct answer is coded as 1 and an incorrect answer as 0. Responses that are made using Likert scales (as with most personality and attitude questionnaires) are simply entered in their raw form – one point if box (a) is endorsed, two if (b) is chosen etc. The responses to these 50 items are then correlated together and factor analysed. The items that have high loadings on each factor measure the same underlying psychological construct and so form a scale. Thus it is possible to determine how to score the questionnaire in future simply by looking at the factor matrix; if Items 1, 2, 10 and 12 are the only items that have substantial loadings on one factor, then one scale of the test should be the sum of these four items and no others.

It is likely that some items will fail to load substantially on any of the factors (i.e., show low communalities). This could happen for a number of reasons; in the case of ability tests, the items could be so easy (or hard) that there is little or no variation in people's scores. Personality items may refer to uncommon actions or feelings where there is again little variation – e.g., 'There are occasions in my life when I have felt afraid', an item with which *everyone* is likely to agree. Or items may fail because they are severely influenced by measurement error or because they measure something different from any of the others that were administered. Test constructors do not usually worry about why, precisely, items fail to work as expected. Items that fail to load a factor are simply discarded without further ado. Thus factor analysis can show at a stroke

- how many distinct scales run through the test;
- which items belong to which scales (so indicating how the test should be scored);
- which items in a test should be discarded.

Each of the scales then needs to be validated, e.g., by calculating scores for each person on each factor and examining the construct validity and/or predictive validity of these scales. For example, scores on the factors may be correlated with scores on other questionnaires, used to predict educational success etc.

CONCEPTUAL SIMPLIFICATION

The second main use of factor is in conceptual simplification. Huge numbers of tests have been developed to measure personality from different theoretical perspectives, and it is not at all obvious whether these overlap. If we take six scales that measure personality traits, it is useful to know how much overlap there is between them. Do they really each assess quite different aspects of personality? At the other extreme, might they perhaps all measure the same trait under different names? Or is the truth somewhere in the middle? To find out, it is simply necessary to administer the test items to a large sample, then factor the correlations between the items. This will show precisely what the underlying structure truly is. For example, two factors may be found. The first factor may have large loadings from all the items in tests 1, 5 and 6. All the substantial loadings on the second factor may come from items in tests 2, 3 and 4. Hence it is clear that tests 1, 5 and 6 measure precisely the same thing, as do tests 2, 3 and 4. Any high-flown theoretical distinctions about subtle differences between the scales can be shown to have no basis in fact, and any rational psychologists seeing the results of such an analysis should be forced to think in terms of two (rather than six) theoretical constructs – a considerable simplification.

REFINING QUESTIONNAIRES

As mentioned in Chapter 7, the third main use of factor analysis is for checking the psychometric properties of questionnaires, particularly when they are to be used in new cultures or populations, or prior to calculating their reliability. For example, suppose that the manual of an Australian personality test suggests that it should be scored by adding together the scores on all the odd-numbered items to form one scale, whilst all the even-numbered items form another. When the test is given to a sample of people in the UK and the correlations between the items are calculated and factor analysed, two factors should be found, with all the odd-numbered items having substantial loadings on one factor and all the even-numbered items loading substantially on the other. This is known as establishing the factorial validity of a scale. If this structure is *not* found, it shows that there are problems with the questionnaire, which should not be scored or used in its conventional form.

SUMMARY

It is easy to see why factor analysis is so important in psychometrics. The same statistical technique can be used to construct tests, resolve theoretical disputes about the number and nature of factors measured by tests and questionnaires and check whether tests work as they should or whether it is legitimate to use a particular test within a different population or a different culture. You may even have wondered whether the size of the eigenvalue obtained when factoring a test that has just one factor running through it has any link to the test's reliability . . .

This chapter has provided a basic introduction to the principles of factor analysis. It has left many questions unanswered, such as:

- How does one decide how many factors are needed to describe a set of data?
- How can computer programs actually perform factor analysis?
- What types of data can usefully be factor analysed?
- How should the results obtained from factor-analytical studies be interpreted and reported?
- Is it possible to correlate *people* together, rather than correlating items together?
- What happens if the correlations between factors are themselves factor analysed?

These and other issues will be explored in the next three chapters.

CHAPTER 9
PERFORMING AND
INTERPRETING FACTOR
ANALYSES

Whilst Chapter 8 gave an overview of the basic principles of factor analysis, it deliberately omitted some of the detail which is needed either to perform factor analyses or to evaluate the technical adequacy of published studies.

Factor analysis involves a serious amount of computation, making it unfeasible to perform calculations by hand. Nor is it straightforward to perform factor analyses using spreadsheets unless these use macros or matrix algebra extensions. And because the underlying mathematics is rather more complex than for the straightforward analyses encountered so far, even if we *were* to write spreadsheets to perform factor analyses, it would be difficult for readers to amend them. To learn how to perform and interpret factor analyses it makes more sense to actually perform different analyses (for example, using different numbers of variables and participants, different types of correlations, different methods of factor rotation and/or different methods for determining the optimal number of factors to rotate) rather than getting into the computational minutiae, which are likely to baffle any readers who do not have a strong mathematical background.

Fortunately, there is an excellent (and free) factor analysis package available for users of Windows (Lorenzo-Seva and Ferrando, 2006), and I will assume that readers have access to this; Macintosh and Linux users can run it using free emulators, such as WineSkin or Wine. Confirmatory factor analyses (see Chapter 11) require other specialised packages. Free versions include the student version of LISREL (although this has limitations on the size of analyses which can be performed) or Onyx (which is Java-based so should run on most systems). Readers who are familiar with the R statistical environment (R Core Team, 2013) can perform all the analyses described in this chapter using Bill Revelle's superb 'Psych' package for R (Revelle, 2017c) for exploratory factor analysis or the Lavaan package for confirmatory analyses – though R can hardly be described as user-friendly. Other statistical packages such as SPSS, SAS and SYSTAT (though not MYSTAT) can be used by aficionados, but with difficulty. For example, it will be necessary to roll up one's sleeves and use syntax commands to persuade SPSS to perform anything but the most basic analyses.

There are 10 basic stages involved in performing an exploratory factor analysis. The first nine are discussed below and the final one in Chapter 11.

- Planning

  - Stage 1: Ensure that the data are suitable for factor analysis.
  - Stage 2: Ensure that the sample size is large enough.

- Analysing

  - Stage 3: Decide how to calculate correlations.
  - Stage 4: Decide on the model – factor analysis or component analysis.
  - Stage 5: Decide how many factors are needed to represent the data.
  - Stage 6: If using factor (rather than component) analysis, estimate the communality of each variable.
  - Stage 7: Produce factors giving the desired communalities (factor extraction).
  - Stage 8: Rotate these factors so that they provide a replicable solution ('simple structure').
  - Stage 9: Optionally compute factor scores.
  - Stage 10: Optionally perform hierarchical analyses, if appropriate.

One of the problems with factor analysis is that the computer programs used will almost always produce an answer of some kind, and by trying to analyse the data using many different techniques, taking out different numbers of factors and concentrating on different subsets of variables, it is possible to pull something semi-plausible from the most ghastly study. Indeed, there are some areas of the discipline, such as personal construct psychology/ repertory grid analyses, where this is the norm. It is vital that those who use the technique or read the literature should have an understanding of the design and execution of factor-analytical studies. Hence this chapter begins with a look at the types of data which may usefully be factor analysed.

STAGE 1: SUITABILITY OF DATA FOR FACTOR ANALYSIS

Notwithstanding Michell's (1997a) critique, most psychologists regard the numbers which they analyse (scores on questionnaires, rating scales, responses to individual items and so on) as having the same properties as real, physical measures. In other words, it is probably safe to assume that anyone reading this far has decided to be pragmatic; readers may need to perform analyses on data from questionnaires and tests in order to pass examinations or to use tests in the real world, and so, whilst they may acknowledge these issues at an intellectual level, they do not have the luxury of taking a stand on it. So the rest of this chapter (and indeed, this book) makes the major assumption that psychologists can measure quantities using tests.

However even the most cavalier test user must sometimes recognise that the numbers which they so revere may give rise to misleading results. Chapter 5 dealt with correlations and showed that the following (among other things) can influence the size and, in some cases, even the direction of the correlation between two variables:

- differences in scores between sub-groups of people;
- variables having different distributions of scores (for example, where one is skewed and the other is not);
- measuring variables which are discreet rather than continuous, particularly when the number of categories is small as when responses to ability items are coded as correct or incorrect;
- using a sample where the range of scores differs from what is normally found in the population – for example, basing an analysis of cognitive tests on scores from university students and people with learning difficulties, or IQ with just a sample of university students;
- making errors when handling missing data.

As the first step of a factor analysis involves correlating all of the variables together, there is plenty of scope for these problems to creep in – an issue that has the potential to make the results of the analysis meaningless.

VARIABLES MUST BE INDEPENDENT

It is also necessary to ensure that all of the variables being measured are independent; in other words, there is no reason (other than perhaps something to do with personality, mood, ability, knowledge or some other psychological variable) why the response made to one item should influence the response made to another item. Readers of Chapter 2 will be familiar with my ascerbic views about questionnaires which essentially repeat the same item several times, a clear example of data which are not suitable for factor analysis (and where the use of factor analysis will seem to give a thin veneer of scientific respectability to what is patently obvious to anyone who bothers to read the items). However, it can also happen when items are combined to form several different scales – as with the old Minnesota Multiphasic Personality Inventory (MMPI; Hathaway and McKinley, 1940). Here one item could contribute to several different scales, and so it makes no sense to factor analyse these scale scores. For example, if individuals produce scores on four test items, it would be permissible to create and factor new variables such as

(Item 1 + Item 2) and (Item 3 + Item 4)

or (Item 1 + Item 2 − Item 3) and (1 − Item 4),

but not (Item 1 + Item 2 + Item 3) and (Item 4 − Item 1)

or (Item 1) and (Item 1 + Item 2 + Item 3 + Item 4)

as in the latter two cases, one of the observed test items ('Item 1') affects two of the variables being factored.

Similar problems can arise when analysing data from behaviour checklists, electrophysiological responses or otherwise coding mutually incompatible behaviours. For example, if a 'time sampling' method is used to record what a child is doing in various 30-second periods, the variables might include 'playing alone', 'playing with other children', 'sleeping' etc. The problem is that, when a child is sleeping, it cannot also be playing – either with other children or alone. When it is playing with other children, it cannot be sleeping or playing alone and so on. The variables are not independent. Likewise, when coding responses to a projective test, one could not have items such as 'says that central figure is their mother' and 'says that central figure is their father'. One has to be careful to ensure that the variables being factor analysed are genuinely independent; in other words, that a person's response to one of the variables does not affect their response to any other variable other than through the influence of the developmental, psychological social or physiological process which the test/ assessment is trying to measure.

THE VARIABLES MUST NOT COME FROM IPSATISED SCALES

It is not possible to factor analyse all of the scores from any test where it is impossible for a person to obtain an extremely high (or extremely low) score on *all* of its scales (known as 'ipsatised tests' and discussed in Chapter 2) as all of the scales of such tests are bound to be negatively correlated. Advocates of these tests claim that it is possible simply to drop one of the scales before factoring. However, the interpretation of the results will be affected by the (arbitrary) choice of which scale to omit, which makes the whole exercise rather pointless.

THE CORRELATION MATRIX SHOULD CONTAIN SOME NON-ZERO CORRELATIONS

Although not strictly a requirement for factor analysis, it is usual to check whether the correlation matrix shows several reasonably large correlations – normally by looking at it and ensuring that some are larger than about 0.3. If all of the correlations are tiny, then one should seriously question whether any factors are there to be extracted – and if an analysis of such a matrix *is* attempted, it follows that because correlations are minuscule, the communalities of the variables will also be small, which means that huge sample sizes will be needed, as described below.

If correlations are small because of the use of tests with low reliability, it may be appropriate to correct for the effects of unreliability, as shown in Chapter 5. Likewise, if poor experimental design led to data being collected from a group of restricted range (e.g., ability scores being obtained from a sample of university students rather than from a sample of the general population), it might be appropriate to correct the correlations for this using the formula of Dobson (1988) as discussed in Chapter 5. However, such pieces of psychometric wizardry should be used with caution and are really no substitute for sound and thoughtful experimental design.

There are statistical tests (such as Bartlett's Test of Sphericity and the Kaiser–Meyer–Olkin [KMO] measure of sampling adequacy; Bartlett, 1950, Kaiser, 1970, 1981) that show whether the correlation matrix contains many non-zero correlations. A useful discussion of their use is given by Dziuban and Shirkey (1974). The Bartlett test is very sensitive to sample size, and minuscule correlations between variables from a large sample will lead the test to indicate that factor analysis is appropriate – a point made by Bartlett (1950) himself. This makes it of limited (if any) use. In addition, there is no way of interpreting the KMO statistic other than by using 'rules of thumb' rather than anything based on empirical data or statistical theory. To misquote Alice in Wonderland, 'What is the use of a statistic . . . without effect sizes or significance levels?' The Bartlett and KMO statistics are widely quoted, probably because they are calculated by popular statistical packages, and quoting them gives authors the appearance of statistical expertise. But, at the end of the day, if the correlations are all close to zero, implying that there are no factors to extract, this is what the factor analysis will show. I cannot see the point of statistical tests such as these.

MISSING DATA

Missing data can be a curse. If a small amount of data is missing and this is scattered randomly throughout the data matrix (for example, if a few people have forgotten to answer the occasional question in a personality questionnaire), there are few problems. There are three options for dealing with it. The first is to drop from the analysis everyone who has any missing data. This is (perhaps) the safest option, though it is worthwhile checking demographics and other test scores of people who omit items to ensure that they are, indeed, a random sample of the population. Second, one can ignore missing data and base the correlation between two items on the scores of people who have answered both of them; this means that the correlations will be based on slightly different numbers of cases. This can be a problem, as discussed in the next paragraph. Finally, the missing data could be estimated, as described in Chapter 3.

It would not be wise to factor analyse data where a proportion of the sample omitted to take complete tests or blocks of items. For example, some people may have taken tests A, B and C. Others may have taken tests A and C only, and others may have taken only tests B and C. Because of this, it would not be legitimate to factor analyse these data although several statistical packages will do so without a murmur.

Ability tests with time limits are particularly problematical as quite a lot of people will not have time to answer the last few items in the scale and those who do so are unlikely to be a random sample of the participants – they are likely to be highly able, which will tend to reduce the size of the correlations between these difficult items (see the discussion of attenuation in Chapter 5). For this reason, it is wise to allow participants (nearly) unlimited time to complete ability tests when developing (and factor analysing) them and only afterwards impose time limits.

STAGE 2: SAMPLE SIZE FOR FACTOR ANALYSIS

Each factor analysis is based on a correlation matrix – and when the number of variables is large, the number of correlations in these matrices becomes huge; it is $N \times (N-1)/2$, where N is the number of variables being factor analysed. Thus if 50 variables are being factor analysed, the analysis is based on 1225 correlations. These correlations are calculated from a sample, which we hope and pray will be sufficiently large and representative to produce correlations that are fairly close to the correlations that we would obtain were we to test all the people in the population. But because we just test a sample, rather than the population, each of these correlations will vary a little from the true (population) value. For example, suppose that the correlation between two variables is 0.25 in the population; if we calculate the correlation between these two variables from a sample of (say) 100 people, we might find that the correlation was 0.22. In another sample of 100 people it might be 0.2 and so on. The problem is that if just one of these correlations is quite a lot larger or smaller than the value in the population, the factor structure will be inaccurate – and with so many correlations being calculated, the chances are high that some of the correlations will be quite a lot larger or smaller than their true values in the population.

There is some good statistical theory underlying this. Every time we calculate a correlation, we can also calculate a statistic known as its 'standard error'. This shows how much larger or smaller than its true value a correlation is likely to be, given the size of our sample. For example, if the true value of the correlation is 0.25, and we gather data from several samples each containing data from 100 people, we should not be surprised if the correlation is as small as 0.06 or as high as 0.43 in some of these samples – for such extreme values will be found in about 5% of the samples.

Of course, when we calculate a great many correlations (as when performing a factor analysis) the problem becomes worse. This is because when we calculate many correlations, the chances of *at least one* of them being quite a lot larger or smaller than it should be, just because of chance variations in the people we sampled, will obviously be larger than the chances of *just one* of them being quite a lot larger or smaller than their true value.

Spreadsheet 9.1 is very simple-minded and shows how much the correlations are likely to deviate from their 'true' values by taking a sample of a particular size. For example, if the true correlation between two variables is 0.6 (in other words, the correlation calculated from all members of a particular population is 0.6) but we sample just 10 people from that population, the correlation calculated from those 10 people could be as low as −0.48 or as high as 0.89. More specifically, the values of the correlation will be more extreme than these values in 0.05 of the samples we draw, which is what alpha=0.05 means. So, if we believe that the correlation between two variables in the population is (say) 0.3, it is possible to see how much larger or smaller a single correlation might be. If it is assumed that all the correlations are zero in the population, the spreadsheet also shows what range of correlations are likely to be found.

EXERCISE 9.1: CONFIDENCE INTERVALS FOR CORRELATIONS

Resources required: Spreadsheet 9.1: Confidence intervals for correlations. From www.routledge.com/9781138228894

Purpose: To show what variation in correlations should be expected by chance

Contents of spreadsheet: Typical values for the number of variables, correlations and significance level (alpha)

Suggested activity:

- Note what happens when the sample size increases for several values of correlation; for example, when the population correlation is 0.1, 0.25 and 0.5. How large does the sample size need to be in order to be fairly sure that the correlation calculated from one sample of people (which is what psychologists normally analyse) is fairly close to the true (population) value? You might like to explore this for various sample sizes by drawing on your 'intuition' and/or knowledge of the sample sizes used in published factor analytic studies.
- If all of the correlations are zero in the population, there are no factors to find. However, sampling variations mean that some quite large correlations may emerge, and it is perfectly possible that factor analysing data from a small sample of people will cause these to be mistaken for genuine factors. When the population correlation is set to zero, the spreadsheet also shows how large the largest correlation in the matrix is likely to be. For example, if 20 variables are correlated based on a sample size of 70, there is a one-in-twenty chance that one of the correlations in this matrix will be as extreme as +/−0.418, rather than zero. Alter the number of people in each sample to see how large the sample needs to be to avoid misleading oneself.

Points to note:

- Alpha here refers to the probability of making a Type I error, *not* reliability.

Learning outcomes:

Readers should now be able to

- appreciate that performing factor analysis with small samples is unwise.

So how large should the sample be in order to perform a factor analysis? Experts vary in their recommendations, but factor analysis should not be attempted if the number of subjects is less than 100. Otherwise the correlations computed from this sample of people will differ substantially from those which would have been obtained from another sample, giving results which are unreplicable and which are not a good approximation of what the relationship between the variables really is in the population.

It used to be thought that it is also necessary to relate sample size to the number of variables being analysed. For example, Nunnally (1978) advocated that there should be at least 10 times as many cases as variables. More recent studies (Barrett and Kline, 1981a; Guadagnoli and Velicer, 1988) show that, so long as there are more people than variables, the ratio of subjects to variables is not as important as absolute sample size and the size of the factor loadings. Thus, if the factors are well defined (e.g., with loadings of 0.7 rather than 0.4), one needs a smaller sample to find them. If the data being analysed are known to be highly reliable (e.g., test scores, rather than responses to individual items), it should be possible to relax these guidelines somewhat. However, attempts to factor analyse small sets of data are doomed to failure as the large standard errors of the correlations ensure that the factor solution will be both arbitrary and unreplicable.

MacCallum et al. (1999) offer one of the best treatments of this issue that I know. Their analysis based on simulated data shows that the following variables influence the replicability of factor analyses:

1   The size of the loadings (or communality of the variables). A set of variables yielding factors with small loadings (e.g., 0.4 rather than 0.6) will be harder to find/ replicate for a given sample size. The guidelines given in the paper assume a factor analysis has been performed – not a component analysis.
2   The number of variables per factor. If a large number of variables have substantial loadings on a factor, it will be easier to replicate the factor structure than if only a few variables have large loadings. For example, if ten variables have factor loadings greater than 0.4, this factor will be easier to replicate than if only four variables have loadings above 0.4.
3   The size of the sample, which interacts with the other two influences.

The problem is that, until one has performed the analysis, one cannot know how large the communalities of the variables will be. If the study is *truly* exploratory, then one will not know how many variables will have large loadings on each factor either. So, when designing a study, it seems sensible to stick to these authors' recommendation of a minimum sample size of 500, bearing in mind that even this will not be adequate if the communalities of the variables are low, which is often the case for personality items. On the other hand, if the communalities of the variables are large (above about 0.7 when performing factor analysis not principal-component analysis), smaller samples and smaller numbers of variables per factor will be acceptable. However, it must be said that I have rarely encountered communalities this large when performing real-life factor analyses. Factor analyses of test items pose a particular problem here; as responses to individual items are severely affected by measurement error, in my experience, the chance of any of them achieving a communality greater than about 0.3 is minuscule. Factor analysing test items will almost always require huge samples, and even then there is no guarantee that the findings would be replicable.

Performing and interpreting factor analyses with small samples and identifying factors on which only a few (say three or four) variables have large loadings is a waste of everybody's time unless the communalities of the variables are large. And, unless there is excellent reason to suppose that the number of variables per factor and the communalities of these variables will be large, it would be foolhardy to perform a factor analysis with fewer than about 500 participants – and even this may not be sufficient, according to MacCallum et al. (1999).

STAGE 3: CALCULATING CORRELATIONS

RATIO-LEVEL DATA

Most statistics packages assume that factor analyses are to be performed on interval or ratio-scaled data – numbers representing proper physical measurements. For example, if we measured the amount of time it took people to correctly solve a set of visualisation puzzles, their heart rate, their skin resistance, the number of books they say they read last year, the amount of time it takes them to recognise a threatening (rather than an unthreatening) word and so on, there would be no problem performing a factor analysis using Pearson correlations, provided that the variables are not too skewed in opposite directions.

ORDINAL DATA

Responses to Likert scales can probably best be regarded as ordinal data – where we can be fairly confident that one response (strongly agreeing versus agreeing, for example) indicates a higher level of some behaviour than another, but we cannot be sure whether the change in the level of the trait between a rating of 'strongly agree' (coded 5) and 'agree' (coded 4) is the same as between – say – 'agree' and 'neutral' (coded 3).

Some psychologists thus used to perform factor analyses using non-parametric correlations, such as Spearman's rho, rather than Pearson correlations. In practice, this can be a laborious process as many popular statistical packages assume that anyone performing a factor analysis will want to use Pearson correlations and so offer no other options. Opinions were divided about the legitimacy of such analyses; Gorsuch (1983) argued that non-parametric correlations might be useful whilst Cattell (1978) and Nunnally (1978) argued against their use in factor analysis – although these comments were, of course, made before Michell's (1997a) critique. That said, it should be remembered that Spearman's rho is identical to a Pearson correlation performed on ranks, and so it shares all of the desirable properties of the Pearson correlation – lying between −1 and 1, and producing a correlation matrix where none of the eigenvalues are negative.

We have already encountered the tetrachoric correlation for correlating together two dichotomous (two-valued) variables – for example, responses to ability items where '1' indicates a correct answer and '0' an incorrect answer. In Chapter 5, we showed that calculating the Pearson correlation was not a good idea for these variables, for, if the items differ in difficulty, the correlation falls. The same problem also affects scores on Likert scales, only to a somewhat smaller extent. It is possible to extend the idea of the tetrachoric correlation to deal with Likert-scaled variables or similar. For example, scores on a five-point Likert scale may be used to give a rough approximation of people's scores on some normally distributed trait. The polychoric correlation between two Likert-scaled variables estimates what the correlation between the two underlying normal variables would have been. This process is mathematically and computationally complex. Furthermore, it is necessary to *assume* that some continuous variable underlies the scores which we observe – and of course there is normally no way of testing whether this assumption is correct.

In addition, Kampen and Swyngedouw (2000) argue that items which ask respondents to rate how much they agree with statements (the format used in most personality questionnaires) are singularly inappropriate for analysis using polychoric correlations because there may not be just one variable which determines how a person will rate their level of agreement.

> A respondent may have one set of arguments for not-agreeing and another set of arguments for agreeing, some of which could be additive, but others may have the effect of a veto (by nature a boolean variable). This implies that not one, but several underlying variables may exist which may or may not be metric.
>
> (Kampen and Swyngedouw, 2000: 94)

So whilst polychoric correlations may be suitable for some variables, they may not be for others; the assumption of a single normally distributed underlying variable just may not apply.

Psychologists are generally uninterested in exploring the cognitive processes that cause a person to answer a personality item in a certain way (but see Arro, 2013; Rosenbaum and Valsiner, 2011). However, without knowing these it is hard to know whether it is sensible to make strong assumptions about the presence of some underlying continuous variable. I have less of a problem using the data for computing Pearson (or Spearman) correlations, for, in that case, if people use very different criteria for answering a question, the analysis will show that it does not load cleanly on one factor. It is when one needs to make assumptions (on the basis of zero evidence) about these processes before calculating the correlations that I start to feel uneasy.

If polychoric correlations are calculated and factor analysed, it will sometimes be found that the factor analysis program fails because the matrix of polychoric correlations yields some negative eigenvalues. Choosing an option such as 'unweighted least squares', also known as 'ordinary least squares' or 'principal-axes factoring' should solve the problem; failing that it is possible to 'smooth' the correlation matrix (e.g., Knol and Tenberge, 1989) – adjusting the correlations slightly to eliminate the negative eigenvalues(s). The R environment has routines which will do so though one might perhaps worry about whether the polychoric correlations cause more problems than they solve if smoothing is necessary.

So what should happen in practice?

It has been shown empirically that if scores on a normally distributed variable are split into categories, the correlations based on the categorised data are rather close to the correlations based on the original, uncategorised data so long as the number of categories is larger than about four (Bollen and Barb, 1983). So, if a variable is measured on a five-point scale or larger, there is arguably little point going to the trouble of computing polychoric correlations, smoothing them etc.

I take a rather pragmatic view about whether or not to use polychoric correlations. Doing so is unlikely to do harm, provided that one is happy with the assumption that the underlying variable is indeed both continuous and normally distributed and that one is happy to discount the issues raised by Kampen and Swyngedouw (2000). In practice, the difference between the polychoric and Pearson correlations is likely to be fairly small by comparison with the other effects noted above (differences in distributions, subgroups with the samples etc.), and, if the number of categories is five or more, it is probably not necessary to compute polychoric correlations.

The Factor program (Lorenzo-Seva and Ferrando, 2006) will calculate either Pearson or polychoric correlations, and it can be fun to compute both and notice if and when they differ appreciably. I would certainly recommend computing polychoric (tetrachoric) correlations when factor analysing binary data – such as ability items which are coded as correct or incorrect. In this case it is evidently reasonable to suppose that the underlying ability is continuous but that items differ in their easiness (proportion of people who answer them correctly). Computing Pearson correlations in this instance is misleading, as large Pearson correlations can only arise when two items have similar difficulties.

EXERCISE 9.2: FACTOR ANALYSIS OF
PEARSON AND POLYCHORIC CORRELATIONS

Resources required: Dataset '1 factor 3 levels of difficulty.dat' from
www.routledge.com/9781138228894. Factor program. Download details are in the
'internet software links document' in the zip files at www.routledge.com/9781138228894

Purpose: To show a situation where Pearson and polychoric correlations can be very
different

Contents of data file: Answers to nine ability items, where 1 indicates a correct
answer and 0 an incorrect answer. Three of the items are easy, three are of average
difficulty and three are difficult. Roughly a third of the 272 participants are highly
able, a third have average ability and a third have low ability.

Suggested activity:

- Use the Factor program (Lorenzo-Seva and Ferrando, 2006) or similar to analyse
  the data file '1 factor 3 levels of difficulty.dat' using both polychoric and Pearson
  correlations.

Points to note:

- The polychoric correlations are much larger than the Pearson correlations (for
  example, the correlation between Item 1 and Item 9 is 0.657, versus 0.252, as you
  should verify).

Learning outcomes:

Readers should now be able to

- appreciate that if the items in a test differ considerably in their level of difficulty and
  the people in the sample differ appreciably in their level of ability, then Pearson
  correlations will tend to be considerably smaller than tetrachoric correlations;
- appreciate that the choice of which coefficient to use can therefore have a major
  impact on the factor structure which is found.

NOMINAL (CATEGORICAL) DATA

It should be obvious, but categorical data, where numbers are assigned arbitrarily to
levels of some variable, are not suitable for factor analysis. For example, suppose that
a researcher gathered data from several towns and decided (quite arbitrarily) to code
location as London=1, Chicago=2 and Toronto=3. Because these codes are arbitrarily

assigned, it makes no sense to correlate them with anything because different results would be obtained if the codes had been assigned differently. So it makes no sense to include any such variables in factor analyses.

STAGE 4: FACTOR ANALYSIS OR COMPONENT ANALYSIS?

One school of thought maintains that factor (rather than component) analysis should never be used because of the difficulty in estimating communalities – the estimation of factor scores when performing factor analysis also turns out to be surprisingly unpleasant. The second school of thought maintains that, as the factor model is a priori much more likely to fit the data, any attempt to estimate communalities is better than none. Interested readers should see Velicer and Jackson (1990) for a more detailed discussion of this topic. My personal preference would normally be to perform factor analysis.

When performing components analysis, the communality of each variable is 1.0 – because variations in the scores on each variable are assumed to be explained entirely by all of the common factors (apart from measurement error). When performing factor analysis, the communality of each variable is assumed to be less than 1 – because the common factors themselves are thought not to explain all of the variation in the scores of the variable. Part of the variation is due to the unique factor belonging to that variable. So, if a variable has a unique factor loading of 0.6, 0.6×0.6=36% of the variation in scores on that variable is due to that unique factor. Therefore the variance to be explained by the common factors (its communality) is only 64%.

There are several ways of estimating the communality of each variable, and these are explored in the factor extraction section later in this chapter.

STAGE 5: TESTS FOR THE NUMBER OF FACTORS

Several tests have been developed to help analysts to choose the 'correct' number of factors. These tests require careful consideration, and one cannot rely on computer packages to make this important decision as many (including SPSS) use a technique which is known to be flawed and fail to incorporate some of the more useful tests. Determining the number of factors to be extracted is probably the most important decision that one has to make when conducting a factor analysis. A faulty decision here can produce a nonsensical solution from even the clearest set of data. There is no harm in trying several analyses based on differing numbers of factors and in using several different tests to guide the choice of factors.

The first guides are theory and past experience. One may sometimes want to use factor analysis to ensure that a test is performing as expected when used within a different culture, patient group or whatever. Confirmatory factor analysis can be used for this purpose (see Chapter 11), but, if exploratory factor analysis is preferred, the previous results can be used to guide one in deciding how many factors to extract. For example, if a (technically adequate) factor analysis of a test in the UK revealed seven factors, any attempt to factor analyse the tests in the USA should at least consider the seven-factor solution.

Theory and past practice are all very well, but many factor analyses are truly exploratory in nature. The researcher may have no good theoretical rationale for deciding how many factors should be extracted. There are a number of other tests which can be used in such circumstances, all of which seek to determine the number of factors that should be extracted from a correlation matrix. The problem is that few of them have been implemented in the computer packages likely to be encountered by non-expert users. Second, the various techniques do not always yield consistent results. One test may point to six factors, another to eight and previous research to nine! In circumstances such as this, it is safest to consider a number of solutions and check them for psychological plausibility. Users should also consider the following:

- Does increasing the number of factors increase the 'simplicity' of the solution (such as decreasing the proportion loadings in the range of –0.4 to 0.4)? If increasing the number of factors does little or nothing to increase the simplicity of the solution, it is arguably of little value.
- Do any large correlations between factors emerge when using oblique solutions? These can indicate that too many factors have been extracted, and that two factors are trying to pass through the same cluster of variables. Correlations between factors larger than around 0.4 could be regarded as suspect.
- Have any well-known factors split into two or more parts? For example, if a myriad of previous studies show that a set of items form just one factor (e.g. extraversion), yet they seem to form two factors in your analysis, it is likely that too many factors have been extracted.

That said, it seems that if there *is* any doubt as to how many factors to rotate, it may be better to extract too many rather than too few.

THE KAISER–GUTTMAN CRITERION

One of the oldest and simplest tests for the number of factors is that described by Kaiser (1960) and Guttman (1954) and known as the 'Kaiser–Guttman criterion'. It has the advantage of being very straightforward. One simply performs a principal-components analysis on the data, extracting as many factors as there are variables but without rotating the factors. The eigenvalues are calculated as usual by summing the squared loadings on each component. One then simply counts how many eigenvalues are greater than 1.0 – this is the number of factors to be used.

There are many problems with this technique, the most obvious being its sensitivity to the number of variables in the analysis. As each eigenvalue is simply the sum of the squared factor loadings, if the number of variables is large, so too will be the eigenvalue. A test for the number of factors should give the same result whether or not there are four or 40 variables representing each factor, and the Kaiser–Guttman test manifestly will not do so. Furthermore, Hakstian and Mueller (1973) observed that the technique was never intended to be used as a test for the number of factors. Because it is extremely easy to implement automatically, most statistical packages will perform a Kaiser–Guttman test by default. It should *always* be overridden.

THE SCREE TEST

The scree test, devised by Cattell (1966) is also conceptually simple. Like the Kaiser–Guttman criterion, it is based on the eigenvalues of an initial unrotated principal-components solution. However, it draws on the *relative* values of the eigenvalues, and so should not be sensitive to variations in the number of variables being analysed. Successive principal components explain less and less variance, and so the eigenvalues decrease. The scree test is based on visual inspection of a graph showing the successive eigenvalues, such as that illustrated in Figure 9.1.

Figure 9.1 Scree test showing eigenvalues from an unrotated principal-components analysis of nine variables. The graph indicates that two factors should be extracted

The basic idea is simple. It is clear that the points on the right-hand side of Figure 9.1 form a straight line, known as a 'scree slope'. It is possible to put a ruler through these points and to determine how many eigenvalues lie well above this line. This is the number of factors which should then be extracted. Thus Figure 9.1 depicts a two-factor solution. Further examples of the interpretation of scree tests are given in the literature (Cattell, 1966; Cattell, 1978; Cattell and Vogelman, 1977). Several popular texts on factor analysis describe the scree test incorrectly by asserting that the number of factors corresponds to the number of eigenvalues above the scree line *plus one*. They would thus advocate extracting three factors from the above solution. It is not obvious where this confusion arose, as Cattell's papers and 1978 book are quite clear on the matter; 'the last real factor is that before the scree begins' (Cattell and Vogelman, 1977: 290).

A problem with the scree test is that it does rely on subjective judgement and may sometimes have several possible interpretations, particularly when the sample size or the 'salient' factor loadings are small (Gorsuch, 1983). Sometimes more than one clearly identifiable straight scree slope is found. In such cases, one simply looks for the eigenvalues which lie above the leftmost scree slope.

PARALLEL ANALYSIS

Simulation studies show that parallel analysis is the most accurate way of determining the correct number of factors to extract (Velicer et al., 2000; Zwick and Velicer, 1986), provided that the data being analysed are measured on a continuous scale or a Likert scale with more than two values (Tran and Formann, 2009). Now that computers are powerful enough to enable its use, it should be the method of choice. The basic principle is quite simple. It involves checking whether each of the eigenvalues that emerges from a principal-components analysis is larger than you would expect by chance.

Suppose that you gather data on 10 variables and 100 people and factor analyse the results (but without rotating the factors). The factor analysis program will produce a list of eigenvalues, as many eigenvalues as there are variables.

Now perform another factor analysis, but, rather than using the data that you have collected, just analyse random data (again using 10 variables, 100 people). You could literally just type in numbers at random into the computer program that you use for factor analysis. Then run the factor analysis again, based on this random data. You would expect the correlations between these random variables to be roughly zero – though some will be a little larger than zero, and some smaller than zero by chance. (The size of your sample will affect how close to zero they are; with a small sample, you might find that some correlations are as large as 0.3 or as small as −0.3; with a large sample, few if any will be above 0.1 or less than −0.1.) This approach, generating lots of sets of data and seeing what happens when you analyse them in a particular way, is known as a Monte Carlo analysis. There are several variations possible – for example, rather than generating random data, one can simply mix up the rows of the data matrix – so one person's response to Item 1 is followed by another person's response to Item 2 and so on. This has the advantage of making sure that the frequency distribution of the variables is always the same although the correlations between them should be close to zero.

It should hopefully be obvious that, if all the correlations are zero, no factors are present in the data. But some of the correlations will be greater or less than zero just because of chance sampling variations. The question is whether the eigenvalues from the data are larger than would be expected by chance – that is, from factor analysing correlations between random numbers.

The problem is that we have only looked at one set of random data – and of course the correlations (and the eigenvalues) will vary depending what set of random numbers we typed in. So it is necessary to repeat the factor analysis many times – a thousand times, for example – using a different set of random data each time to get an idea of how large the eigenvalues typically are; a statistician would say that you find the 'sampling distribution' of the eigenvalues. Then you simply work out the average size of the first eigenvalue, the second eigenvalue etc. by averaging across all 1000 analyses. You also find the 95% confidence limit; this is the value of each eigenvalue that is only exceeded on 5% of the 1000 trials. We call this the critical value.

That is all there is to performing parallel analysis. The first eigenvalue from the analysis of the real data is compared with the critical value found from the random data. If the real eigenvalue is larger than the critical value for the first eigenvalue from random data, there is at least one factor in the real data and the process is repeated for the second, third, fourth factors etc. – until one of the eigenvalues is smaller than the corresponding critical value.

For example, suppose that, when correlations between 10 variables derived from 100 participants were factor analysed, the first few eigenvalues were 2.9, 1.63, 1.27, 1.14 and 0.97. Scores on 10 random variables were also generated from 100 participants, a principal-components analysis was performed and the 10 eigenvalues were calculated. This procedure was repeated 1000 times, and the average value for each eigenvalue was found – and also the value for each eigenvalue that was only exceeded in 5% (50) of the 1000 replications. How many factors are present in these data? To answer this question using parallel analysis, the critical values in the final column of Table 9.1 should be compared with the eigenvalues from the real data. The first eigenvalue from the real data (2.9) is larger than the critical value for the first eigenvalue in the table (1.68), so it is unlikely that one would find such a large eigenvalue by chance (i.e., by factor analysing random data). So there is at least one factor in the data. Likewise, the second

Table 9.1 Eigenvalues obtained from factor analysing 1000 random correlation matrices based on 10 variables and 100 participants

Eigenvalue number	Average eigenvalue from the analysis of 1000 sets of random data	Critical value based on the 95% confidence limit; only 5%, or 50, of the random eigenvalues were larger than the values shown here
1	1.53	1.68
2	1.36	1.47
3	1.23	1.31
4	1.12	1.20
5	1.02	1.09
6	0.93	1.00
7	0.84	0.91
8	0.75	0.82
9	0.66	0.74
10	0.56	0.64

eigenvalue (1.63) is bigger than 1.47, so there are at least two factors present. The third eigenvalue (1.27), however, is smaller than the critical value of 1.31; it is therefore quite possible that a third eigenvalue as large as 1.27 could have arisen by chance. So one would conclude that there are just two factors in the data.

You should be concerned about where the numbers in Table 9.1 came from. I did not spend weeks typing 1000 sets of random numbers (each involving 10 variables and 100 participants) into a spreadsheet and performing 1000 factor analyses, laboriously tabulating the results. The Factor computer program (Lorenzo-Seva and Ferrando, 2006) will perform this analysis. It generates the table of simulated eigenvalues automatically and will use the parallel analysis method to advise on the number of factors in the data. Several other computer programs and websites (search for 'parallel analysis') also perform parallel analysis. It is just necessary to specify the number of variables and participants in your real data and the number of replications to be performed, and the program or website will produce a table such as that shown in Table 9.1 within a few seconds. This may be used to determine the appropriate number of factors, as shown above. It is then necessary to analyse your 'real' data using your favourite statistical package and specify that it should extract this number of factors (rather than using the default test).

One word of warning: the critical values for the eigenvalues depend on the number of variables and the number of participants in the factor analysis. The values shown in Table 9.1 will only be correct should you want to find the number of factors present when analysing 10 variables and have gathered data from 100 participants. It will be necessary to produce your own version of this table for every set of real data that you need to analyse.

OTHER TECHNIQUES

The Minimum Average Partial ('MAP') test (Velicer, 1976) is another consistently accurate technique for estimating the appropriate number of factors (Zwick and Velicer, 1986) and the Factor package (Lorenzo-Seva and Ferrando, 2006) is one of the few programs that will also perform it. If too many factors are extracted from a correlation matrix, the last ones tend to have only one or two large loadings. The MAP test tries to identify when this happens by looking at the size of the partial correlations between the variables after extracting successive principal components. When the average of the partial correlations reaches a minimum, this indicates the point at which all the common factors have been removed.

Another useful (but straightforward) technique is Revelle and Rocklin's (1979) 'Very Simple Structure' (VSS) test for the number of factors. The rest of this paragraph will probably only make sense after reading the 'factor rotation' section of this chapter. If there are n variables, the VSS test involves performing n factor analyses, extracting and rotating[1] one, two, three . . . n factor solutions. In each case a simplified factor pattern matrix is calculated from the factor pattern matrix, where each variable's largest loading[2] is kept unchanged but all other loadings are changed to zero. This resembles the way in which factor matrices are generally interpreted. A statistic is calculated which evaluates how well this simplified factor matrix fits the original correlation matrix; the authors demonstrate that when too many factors are extracted, the goodness of fit becomes worse. Thus the solution where the simplified pattern matrix best fits the data indicates the optimal number of factors. It can be run from the R environment (Revelle, 2017b).

Reliable component analysis (Cliff and Caruso, 1998) is another method which is sometimes used, and preliminary studies suggest that Exploratory Graph Analysis (EGA) may be particularly useful when the correlations between factors are large – a condition where some other techniques struggle (Golino and Epskamp, 2017; Golino and Demetriou, 2017). Though promising, this last technique is very new, and the methodology (a network model, rather than conventional statistics) is best described as 'challenging'. There are other methods too, and the Factor program (Lorenzo-Seva and Ferrando, 2006) implements some other little-researched techniques whose value is uncertain. So how to choose between them?

Many of these tests have been applied to the same sets of simulated data, where the number of 'actual' factors is known. If we assume that these artificial data behave in much the same way as any set of real-life data (a rather major assumption), it is possible to determine which of these tests can best identify the true number of factors. There are several such studies (Golino and Epskamp, 2017; Velicer et al., 2000; Zwick and Velicer, 1986). To précis the main findings from these papers, parallel analysis, the MAP technique and the VSS criterion seem to generally perform well. The scree test sometimes does, whilst the Kaiser–Guttman is of little use. The VSS method does not work well if variables have large loadings on more than one or two factors – although in most practical applications this is unlikely to be an issue. Thus, when performing a factor analysis it makes sense to use parallel analysis (because of its sound statistical basis and its proven utility) in conjunction with one or two other techniques, such as the MAP or VSS. The VSS procedure is not particularly accessible (other than to users of the R package), however.

STAGE 6: COMMUNALITY ESTIMATION

We must first admit that the previous chapter deliberately oversimplified the process by which factors are positioned through the clusters of variables. In practice, this is performed in two stages. First, communalities are estimated, and the factors are placed in some arbitrary position relative to the variables (*factor extraction*); the factors are almost invariably at right angles at this point and will probably *not* pass neatly through the clusters of variables. Then another procedure (called *factor rotation*) is used to move the factors through the clusters of variables, possibly allowing the factors to become correlated.

The estimation of communalities is a process which worries factor analysts as there is no easy way of checking that one's estimates are correct. Indeed, the problems associated with this can drive some researchers to use the simpler component model, which assumes that the communality of each variable is 1.0. My own preference is clear. When analysing psychological data, it is better to try to estimate communalities rather than to make a completely unrealistic assumption about the data for the sake of mathematical convenience. That said, it would be unusual for the two techniques, factor analysis and component analysis, to give radically different results.

It used to be assumed that the square of the largest correlation between a variable and any other variable in the correlation matrix would give an estimate of the variable's communality. This is because the correlation between a variable and anything else cannot possibly be larger than the square root of the communality of the variable. (The obvious problem is that, if the variables measure different things, this will lead to a serious underestimation of the communality. And, if all of the *other* variables in a correlation matrix have a lot of measurement error associated with them, this will also underestimate a variable's communality.)

Then it was appreciated that the multiple correlation might be the way to go; the square of the multiple correlation obtained when trying to predict scores on a variable from all of the other variables in the correlation matrix might be better. Since the communality is defined as the proportion of a variable's variance that can be shared with the other variables in the analysis, it has been claimed that this gives the lower bound for the communality – the smallest value that the communality could possibly have, although a paper by Kaiser (1990) challenges this view.

Then an iterative process was developed – one starts off with some guess as to what the communalities might be (such as the largest correlation each variable has with any other variable, the squared multiple correlation – or just a number such as 0.8). Then one performs a 'principal-axes' factor analysis, as described below, and calculates what the communality is from the number of common factors extracted. This replaces the original estimate of communality, and the factor analysis is repeated. This sequence is repeated again and again until the estimate of communality does not change – or something goes hideously wrong and the communality exceeds 1.0. This last situation is known as a 'Heywood case' – a term which will occasionally be seen in an error message when performing factor analysis.

Two things should be noted about this iterative procedure.

First, the iterative process often seems to need far more steps than are specified by the default settings in computer packages before the communalities become stable, so it is well worth changing the default values used by packages such as SPSS to something large – e.g., 1000.

Second, according to Gorsuch (1983: 107) 'no proof has yet been presented to show that [the communalities] either must converge or that the value to which they converge is either the theoretical communality or less than the variable's reliability'. In other words, the estimate of each variable's communality might not be accurate.

These days, the communality of each variable can also be estimated without iteration by using maximum likelihood estimation when performing the factor analysis, and this is arguably the most appropriate procedure.

STAGE 7: FACTOR EXTRACTION

There are plenty of techniques for performing factor analysis, rejoicing in names such as Maximum Likelihood, Principal Factors, Generalised Least Squares, Weighted Least Squares, Alpha factoring and Image Analysis. They all use different mathematical methods to estimate communalities and position the factors relative to the variables before rotation takes place. The good news is that it does not matter much which method is used; Harman (1976 – and still a classic) demonstrated this by analysing the same sets of data by just about every conceivable method, and the consensus view about this has not changed.

Maximum-likelihood estimation is useful for two reasons; it is mathematically elegant, and it provides statistics which show how well the factor model fits the data although the interpretation of these statistics is still contentious as some of them are heavily influenced by sample size. The technique also has two disadvantages. It requires the assumption of 'multivariate normality' (the discussion of which is a little too mathematical for this book), and it will sometimes not work when analysing polychoric/tetrachoric correlations. Principal Factors/Principal Axis or Unweighted Least Squares/Ordinary Least Squares are good substitutes; the other methods are a little more esoteric, and so might require some justification for their use. The details of the mathematical methods described here are somewhat complex and so will not be explored further. Any good text on factor analysis such as Harman (1976), Gorsuch (1983) or Tabachnick and Fidell (2007) will allow the mathematically astute reader to master these issues.

All of the above-mentioned techniques for factor extraction therefore place the factors in essentially arbitrary locations relative to the variables. Typically, the factors are positioned so that each successive factor is placed

• at right angles to previous factors; and
• in a position where it 'explains' a substantial proportion of the variance of the items (i.e., so that it is close to as many variables as possible; this means that the correlations between the factor and at least some of the variables will be appreciable, and so the eigenvalue of the factor will also be large).

However, as these factors are placed in arbitrary positions, it makes no sense to interpret this 'unrotated factor matrix'.

STAGE 8: FACTOR ROTATION

Factor rotation changes the position of the factors relative to the variables so that the solution obtained is easy to interpret. As was mentioned in Chapter 8, factors are identified by observing which variables have large and/or zero loadings on them. The solutions which defy interpretation are those in which a large number of variables have 'mediocre' loadings on a factor – loadings of the order of 0.2 or 0.3. These are too small to be used to identify the factor yet too large to be treated as if they were zero. Factor rotation moves the factors relative to the variables so that each factor has a few substantial loadings and a few near-zero loadings. This is another way of saying that the factors are spun round until they pass through the clusters of variables, as was seen in Chapter 8.

Thurstone (1947) was probably the first to realise that the initial position of the factor axes was arbitrary and that such solutions were difficult to interpret and harder to replicate. He suggested that factors should be rotated and coined the term 'simple structure' to describe the case in which each factor has some large loadings and some small loadings, and, likewise, each variable has substantial loadings on only a few factors. Specifically, he made the following suggestions:

a) Each variable should have at least one near-zero loading on a factor.
b) Each factor should have at least as many near-zero loadings as there are factors.
c) Every pair of factors should have several variables whose loadings are near zero for one factor but not the other.
d) Whenever more than about four factors are extracted, every pair of factors should have a large portion of variables with zero weights in both factors.
e) Every pair of factors should have few variables with non-zero loadings in both factors.

For example, if two factors are extracted from the correlations between six variables, the correlations between each of the variables and each of the tables could resemble one of the five models shown in Table 9.2. Here a 'large' loading (one that lies between −0.4 and +0.4, by convention) is shown as an asterisk, a 'small' loading (between −0.39 and +0.39) is shown as a blank.

It is worth spending a little time appreciating what simple structure looks like by perusing this table as it is important to recognise it when interpreting factor matrices.

Table 9.3 demonstrates how much easier it is to interpret rotated rather than unrotated factor solutions. The unrotated solution has several loadings in the order of 0.2 or 0.3

Table 9.2 Five different two-factor solutions, only one of which demonstrates simple structure

	Simple structure			Fails Rules 1 & 2			Fails Rule 2			Fails Rule 3			Fails Rule 5	
	F1	F2		F1	F2		F1	F2		F1	F2		F1	F2
Var. 1	*			*			*	*		*			*	*
Var. 2		*		*	*			*					*	*
Var. 3		*		*				*					*	*
Var. 4	*			*	*		*						*	
Var. 5		*		*	*			*						*
Var. 6	*			*			*	*		*	*		*	

Note: An asterisk denotes a large factor loading. A blank entry denotes a near-zero loading.

Table 9.3 Rotated and unrotated factor matrices

Variable	Unrotated solution				VARIMAX rotated solution		
	F1	F2	Communality		F1	F2	Communality
Comprehension	−0.766	0.170	0.616		0.780	0.086	0.616
Spelling	−0.717	0.288	0.597		0.772	−0.042	0.597
Vocabulary	−0.718	0.143	0.535		0.725	0.096	0.535
Multiplication	−0.148	−0.684	0.489		−0.080	0.695	0.489
Matrices	−0.364	−0.524	0.408		0.176	0.614	0.408
Geometry	−0.244	−0.602	0.422		0.037	0.649	0.422
Eigenvalue	1.830	1.237	Sum=3.067		1.769	1.300	Sum=3.067

which are too large to ignore but not large enough to get excited about. After rotation, the solution could not be clearer. The first factor looks as if it measures language ability (because of its substantial loadings from the comprehension and spelling tests), whilst the second factor corresponds to numerical ability. The eigenvalues and communalities of the variables are also shown. This indicates that, during rotation, the communality of each variable stays the same, but the eigenvalues do not. However, the sum of the communalities (which equals the sum of the eigenvalues) stays the same. The rotated solution explains exactly the same amount of variance as the unrotated solution; it just distributes it differently between the factors.

One crucial decision has to be made when rotating factors. Should they be kept at right angles (an 'orthogonal rotation'), or should they be allowed to become correlated (an 'oblique rotation')? Since one never knows whether factors will be correlated, it is probably good practice to always perform an oblique rotation. However, the computation and interpretation of orthogonal solutions is considerably more straightforward, which accounts for their continued popularity.

Kaiser's (1958) VARIMAX algorithm is a method of rotation which MAXimises the VARIance of the squared factor loadings in order to find the best orthogonal simple structure rotation. Variance is maximised when each factor contains some large and some very small loadings – in other words, when simple structure has been reached. It is the overwhelmingly popular choice for orthogonal rotations, and many computer packages will perform it by default. Its rationale is quite straightforward and is best demonstrated using Spreadsheet 9.2 which allows you to perform a factor rotation 'by eye' and compares these results with the VARIMAX solution. It should provide evidence that the VARIMAX solution finds the same answer as eyeballing the data.

EXERCISE 9.3: VARIMAX ROTATION

Resources required: Spreadsheet 9.2: VARIMAX rotation. From www.routledge.com/9781138228894

Purpose:

- To show how VARIMAX works.
- To demonstrate that it produces the same solution as rotating factors by eye.
- To introduce the hyperplane count.

Contents of spreadsheet:

Four datasets (A–D), each showing an unrotated factor matrix with six variables and two factors

Suggested activity:

a) Copy and paste dataset A into the unrotated factor loading matrix. The rotated factor matrix is shown below, and a graph also shows a plot of the rotated factor loadings. The blue squares on the graph represent the arrowheads in Figure 8.2. You should convince yourself that the blue squares on the graph represent the values in the rotated factor matrix.

  o Does the unrotated matrix meet the criteria for simple structure shown in Table 9.2?
  o Underneath the graph is a green slider. Moving this sideways will rotate the variables relative to the factor axes.
  o Adjust the slider to identify the best 'simple structure' solution by eye – that is, find the position where each variable has a large loading on one factor but a small loading on the other. Note down the 'normalised VARIMAX' figure, below the slider.
  o Now adjust the slider without looking at the graph; instead, find the position where the value of the 'normalised VARIMAX' statistic is at a maximum. Does your eyeball come to the same conclusion as this statistic?
  o Check Table 9.2 to determine whether the solution has reached simple structure.

b) Repeat the process for Datasets B–D. For each dataset, notice how the information in the diagram is reflected in the rotated factor matrix. This is important, as computer programs do not usually print out diagrams, and so the interpretation of the results from a factor analysis relies entirely on how well one can understand the factor matrix.

Points to note:

- Dataset B clearly requires an oblique solution; it is impossible to position the variables on top of the right-angled factors.
- Dataset C represents random data without any real factor structure; it is hard to decide whether one position is better than another. None of the loadings in the rotated factor matrix are above 0.4.
- Dataset D: two factors are used to represent a one-factor solution; once again, the loadings fail to reach simple structure. The best solution places the variables at 45° to each of the factors.
- There is a correlation matrix at the bottom of each spreadsheet. Copying and pasting this into a text document allows the datasets to be analysed using the Factor program or similar.

Learning outcomes:

Readers should now be able to

- recognise simple structure when they see it;
- appreciate that the VARIMAX criterion positions factors sensibly and tries to ensure that they reach simple structure;
- appreciate that when there are the wrong number of factors or if orthogonal rotation is performed when oblique rotation is required, the solution may not reach simple structure.

Table 9.4 also shows these four sets of unrotated factor solutions.

Computer programs for factor rotation simply find the solution which maximises some mathematical criterion, such as the normalised VARIMAX criterion shown on the spreadsheet. They can deal with more than two factors (imagine a third axis sticking out from the spreadsheet with another slider under it). However, you may have noticed that when rotating the factors using the spreadsheet, the normalised VARIMAX criterion sometimes does not change very much even though the factor loadings do. In other words, there can be a range of almost equally good solutions, with slightly different factor loadings. Worse still, there may be two almost equally good solutions which have very different patterns of loadings. Computer programs will not warn you if/when this happens. It is therefore important to realise that factor loadings are really fairly crude; it would make no sense to argue that a variable with a loading of 0.5 is in some sense 'better' than one with a loading of 0.45, for example. All one can sensibly say is that both are reasonably large.

Table 9.4 Four sets of factor loadings for rotation using Spreadsheet 9.2

Dataset A: Two orthogonal factors				Dataset B: Two oblique factors		
	Factor 1	Factor 2			Factor 1	Factor 2
Var. 1	0.63	0.47		Var. 1	0.42	−0.54
Var. 2	0.53	0.56		Var. 2	0.63	−0.43
Var. 3	0.59	0.43		Var. 3	0.43	−0.27
Var. 4	0.42	−0.56		Var. 4	0.54	0.08
Var. 5	0.55	−0.33		Var. 5	0.60	0.20
Var. 6	0.47	−0.45		Var. 6	0.54	0.24
Dataset C: No factors				**Dataset D: One factor**		
	Factor 1	Factor 2			Factor 1	Factor 2
Var. 1	−0.20	0.22		Var. 1	−0.46	0.12
Var. 2	0.00	−0.30		Var. 2	−0.59	0.02
Var. 3	−0.20	−0.27		Var. 3	−0.44	−0.03
Var. 4	0.15	0.22		Var. 4	−0.48	−0.08
Var. 5	0.23	0.00		Var. 5	0.42	0.10
Var. 6	0.17	−0.32		Var. 6	0.43	−0.16

Sometimes it makes little sense to keep the factors at right angles; it can be seen that in the second dataset it is not really possible to position the factors close to the clusters of variables. Examining the rotated factor matrix shows that, rather than having a large loading on one factor and a near-zero loading on the other factor, variables sometimes have one large and one moderate loading, 0.2 or so. Seeing this in the VARIMAX rotated factor matrix can indicate that an oblique rotation is needed.

In the third case, there is no discernible simple structure – all of the data points are scattered around, and it is impossible to rotate the axes anywhere sensible. Again, this is reflected in the rotated factor matrix; just note how large the factor loadings are.

The fourth case is interesting. Here we have extracted too many factors; the correlation matrix contains one factor, but we attempt to rotate two factors. Rotating the factors to maximise the normalised VARIMAX criterion does not place the variables where one might expect if performing the rotation 'by eye'. Instead the rotation algorithm places the variables along a line midway between the two factors, as you should determine. This is reflected in the factor matrix, where there are no near-zero loadings, indicating that the rotation has not reached simple structure. This is an important point to remember. If a pair of factors have similar loadings and few near-zero loadings, this may indicate that either too many factors have been extracted or that an orthogonal rotation has been performed where an oblique one would be more appropriate (see Dataset B). The analysis should be run again using oblique rotation or with one fewer factor being extracted.

What is the difference between the 'normalised' VARIMAX criterion and the non-normalised one? Where the variables which form one factor have lower communalities than the variables which form the other factor, the VARIMAX criterion defined above (the variance of the squared loadings) tends to give more weight to the variables with the largest loadings. Hence the normalised VARIMAX criterion is generally used; this gives equal weight to all variables when deciding where to position them. The variables in Dataset A and Dataset B have somewhat different communalities, so it is worthwhile looking what happens when these are rotated using both criteria. For Dataset A the difference is fairly small; it is larger for Dataset B. As Revelle (2017a) observes, some statistical packages use the normalised criterion whilst others do not, and some (e.g., Factor) give users the choice of which to use. It always makes sense to choose the normalised version of any rotation algorithm.

OBLIQUE ROTATIONS

Whilst the factor structure matrix shows the correlations between all of the variables and all of the factors in Figure 8.3 we showed that, although each factor passes neatly through a cluster of variables, because the factors are correlated, it is no longer the case that each variable has a large loading (correlation) with just one factor. Alarmingly, opinions are divided as to whether the factor structure matrix or the factor pattern matrix should be interpreted in order to identify the factors or to report the results of factor analyses. For example, Kline (1994: 63) states that 'it is important . . . that the structure and not the pattern is interpreted', yet Cattell (1978, chapter 8), Tabachnick and Fidell (2007) and most others hold precisely the opposite view. Brogden (1969) suggests that, if the factor analysis uses well-understood tests but the interpretation of the factors is unknown, then the pattern matrix should be consulted. Conversely, if the nature of the factors is known but the nature of the items is not, then the structure matrix should be consulted. Brogden's justification for this position seems to be sound, and so one should normally interpret the pattern matrix.

Readers may wonder how one would ever be able to identify a factor but not the variables which load on it. However, this is possible. For example, a selection of behavioural or physiological measures may be correlated and factored. Factor scores might be computed for each person, and these may be correlated with other tests. If a set of factor scores shows a correlation of 0.7 with the subjects' scores on a reputable test of anxiety, it is fairly safe to infer that the factor measures anxiety. Alternatively, a few well-trusted tests may be included in the analysis to act as 'marker variables'. If these have massive loadings on any of the rotated factors, this clearly identifies the nature of those factors.

Several programs have been written to perform oblique rotations, and Clarkson and Jennrich (1988), Harman (1976) and Sass and Schmitt (2010) are among those who discuss the relationships between the various methods and evaluate their usefulness. However, the *important* decisions are whether to perform a component or a factor analysis, how many factors to rotate and whether to use an oblique or orthogonal rotation. In practice, it does not seem to matter too much which particular rotation technique is used. 'In reality, the selection of "best" rotation criterion must be made by the researcher. In many circumstances, different rotation criteria yield nearly identical rotated pattern loading matrices' (Sass and Schmitt, 2010: 99). Techniques such as (normalised) Direct Oblimin (Jennrich and Sampson, 1966) are among the more useful.

A point which is often overlooked is that oblique rotation programs need 'fine tuning' in order to reach simple structure (Harman, 1976), usually by means of a parameter (usually called delta or gamma) which controls how oblique the factors are allowed to become. This is set by default to a value which the program author rather hoped would be adequate most of the time. Using this value blindly is a dangerous, if common, practice. Harman suggests performing several rotations, each with a different value of this parameter, and interpreting that which comes closest to simple structure. Using normalised Direct Oblimin from the Factor program, it is possible to adjust gamma in the 'configure rotation' section; a large negative value (e.g., −100) will produce a factor pattern matrix which looks very much like the VARIMAX solution. Larger values (e.g., −30, −10, −1, 0, +0.2) will allow the factors to become more and more correlated. Values of delta larger than about +0.2 can cause problems as the program may try to place the factors on top of each other, which will crash the program. It is sensible to rotate the factors several times using several different values of delta and then interpret the solution which shows the best simple structure. One method for determining the 'best' simple structure might be to monitor the hyperplane count, as described below.

FACTOR ROTATION BY MONITORING HYPERPLANE COUNT

An alternative to the so-called 'analytic' methods of factor rotation, which rely on finding the maximum of some mathematical function, is to simply position the axes so that as many variables as possible have near-zero loadings on the factors. Variables with near-zero loadings are 'in the hyperplane'. It is possible to perform such a rotation using Spreadsheet 9.2. One simply specifies how wide the hyperplane should be (in other words, what value of factor loadings should be regarded as trivially small). Figures such as 0.1 or 0.2 are usual, implying that loadings between −0.1 and +0.1 or −0.2 and +0.2 are 'in the hyperplane'. One then rotates the solution to simply maximise the hyperplane count. What could be simpler?

EXERCISE 9.4: FACTOR ROTATION
BY MAXIMISING HYPERPLANE COUNT

Resources required: Spreadsheet 9.2: VARIMAX rotation. From www.routledge.com/9781138228894

Purpose: To explore rotation by maximising hyperplane count

Suggested activity:

- Use Spreadsheet 9.2: VARIMAX rotation to rotate factors so that the hyperplane count (shown below the graph) is maximised.
- Does this generally suggest the same rotation as normalised VARIMAX?

Points to note:

- Several rather different patterns of loadings have similar hyperplane counts, which may make the technique of limited use when the number of variables and factors is small.

Learning outcomes:

Readers should now be able to

- appreciate that maximising hyperplane count is a simple method of rotation to simple structure.

There are two main problems with this technique:

- First, the width of the hyperplane is arbitrary. If one gets a different set of factor loadings by maximising the number of variables in the 0.1 hyperplane and 0.2 hyperplane, how does one decide which solution is better?
- Several very different factor matrices can sometimes give the same (high) hyperplane count. This can be seen by rotating Dataset B. How does one decide which is the best?

This approach to factor rotation has not received much attention in the literature. This is partly because it was developed at more or less the same time as the mathematically elegant analytical solutions (VARIMAX, PROMAX etc.) beloved of psychometricians, and it also required a great deal of computational power, given the facilities then available. It also had the annoying habit of producing *very* highly correlated factors unless care was taken to prevent factors from piling up on top of each other.

Cattell's 'Maxplane' technique (Cattell and Muerle, 1960) was the first program to attempt this form of rotation and appears to give similar results to other methods of rotation (Gorsuch, 1970). Functionplane (Katz and Rohlf, 1974) is a later development which seems to overcome the two problems shown above. However, it does not seem to be implemented in any popular statistical packages – or even in R.

STAGE 9: FACTOR SCORES

Suppose that one factor analyses a set of test items which measure some mental ability, e.g., the speed with which people can visualise what various geometric shapes would look like after being rotated or flipped over. Having performed a factor or component analysis on these data, one might find that a single factor explains a good proportion of the variance, with many of the test items having substantial loadings on this factor. It is possible to validate this factor in exactly the same way as one would validate a test (as discussed in Chapter 7). For example, one can determine whether the factor correlates substantially with other psychological tests measuring spatial ability, measures of performance etc. However, in order to do this, it is necessary to work out each person's score on the factor – their 'factor score'.

Most readers will never need to compute a factor score and so can safely skip the remainder of this section. In any case, if factor analysis is being used to identify a group of items that will be put together as a scale, it makes more sense to determine how well scores on this scale correlate with behaviour rather than dealing with scores on the 'factor'.

One obvious way of calculating a factor score is to identify the items which have substantial loadings on the factor and to simply add up each person's scores on these items, ignoring those with tiny loadings on the factor. For example, suppose that four Likert-scaled items were factor analysed and that these had loadings of 0.62, 0.45, 0.18 and 0.73 on a factor (after rotation). This suggests that Items 1, 2 and 4 measure much the same construct, whereas Item 3 measures something rather different. In this case, adding together each person's scores on Items 1, 2 and 4 might be sensible.[3] There is a lot to be said for this simple approach, which is exactly equivalent to identifying which items form a scale and then adding the scores on these items together. It is simple to perform and easy to understand.

An alternative way of writing the same thing is to say that each standardised variable should be multiplied by a weight to give the score for each factor. In the above example, the weights for Variables 1–4 are 1, 1, 0 and 1. These are known as *factor score coefficients*. If more than one factor is extracted/rotated, then each factor will have a separate set of factor-score coefficients.

It is, however, possible to have factor-score coefficients which are not just 0 or 1. For example, if Variable 2 has a larger loading on the factor than Variable 1 (meaning that it is a better measure of the factor), it might be sensible to give it a larger weight; the first two factor-score coefficients might be 0.6 and 0.8, for example. All the factor-score estimation procedures described below are different ways of achieving this end.

In the case of principal-components analysis and orthogonal rotation, the calculation is straightforward; one simply divides the factor loadings by the sum of the squared loadings of the *rotated* factor (its eigenvalue) to obtain the factor-score coefficients for that factor. Then to calculate each person's score on that principal component, one simply standardises the scores on each of the variables (divides each person's score on each variable score by the standard deviation of the variable) and multiplies these standardised scores by the appropriate factor-score coefficient. Then one adds together each of these scores for each person to obtain a factor score.[4] Spreadsheet 9.3 gives a worked example, for those who are interested.

The process is slightly more complex when performing oblique rotation, but the same basic principles apply; one obtains a matrix of factor-score coefficients, standardises the raw data and multiplies a person's standardised scores on all variables by the component-score coefficients for a principal component. Summing these gives the score of that person on that component.

Deriving the factor-score coefficients from a factor analysis is more complex than for principal components, and there are several different ways of estimating factor scores – often yielding rather similar results (McDonald and Burr, 1967) though Bartlett's method is arguably the best. Good discussions are given by Harman (1976, chapter 16), Comrey and Lee (1992, section 10.3) and Harris (1967), for those who are interested. A useful (though somewhat mathematical) history of methods of calculating factor scores is given by Bartholomew et al. (2009).

SUMMARY

Factor analysis is a tremendously useful technique for clarifying the relationships between a number of interval-scaled or ratio-scaled variables. It can be applied to any such data – from physical and physiological measures to questionnaire items. This chapter has described how to perform a technically sound factor analysis and has highlighted some common errors which occasionally creep into published papers.

NOTES

1 Except in the case of the one-factor solution.
2 Or, in some implementations, two largest loadings.
3 It is better to add together the standardised scores rather than the raw scores for each variable. This is because if the variables have different standard deviations, the variables with the largest standard deviations will have a greater influence on the total score. However, this is rarely done in practice when computing scale scores from several Likert items. Nevertheless, it should definitely be done when combining scores from several different scales if the standard deviations vary considerably.
4 It is common practice, though not necessary, to subtract the mean of each variable from each person's score before dividing by the variable's standard deviation.

CHAPTER 10
ALTERNATIVE FACTOR
ANALYSIS DESIGNS

Thus far we have seen how factor analysis can be a useful tool for analysing the correlations between test scores, item responses or other variables. Up to this point, we have assumed that a large sample of people provide data on a smaller number of tests or items and that these test scores or items are correlated together. Factor analysis can then be used to examine the correlations between the tests and determine whether they all measure different things or whether they instead measure a smaller number of factors.

The vast majority of factor analyses in the literature operate in this way. However, there are plenty of other possible designs for using factor analysis. This chapter explores some of these and gives some examples of how and why they may be useful in a wide variety of settings – including case studies of individuals, classification of people and the study of mood and motivation. In particular, the idea that factor analysis can provide valuable insights when studying individuals (for example, in clinical work or case studies) does not seem to be well known. What follows draws heavily on the work of Cattell (1946, 1978) who seems to have been the first to see the huge potential that these techniques offer for academic and applied psychologists.

The basic idea is very simple. So far, we have used factor analysis to analyse the correlations between a number of pieces of data (e.g., scores on tests or responses to items) obtained from a sample of people. The number of people is larger than the number of variables. Cattell suggests that this form of factor analysis is termed 'R-analysis' – for 'regular' analysis – simply because it is the most familiar and most popular form of factor analytic design.

Putting R-technique in context, Figure 10.1 shows people, variables and occasions. As R-analysis involves testing a lot of people on a few variables on one occasion, R-analysis can be represented by

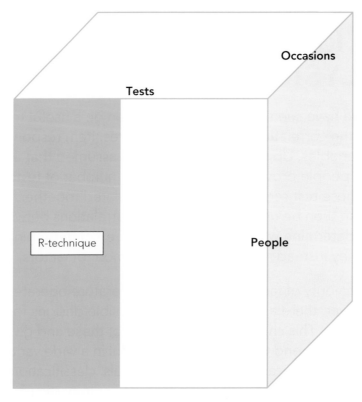

Figure 10.1 Regular (R-technique) factor analysis in context. This involves factor analysing the correlations between a moderate number of variables, based on the responses of a large number of people

the dark blue rectangle as shown. The fact that it is taller than wide indicates that the number of people will always exceed the number of variables.

It should be obvious from the diagram that there are other possible designs, too. What if a lot of data were gathered from a few people on one occasion? For example, suppose that a developmental psychologist has data on 30 children whose behaviour has been measured on one occasion using the Child Behaviour Checklist (Achenbach and Rescorla, 2001). Typical items on this checklist are 'eats things which are not food or drink', 'gets in many fights' and 'acts too young for age', each of which is scored using a three-point scale.

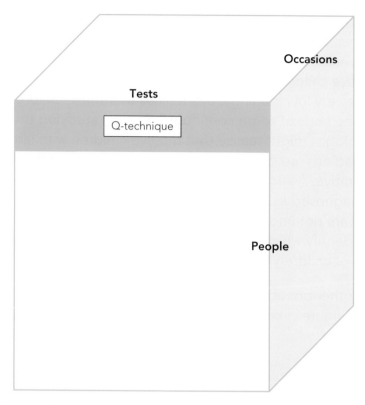

Figure 10.2 Q-technique factor analysis in context. This involves factor analysing the correlations between a moderate number of people, based on a large number of variables

This checklist consists of 113 items, and so it would clearly be impossible to perform an R-factor analysis in order to determine which of the checklist items form factors because there are more items in the checklist than there are people in the sample. Anyway, this might not be the question which the child psychologist wants to address. She might be much more interested in knowing how many different 'types' of children there are in her sample. For example, does the checklist allow the children to be categorised in terms of disruptive behaviour? Or can it also identify children who are anxious/depressed?

One possibility would be to perform what Cattell terms a Q-technique factor analysis. Instead of correlating the items together, *people* are correlated together on the basis of their scores on the items, as shown in Figure 10.2. People who respond similarly to the test items correlate substantially and will form a factor. For example, five children may have large loadings on Factor 1, and four might have very low loadings; this tells us that these children are on the opposite ends of some continuum. And on studying the results, the psychologist might realise that the five children with large positive loadings are disruptive, whilst the four at the other extreme are cooperative. A second factor might separate out the children who are diagnosed as having affective disorders (anxiety etc.) from those who are not and so on. It is also possible to calculate factor scores to identify which items in the checklist lead to the particular groupings of children that are found.

There are other possible designs too, and rather than drawing many more figures like Figure 10.1 and 10.2, these are all shown

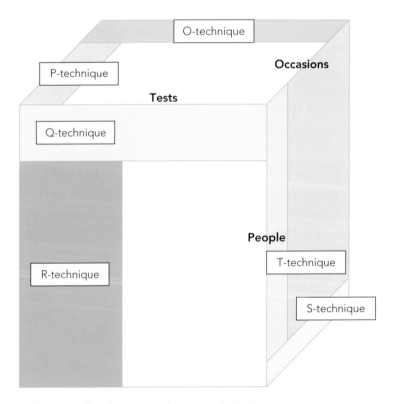

Figure 10.3 Cattell's classification of factor-analytic designs

together in Figure 10.3. In each case, the variables to be correlated are represented by the smaller end of a rectangle. Thus T-technique involves administering one test to many people on several occasions and correlating/factor analysing the occasions. Techniques which are particularly useful in psychology include P-technique and S-technique. P-technique involves gathering data from just one person on a large number of occasions – although as we shall see below, it can be modified to allow data from several people to be used. It is very useful in studying mood or motivation, as it shows which mood variables change together from occasion to occasion. The other techniques are rarely – if ever – used, even though they may be useful in some contexts. These are described briefly.

S-TECHNIQUE, T-TECHNIQUE AND O-TECHNIQUE

Like Q-technique, S-technique involves identifying types of individuals – but based on their responses to a single test, which is administered on a large number of occasions. For example, suppose that an occupational psychologist wanted to discover how stress affected members of a university psychology department, with the objective of discovering which individuals were stressed at which periods of the year, so that additional support and/or changes to working practices might be put in place. A key question is whether all members of staff experience stress at the same times, and so a sample of undergraduate students, graduate students, professors, clerical support staff, teaching staff, technical staff and administrators might each be given a stress questionnaire to complete once a day for a year. The total score on this scale is analysed; S-factor analysis might show that the undergraduate students, some administrators and some clerical staff all load on the same factor, indicating that they experience stress at much the same times of the year, whilst professors might fall onto a different factor, indicating that they experience stress at different times. The key point is that the factor analysis will show how many distinct groups of people exist within the sample and which people belong to which group.

T-technique, on the other hand, is more likely to be of interest to those who study moods or are interested in the psychometric properties of a particular test which measures a personality trait of some sort – conscientiousness, for example. (It would make little sense to use it to explore an *ability* trait such as general intelligence because T-technique involves measuring the trait on multiple occasions, and participants would remember how they solved the various items in an ability test.) T-technique involves giving a large group of people the same test on a smaller number of occasions; the correlations between the scores that the people obtain on the various occasions are then intercorrelated and factor analysed. The size of these correlations says something about the temporal stability (test-retest reliability) of the scale, and if just one factor is found it will indicate that the test produces consistent scores on every occasion. T-technique might also be useful when studying moods. For example, several mood induction techniques have been developed to change people's moods, and one way of testing their effectiveness would be to administer a mood scale on several occasions, some of which followed a mood induction. If the mood induction was generally successful, a factor should emerge consisting of the occasions on which the mood induction took place; as the participants lived different lives, one would not expect their mood scores to be correlated on the other occasions. That said, I know of no studies which have used T-technique.

O-technique involves one person completing a large number of tests (or test items) on a smaller number of occasions corresponding to different situations, perhaps. The scores obtained on the various occasions are then correlated together. It could therefore show which situations similarly influence a person's entire personality profile or their entire range of mood states. Being based on a single individual, it could conceivably be useful in clinical psychology, although I am not aware of any published research (clinical or otherwise) which uses this technique.

P-TECHNIQUE AND ITS VARIANTS

P-technique is very useful in developing and evaluating scales that measure moods, emotional states, motivational states and anything else which is likely to vary over time. Whilst the definition of P-technique given above allows for the analysis of a single individual (for example, discovering which items in a questionnaire measuring mood or behaviour tend to change together), two other techniques – called Chain-P technique and dR or Differential-R technique) have been developed which allow the use of larger samples of people.

It is very important that regular (R-technique) factor analysis should *not* be used when designing a questionnaire to measure states such as mood or motivation, and any scales which are developed in this way should be treated with scepticism. The reason for this is simple. R-technique only considers the correlations between variables which are measured on one occasion. The key thing about moods and levels of motivation is that they vary over time. So to measure mood it is necessary to discover whether (for example) the days on which a person feels energetic are also the days on which they feel apprehensive, healthy, alert, confident and strong, and to find that on days when someone's score on one of these variables dips, their scores on all of the others decrease too. If so, these behaviours go together and form a mood state. Only by studying which items vary together over time *within an individual* can we be sure that the test is measuring states, rather than stable personality traits. P-technique is ideal for this purpose. Suppose that a person is given a 20-item mood questionnaire to complete at random times of the day on 50 or more occasions. It might be found that when the person's responses to the items are intercorrelated and factor analysed, whenever the person feels healthy they also tend to feel alert, confident and strong; on occasions when their scores on one of these variables dips, the scores on the other variables dip too. In other words, these four items form a factor of mood. Much the same can be done with a test of motivation.

If a mood scale is constructed by administering a set of items to a group of people on just one occasion (R-technique), there is absolutely no guarantee that the scale measures mood at all. It could instead just measure personality. Of course, the instructions may *ask* participants to respond as they feel right at this moment (rather than how they generally feel), but there is no guarantee that people's responses actually do vary from time to time or across situations. The questionnaire might be measuring a trait and not a state. After all, it is only the psychologist's intuition that leads them to believe that responses to these items might vary systematically over time. It might just be the case that any 'variations' which are noticed when one looks at responses to questionnaires are just random fluctuations; just because scores on an item vary from time to time or situation to situation, it does not follow that the item measures any sort of mood, emotional state or motivational state. People might be giving random answers! Only if one can determine that groups of items which look as if they refer to different moods, feelings or motivations all change together, can one be sure that one is measuring a genuine mood, emotion or emotional state. And to do this, P-technique (or one of its variants) is needed.

The reason why many psychologists (it would be unkind to give a reference) try to construct mood scales using R-technique is probably just expediency. It is very easy to administer a set of items to a group of students in a class, whereas gathering data from a person on multiple occasions requires more effort. And, of course, this approach has other problems too. Completing a mood scale (and possibly a bundle of other questionnaires too) in a classroom is a pretty horrible experience for anyone, and this will surely have an impact on the very moods that the questionnaires try to assess! It really is far better to administer the questionnaires on a mobile device as people are living their normal lives and then identify groups of items which intercorrelate from occasion to occasion.

P-technique involves gathering data on a few items (or scales) on multiple occasions; there should be more occasions than items. Any of the usual factor analytic methods may be used (e.g., using parallel analysis to identify the optimum number of factors, plus some form of oblique rotation). The interpretation of the results is quite straightforward. Each of the factors which emerges corresponds to a group of items which tend to rise and fall together over time and so which measure the same mood or level of motivation. Scrutiny of the items will allow each factor to be tentatively identified, and each factor should then be validated in the usual way.

There are, however, some problems with P-technique. The most obvious is that it is based on the responses made by a single person. Whilst there are times when exploring the responses of just one individual may be extremely useful – for example, in clinical psychology – many researchers will want to reassure themselves that the results obtained from this analysis will generalise to other people. One way round this might be to perform several different P-technique factor analyses, each based on a different person, to determine whether the same mood items have substantial loadings for each individual. However, it would be hard to decide what to do if there were substantial differences between the number or nature of factors found for each person. It might be advisable to use a technique called multiple-group structural equation modelling to determine whether the same factor structure fits the data from all of the participants.

The second issue is more practical. If the mood questionnaire is long, then it will be necessary to administer it on a great number of occasions in order to perform the factor analysis, given that there need to be more occasions than items. This may create practical difficulties as it might be hard to find volunteers who will diligently answer the mood items on (say) 50 occasions. If there are more items than occasions, one solution might be to use item parcelling – grouping items together in order to reduce the number of variables to be factor analysed (Barrett and Kline, 1981b; Little et al., 2002). However in a truly exploratory study, deciding how to form the parcels may be difficult. Unless parcelling is performed very carefully, the results of the factor analysis can be misleading or hard to interpret, and, of course, the problem with an exploratory analysis such as we describe here is that very little evidence is available about the psychometric properties of the items. It is therefore hard to decide how or whether to combine them into parcels.

Two modifications of P-technique may therefore be more useful.

CHAIN-P TECHNIQUE

Chain-P technique involves gathering data from each of several people and stacking their data on top of each other before performing the factor analysis. For example, if a mood questionnaire consists of six items, the data file might resemble Table 10.1.

Here the first person provided data on four occasions: for this example, we pretend that the six mood items have been answered using a five-point scale, so the responses are numbers 1–5. The second person provided data on just three occasions and so on. The factor analysis would be performed on the whole data file.

Table 10.1 Stacked data for a Chain-P factor analysis

		Item 1	Item 2	Item 3	Item 4	Item 5	Item 6
Person 1	Occasion 1	2	3	5	3	4	3
	Occasion 2	1	2	3	4	3	3
	Occasion 3	4	2	2	5	2	1
	Occasion 4	4	5	2	1	1	4
Person 2	Occasion 1	5	4	5	4	4	5
	Occasion 2	4	3	5	5	4	5
	Occasion 3	5	5	3	4	5	4
Person 3	Occasion 1	5	2	5	1	2	3
	Occasion 2	4	3	3	3	2	3
	Occasion 3	2	3	2	3	3	3
	Occasion 4	2	5	5	3	2	2
	Occasion 5	3	3	4	2	4	1
Person 4	Occasion 1	5	4	5	5	5	4

This method is widely recommended – but there can be a problem with analysing the scores as shown. A cursory look at the data in Table 10.1 shows that Person 2 tends to use the 4s and 5s on the rating scale far more than the other participants. This might be because of some sort of response style, such as the tendency to agree with statements. It could be because they have higher scores on a trait which is related to mood; indeed Cattell (1973) has suggested that each trait may have a corresponding mood state. This is hardly surprising. If items are written to measure the state of anxiety, people who are habitually highly anxious (a trait) will tend to rate themselves higher on these 'mood' items than will people who are low on trait anxiety. And this causes problems with Chain-P analyses.

EXERCISE 10.1: P-TECHNIQUE

Resources required: Spreadsheet 10.1: P-technique. From www.routledge.com/9781138228894

Purpose: To show why data must be standardised by person before performing Chain-P-technique factor analysis

Contents of spreadsheet: Table 1 shows data from a six-item Likert scale administered to one person on 11 occasions

Suggested activity:

- Scroll down and note the correlations in Table 2, which show that Items 1–3 measure one state and Items 4–6 another state. (You may wish to factor analyse the correlations to check.)

- Table 4 shows the same data – plus the data from four additional people: a Chain-P design. By some huge coincidence, all of the people have exactly the same scores on the questionnaires, and so the correlations between the items in Table 4 are identical to the correlations in Table 2. A moment's thought will reveal why. The scatter diagrams for these two sets of data would look identical, the only difference is that each data point is based on five people, not one.

- What happens if some people have higher average scores than others on one or both of the moods? For example, if one of the moods is state anxiety, what if some of the participants are more anxious in all situations than are other people? Adjusting the values on the green 'Offset' cells in Table 3 adds a constant to a person's scores on Items 1–3 and/or their scores on Items 4–6 on every occasion. Entering an offset of 1 for Person 2 on Items 1–3 will add one to each of that person's scores on these items; it will increase their average score (but not their standard deviation). Do this now and check its effect on the data by comparing the scores of Person 1 and Person 2 in Table 4 and the means and standard deviations in Table 6!

- Just slightly increasing all of one person's scores on Items 1–3 affects the correlations between Items 1–3 more than one might perhaps expect; for example, the correlation between Items 2 and 3 rises from 0.39 to 0.56. Now choose some more offset values for Items 1–3 in Table 3 and note what happens to the correlations between the items in Table 5. It can be seen that the more that people's mean scores (offsets) vary, (a) the larger the correlations between Items 1–3 become whilst (b) the correlations between Items 1–3 and Items 4–6 do not change much. Try entering some different values for the offsets for Items 1–3 to convince yourself of this.

- If people's scores on Items 4–6 are also allowed to vary, the correlations between Items 4–6 will also increase. You may want to enter some values in the offsets for Items 4–6 in Table 3 to check this. But what if, the mean scores of the participants are correlated? What if the person with the largest offset (highest mean score) for Items 1–3 also has the largest offset for Items 4–6? This is quite likely to happen in practice. For example, suppose that Items 1–3 measure state anxiety and 4–6 measure state depression. Although the biological mechanisms for anxiety and depression appear to be distinct, people who tend to be anxious also tend to be depressed, and so it is highly likely that, in real-life data, people with elevated scores on one mood will also have elevated scores on the other. Observe what happens to the correlations between Items 1–3 and 4–6 (towards the bottom left of the correlation matrix in Table 5) if the offset for Items 1–3 is chosen to resemble (or be roughly proportional to) the offset for Items 4–6.

For example, the offsets for Persons 2–5 on Items 1–3 might be 1, 2, 3 and 4; their offset for Items 4–6 might be 1, 2, 2 and 3. It can be seen that this causes the correlations between Items 1–3 and Items 4–6 to increase dramatically. For example, using the values suggested above, the correlation between Items 2 and 5 rises from 0 to 0.76! This will completely change the factor structure from what it should be.

Points to note: –

Learning outcomes:

Readers should now be able to appreciate that

- if people differ in their mean scores, this can influence the number of factors found in the correlation matrix when performing Chain-P factor analysis;
- to avoid this it is necessary to standardise scores on each item for each person before performing the factor analysis.

When people who have elevated scores on one set of items also happen to show elevated scores on another set of items,

a)   correlations within a set of items which measure the same mood state will increase, and
b)   correlations between items which measure *different* mood states will increase.

Here, (a) just suggests that the correlations between items which measure the same mood state – and hence their factor loadings – will become larger. But (b) implies that the number of mood factors identified by P-technique will be incorrect. In the examples given above, factor analysis will identify one mood factor, not two, as the correlations between items which measure different mood factors can become large.

There is, however, an easy way to avoid this problem. If the mood scores for each person are standardised (so that each person's scores on each item, averaged across occasions, have the same mean), the problem vanishes. It is also normal to ensure that each person's scores are brought to the same standard deviation, as consistent differences in standard deviations from person to person can also influence the correlations. And it is conventional to standardise scores such that each person's scores on each item have a mean of 0 and a standard deviation of 1.

DIFFERENTIAL-R TECHNIQUE

If moods are measured on just two occasions, a simpler technique known as Differential-R technique can be used; it is far simpler than it sounds.

It simply involves subtracting each person's score on an item on Occasion 2 from the score which they gave on Occasion 1. Thus items which move in the same direction will be identified as states when these difference scores are correlated together and factor analysed.

The problem with difference scores is that it is necessary to assume that each person in the sample uses the scales in the same way and that someone whose score on an item shifts from 7 to 6 (on a Likert scale for an item) shows the same amount of mood change as someone whose mood changes from 2 to 1 – which Michell argued is unlikely to be the case. Person 6 in Spreadsheet 10.2 shows massive shifts in mood between the two occasions. This is not unusual; some people's moods swing enormously, whilst other people's moods are extremely stable (McConville and Cooper, 1992) – plus we may not know the situations under which the participants filled in the mood scales that might explain their extreme shift in moods. But does this matter?

EXERCISE 10.2: DR TECHNIQUE

Resources required: Spreadsheet 10.2: dR technique. From www.routledge.com/9781138228894

Purpose: To show how individual differences in mood variability can affect the factor structure found using dR technique

Contents of spreadsheet:

- Sample data from seven people, each of whom completed some mood items on two occasions.
- Table 1 shows the raw data.
- Table 2 shows the difference scores.
- Table 3 shows the correlations between these difference scores.

Suggested activity:

- Looking at Table 3, it is clear that one mood factor is found. (Factor analysis reveals a one-factor solution where all variables except for Variable 4 have large loadings on the factor.)
- Figure 1 of the dR technique spreadsheet plots the scatter diagram showing the correlation between Item 1 and Item 2. It can be seen that the huge mood shifts experienced by Person 6 make them an outlier, and their data alone is responsible for the massive and statistically significant correlation between these two items.

- It is therefore clear that, if some people's moods shift more than others, this will affect the correlations between the difference scores.
- It might be prudent to recode the mood-shift data as showing an increase, decrease or no shift between the two occasions. Tables 4 and 5 and Figure 2 of the dR technique spreadsheet show how this affects the correlations. Analysing the data in this way would lead the researcher to a completely different conclusion about the number and nature of the mood factors.

Points to note:

- If people vary in the extent to which their moods change, this can affect the correlations and factor structure found using dR technique.
- Possible solutions might include recoding scores as negative, zero or positive or standardising scores within individuals before calculating correlations.

Learning outcomes:

Readers should now be able to

- appreciate that if some people's moods vary more than others', it is unwise to perform dR technique on raw difference scores.

The purpose of this is to show that correlating and factor analysing difference scores in dR technique requires considerable care. Individual differences in mood variability mean that some people will show larger mood shifts than others, as will the fact that some people's lives are more eventful than others. There is a danger that these variables – which have nothing at all to do with the structure of moods – will tend to inflate correlations between items which are based on difference scores. One possible solution might be to code difference scores as just being negative, positive or zero.

Q-TECHNIQUE

Q-technique involves correlating people together on the basis of their scores on a large number of variables. For example, suppose that a group of undiagnosed psychiatric patients answered a large number of items in a questionnaire. The depressed patients would answer all of the items which enquired about low mood, sleep disturbances, concentration difficulties etc. in much the same way; the schizophrenic patients would answer items enquiring about hallucinations, delusions, feelings of being controlled etc. in much the same way. So when people are correlated together on the basis of these responses and a factor analysis is performed, then two factors should emerge – one with large loadings from all of the people with depression (remember that it is people,

not variables, who show factor loadings in Q-factor analysis) and the other with high
loadings from all of the people with schizophrenic symptoms.

Historically Q-technique has been applied to a form of data known as the Q-sort
(Stephenson, 1953). Here, people are presented with a large number of printed cards,
each with a statement written on it (e.g., 'sociable'). Each participant decides how
accurately the word or phrase on each card describes them and show this by sorting
them into piles – typically along a scale from 'extremely inaccurate' to 'extremely
accurate'. They are usually given instructions to put a certain number of cards in each
pile with most near the centre. (The order of the cards within each pile does not
matter.) Figure 10.4 shows an example where a person was asked to sort 22 cards so
that there was one card in the leftmost pile, two cards in the next pile, then 4, 8, 4, 2
and 1 cards in subsequent piles.

Each card is given a score corresponding to the number at the bottom of the table:
this score reflects how well the person believes that the description on the card
describes them. These data are then put into a table rather as shown in Table 10.2.
Here the *people* form the columns, and the *items (cards)* the rows – unlike the data
tables used for R–factor analysis. The column titled 'Person 1' holds some of the data
from Figure 10.4, as you should verify.

That is the Q-sort. However, it is not necessary to perform a Q-sort in order to
conduct a Q-factor analysis. All that is needed is a large number of quantitative
variables, which are administered to a rather smaller number of people. These variables
might be responses to questionnaire items, test scores, physiological measures, ratings of
behaviour or a whole host of other things. The aim of the Q-factor analysis will be to

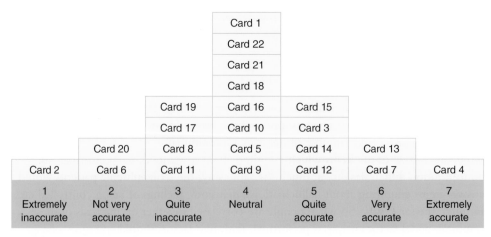

Figure 10.4 Diagram of how one person might arrange 22 cards describing
themselves when performing a Q-sort

Table 10.2 Data matrix for Q-technique factor analysis

	Person 1	Person 2	Person 3	. . . etc
Card 1	4			
Card 2	1			
Card 3	5			
Card 4	7			
etc.				

determine how people vary in the way in which they respond to these variables: that is, which people show similar profiles of responses to all of the items.

In order to perform a Q-analysis there should ideally be rather a lot of data from each person, and, of course, these pieces of data should be independent: the way in which a person responds to one item should not determine how they must respond to another, unless this correlation is caused by some personality trait, ability trait or other psychological phenomenon. For example, whilst 'Do you believe in ghosts?' and 'Do you believe in fairies?' would be fine, 'Do you believe in the supernatural?' and 'Do you believe in ghosts?' would not, as people who said that they did not believe in the supernatural could not, by definition, believe in ghosts.

It is also vitally important that the variables should be selected carefully so that no variables are answered in the same way by (almost) all people in the sample. Any such variables will increase the correlations between *all* people: there will be a general factor of 'humanness' (because all of the humans in the sample answer these items in exactly the same way). This is demonstrated in Spreadsheet 10.3. This generates some simulated data for Q-factor analyses using a statistical package such as Lorenzo-Seva and Ferrando (2006).

EXERCISE 10.3: Q-TECHNIQUE

Resources required: Spreadsheet 10.3: Q-technique. From www.routledge.com/9781138228894

Purpose: To show why non-discriminating items should be removed before performing Q-factor analysis

Contents of spreadsheet: Simulated data from three groups with different psychiatric diagnoses (depressive, schizophrenic and psychopathic). Each group contains three people, and everyone answered the same 21 questionnaire items.

Suggested activity:

- The first set of data (Table 1) in this spreadsheet shows the responses from nine people (columns) who have each answered 21 questions (rows) on a nine-point Likert scale. The spreadsheet is constructed such that Person D1 is given a random score on each item. Person D2's score and Person D3's score are based on Person D1's score: they are just randomly nudged up or down a little. A similar procedure is followed for People S1–S3 and P1–P3. Thus the scores obtained by Persons D1–D3 are similar: so too are the scores from S1–S3 and P–P3. But the correlation *between* people from the different groups should be small. The correlations are shown in Table 2 of the spreadsheet, and a scatter diagram showing the correlation between Persons D1 and P3 is shown next to Table 2. (The correlation between other pairs of people from different groups should be similar.)
- Cut and paste the scores of the nine people into a text file and use a program such as Lorenzo-Seva and Ferrando (2006) to convince yourself that Q-factor analysis can identify three groups of people. However, as such programs are designed to perform an R-factor analysis (correlating items together, rather than people) when specifying the model it is necessary to specify nine variables and 21 cases – not 21 variables and nine cases. After rotation, the factor analysis will reveal three factors, with the first three people having large loadings on one factor, Persons S1–S3 having large loadings on the second factor and Persons P1–P3 having large loadings on the third.
- What happens to the correlations between the people if more variables are added which (a) are extreme and (b) do not discriminate between people? In other words, what if there are some items with which (almost) everyone strongly agrees or strongly disagrees? With Table 2 visible on screen, add some more values in the green cells below the existing data – but put the same large (or small) value in each column – 1s or 9s.
- As a row or two of such data are added, it is clear that the correlations between people from different groups (e.g., D1 and P3) increase quite rapidly, as can be seen in the scatter diagram to the right of the correlation matrix in Table 2. Factor analysing the data now shows that the number of factors is less than three, and that the structure is not nearly as clear-cut as previously.

Points to note:

- Non-discriminating items reduce the number of Q-factors.
- Non-discriminating items should be dropped, or the bifactor model or Schmidt–Leiman technique might be used (see Chapter 11).

Learning outcomes:

Readers should now be able to

- identify a problem with performing a Q-technique factor analysis.

It is therefore important to remove any items to which all participants give extreme and similar answers before performing a Q-factor analysis. Such items are not uncommon: any item with which virtually everyone strongly agrees or with which almost everyone strongly disagrees will affect the clarity of the results by increasing the correlation between the factors and/or reducing the apparent number of factors. The easiest way of identifying and removing them is to examine the mean and standard deviation of each item, to identify those which (a) do not discriminate between people and (b) have a very high or very low mean. The bifactor model or Schmidt–Leiman technique could also presumably be used to eliminate the effects of the general factor; these methods are discussed in Chapter 11. However, I know of no studies which have done so.

G-ANALYSIS

G-analysis is simply a form of Q-analysis that is based on dictotomous (two-valued) data. It is useful when a checklist is used to describe a person's responses to some stimulus or when their behaviour is assessed using a 'true/false' format. One of the earliest uses of the technique was to objectively score people's responses to a projective test, such as the Rorschach inkblots: a series of checklist items could be drawn up, perhaps (but not necessarily entirely) based on some theoretical or practical considerations. For example, if people are shown a black-and-white inkblot and one starts by saying that they see 'Two witches dancing round a bright red fire . . .' it would be possible to code this data by using items such as:

- Item 1   mentions colour
- Item 2   mentions movement
- Item 3   mentions an alligator
- etc.

It is normal to gather the data first and then develop a coding system to capture its most salient characteristics: in the above example, the aim would be to capture all the richness of the participants' descriptions in a list of features, each of which is coded as present or absent from each person's response to the picture.

For reasons discussed by Holley (1973) it is inappropriate to use the more usual Pearson correlation when correlating people together from binary-coded data. A different correlation called the G-coefficient overcomes the problem: it is shown on Spreadsheet 5.3 in Chapter 5. It is very simple to calculate. Suppose that two people are to be correlated together based on their responses to 20 two-value items. To calculate G, all one needs to know is how many times they give the same response: multiply this by two, divide by the number of items and subtract one. For example, if the two people give the same responses to 13 of the 20 items, $G=(2\times13)/20-1=0.3$.

Table 10.3 Tables showing amount of agreement between two people, based on items coded 0/1

Table 10.3a

		Person 2	
		0	1
Person 1	0	4	4
	1	4	4

Table 10.3b

		Person 2	
		0	1
Person 1	0	8	4
	1	4	4

Some more data are shown in Table 10.3. In part (a) the responses of two people to 16 items are shown. It can be seen that $G=(2\times8)/16-1=0$, which looks eminently sensible. However, suppose that the checklist contains some items to which everyone gives the same answer: for example, suppose that no one reported seeing an alligator in the inkblot, and there were three more items like this. The data would be as shown in Table 10.3b, and G would be $(2\times12)/20-1=0.2$. Including items which do not discriminate between people will increase the correlation between people and consequently affect the factor structure in much the same way as shown in Spreadsheet 10.3. For this reason, G-analysis is best used when the items show a similar split – where the proportion of people coded as '1' is roughly similar for all items.

Fortunately, it is not that difficult to achieve this, especially if the data are being coded without much in the way of theoretical knowledge. In the above example, rather than coding 'mentions an alligator' (when virtually no one ever does so), it might be possible to change the item to 'mentions any non-human animal', which might perhaps be endorsed by 50% or so of the sample.

When faced with few theoretical expectations, plus a mass of data on a rather small sample of people – a not uncommon problem in clinical or educational research – it can make sense to perform a G-analysis because the usual R-technique factor analysis would not be appropriate as there are more variables than people. However, care must be taken to ensure that all of the items show individual differences, otherwise a large general factor will mask any more subtle groupings of people unless bifactor analysis etc. is used as described in Chapter 11.

IDENTIFYING Q-FACTORS

When performing a normal R-technique factor analysis, identifying the factors is generally quite straightforward as one merely observes which variables have large positive or negative loadings on the factor. These can then be used to tentatively name the factor; the large-loading items can be put together to form a scale, and this scale can be administered alongside other tests to different samples and cross-validated, as discussed in Chapter 7. But Q-technique merely reveals that certain people show similar responses to certain other people. How then can one tell which of the many items that were analysed are responsible for these groupings? How can one tell which items cause several people to correlate together?

There are two main options. The first is to rely on other sources of information about the participants. If factor analysis reveals that Participants 2, 5 and 8 all show large loadings on a factor, it might be appropriate to consult case notes, diagnoses and so on in order to hypothesise what they have in common. The problem with this approach is that it is not terribly scientific and does not give any hint as to which particular items *cause* these people to form a factor. If the factor analysis is based on a hundred or more items, it might well be the case that only a couple of dozen of these are responsible for differentiating these people from the rest – and it would clearly be useful to know which these are so that the list of items can be shortened for future applications.

Another way of identifying which items cause people to correlate together and form a factor is to calculate factor scores and note which items have the most extreme (positive or negative) factor scores for each Q-factor. These are the items which are largely responsible for grouping people together on the factor. Alternatively (and more pragmatically), one could just perform many independent sample t-tests using each of the items as the dependent variable. For each variable, one would first test whether the mean score of everyone who had large loadings on Factor 1 differed appreciably from the mean score of everyone else in the sample. Then the analysis would be repeated to find out which items differentiated the people who formed Factor 2 from the rest of the sample and so on. Having identified which items best discriminate the groups, it should be possible to provisionally name the Q-factors – although as with any form of factor analysis, validation and replication on different samples is necessary.

THREE-MODE FACTOR ANALYSIS

The techniques outlined in this chapter have used factor analysis to analyse the responses of several *people*, each of whom yield scores on several different *variables* on multiple *occasions*. These are known as the three modes. Rather than use messy approximations (such as stacking people together when performing a Chain-P analysis), it might be possible to analyse variables, people and occasions together. Tucker (1966) and Bloxom (1968) developed a technique called three-mode factor analysis to analyse just this sort of data. It basically reduces the number of variables down to a smaller number of factors, as in standard R-technique factor analysis: the reduced number of variables is known as the *attribute factor matrix*. But it simultaneously reduces down the number of people, as does Q-technique factor analysis, forming the *object matrix*. And the number of occasions is also reduced, into the *occasion matrix*. The basic aim of three-mode factor analysis is to estimate values for the attribute matrix, the object matrix and the occasion matrix, together with what Tucker terms a *core matrix*, which shows the size of the relationship between each of the factors in the attribute matrix, the occasion matrix and the object matrix, such that each person's score on each test on each occasion can be closely approximated by multiplying these four matrices together. The underlying mathematics is quite complex, computational and estimation issues are still being addressed and so, despite recently celebrating its 50th birthday, the technique has rarely been used except by avid psychometricians. It is possible to use it in the R environment (Giordani et al., 2014).

SUMMARY

It is clear from this chapter that factor analysis can do far more than just identify groups of items which form scales. It can help to identify items which measure moods and may be useful in differentiating various groups of people within a heterogeneous sample. It can also help us understand how test scores vary over occasions, even when there is no regular (periodic) pattern in these changes.

Of course, all of the normal caveats apply: the need for proper sampling of people and/or variables and/or occasions, together with independence of measures, adequate sample sizes and so forth. It is also clear that there is plenty of scope for statistical artefacts to creep in to such analyses – e.g., by not standardising variables (in P-technique) or having items which most people answer in the same way (Q-technique; G-analysis).

One of the most important lessons to emerge from this chapter is, I think, the importance of keeping close to one's data. It is all too easy to run numbers through a powerful statistical package without thinking too much about the legitimacy of what one is doing. When performing any unusual form of analysis, it makes huge sense to ask 'What if . . . ?' – particularly if one stacks data from several participants who may show different average scores or different levels of variability. But these research designs can be useful when performing exploratory analyses on a wide range of variables.

CHAPTER 11
DEVELOPMENTS IN FACTOR ANALYSIS

Chapters 8 and 9 introduced the basic procedures of exploratory factor analysis; many readers will find this sufficient to understand how to develop a scale or interpret the results from an analysis of several different variables. However, these chapters did not consider one very important and very popular extension of factor analytic methodology, namely hierarchical factor analysis.

This chapter therefore considers this technique (plus some variants) and also briefly outlines a technique known as confirmatory factor analysis, which is useful when the researcher has a clear expectation about what factor structure should emerge. For example, previous research may have shown that Items 1, 3 and 5 of some questionnaire form one scale, whilst Items 2, 4 and 6 form another. Confirmatory factor analysis allows this hypothesis to be tested and produces a wealth of statistics showing how well the theoretical model actually fits the data.

HIERARCHICAL FACTOR ANALYSIS

The basic idea behind hierarchical factor analysis is very simple. If a large number of pieces of data – responses to test items, for example – are administered to a still-larger sample of people and the results are factor analysed, then, as long as oblique rotation is performed, some of the factors may well be correlated. For example, a researcher might wish to administer a huge range of ability items to a vast number of people and then ask how many distinct ability factors there are. Carroll (1993, 2003) reports the results from a great number of studies which show that the results can best be represented as shown in Figure 11.1.

The bottom layer of Figure 11.1 represents individual test items. Above these items are factors – labelled P1, P2, P3 etc. – measuring different cognitive abilities ('primary mental abilities' is the usual name for them in intelligence research; hence the labels of P1, P2 etc.). Once again, there many hundreds of these primary mental abilities – far more than can be shown in the figure. Each of these is measured by a large number of

Figure 11.1 Part of a very large hierarchical model of abilities

variables (perhaps 20 or 30 per factor) so there would be several thousand boxes on the lowest level of Figure 11.1.

Lines linking items to factors represent large factor loadings. Thus Items 1–4 (for example) have large loadings on Factor P1 and near-zero loadings on the other factors as there are no lines linking them to other factors. If the items have been carefully developed, each item should only measure one factor, and so each item should be linked to only one primary mental ability.

If an oblique rotation is used when factor analysing the correlations between the items, the primary factors can themselves be correlated, and all factor analysis programs will show the correlations between the factors as part of the output from an oblique factor analysis.

It is possible to factor analyse the correlations between the rotated primary ability factors. This produces 'second-order' factors, of which eight are shown in Figure 11.1. What if these eight second-order factors are also correlated? The factor analysis process can be repeated at each level until either (a) all of the factors are uncorrelated or (b) only one factor remains. In the case of human abilities, a single factor ('general ability') can be extracted from the correlations between the second-order factors, as shown in Figure 11.1. However, this is not invariably the case; when factor analysing the correlations between personality traits, most (though not all) theorists identify five major personality traits and stop there, rather than extracting a single 'general factor' of personality because the correlations between the five main personality factors are rather small (Costa and McCrae, 1992).

Hierarchical factor analysis is basically the process outlined in the previous paragraphs. However, it is rarely performed precisely as I have described it, starting with a large number of items, factor analysing the correlations between them and then factor analysing the correlations between the first-order factors and the second-order factors and so on. Instead, it is more usual to work at the structure piecemeal and to investigate the correlations between *tests* measuring the various primary factors (P1, P2 etc. in Figure 11.1) rather than the correlations between *factors*, which stem from factor analysing a large number of items.

Rather than trying to write items measuring every possible cognitive ability, one researcher might focus on measuring abilities which seem to involve visualisation (sometimes called Gv in the literature). They may develop six different tests which appear to involve different aspects of visualisation – for example, finding routes through mazes; imagining what landscapes of blocks, cylinders and cones would look like if viewed from another position; being able to identify the outline of a simple shape hidden inside a more complex line drawing and so on. Factor analysing the correlations between people's scores on several such tests might reveal that they all intercorrelate and form a single visualisation factor. Another researcher might do the same with eight puzzles which involve reasoning – and might perhaps find that *two* factors emerge – one from puzzles that involve unfamiliar content and another from those that rely more on knowledge gained at school. (These abilities are sometimes called fluid ability or Gf and crystallised ability or Gc.) A third researcher may explore performance on seven tasks measuring memory and find evidence for a single memory factor Gm. It is then necessary to check that when some or all of the visual tests, reasoning tests and memory tests are given to the same group of people, the factors emerge as expected. This is necessary because it is possible that some of the second-order factors identified by different researchers might be identical.

REASONS FOR NOT PERFORMING A SINGLE, HUGE, HIERARCHICAL FACTOR ANALYSIS

PRACTICALITY

According to Carroll (1993) there were 241 factors of reasoning ability, plus many others measuring memory, attention, language ability etc. – well over 500 in total. So, in order to understand the structure of human abilities using hierarchical factor analysis, it would be necessary to give items measuring these 500 factors to a sample of people. Even if there were a mere 10 items measuring each factor, this exercise would involve each participant completing 5000 items – a process which would take several days, once instructions and rest breaks were included: it is not at all obvious how one would recruit volunteers who would solve such problems conscientiously for such a long time.

When diverse items are factor analysed, the communalities are usually rather low, indicating that each of the items is only weakly related to the factor(s). As a consequence of this, vast samples of people are required in order to correctly identify the number and nature of the factors: the number of people would, in any case, need to be larger than the many thousands of items. This would turn into a massive and expensive research project.

Then there would be the problem of how to factor analyse a 5000×5000 correlation matrix; it is not obvious that any existing computer system is powerful enough to perform such an analysis, given that the amount of time taken to perform a factor analysis will be (very roughly) proportional to the cube of the number of variables (Press et al., 1993). So, if it takes 1 second to factor analyse 10 variables, it might take $5000/10 \times 5000/10 \times 5000/10$ seconds (4 years) to analyse 5000 variables.

ESTIMATION OF CORRELATIONS BETWEEN FACTORS

Estimating the correlations between factors with precision becomes particularly important when performing hierarchical analyses, as the correlations between the factors will form the correlation matrix to be analysed at the next-highest level of the hierarchy. We mentioned in Chapter 9 that rotation algorithms generally include a parameter which determines how oblique the factors are allowed to become; see Harman (1976). In the case of Oblimin, this parameter is known as gamma; SPSS calls it delta, for reasons best known to itself. So how does one go about choosing a value for gamma? Most computer programs will simply use a default value (zero for Oblimin in the case of SPSS), but, when performing the rotation, neither the rotation algorithm nor the user can know in advance how oblique the factors really are. There is no theoretical rationale nor empirical data to suggest choosing a gamma value of 0 rather than (say) 0.4 or −100 for a particular set of data, and this matters because it will influence the size of the correlations between the factors. It is clearly important to estimate these correlations as accurately as possible when performing a hierarchical factor analysis, so using standard packages is risky, to put it mildly.

Paul Barrett (e.g., Barrett and Kline, 1980) came up with a good solution to this problem. He conducted hundreds of rotations, each with a different value of gamma, and chose the one which gave the best approximation to simple structure. For each rotation, he calculated the percentage of loadings which were between −0.1 and +0.1 ('the hyperplane') and chose the solution with the largest hyperplane count. This was repeated for several hyperplane widths to make sure that all solutions gave similar results.

The bottom line is that it is hard to determine the correlations between factors with great accuracy, and errors in these correlations may well influence the higher-order factor structure – the number and nature of the second-order factors. Given that factor analysing items is known to be problematical, it might make more sense to replace the primary factors with scores on well-constructed tests and correlate these together in order to explore the higher-order factor structure.

FACTOR ANALYSING SMALL DATASETS

One problem which is often encountered when performing hierarchical factor analyses is that the number of variables becomes small as one approaches the apex of the pyramid, for the number of variables being factored is equal to the number of factors at the next level down the pyramid. In Figure 11.1, *g* is found by analysing the correlations between eight second-order factors, which should present few problems (as long as the factor analysis suggests no more than one or two factors!). However, it can be the case that the researcher needs to extract and rotate higher-order factors from the correlations between very few lower-order factors, and, when the number of variables is small, it is sometimes hard to know where to position the factors relative to the variables.

Hendrickson and White (1966) provide a useful technique to overcome this problem. Rather than using factor rotation to align the (small) number of first-order factors relative to the second-order factors, as shown in the top part of Spreadsheet 11.1, it expresses the loadings of the *original variables* on the second-order factors. There are two advantages to this.

First, deciding where to place the variables relative to the factors can be tricky when the number of variables is small. In the present example, there are only four first-order factors and deciding how to rotate the loadings of these four first-order factors on the two second-order factors will be problematical. It is a particular difficulty for those who use the hyperplane count to judge the goodness of fit because the proportion of loadings in the hyperplanes with four variables can only be 0, 25, 50, 75 or 100% – and there may be several rather different rotations which give the same hyperplane count. Showing how the original variables map on to the second-order factors allows for a much larger range of hyperplane counts, which may prove useful in identifying the most appropriate solution.

The second problem with positioning first-order factors relative to second-order factors is the issue of interpretation. It might be that the psychological meaning of one or more of the first-order factors is unclear. If this first-order factor (plus another) show large loadings on a second-order factor, it can be very difficult indeed to attempt an interpretation of what the second-order factor might represent. On the other hand, if one can see which of the original *variables* show large and small loadings on each second-order factor, it can be much easier to interpret what the second-order factor might mean.

EXERCISE 11.1: HIERARCHICAL FACTOR ANALYSIS

Resources required: Spreadsheet 11.1: Hierarchical factor analysis. From www.routledge.com/9781138228894

Purpose: To demonstrate the Hendrickson–White technique

Contents of spreadsheet: Direct-Oblimin rotated factor solution – 24 variables, four factors

Suggested activity:

- Section A of the spreadsheet shows the Direct-Oblimin rotated first-order factor matrix. It also shows the correlations between these first-order factors.
- Section B and the top chart show the conventional second-order factor loadings; the first-order factors have loadings on two second-order factors. Adjust the top slider and note how difficult it is to decide where best to place the axes.
- Section C performs the Hendrickson–White transformation and shows the loadings of the variables on the two second-order factors. Adjust the bottom slider and note how much easier it is to position the factors now that more data points are present.

Learning outcomes:

Readers should now be able to

- perform a Hendrickson–White transformation using the spreadsheet;
- appreciate its usefulness in performing hierarchical factor analyses.

SCHMID–LEIMAN TRANSFORMATION

The Schmid–Leiman technique (Schmid and Leiman, 1957) is conceptually very similar to the Hendrickson–White methodology. The main difference from the user's point of view is that it produces a factor matrix showing both the second-order factors and the first-order factors; the influence of the second-order factors has been partialled out from each of the first-order factors.

Take the example of ability tests. It might be found that four tests of verbal skills (reading, comprehension, anagrams, vocabulary) which correspond to first-order factors in Figure 11.1 form a second-order factor when these tests plus a lot of other tests are given to a sample of people, correlated and factor analysed. A hierarchical analysis might produce a third-order factor of general intelligence. Some part of the correlation between the verbal tests will arise because of general intelligence, which, by definition, influences performance on all tasks which are below it in the hierarchical model. Someone with a high level of general intelligence will tend to perform well at all the verbal (and all the other) tasks; someone with a low level of general intelligence will probably perform less well at all of the tasks. So, if the average correlation between the verbal tasks is – say – 0.5, how much of this is due to general intelligence and how much is due to differences in verbal ability alone? This is the question which the Schmid–Leiman technique addresses.

It produces a factor matrix which shows all of the first-order factors plus all of the second-order factors, third-order factors etc. in one table. The difference between this and a traditional hierarchical factor analysis is that the factor loadings on the first-order factors are corrected for the influence of the second- and third-order factors. The Schmid–Leiman technique shows the relationship between the variables and the second-order factors, rather like the Hendrickson–White method discussed above. So it shows the loadings of each of the variables on each of the second-order factors – after correcting for the influence of any third-order factors. (The Hendrickson–White technique does not partial out the influence of the higher-order factors.)

The practical advantage of this technique is that it allows users to see how important primary and second-order factors are, after controlling for higher-order factors. To select a paper at random, Dombrowski and Watkins (2013) factor analysed the correlations between adolescents' scores on a widely used battery of ability tests. Table 11.1 shows a part of their results. They analysed 42 tests which corresponded to first-order factors and extracted five second-order factors, then one general factor (g).

The initial factor analysis, which showed that the 42 variables formed five factors, indicated that the first factor (F1) was impressively large; it explained 39% of the variance in the correlation matrix. And as the test scores that were factor analysed seemed to involve language, most users of this test would probably conclude that this is some sort of verbal ability factor. However, the Schmid–Leiman analysis shows the presence of a large general ability factor. It explains 33% of the variance. Tellingly, this general intelligence factor was largely responsible for the variance explained by the second-order F1. For the Schmid–Leiman analysis shows that after correcting for the effects of general intelligence, F1 only explains 5% of the variance in the correlation matrix.

Table 11.1 Part of a Schmid–Leiman analysis of scores on various ability tests

Tests corresponding to first-order factors	Second-order factor	Results from Schmid–Leiman analysis	
	F1	g	F1
Picture vocabulary	0.85	0.60	0.52
Verbal comprehension	0.83	0.76	0.51
General information	0.82	0.69	0.50
Academic knowledge	0.79	0.70	0.48
Story recall	0.72	0.56	0.44
Oral comprehension	0.68	0.60	0.41
etc.			
% variance	38.9	33.1	5.0

Source: Adapted from Dombrowski and Watkins (2013)

Why is this important? The most obvious reason is to help practitioners understand what they are measuring. It would be very tempting for educational psychologists or others to give children the Picture Vocabulary test, the Verbal Comprehension test etc. in the belief that they are measuring their verbal skills – whereas the Schmid–Leiman shows that these tests are rather better measures of general intelligence than verbal ability (their loadings on the g factor are higher than their loadings on F1). So the tests which have large loadings on F1 are not 'pure' measures of language skills at all. Instead they measure a mixture of general intelligence and language skills – and so, if scores on these tests predict school performance, it is impossible to tell whether language skills, general ability or both are responsible for this correlation.

The Factor program (Lorenzo-Seva and Ferrando, 2006) for Windows and the Psych package in R (Revelle, 2017c) perform Schmid–Leiman analyses.

BIFACTOR MODELS

Psychologists have recently rediscovered bifactor models – originally due to Holzinger and Swineford (1937). Confusingly, perhaps, 'bifactor' models do not involve just two factors – but instead two *levels* of factors. Each variable is presumed to be influenced by both a general factor and one of several group factors, as shown in Figure 11.2. (Each variable may also have a unique factor associated with it, but these have been omitted for the sake of clarity.) A key assumption is that the general factor is uncorrelated with all of the group factors, which is rather different from the hierarchical model considered above.

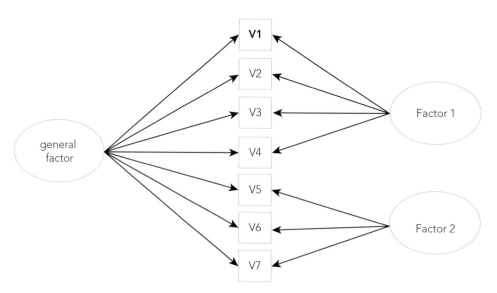

Figure 11.2 The bifactor model (unique factors are omitted for the sake of clarity)

In addition, all of the group factors are assumed to be uncorrelated; there is no curve denoting a correlation between Factor 1 and Factor 2 in Figure 11.2. Third, it is assumed that each variable is influenced by the general factor plus only one group factor; it is not possible for two different group factors to influence a variable. A final difference from the hierarchical model described above is that the loadings on the general factor and the loadings on the other factors are all estimated together, rather than sequentially after factor rotation. Reise (2012) gives an excellent introduction to these models.

So when and why can this technique be useful? One possibility is to check for social desirability. Suppose that the variables being analysed are scores on different personality tests and that there is good reason to suppose that they may all be influenced by social desirability. For example, one test might consist of items asking about how good one's sense of humour is, a second test might ask about honesty and so on. Social desirability is likely to influence scores on all of the tests; some people will be more likely to make socially desirable responses than others, and this will lead to all tests loading a general factor of social desirability. For this reason, it might make sense to fit a bifactor model to the data. The general factor would represent social desirability, which should influence every test. The group factors would represent the relationships between the variables after controlling for the effects of social desirability.

In the previous example, the general factor is a 'nuisance', and the interesting part of the analysis centred on the group factors. However, it is also possible to treat the general factor as being the one of main interest. Suppose that a large national sample of children were given two stories to read, and their comprehension was assessed in each of them. One of the stories involved life on the farm, and the other dealt with travel in the city. To their horror, the researchers then realised that children who lived in the country might be more familiar with farming terms, whilst urban children might perhaps find the city-based items easier. To see whether all of the items form a general 'verbal comprehension' factor after allowing for this, a bifactor analysis could be performed; Factor 1 and Factor 2 would control for the influence of the two different scenarios on comprehension.

Whether to perform a bifactor analysis or Schmid–Leiman analysis of correlated factors is not a straightforward decision to make; in many cases they seem to yield broadly comparable results. However, Mansolf and Reise (2016) outline some problems with the Schmid–Leiman which may make some form of bifactor model preferable. Jennrich and Bentler (2011, 2012) have made an important methodological advance by developing a technique where the user does not need to specify beforehand which group factors influence each variable; their software allows this to be determined empirically, rather than on a priori grounds as with the comprehension example. The technique is known as exploratory bifactor analysis (EBFA); their 2012 paper is a development which allows the group factors to be correlated. However, EBFA is still rather new, and, though it looks promising, it should probably be used with caution.

ARE HIGHER-ORDER
FACTORS IMPORTANT?

My own view is that it makes far more sense to explore and interpret higher-order factors (second-order, third-order factors and above) rather than primary abilities. There are two reasons for this.

First, the literature seems to show that higher-order factors can have considerable explanatory power in practical settings. Take general intelligence, for example. The paper mentioned in the previous section is typical of a large number of studies showing that g is the 'active ingredient' which allows ability tests to predict performance at school or at work (Thorndike, 1985) and that lower-order ability factors are generally of little use for the prediction of behaviour. Suppose that one used a range of ability tests to predict who would succeed at learning to fly fighter aircraft. Training novices to fly such aircraft is hugely expensive, and so administering tests to identify applicants who are likely to perform well is likely to be highly cost-effective.

Suppose that one administers 20 tests measuring coordination and mathematical, spatial and similar skills; these might each show some correlation with flying performance. But, without performing some sort of hierarchical analysis, it is impossible to tell whether these correlations arise because each of the tests measures general intelligence to some extent or whether the narrower skills (coordination etc.) are what predict flying performance. If g is far more important than the lower-level skills, then any test that is a good measure of g should be able to predict flying performance; it need not have any obvious relevance to flying an aircraft at all. So a simple test which is known to be a good measure of g (such as one which asks participants to identify the next shape in a pattern or spot the rules linking groups of objects) might work as well as a larger selection of lower-level tests which appear to be relevant to aviation but which may, in fact, only work because they each measure g to some extent.

Understanding the extent to which a low-level factor is influenced by higher-order factors is therefore of practical use – and also has major theoretical benefits, as it can guide users as to the most appropriate variables to measure – lower-level factors (or 'facets' as they are sometimes called) or broader personality traits.

For completeness, we ought to add that higher-order factors do not *always* predict behaviour better than narrower factors – see for example Judge et al. (2013), although this study did was not able to perform Schmid–Leiman analyses but instead relied on a meta-analysis of correlations between personality traits and job performance.

Second, the number of primary abilities is virtually infinite. In Chapter 2 we bemoaned the fact that many of the items which are administered in personality questionnaires are very similar in content: 'Do you often seek out the company of others?', 'Are you a sociable person?', 'Do you really enjoy a lively party?' and so on. If you loathe and detest the company of other people, then you *have* to answer 'no' to these three items; if you are a convivial type then you *have* to answer 'yes' to all of them, just because they ask the same question with slightly different words. This similarity of meaning guarantees that these items will form a factor. But this is not an interesting psychological discovery but a necessary consequence of asking virtually the same question several times. It is possible to create any factor one wants by writing subtle variations of the same question, so the discovery of factors such as these says nothing about the structure or nature of personality (or ability). If participants understand the meanings of the words in the questions and answer them honestly, then such items are *bound* to correlate and must *inevitably* form a factor.

Anyone can create the most wonderful sounding trait by writing some items which essentially ask the same question several times; it would be unkind to give real-life examples, though the widely used Rosenberg (1965) self-esteem scale deserves a dishonourable mention. But it would be trivially easy to develop scales such as 'fear of overeating', 'introverted melancholia', 'antisocial hedonism' . . . The list is literally endless, and the problem is that many psychologists spend their careers focused on such trivia. In my opinion, such work is of little value because the scales that are developed using factor analysis only show that participants recognise the meaning of the words and respond consistently.

Michael Eysenck once reminded me that participants who have taken personality tests frequently comment, 'I noticed that you asked the same question twice, in order to ensure that we were responding consistently'. I know of no personality scale which does this; participants may instead detect the lamentable similarity of the items.

Creating a vast number of traits seems to me to miss the whole point of using factor analysis in psychology; to identify *unexpected* relationships between seemingly quite *different* traits. We argued earlier that if the factor reflects some real characteristic of the individual (linked to individual differences in brain structure or function, developmental history, cognitive skills, social background or whatever) it is likely to influence several rather difference aspects of behaviour; post-traumatic stress disorder, for example, involves increased arousal (so difficulty sleeping etc.), emotional numbness and intrusive thoughts – three symptoms which look as if they are different yet which we know have a common cause. The strength of factor analysis is that it can identify such unexpected relationships. Finding (through factor analysis) that people who feel optimistic also tend to be sociable, assertive and talkative is a genuinely interesting discovery. So too is the finding that people who are highly creative also tend to perform well on tasks as diverse as memory, visualisation, logical reasoning and so on. These traits certainly sound as if they measure quite different aspects of cognitive functioning; the finding that they are all correlated is intriguing and suggests that they have some common origin, which needs to be established through interview, experiment etc. So it is my firm belief that whilst using factor analysis to map out the primary mental abilities at the bottom of the pyramid shown in Figure 11.1 is probably good sense, as the items in these scales will be so similar in meaning or in the cognitive processes which are required to solve them, they are of little or no intrinsic interest. Instead, it is necessary to explore the correlations between the factors derived from these items – the higher-order factors, in other words.

There are two possible solutions to this problem. First, one can try to eliminate all questions that are synonyms. Thus, if we were constructing a questionnaire to measure depression, one question might ask about sleep patterns, another about mood, another about changes in eating habits, a fourth about feelings that things will never get better and so on; the number of questions in the questionnaire would reflect the number of behaviours which are thought to be related to depression. Each item is written to tap a different aspect of depression, and if these items form a factor, then there is evidence for a source trait of depression. This is essentially the approach which Eysenck, Cattell (Cattell et al., 1970) and others claim to have followed when developing their personality scales; items were written, synonyms were dropped and the remaining items were given to samples of people whose scores were then factor analysed. There are four obvious problems with this approach:

- Only one item is written to measure each aspect of behaviour, and we discussed the problem of 'one-item scales' earlier (Chapter 6). Using only a very few items – one for each different aspect of behaviour – means that the occasional 'slip of the brain', uncertainty about the meanings of words and other random errors can have quite a marked influence on a person's total score.
- The resulting scales will generally be quite short and will be determined by the number of different behaviours which define the trait. For the 'depression' example, there could be only nine items, as the DSM-5 definition of depression involves only nine different behaviours.
- Although it sounds very straightforward to 'eliminate synonyms', this is a time-consuming and highly subjective procedure. Do 'unhappy' and 'depressed' and 'miserable' mean precisely the same thing? It is difficult to tell; Cattell recruited panels of language specialists and consulted dictionaries, but, in the end, there is a lot of subjective judgement involved.
- Eliminating synonyms disregards the possibility that items measure different degrees of the same characteristic. For example, the words 'happy' and 'content' may describe different points along a scale of happiness; someone who says that they are happy must also (logically) say that they feel content, whereas someone who says they are content may or may not describe themselves as happy. Simply identifying words as synonyms (or not) ignores this type of dependency.

The second solution would not require synonyms to be eliminated. Several items could be written to tap each aspect of depression – 'Do you sometimes feel "down" for no

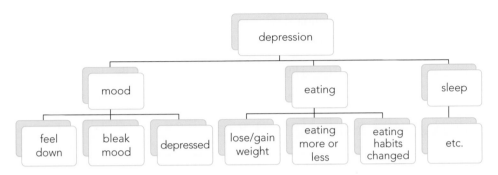

Figure 11.3 Hierarchical factor analysis of semantically similar items related to depression

good reason?', 'Does your mood often feel bleak?', 'Do you usually feel depressed?', 'Have you lost or gained weight recently?', 'Have you noticed yourself eating more or less than normal?', 'Have your eating habits changed in the last few months?' and so on. These could all be thrown into a factor analysis. The factor analysis will produce factors consisting of groups of items which are near-synonyms – a 'mood' factor and an 'eating' factor in the case of the six items in the previous sentence. *However, I suggest that these factors should not be interpreted.* This is because they are *bound* to emerge because several of the questions are semantically related; someone who 'usually feels depressed' *must* 'often feel bleak', for example.

Rather than paying much heed to these factors, which will necessarily reflect groups of items whose meanings overlap, one should instead perform a hierarchical factor analysis to determine whether the correlations between these *factors* produce a second-order factor, rather as shown in Figure 11.3.

If a trait represents some physical or psychological characteristic of the individual (rather than a social construction), Cattell (1946) argues that it will influence several different behaviours, just as the influenza virus leads to a whole range of seemingly different symptoms (feeling of malaise, aching limbs etc.). So, from a psychological point of view, it may make sense to use the first-order factors as the building blocks for discovering interesting but unexpected relationships between variables through hierarchical factor analysis. In other words, the lowest-level factors are treated rather as if they were mere items, and only the higher-order factors should be interpreted.

COMPARING FACTORS

Suppose that two researchers have factor analysed the same variables. Are all (or any) of the factors the same in the two studies? It can be hard to tell just by looking at the factor loadings. If the 'replication' of a factor lacks a few substantial loadings and has

Table 11.2 Data from an original study plus three 'replications', showing correlations and congruence coefficients as measures of factor similarity

	Original study			Replication (a)			Replication (b)			Replication (c)	
	F1	F2		F1a	F2a		F1b	F2b		F1c	F2c
Var. 1	−0.6	−0.1		0.1	0.7		−0.1	0.7		−0.5	−0.3
Var. 2	0.4	0.2		0.6	−0.1		0.1	−0.6		0.3	0.3
Var. 3	−0.4	0.1		0.2	−0.5		0.1	0.2		−0.3	0.0
Var. 4	0.0	0.8		0.4	0.1		0.4	−0.1		0.2	0.7
Var. 5	−0.2	−0.8		0.3	−0.4		−0.4	0.1		−0.3	−0.6
Var. 6	0.2	0.4		0.5	0.5		0.2	0.4		0.4	0.4
Correlations with factors from original study	F1	1.0		0.41			0.41	−0.75		0.93	0.61
	F2	0.4		0.33			0.99	−0.2		0.62	0.96
Congruence coefficients with factors from original study	F1	0.17		0.33			0.33	−0.73		0.91	0.53
	F2	0.35		0.35			0.99	−0.13		0.55	0.97

a couple of substantial loadings which were not expected, is it the same factor? There is plenty of scope for confirmation bias to creep in when looking at tables of factor loadings, so just looking at the factor matrices cannot be recommended.

There are five main ways of testing whether factors replicate.

CORRELATIONS BETWEEN FACTORS

The obvious procedure is to correlate the factor loadings from the original factor pattern matrix with the factor loadings from the replication. Whilst intuitively appealing, it is best avoided. For example, F1 in the original study does not look much like F1a from Replication (a) in Table 11.2. The original factor consists of Variable 1 (reverse scored), Variable 2, and Variable 3 (reverse scored). The substantial loadings on F1a (i.e., loadings above 0.4 or less than −0.4) are Variable 2, Variable 4 and Variable 6. These two factors do not look remotely similar – yet their loadings correlate perfectly together (r=1.0) as you might care to verify. Correlations will not suffice.

CONGRUENCE COEFFICIENT

Unlike the correlation, the congruence coefficient takes the absolute difference between the factor loadings in the two studies into account; Table 11.2 also shows the congruence coefficients.

Looking at the congruence coefficients, it seems at first glance that Replication (a) does not provide any factors which resemble the originals, Factor 1 from

Replication (b) resembles Factor 2 from the first study (congruence of 0.99) and that the factors in Replication (c) resemble those found in the first study quite closely. But what value of a congruence coefficient constitutes 'good' agreement? There have been attempts to determine significance levels for congruence coefficients, although Davenport (1990) demonstrates that these are inappropriate. As far as I am aware, no one else has addressed this issue – and it seems rather silly to quote a statistic without knowing what it implies about a set of data. Asking experts to identify which factors look similar and relating this to the congruence coefficient suggests that congruence coefficients larger than about 0.85 indicate that the same factor has been found in two different studies (Lorenzo-Seva and ten Berge, 2006). Although this is hardly the most scientific approach, it is probably the best that is available to date. Spreadsheet 11.2 computes congruence coefficients to help users decide whether the same factor is found in up to three different samples of people.

THE KAISER, HUNKA AND BIANCHINI (1971) CRITERION

This is an alternative to the congruence coefficient, but, since Barrett (1986) demonstrated that this technique is both more complicated and less useful than the congruence coefficient, it will not be discussed further.

PROCRUSTES ROTATION

Procrustes rotation[1] (Hurley and Cattell, 1962) allows one to determine whether one set of factor loadings resemble those from another study. One simply specifies the 'target' factor matrix from a previous study, and the software rotates the variables to match this as closely as possible (maximising congruence coefficients). However, Procrustes solutions seem to be too powerful in that almost any set of data – even random data – seem to be able to be coaxed to fit any model that one wants (Horn and Knapp, 1973; Paunonen, 1997). It cannot be recommended, although the Factor program (Lorenzo-Seva and Ferrando, 2006) allows such rotation to a target matrix to be performed.

CONFIRMATORY FACTOR ANALYSIS

This technique is discussed below. There are several variants of the technique, but its most common use is to determine whether the factor loadings, factor correlations, communalities etc. found in one sample are also found in one (or possibly more) different sets of data. For example, if a set of personality variables are administered to a sample of people, an exploratory factor analysis will reveal their factor structure; this can be a hierarchical model or something much simpler. Then confirmatory factor analysis can be used to determine whether the same structure is found when the same variables are administered to another sample (or samples). It performs a chi-square test to determine the degree of fit – which all sounds very good, except that the significance

Table 11.3 Examples of model specification for confirmatory factor analysis

	Factor 1	Factor 2	Factor 3
Var. 1	*		
Var. 2	*		
Var. 3	*		
Var. 4	0	a	
Var. 5	0	a	
Var. 6	0	*	
Var. 7	0	*	
Var. 8	0	0	0.36
Var. 9	0	0	*
Var. 10	0	0	0.43
	Factor correlations		
Factor 1	1		
Factor 2	*	1	
Factor 3	0.3	*	1

of the chi-square test depends on the size of the sample. If the sample is large, then a significant chi-square is almost guaranteed, indicating that the fit is poor. If the sample size is small, even rather different structures appear to fit. Fortunately, however, there are also other indices which may be used to check model fit. For details see Byrne (1995) or Kline (2011).

Though I did not make it explicit, the Procrustes rotation discussed above is an example of confirmatory factor analysis; a method which is used to test whether a particular factor model fits the data. For example, one can use a program such as EQS AMOS, LISREL, MPLUS (or the freeware MX) to analyse a set of data, specifying the model which one wants to fit. Those who are happy using the R-environment may prefer a package such as LAVAAN.

For example, one could specify that the data (10 variables, 200+ cases) should produce a factor matrix with the constraints shown in Table 11.3.

The symbols in Table 11.3 need some explanation. The entries in this table are known as 'parameters', and these can be fixed, estimated or estimated with an equality constraint.

- 0 or some other numerical value implies that the factor loading (or correlation between factors) is precisely the value which is shown; it is a fixed parameter.
- * indicates that the program should provide the best possible estimate of the value of this parameter; a free parameter.

- a, b etc. indicates that the value is to be estimated but should be the same as another loading or correlation with the same label; in the above example, Variable 4 and Variable 5 would both be forced to have exactly the same loading on Factor 2, though the program would determine what this value should be.

The method of specifying these relationships differs between programs, but the basic logic is the same for all of them. It is also possible to specify communalities for the variables (i.e., to test a factor or a component model), and allowing the unique factors associated with each variable to be correlated is common practice – though as mentioned earlier, making post hoc modifications to a model purely to improve its fit to the data is scientifically extremely dubious as it will capitalise on chance variations in the data, meaning that another sample of people cannot possibly be expected to show such good fit to the model. And we cannot tell how much we are overestimating the fit of the model by 'tweaking' it in this way.

Confirmatory factor analysis is a special case of structural equation modelling (Hu and Bentler, 1995), and it is not possible to give a detailed account of the methodology here; my favourite books on the subject are Loehlin (2004) or Kline (2011), whilst David A. Kenny currently provides an excellent online resource at http://www.davidakenny.net/cm/causalm.htm. It is essential to consult some of these sources before performing a confirmatory factor analysis.

This is because the technique holds many traps for the unwary. For example, not all models can be tested. If the user specifies too many parameters to be estimated, it is mathematically impossible to find a unique solution. This should be obvious from the previous factor analysis chapters. If all of the factor loadings on all of the factors were to be estimated, an infinite number of solutions is possible. This is why we use factor rotation in exploratory factor analysis – to impose additional constraints to identify the 'best' of these solutions. In addition, equality constraints (specifying that one parameter should equal another but leaving the program to estimate the best value for the parameter) can pose problems, though thankfully they are rarely used in confirmatory factor analysis.

All of the software programs mentioned above produce a chi-square statistic which shows whether the model is a significantly *bad* fit to the data. This value of chi-square is influenced by the sample size; increasing the sample size will increase the value of chi-square which will make it more likely that the value of chi-squared will be statistically significant, implying that the model is wrong. So (as mentioned earlier in this chapter) a bewildering range of ad hoc indices have been created to measure how well a model fits the data (Hu and Bentler, 1995). There are rules of thumb for interpreting what these mean, but (in my opinion), although it sounds terribly learned to rattle off a lot of values for these indices when publishing a paper using the technique, they actually tell us rather little about how useful the model actually is – see Barrett (2007). Rather than providing an absolute indicator of goodness of fit, these fit indices are much better at showing relative fit – in other words, whether one model is better than another.

One sometimes encounters 'nested models', which are two models where the simpler model is a special case of the more complex one. For example, a two-factor model in which each variable has an appreciable loading on just one factor can be seen as a special case of a one-factor model. This is because, if the correlation between Factor 1 and Factor 2 of the two-factor model is 1.0, this is equivalent to a one-factor model where every variable loads the factor. It is possible to conduct a chi-square test to determine whether the two-factor model fits the data significantly better than the one-factor model. To do so, all that one does is subtract the value of chi-square for the simple model from the chi-square value of the more complex model. One also subtracts the degrees of freedom of the simpler model from the degrees of freedom of the more complex model. Then one simply tests whether the difference in chi-square is significant, using the difference of degrees of freedom.

How then should one use confirmatory factor analysis? If one researcher reports a particular factor structure, how can one check whether it replicates in a different sample?

The obvious technique is to simply set all of the parameters to the values from the rotated factor solution reported by the first author; this tests whether each of the factor loadings, communalities and factor correlations are the same in the second sample. Although this is the most straightforward analysis to perform, I have never seen anyone report such a study. Correlations each have a certain degree of standard error, so we would not expect them to be identical in a second sample; the model would probably not fit that data for this reason, and journals tend not to report failed replications, so authors are under pressure to improve model fit somehow.

The second possibility is to specify the factors as shown for Factor 1 in Table 11.3. In other words, the 'small' loadings from the original study are set to zero, and the 'large' loadings for each factor (perhaps those above 0.4 . . . or the three largest loadings . . . or whatever criterion the author chooses) are set to be estimated, the expectation being that these will be rather different from zero. It is usual to estimate all the correlations between the factors, too, if the original researchers performed an oblique rotation. Assuming that each variable has a substantial loading on each factor, there will be no problems estimating the values for the parameters of this model. The only problem is whether, if the model does not fit the data particularly well, one consults 'modification indices' provided by the software to identify which parameters could be changed in order to improve the fit of the model – the start of what could be a long and dangerous iterative process. The real danger arises when researchers have clearly modified their model to fit the data – but then pretend that this was the model that they planned to test at the outset. Given the pressure to publish positive findings, my advice would be to be very wary of any study which sets out to test a complex model because that model may have come from post hoc analyses and so will very probably not be replicable.

Confirmatory factor analysis is extremely popular, although it may not fare well when applied to personality test items (McCrae et al., 1996). This may be because some personality items may load on more than one factor (for example, Impulsivity is thought to be related to both Extraversion and Neuroticism). The obvious riposte is that one should then perhaps consider trying to write better items that are only influenced by one personality factor, or, if such relationships are well known, the factor model should be amended to allow such variables to load more than one factor.

One word of warning is in order. It is meaningless to perform exploratory factor analysis and confirmatory factor analysis on data from the same sample of people. This is because sampling variations will tend to inflate some factor loadings (and underestimate others) when performing the exploratory factor analysis. If the confirmatory factor analysis uses the same sample, it will encounter the same sampling variations – and so will appear to fit the data much better than it ought.

SUMMARY

This chapter has addressed some slightly more advanced topics in factor analysis. Key amongst them is the idea of a hierarchy of factors, with factors corresponding to very narrow personality traits, ability traits or behaviours at the bottom of a pyramid, and (assuming that some of these are found to intercorrelate appreciably) second-order factors describing the correlations between these factors, third-order factors describing the correlations between the second-order factors and so on. This approach to factor analysis circumvents what may be one of the major problems in modern research – the proliferation of scales containing items which all mean much the same thing. By focusing on how they relate to other, quite different scales, it is possible to discover interesting, unexpected relationships; simply expanding a list of more and more low-level factors does not seem likely to advance the discipline.

Several useful statistical techniques have been introduced, including the bifactor model and techniques for identifying whether the same factor (or factors) has emerged in several different exploratory factor analyses. The chapter ended by giving a glimpse of a technique known as confirmatory factor analysis, which can be used to determine whether the factor structure found in one sample also appears in another group.

NOTE

1 Procrustes was a son of Poseidon in Greek mythology who waylaid travellers and forced them to fit his bed – either by stretching them or by cutting pieces off. Procrustes rotation likewise makes factor loadings larger or smaller in an attempt to get them to fit a target.

CHAPTER 12
ITEM RESPONSE THEORY

This chapter introduces a completely different approach to assessing ability from test scores, one that does not require the use of norms and does not even require that respondents should all take the same items. As its name suggests, the technique considers how people respond to individual items in a test, rather than people's total scores. It leads naturally to 'tailored testing' – the administration of test items by computer, such that the difficulty of the items presented is appropriate for each individual's ability level – and is one of the most exciting recent developments in psychometrics.

ITEM RESPONSE THEORY (IRT)

Thus far we have always assumed that a person's total score on a psychological test provides the best measure of their ability or endowment with a particular personality trait. We are so familiar with adding up the number of items answered correctly (or totalling up scores on Likert scales) and comparing these scores with norms to interpret their meaning for an individual that it is difficult to see an alternative – despite paying lip-service to Michell's criticisms of doing so. In this chapter, I will mainly refer to ability scales, as the mathematics for these is somewhat easier given that each item is only scored 1 (correct) or 0 (incorrect). However, the principles outlined here apply to Likert-scaled items too – these are known as 'ordered-response' scales in the item response literature.

One problem with using the total score as a measure of ability is that someone who gets four easy items correct but fails all the hard items ends up with the same score as someone who (through boredom?) gets one easy item and three of the hard items correct. For the total score completely ignores the available information about the difficulty of the test items. A person will obtain a high score given an easy test and a low score if they are given a hard test, even though their level of ability is exactly the same when taking both tests. In other words, a person's level of ability is confounded with the difficulty of the items which are administered to them; their score on a scale depends on both their ability and the difficulty of the items which they were given. Because conventional tests cannot separate these two things, it is necessary to use tables of norms to interpret test scores.

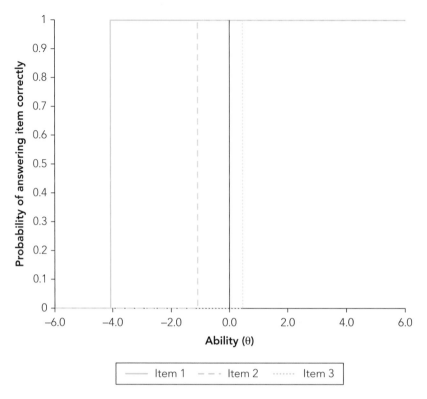

Figure 12.1 Three items forming a Guttman scale

Of course, this would not be an issue if the items formed a Guttman scale (see Chapter 3). Here everyone would pass all of the items that were below their ability level and fail all the ones that were above it. But we saw in Chapter 3 that items simply do not form Guttman scales in real life unless they differ *enormously* in difficulty. However, Guttman scaling introduces two important principles; it is possible to link each person's level of ability to the pattern of items which they answer correctly.

When plotting the responses to items that form a Guttman scale as in Figure 12.1, a person's ability is defined by their position along the horizontal axis. The three lines (known as item characteristic curves, or ICCs) each represent one item. Each line shows the probability that a person with a particular level of ability will answer the item correctly. So (for example) someone with an ability of zero has a 100% chance of answering Items 1 and 2 correctly, and no chance at all of answering Item 3 correctly (the three probabilities are 1.0, 1.0 and 0.0).

Defining item difficulty in terms of ability level is something rather new and rather interesting because it should be obvious that if these data fit the model, the same graph will be obtained *no matter how many people in the sample have each level of ability*. It will not matter whether 5% or 90% of the people in the sample have an ability level between (say) −4 and −2. As long as the data fit the model, the ICCs will look the same. In other words, it might be possible to interpret the meaning of a test score without having to use tables of norms. If true, this could be a huge step forward for psychometrics.

For the sake of simplicity, we shall assume that we are dealing with a 'free-response test' where respondents are asked to produce an answer rather than choose between several alternatives. Otherwise, guessing complicates matters as someone with a very low level of ability may have an above-zero chance of answering an item correctly, just because of lucky guessing.

We pointed out earlier that one of the problems with Guttman scaling is that data simply do not fit that convenient model in real life unless the items differ so enormously in difficulty that administering them would make little sense. But what if the chances of answering an item correctly do not switch suddenly from 0.0 to 1.0? What if there is a more gradual increase in the chances that a person will correctly

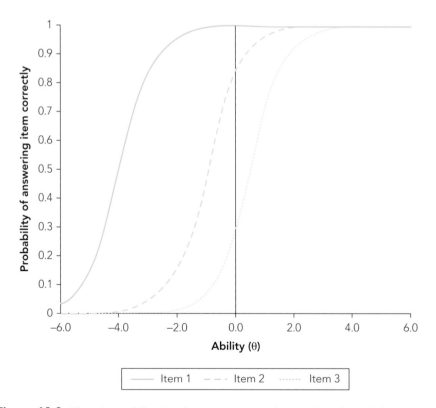

Figure 12.2 Three items following the one-parameter logistic (Rasch) model

answer the item as the ability level increases? In this case, the curves showing the probability that a person with a particular level of ability will answer an item might be as shown in Figure 12.2. They resemble the Guttman model but have the hard corners smoothed off. For now, we will assume that the spread of scores is the same for each curve (i.e., the ICCs all run parallel to each other; they have the same slope), though this assumption will be relaxed later.

The difficulty of each item is defined in terms of the ability of the participants. The difficulty level of an item corresponds to the point at which there is a 50% chance that a person will answer it correctly. This can be read off the graph. One simply identifies the point on the Y-axis where the chances of passing an item is 0.5 and then reads left or right to find where each ICC crosses this line. For Item 1 it is at the ability level of −4, for Item 2 it corresponds to an ability of −1 and for Item 3 it is an ability of 0.5. Do not worry that some of the abilities are positive numbers and some are negative – this is arbitrary, and we have seen above that a person with a zero level of ability will pass two of the three items. So, when using item response theory, it should be remembered that an ability (θ) of zero does not imply that someone scores zero items correct.

Note that the difficulty levels of these items are the same as with the Guttman example (−4, −1 and 1.5), as can be seen by identifying the ability level where there is a 0.5 chance of correctly answering each item.

THE ITEM CHARACTERISTIC CURVE

At this stage we need to make five assumptions about the items in a scale and the ICCs which they produce:

a) The chance of someone getting an item correct depends on both their ability and the difficulty of the test item.
b) All the items in a scale measure just one construct; this can be checked using factor analysis.
c) All of the items have the same 'discrimination' – in other words, the ICCs all have the same slope (are parallel).
d) The chances of someone getting a particular item correct are not influenced by the correctness of responses to any other items, other than as a function of the person's ability. (This is known as the assumption of 'local independence'.)
e) No one gets all of the items correct or all of the items incorrect.

The last two assumptions probably need some explanation. The assumption of local independence means that each item should be an entirely novel problem, and there should be no carry-over from one item to the next – either positive (where a correct answer to one question is either necessary or provides a clue for how to answer another) or negative (where it may be necessary to break the 'set' used in previous questions to arrive at the correct answer). Thus the assumption of local independence would not hold for items such as

Item 1   What is 4+5, and

Item 2   What is the square root of the previous item?

as, if Item 1 is answered incorrectly, so too must be Item 2.

We also need to assume that no one gets all of the items incorrect or all of them correct. This is necessary because values of ability can range (in theory) from minus infinity to infinity. If someone answers all three items in Figure 12.2 correctly, we can see from the figure that their level of ability will almost certainly be greater than 4.0. However, there is no way of telling how *much* bigger than 4 it is, because there is no more difficult item in the scale. Their ability level could be 4.1 or 4000.

For now, we assume that the ICCs run parallel to each other, with the more difficult items to the right of the ability scale. Since item difficulty is the only thing ('parameter') that makes one ICC different from another, the ICCs shown in Figure 12.2 represent the 'one-parameter model', which is also known as the Rasch model after the Danish psychometrician Georg Rasch who developed it (Rasch, 1960). When performing a Rasch analysis it is necessary to estimate the ability of each person in the sample together with the difficulty of each item in the scale. So the number of parameters to be estimated increases as the sample size increases – unlike techniques such as factor analysis, where only factor loadings and communalities are estimated. Thus, whilst using huge samples is advisable for techniques such as structural equation modelling, because large samples result in smaller standard errors of measurement whilst not increasing the number of parameters to be estimated, the same principle will not apply to Rasch scaling.

The graphs shown in Figure 12.2 can be described by a fairly simple mathematical equation, known as the 'logistic function'. There are two main reasons for working with the logistic function. First, the shape of the curve looks sensible according to the criteria outlined above, and it guarantees that the probability of a person's passing an item can never stray outside the range of 0.0 to 1.0. Second, it is easy to work with mathematically in that it does not require any integrations or similar messy techniques to be performed. It starts off at zero, moves smoothly upwards at a point determined by the item's difficulty and then flattens out as it approaches a probability of 1.0.

Rather than plotting graphs, it is possible to calculate the chances that a person with a particular level of ability will correctly answer an item which has a certain level of difficulty. For example, what are the chances that a person whose ability is −1.0 will correctly answer an item whose difficulty is −1.5?

The equation for the one-parameter logistic function is

$$P_i(\theta) = \frac{e^{(\theta - b_i)}}{1 - e^{(\theta - b_i)}}.$$

The left-hand side of the equation reads 'the probability that a person will get item "i" correct given that they have a level of ability that is θ'. On the right-hand side of the equation, e is simply a number whose approximate value is 2.718, θ is the person's ability and b_i is the difficulty level of item 'i'.

So to calculate the chances that a person whose ability is -1.0 will correctly answer an item whose difficulty is -1.5, we simply substitute

$$P_i(1.0) = \frac{e^{(1.0 - 1.5)}}{1 + e^{(1.0 - 1.5)}}$$

$$= \frac{e^{(-0.5)}}{1 + e^{(-0.5)}}$$

$$= \frac{.6065}{1 + .6065}$$

$$= 0.378.$$

which agrees with Figure 12.2.

The only step that may have given any problem here is the evaluation of $e^{-0.5}$. Many websites or calculators will evaluate it.

We have not so far mentioned what the x-axis scale represents. It is a measure of ability in 'logits'. Despite some claims to the contrary, this does not form an interval scale (Salzberger, 2010) but is instead something rather stronger than ordinal measurement – 'linear measurement' which may allow people's abilities (and item difficulties) to be compared so long as the data fit the model. Its scale is set by assuming that all items have a discrimination power of 1.0. A good discussion of these issues is given by Wright and Linacre (1989).

A useful feature of the Rasch technique is that a process called 'conditional maximum likelihood estimation' makes it possible to estimate the difficulty of all of the items in the scale *independently of the abilities of the sample of people who took the items*. Thus, if the assumptions of the model are met, it should be able to give the same set of items to a group of people who are highly able and to another group of less-able individuals – and the difficulties of the items will be the same in both samples. In other words, the numbers (parameters) which specify the difficulty of the items can be estimated without reference to the abilities of the people who take the items. This is known as 'specific objectivity'. Something similar is found when performing a regression. The slope and intercept of the regression line is exactly the same, no matter whether there are a lot of high-ability or low-ability people in the sample. All that matters is that everyone's data fits the model.

Specific objectivity, being able to estimate item difficulties without having to consider the abilities of the people in the sample, is hugely important. For it follows that norms are not needed, as pretty much any sample of people can be used to establish the difficulty of the items, as long as there are several people who pass and fail each item. Unlike conventional tests, it is not necessary to track down a representative sample of the population, administer the scale and tabulate their scores in order to calculate the difficulty of each item in the scale and establish tables of norms. It can be seen that this makes Rasch scaling particularly useful when assessing children, where there is a very wide range of abilities as children mature (Elliott et al., 1996). Then, once the difficulties of the items are known, these items can be used to estimate the ability of a new individual.

RASCH SCALING AND MICHELL'S CRITERIA FOR SCIENTIFIC MEASUREMENT

Because the Rasch model supposedly tests whether data are quantitative (Perline et al., 1979; Wright, 1985), rather than assuming it, a lively debate has arisen about whether Rasch scaling overcomes the objections raised by Michell (1997a). Borsboom and Scholten (2008) give an excellent and accessible précis of some of the issues; it is well worth consulting. Their conclusion is that opponents of Rasch scaling have not proved that it does not overcome Michell's objections (with apologies for the quadruple negative). However, Michell's (2004: 28) view is uncompromising:

> If a person's correct response to an item depended solely on ability, with no random 'error' component involved, one would only learn the ordinal fact that that person's ability at least matches the difficulty level of the item. Item response modelers derive all quantitative information (as distinct from merely ordinal) from the distributional properties of the random 'error' component . . . Here, as elsewhere, psychometricians derive what they want most (measures) from what they know least (the shape of 'error') by presuming

to already know it. . . . By any fair-minded reckoning, our state of knowledge at present does not support claims to be able to measure psychological attributes using item response models.

Paul Barrett (2011: 28) also makes a remarkably clear assessment of the situation:

The idea that a statistical model of questionnaire item responses can somehow reveal quantitative structure for an attribute constructed by that very same statistical model seems unreal to me. Describing the constructed attribute as a 'latent variable' is an attempt to avoid admitting the variable is just something constructed from data observations using a particular form of data analysis. There is nothing 'latent' about such variables.

The debate rumbles on without any obvious conclusion in sight, but it certainly seems that (despite what its proponents sometimes claim) the Rasch model is not a statistical panacea which can determine whether or not a set of items measure some quantitative attribute. The problem is that the debate centres on philosophical definitions of 'measurement', and, ironically enough, many of us who were brought up in the tradition of actually trying to assess individual differences may not have the relevant background or inclination to take part in the debate; it is far easier to just carry on as before with one's head in the sand and hope that someone else will decide that what we are doing is justifiable. However, if psychometrics is to be regarded as a science (rather than a technology which just counts arbitrary things), it is surely necessary to consider these issues in depth.

TWO- AND THREE-PARAMETER MODELS

Thus far we have assumed that every item has an equal 'spread' either side of its difficulty value. This is actually quite a restrictive assumption; it seems quite probable that items' ICCs may have different slopes (or levels of 'discrimination') as shown in Figure 12.3. A small value of discrimination indicates that people with a broad range of abilities have a reasonable chance of getting the item correct. A high value of discrimination indicates that the ICC is much more upright. (The mathematically minded might like to view the discrimination parameter as being the slope of the ICC at its point of inflection.)

In Figure 12.3, Item 1 has a high level of discrimination, Item 2 has a moderate level and Item 3 has a low level, indicating that people of a very wide range of abilities have a chance of answering this item correctly. The two-parameter IRT model thus includes a second parameter ('a') denoting item discrimination. As well as estimating the ability of each person and the difficulty of each item, it is possible also to estimate the discrimination power of each item.

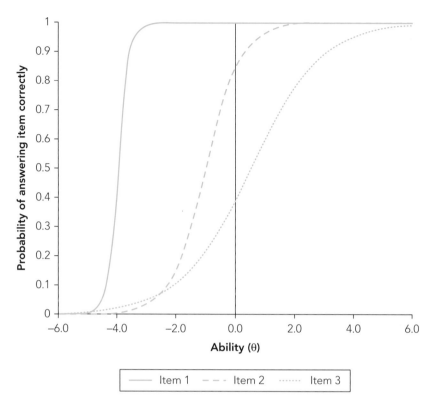

Figure 12.3 Three items following the two-parameter logistic model

The ICCs shown above will clearly be inappropriate for multiple-choice tests. Here even someone with very low ability will have an above-zero chance of getting an item correct by lucky guessing. But what *should* the probability of correctly answering an item be when a person is offered several alternative answers and is asked to choose the correct one? It all depends what one wants to assume. One possibility would be to assume that someone who did not know the answer just guessed one of the answers at random, in which case the probability would simply be

$$\frac{1}{\textit{number of alternatives}}.$$

However this may not be realistic. Some of the alternatives may be so obviously incorrect that even someone of very low ability can eliminate them when choosing an answer. So for each item it might be better to *estimate* what the probability is that a person of very low ability would answer it correctly, rather than assuming that it will be a constant, based on the number of alternative answers offered by a multiple-choice item. This guessing parameter ('c') can be estimated using the three-parameter IRT model – although, as we shall see, it can be difficult to obtain good estimates of its value.

Figure 12.4 shows the same items as in Figure 12.3, only now with guessing parameters of 0.15, 0.2 and 0.25. (Note that when c is not zero, the difficulty of an item is defined slightly differently; it reflects the probability value which is halfway between the lower asymptote and 1. Thus in the case of Item 2 which has c=0.2, the difficulty of the item is determined by a probability of passing it which is

$$0.2 + \frac{1.0 - 0.2}{2}$$

or 0.6.)

It is very easy to modify the formula for the one-parameter logistic formula to take account of the discrimination parameter a_i and the guessing parameter c_i. The modified formula is

$$P_i(\theta) = c_i + (1 - c_i)\frac{e^{a_i(\theta - b_i)}}{1 - e^{a_i(\theta - b_i)}}$$

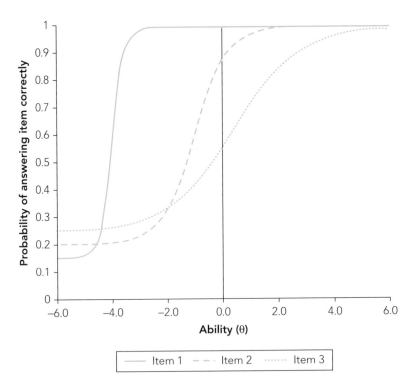

Figure 12.4 Three items following the three-parameter logistic model

where a_i represents the item's discrimination, b_i its difficulty and c_i represents the probability that a respondent of very low ability answers the item correctly.

The above formula is a slight elaboration of the previous one. Thus if c_i=0 and the item discrimination parameter a_i=1.0 we have the equation for the Rasch model.

Although this discussion has been based on an ability model where each person's response to an item is coded as either correct or incorrect, both the Rasch and two- and three-parameter models have been extended to allow the analysis of responses from Likert scales and similar. These are known as 'graded-response models' in the case of the two- and three-parameter models and 'polytomous models' in the case of Rasch scaling.

ITEM- AND TEST-INFORMATION FUNCTIONS

Suppose that we want to use a scale to discriminate between people who have levels of ability between 2 and 6. It should be obvious that only one of the three items shown in Figure 12.4 can help us distinguish between people whose abilities lie in that range; Items 1 and 2 are so easy that everyone with an ability between 2 and 6 will get them correct. Items which everyone passes, or items which everyone gets incorrect, can tell us nothing about individual differences in people's ability. So it is necessary to find a way of determining which items will be useful for measuring abilities within a certain range. The information function does this. It shows the precision with which a parameter can be estimated at a particular ability level. For, whenever a parameter is estimated using item response theory, the software produces a standard deviation, which shows how much measurement error is present. The information function is simply one divided by the square of this standard deviation. Thus, the smaller the standard deviation (implying the more accurate the measurement), the larger the information function is.

The usual warning applies; if the model does not fit the data, none of these clever statistics have any value whatsoever. But when the data do fit the model, the item-information function is a very useful statistic that can show the range of abilities for which a particular item can discriminate between people with accuracy. It shows the precision with which an item can measure the trait at a particular level of ability.

Figure 12.5 shows three ICCs (solid lines) and their associated information functions (dotted lines). The point at which each information function reaches its peak shows for which ability level each item can most accurately measure a person's ability, and its height at any ability level indicates how accurately it can measure an ability of that level.

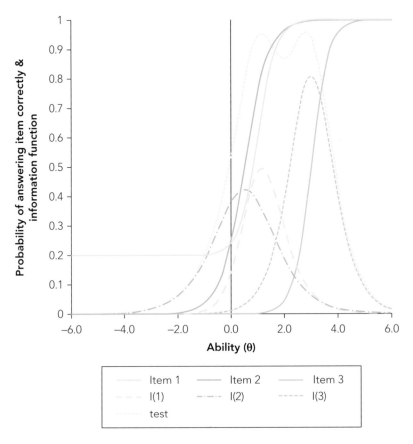

Figure 12.5 Item characteristic curves, information functions and the test–information function from three items

It should be clear that the information function sits (almost) directly underneath the corresponding ICC; the position of its maximum is close to (but not necessarily identical to) the difficulty of the item.

EXERCISE 12.1: INFORMATION FUNCTION

Resources required: Spreadsheet 12.1: Information function. From www.routledge.com/9781138228894

Purpose: To show how the item-information function and test-information function can be used to select items to measure a particular range of abilities

Contents of spreadsheet: Item parameters from three items

Suggested activity:

- Try adjusting the three parameters of Item 1 to allow it to make as good a discrimination as possible between people whose abilities are in the range of −4 to −2. You might want to start by noticing how varying the item difficultly affects the information function. Then perhaps vary the discrimination power of the item. Finally, see what effect changing the guessing parameter has on the information function. Note that the maximum value of the information function can be (and often is) greater than 1.
- What do you notice if the c parameter is greater than zero?
- What do you notice if the a parameter is small – i.e., less than 1?

Learning outcomes:

Readers should now be able to

- appreciate how selecting items with particular parameters may be used to determine the ability range for which a test provides maximum information.

Exercise 12.1 shows that the width of the information function is determined by the discrimination parameter. The larger the c parameter, the lower the information function is. The information functions are not normal distributions (try item parameters of 4, −3 and 0.5 and notice the slight skew of the information function, which peaks at an ability level of −2.9). However, the most interesting thing to come out of this analysis is that an item with low discrimination power is of little use for measuring anything at all, as can be seen by its low information function. This is well worth remembering when using IRT to develop scales.

It is also possible to calculate the test-information function simply by adding together all the item–information functions. This shows, for each level of ability, how accurately the scale can discriminate between people of that ability level. The test-information function is also shown in Figure 12.5. It shows that for these three items, the test performs best when discriminating between people whose abilities are roughly between 1 and 3.5.

It should now be apparent how massively useful item response theory can be. For once the item parameters are known, it is possible to put together items to form a test with just about any desired test characteristic curve, depending on the purpose of testing. One just estimates the parameters for a large set of items and selects a few items which will produce the desired test-information function. For example, an employer might be interested in discriminating between borderline applicants; they may not be particularly interested in accurate assessments of the very best applicants or the very weakest. They would want a test-information function that is as high as possible towards the middle of the ability spectrum – their experience with previous applicants should give an idea of which levels of ability should be assessed with great accuracy. Or a school may wish to administer items to assess students' progress in mathematics, and, in contrast, they might want the test to measure all abilities equally accurately – in other words, for this application the test-information function should be as high, wide and as rectangular as possible.

EXERCISE 12.2: HOW ITEM PARAMETERS INFLUENCE THE INFORMATION FUNCTION

Resources required: Spreadsheet 12.1: Information function. From www.routledge.com/9781138228894

Purpose: To give further experience at identifying items which are appropriate for a particular ability level by using the information function

Contents of spreadsheet: Item parameters from three items

Suggested activity:

Adjust the item parameters in Spreadsheet 12.1 to

- create a test which discriminates between people with abilities between 0.0 and 2.0;
- create a test which discriminates between people with abilities between −4 and +4.

Learning outcomes:

Readers should now be able to

- appreciate how and why low item discrimination and substantial guessing parameters are best avoided when selecting items using IRT.

It can be seen that unlike reliability coefficients for conventional scales which attempt to estimate the correlation between scores on a scale and the participants' true scores, item response theory allows the accuracy of measurement to be ascertained *for each particular ability level*. The test-information function in Figure 12.5 is 0.5 for a person having an ability of zero. Therefore, if this three-item test estimates someone's ability to be 0, the standard error of measurement is

$$\frac{1}{\sqrt{0.5}} = 1.41$$

This allows one to say (for example) that there is a 95% chance that this person's true ability lies somewhere between $0 - 1.96 \times 1.41$ and $0 + 1.96 \times 1.41$; between -2.77 and $+2.77$, in other words.

RASCH VERSUS TWO- AND THREE-PARAMETER MODELS

Although they are closely related, there are strong differences of opinion about whether it is better to use the one-parameter (Rasch) model or adopt the two- or three-parameter models. Those who favour Rasch scaling have outlined their position clearly in working papers and other useful references at http://www.rasch.org, and it is worthwhile browsing these resources to obtain a deeper understanding of the issues outlined below. The (sometimes abrasive) dispute between those who follow the Rasch model and those who favour the more complex models basically hinges on whether one should make a strong assumption about the relationship between item difficulty and ability – namely that every item has exactly the same slope – and ruthlessly remove any items from a scale which do not meet this assumption. Under the Rasch model, differences in the discrimination power of items are regarded as error variance, whereas the two- and three-parameter models estimate these parameters, and so they will inevitably provide better fit to the data than the Rasch model. As will be seen, the one-parameter model does have certain advantages over the two- and three-parameter models, which may make its use worthwhile. For example, the ICCs are always parallel under the Rasch model, whereas under the others they can cross each other. Thus a person might be expected to fail an easy item and pass a harder one; this could happen if a person whose ability was −4 took Items 2 and 3 whose ICCs are shown in Figure 12.4. However, it means that it is not possible to apply the technique to all sets of items; one will only realise that they do not fit the Rasch model after analysing them, and so it may take several iterations to develop a scale which fits the Rasch model.

Advocates of the Rasch model stress that it has the following merits. Only the Rasch model allows the item difficulties to be estimated separately from the person abilities, and so only the Rasch model allows 'sample-free' estimates of item difficulty to be calculated ('specific objectivity'). In a section entitled 'illiterate theory' Wright (1984: 1) writes, 'The estimation virtues extolled by Swaminathan in a chapter featuring the three-parameter model apply, in fact, only to the one parameter Rasch model' – strong words, indeed. In addition to specific objectivity, proponents of the Rasch model argue that there are several other reasons to prefer it to the more complex two and three-parameter models.

- Differences in item discrimination power can be regarded as examples of items failing to fit the model; scales can be constructed by simply removing such aberrant items, making more complex models unnecessary.
- Rasch scaling can be used to analyse multiple-choice data, and, when it is, the degree of fit can be surprisingly good (Holster and Lake, 2016). In some cases, it seems that estimates of ability are little affected by using the Rasch rather than the three-parameter model.
- Empirically it sometimes seems that item difficulties estimated by the Rasch technique are not very different from those estimated by the three-parameter model (Linacre and Wright, 1995) though it would be naive to assume that this will be the case for all sets of data.
- The Rasch model is parsimonious, which is usually regarded as a virtue in science. Why develop a model requiring the estimation of more parameters if a simple one (which has the advantage of 'specific objectivity') will suffice?
- When estimating parameters took hours or days of computer time, it used to matter that Rasch analysis required less computing power than two- or three-parameter models. However, this is now of trivial importance.

Advocates of the two- and three-parameter models counter with the following points:

- No model ever shows perfect invariance because no model (especially the Rasch) ever perfectly fits the data. Invariance is thus not an all-or-nothing phenomenon – there are degrees of invariance, and parameter estimates will thus always show some 'drift' from sample to sample. Empirically, item difficulty parameters taken from several different samples fitted by the two- and three-parameter models correlate very substantially indeed, typically with R-squared of 0.9 or above (Lord, 1980; Rudner, 1974; Rupp and Zumbo, 2006), perhaps indicating that two- or three-parameter models show 'good-enough' invariance.
- 'Common sense rules against the supposition that guessing plays no part in the process for answering multiple-choice items. The supposition is false, and no amount of pretense will make it true' (Traub, 1983).
- Hambleton and Traub (1973) demonstrated that for short tests where items varied in their discrimination power, the two-parameter model provided more accurate ability estimates than the Rasch model; Hambleton and Cook (1983) further found that for scales comprising 20 items, the three-parameter model gave a better fit to the true structure of the data than did the one-parameter model, although this difference became smaller as the number of variables increased.

Pragmatically, the choice of whether to use the one-parameter model or something more complex boils down to personal preference, the length of the scale, whether or not one is willing to remove what *look* like good items just because they do not fit the model and how well the data fit the model – bearing in mind that the statistical significance of goodness-of-fit indices will be influenced by sample size. An excellent discussion of how to check whether a model fits the data is given by Hambleton et al. (1991).

ESTIMATING ABILITIES AND ITEM PARAMETERS

As mentioned above, the basic aim of item response theory is to estimate the difficulty level of each item in the test, and (at the same time) estimate the ability of each person who takes the test. So, if a test comprises 20 items and the responses of 100 children are analysed, it will be necessary to estimate 20 measures of item difficulty and 100 measures of ability for the one-parameter model, plus 20 item discriminations if the two-parameter model is used, plus another 20 item difficulty indices if a three-parameter model is adopted. How can all these numbers be estimated?

We argued earlier that the item characteristic curve shows the chances of people with various levels of ability passing a particular test item. Perhaps a computer program can be written to firstly make a rough estimate of the abilities of the various people (perhaps on the basis of the number of items answered correctly) and, given these abilities, then estimate the difficulty levels of each of the items. Then the same process could be repeated backwards, with the people's abilities being estimated from the item-difficulty statistics. This process could be repeated time and time again, obtaining better estimates of the ability and item parameters at each stage, until the estimates of the people's ability and the items' difficulties cannot be improved any more. In other words, the program can attempt to find the most appropriate values for all of the item parameters and abilities. Swaminathan and Gifford (1983) have shown that when the number of items and persons is fairly large, the estimates of the parameters that are obtained in this way are quite close to their true values for the one- and two-parameter models, whilst the three-parameter model is rather more problematical.

It is fairly straightforward to develop a goodness-of-fit statistic which shows how well a particular set of item parameters and abilities fit the data. Altering any parameter will increase or decrease the value of this fit statistic – so all one needs to do is adjust the several-hundred item parameters and abilities until one finds the combination which provides the best value for the goodness-of-fit statistic. Put like this, it sounds a simple-enough procedure, but numerically estimating all these parameters is not simple and can go wrong. This is why there is no spreadsheet to perform IRT analyses to accompany this book; it is just too computationally demanding. The whole procedure is exactly analogous to a blind explorer wandering through a landscape, trying to find the lowest point. If the landscape consists of gentle slopes downwards all leading into a single bowl-shaped crater this is easy – one just keeps walking downhill until one can go no further. But what if the landscape is fairly flat, with many shallow valleys and depressions? You would need to do a lot of exploring to cover them all – and there is always the danger that, although you *think* you have found the lowest point, this is in fact a 'local minimum' because there is another, lower, point ('global minimum') in an area which has not been thoroughly explored. If a program invites the user to specify the number of iterations to be performed, this is a rough analogy for how much walking should be done in an attempt to find the global minimum. The 'tolerance' or 'convergence criterion' usually specifies how flat the ground has to be before one is sure that one has reached the lowest point.

This problem affects several types of software, including structural equation modelling, but is a particular issue with the three-parameter model. The 'solution' is to repeat the analysis several times, starting from a different point each time, to check that you end up in the same place – though there is no guarantee that this will be the true global minimum, especially if there is a small deep hole with steep sides somewhere in an otherwise flat region. And, like the hapless explorer, one has no idea what the terrain looks like. Mathematicians have developed several techniques for performing such non-linear optimisation routines, but one can never be quite certain that they will find the single best solution to a particular problem. And suppose that there are three points on the landscape all within a hairsbreadth of being the same height above sea level. If one is lucky, the program will consistently find the lowest point and base the parameter estimates on its location. What it will *not* show is that there are a couple of other, very different, solutions which are almost as good – and which may well yield very different estimates of the parameters in the model. It would be good to know that this is happening so that one can treat the set of parameter estimates with some scepticism, but as far as I know no programs do this.

Several computer programs have been written to simultaneously estimate abilities and item difficulties (and, optionally, discrimination and guessing parameters). An internet search will locate the software. Commercial software includes Xcalibre and Winsteps (for Rasch); free student and trial versions are available. Bilog and Multilog are also widely used. All run on Windows. jMetrik is a freeware Java-based program by J. Patrick Meyer at the University of Virginia which runs on a variety of platforms and is fairly straightforward to use. Param by Lawrence Rudner is another Windows freeware offering which is exceptionally straightforward though it only estimates item and person parameters and their standard errors. Any readers who enjoy using the R environment may find routines such as ltm, TAM, eRm and mirt appealing.

ITEM RESPONSE THEORY AND TEST-ITEM BIAS

One important application of item response theory is the detection of bias in tests. All one needs to do is estimate the item–difficulty parameters for two groups of people – generally a majority and a racial minority group. To determine whether an item is biased against (or in favour of) a minority group, all one needs to do is estimate the item parameters for each group separately. If the item shows no bias, these two ICCs, which show how likely it is that a person of a particular ability from a particular group will pass the item, should be identical. If the item shows bias, they will be different. If a two-parameter model is used, this approach can also show which *level* of ability bias is found. For example, it could be the case that there is no difference at all between the groups at high levels of ability but that the item becomes much harder for minority group members of low ability than for majority group members of low ability. This method of detecting bias is particularly important, given that the difficulty parameters are sample free, and so it should not matter whether one group has higher average scores than the other.

It is possible to calculate a chi-square statistic to test whether or not the item–parameter estimates for a scale differ significantly; this essentially tests whether the test-information functions are the same for the two groups. Several other approaches are possible too (Hambleton and Swaminathan, 1985; Millsap and Everson, 1993), but this area can get technical.

One simple way of detecting bias is to analyse the data item by item. One can simply plot the ICCs for two (or more) groups on the same graph. The area between the two graphs can give some indication of the degree of bias shown by that item. For example, suppose that in one group, an item has $a=0.8$ and $b=1.2$, whilst in another group $a=1.0$ and $b=0.9$; $c=0$ for both groups. Plotting these two ICCs (using Spreadsheet 12.1) shows that the two items are unbiased for ability levels less than about 0 but that they show appreciable bias for higher abilities.

Once the parameters defining each curve are known, determining the area between the two curves is a simple problem to solve using calculus or numerical integration – although it is difficult to know what to do with this information once one has obtained it. However, it might be useful for identifying the most and least biased items in a scale. Of course, this approach precludes the use of the three-parameter model, unless the guessing parameter ('c') is fixed to be the same for both groups. This is because as ability scores theoretically range down to minus infinity, if there is any discrepancy between the c-parameters of the two ICCs, the area between the two ICCs will also tend to infinity.

TAILORED TESTING

The second really important consequence of item response theory is that estimates of the ability of people can be made from different items. For example, Alan might be given Items 1, 3 and 6; Joel might be administered Items 2, 4 and 5 – but despite them having taken quite different sets of items, it would be possible to compare their scores on the ability scale.

In order to develop a tailored test, it is first necessary to develop an 'item bank' – a set of items which form a scale, whose difficulties (and perhaps their discrimination powers and guessing parameters) are known and each of which can be administered by computer. To establish their parameters, they are all administered to a sample of people. Because of specific objectivity, it does not matter too much which sample is used to estimate item difficulty, as long as a reasonable number of people (say 30 or more) in the sample pass each item and another 30+ fail each item. This is necessary because – obviously – if everyone passes or fails an item, its difficulty cannot be determined.

The results are analysed using scaling software, and three sets of things are estimated:

- the difficulty (and perhaps discrimination and guessing parameter) for each item;
- its goodness of fit to the chosen model (Rasch, two-parameter or three-parameter);
- ideally, its degree of bias, assuming that the sample comprises two or more reasonably large sets of people.

If the bank of items being developed is large, it might not be feasible to administer them all to the same group(s) of people as the test is being developed. It is possible to administer some of the items to one sample of people and another set of items to a second sample of people *as long as some items are taken by everyone*. A process known as test equating may then be used to place all of the items on the same scale – even though just a few of them have been taken by members of both samples. Most scaling software will perform such analyses.

Items which do not fit the model need to be dropped, and, as mentioned earlier, more items will be dropped if Rasch scaling is used than if the two-parameter or three-parameter models are employed. Items showing bias should also be dropped at this stage. We now have a database containing the item content and between one and three parameters for each item. All of these items measure a single scale. Specialised software is then used to select items from this database and administer them to a participant.

The test starts by guessing that the participant will be of roughly average ability. An item of average difficulty is selected at random and is presented on screen, the participant's response is recorded and scored (as correct or incorrect) and this is used to refine the estimate of the person's ability. This process is repeated over and over again. As more and more data are gathered, the computer program will be able to predict ever more accurately which not-yet-taken items a person will be able to answer correctly and which they will fail. This allows the person's ability to be determined very rapidly. The information function guides this process of item selection. It identifies which level of item difficulty will give most information about a person's ability, given their performance on previous items. The software will then find an item of the appropriate difficulty, administer it and recalculate the estimate of the person's ability. The process continues until the program has estimated the person's level of ability with sufficient accuracy.

This process, known as 'tailored testing' has several advantages over conventional assessments.

One of the problems with conventional testing is knowing which scale to select. One has to rely on experience, 'gut feeling' or something equally unscientific when deciding which ability test to lift from the shelf, for some are designed for college students, some for young children, some for the general adult population . . . If one chooses an inappropriate test, the participant will either have to take a lot of insultingly easy items (making them bored or careless) or else find that most of the items are impossibly difficult (making them give up). Adaptive testing overcomes this problem. The participant will always be answering items that feel challenging but not impossible, which makes the whole experience more enjoyable.

The second issue is shorter assessment times. Because participants do not have to waste time taking items which are insultingly easy or impossibly difficult for them and so which yield no real information about their ability, adaptive tests can gain relevant information about the participant's ability more quickly.

Third, it overcomes problems of test security. It does not matter too much if someone posts online about the items they were asked to answer when applying for a job – since another applicant will probably be given a completely different set of items.

MOKKEN SCALING

How sensible is it to make extremely strong assumptions about the relationship between people's abilities and the way in which they actually perform when answering test items? No one ever pretends that any model (Rasch or something more complex) ever fits the data exactly – and yet all the desirable properties of item response theory assume that the fit is perfect. So, whilst the mathematical sophistication of the technique appeals to psychometricians, it is not entirely clear how useful the techniques are for day-to-day assessments. Also, in many practical applications, one does not really need to try to measure people's ability with the sort of precision that item response theory claims to offer; very often an employer will just wish to know which 10 candidates performed best on some scale, without worrying too much about whether the candidate ranked no. 6 is a lot or just slightly more able than the candidate ranked no. 7. Mokken scaling is a form of item response theory that does not require such stringent assumptions as the Rasch or two- or three-parameter models. Like other forms of item response theory, Mokken scaling can be applied to data which are scored 0/1 (as in most ability-test data) or to data from Likert scales or similar. However, Mokken scaling of Likert (and similar) data raises some theoretical complications – see for example the explanations given by Wind (2017).

Mokken scaling (Mokken and Lewis, 1982) is a non-parametric approach to item response theory which orders the items in terms of difficulty and orders the participants according to their levels of ability, whilst making far fewer assumptions about the relationship between ability and performance on test items. There are actually two different forms of Mokken scaling, which make different assumptions about the relationship between the ICCs and ability. Rather than assuming that the ICC follows a specified mathematical function, such as the logistic curve, the first version of Mokken scaling (known as 'monotonic') just assumes for each ICC that the probability of passing an item increases (or stays constant) as one moves from low ability to higher-ability candidates; it is never the case that the probability of passing the item decreases as ability increases. The second form of Mokken scaling ('doubly monotonic') imposes a second constraint. Like Rasch scaling, it assumes that the ICCs never cross – but unlike Rasch

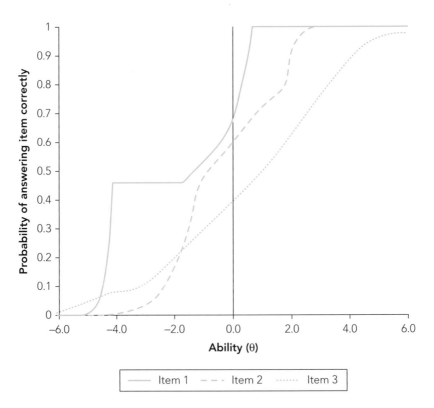

Figure 12.6 Item characteristic curves meeting the demands of Mokken scaling

scaling it does not assume that the ICCs follow any particular mathematical function. Only the doubly monotonic model allows the items to be placed in (invariant) order.

All of the ICCs in Figure 12.6 would be acceptable for Mokken scaling because, although they follow no particular function, they never move downwards as ability increases. Note that Items 1 and 2 fulfil the requirement for double monotonicity.

The other two assumptions made by both forms of Mokken scaling are that of local independence and unidimensionality. These will be familiar from our discussion of Rasch scaling. Local independence means that there is no 'carry-over' from one item to the next, whilst unidimensionality assumes that all of the items in a scale measure the same trait. Taken together these imply that the only reason a person produces a particular response to a test item is their level of the trait being measured plus random error.

Mokken scaling starts off by performing Guttman scaling (see Chapter 3). Suppose that eight people take four items and each answer is coded as correct or incorrect. This trivially small set of data is shown below. The left part of Table 12.1 shows the responses as they are collected (i.e., in a random order), whereas in the right-hand side of the table the columns have been rearranged so that the hardest item (most incorrect answers) comes first and so on. And the right-hand side of the table also roughly orders people so that the most able people (in terms of the number of items answered correctly) are near the top. This does not need any fancy mathematics at all – it just involves sorting the data.

It should be clear from this analysis that the data do not form a Guttman scale. Item 4 appears to be the most difficult one, with only two people passing it. However, one of these (Person 1) got Item 1 incorrect – and as it is easier, this should not happen if the data form a perfect Guttman scale. There are other anomalies too (look at Person 6).

Table 12.1 Responses of eight people to four test items; unsorted and sorted by item difficulty and ability

Unsorted					Sorted by difficulty and ability				
	Item 1	Item 2	Item 3	Item 4		Item 4	Item 1	Item 3	Item 2
Pers. 1	0	1	1	1	Pers. 4	1	1	1	1
Pers. 2	0	1	1	0	Pers. 5	0	1	1	1
Pers. 3	0	0	0	0	Pers. 1	1	0	1	1
Pers. 4	1	1	1	1	Pers. 8	0	0	1	1
Pers. 5	1	1	1	0	Pers. 2	0	0	1	1
Pers. 6	1	1	0	0	Pers. 6	0	1	0	1
Pers. 7	0	1	0	0	Pers. 7	0	0	0	1
Pers. 8	0	1	1	0	Pers. 3	0	0	0	0
Sum						2	3	5	7

Table 12.2 Contingency table showing Items 1 and 4 from Table 12.1

		Item 4	
Item 1	score	0	1
	0	4	1
	1	2	1

In order to tell how well these data form a Guttman scale, it is possible to perform some statistical analyses by looking at the 2×2 contingency tables for each pair of items. So for four items there would be six tables similar to Table 12.2.

For a perfect Guttman scale, everyone who passed the harder item (Item 4) would also pass the other. Table entries which do not fit this model are known as 'Guttman errors'. It is possible to calculate a statistic called Loevinger's H (Loevinger, 1948), which is simply the value of the phi correlation coefficient divided by its maximum possible value. It can be calculated using Spreadsheet 5.3. Dividing phi by its maximum possible value provides an index which varies between 0 (randomness) and 1 (agreement which is as good as possible, given any difference in difficulty between the items). Loevinger's H is therefore 1.0 if the two items form a perfect Guttman scale (i.e., everyone who passes one item fails the other) or 0 if there is no relationship between scores on the two items. For the data shown above, Loevinger's H is 0.2. If one follows the same logic as Rasch scalers (i.e., removing items that do not fit the model), it might be appropriate to remove items with low H-values from a scale before using it.

It is also possible to average these correlations (six of them, in the case of four variables) to obtain an index for the scale as a whole; this basically shows how well the scale as a whole fits the Guttman model.

Mokken defines a scale as any set of items which all have positive correlations between them and which also show positive values of H. A quick factor analysis beforehand will ensure that all of the items measure just one trait. A rule of thumb seems to be that a value of H above 0.3 for each item is good enough for the items to form a 'satisfactory' Mokken scale (Mokken, 1971), though obviously the larger the value of H, the better each item fits the Guttman model. A value above 0.5 is regarded as 'good'. These figures are arbitrary guidelines, based on experience using the technique rather than any firm statistical theory. However, they seem to be widely used.

Roskam et al. (1986) point out several problems with using H for Mokken scaling:

- The discrimination power of the items (the steepness of the ICC). Items with near-vertical ICCs will lead to larger values of H, all other things being equal.

- The difference in difficulty between two items matters. Items which differ substantially in difficulty will tend to have higher values of H.
- The value of H will be linked to the variance of people's scores on the trait. H will be low if the variance is either very low or very high.

These points seem to have merit, and Sijtsma's (1998) excellent review considers these and other problems with the technique. Several 'how to' guides give excellent accounts of Mokken scaling (Sijtsma and van der Ark, 2017; van Schuur, 2003; Wind, 2017) of which Sijtsma and van der Ark is perhaps the most accessible for non-specialists. That paper summarises much recent research on Mokken scaling and gives particular emphasis to the problem of assessing model fit for the doubly monotonic model, which is the one that most users would probably want to adopt. It also gives a step-by-step guide of how to perform Mokken scaling, complete with a worked example. As far as software for Mokken scaling is concerned, there are a few reasonably modern choices – the Mokken routine, which runs in the R statistical environment, or the Mokken or MSP modules for users of Stata.

SUMMARY

This chapter has explored several techniques that estimate people's abilities and item difficulties simultaneously. They may allow test scores to be interpreted directly (i.e., without using norms) as the item difficulties can be estimated independently of the distribution of abilities within the sample. However, it is not obvious that these techniques are able to produce ability estimates that satisfy Michell's criteria for scientific measurement. It has been shown that these techniques have great potential for adaptive testing. However, the strong assumptions that they make about the way in which people respond to test items make some psychometricians uneasy. Mokken scaling is a quick, simple technique which makes far fewer assumptions and merits serious attention.

CHAPTER 13
CONSTRUCTING A SCALE

Obviously, writing good items is *the* crucial step in developing a scale. If the items are poorly written or tested on an inappropriate sample of people, then no amount of psychometric wizardry will ever be able to produce a reliable and valid scale. Kline (1986) and Most and Zeidner (1995) have given some common-sense 'rules of thumb' for writing items and developing scales which might also be useful for those who plan to construct a scale. Gulliksen (1986) is an excellent, non-technical paper on the assessment of abilities and attainment. It considers several other forms of test items and makes vital reading for anyone who is interested in constructing tests in this general area.

It is also necessary to consult the guidelines for the construction and use of psychological tests and the code of human research ethics of one's professional association (e.g., British Psychological Society, American Psychological Association, Canadian Psychological Association) when designing and developing a test.

Developing a test or scale involves developing the items, analysing the items to discover which ones work and which do not, checking reliability as described in Chapter 6, validating the scale as described in Chapter 7 and producing documentation for others who might be interested in using the measure.

DEVELOPING ITEMS

SAMPLING ITEMS FROM THE DOMAIN

This book has stressed that any scale is simply a sample of items from the domain which the scale seeks to measure. There are two ways of doing this: trying to sample items at random (for example, opening a dictionary at random and selecting a word on the page at random) or by some sort of stratified sampling. I would favour ensuring that the scale is a stratified sample of all of the items which could conceivably be written; that is, a sample where equal numbers of items are drawn from a number of different sub-domains, called 'facets'. The simplest example is an attainment test where students are assessed on knowledge and skills which they acquire over a series of weeks. Here the sensible choice of a facet would be knowledge gathered in a particular class or in a particular week. This will presumably be defined in the course syllabus and so is easy to access. Ensuring that each facet contains the same number of items is a simple way of ensuring that the assessment covers what was taught. Without such discipline it is possible that some areas of the syllabus may be omitted whilst others are over-represented.

Using this approach to measure psychological traits, it is usually necessary to look at the literature to determine what the facets should be. Without the discipline of thinking in terms of facets it is very easy to write an item with which one feels proud . . . and so write another, which is quite similar to it, and then another . . . whilst quite forgetting to cover the whole breadth of the trait. It would probably be better if several people wrote items without collaborating because this should prevent one writer producing items which are too similar in content or format. However, this does not seem to be common practice.

Items which virtually everyone answers in the same way (personality items) or which almost everyone gets correct or incorrect (ability items) cause problems if they are concentrated in one facet rather than being distributed randomly. Such items cannot discriminate between people and so will mean that facet is essentially ignored when assessing differences between people. An experienced or omniscient instructor could avoid this by trying to ensure that all items were of equivalent difficulty or by ensuring that each facet was assessed using, for example, one easy, one moderately difficult and one difficult question. However, the problem is that one does not know for sure how difficult an item will be or how similarly people will respond to an item when one writes it.

Constructing ability scales, rather than knowledge-based scales, is more difficult because it is less obvious how one should sample the whole domain of possible items. Whilst some scales (e.g., Heim et al., 1970) include a mixture of items ranging from vocabulary items to series completion, they are unusual. Instead, most scales contain items which are highly similar in content. Indeed, we have speculated that a typical scale designer thinks of some task ('What is the next shape in the series . . . ?', or 'Which three-letter word can be inserted in place of the asterisks to form another word?', or 'How many words can you think of to describe [an object] within 2 minutes?') and then claim to have discovered a new ability trait by measuring performance on this scale. This is why discovering the higher-order traits is far more important than focusing on low-level factors, as was argued in Chapter 11. Otherwise the number of ability traits equals the number of possible scales which could be devised, which is near infinite.

There is another problem, too. In the case of ability items, it is necessary to ensure (as far as possible) that each item involves the same cognitive processes. Just because two items share the same format, it does not follow that they are difficult for the same reasons. For example, consider the two items 'Food is to mouth as seed is to (a) earth (b) plant . . .', which is difficult because it is necessary to recognise that the relationship between the first two items is 'goes into' making (a) the correct answer. On the other hand, 'Oblimin is to oblique as VARIMAX is to (a) orthogonal (b) eigenvalue . . .' is difficult because only those who know about psychometrics would know what Oblimin etc. are. The relationship ('performs this form of rotation') is trivially easy to spot if one knows the meaning of the terms. So, although the format of the two items is identical, the first relies on reasoning whilst the second requires quite detailed knowledge for its successful solution. When writing items, it is necessary to consider both the knowledge needed and the cognitive processes which may be required to solve each problem.

Specifying the areas of content which a scale should measure is probably the most important, yet overlooked, aspect of scale design. Writing items is fairly easy; determining what, precisely, the scale should measure requires some grasp of the theoretical background plus a thorough knowledge of the literature in the area. There is also the possibility that the trait one wishes to assess simply does not exist. Just because one *thinks* that some people fear succeeding whilst others do not and that this is an important determinant of behaviour, it does not follow that this is true. So, whilst it is perfectly possible to write items that are close paraphrases of each other and so form a highly reliable scale and go on to discover that people who fear success tend to be more anxious than those who do not, it does not follow that the scale will show incremental validity or predict behaviour any better than a broader anxiety scale. Test developers need to be aware that all their effort may come to nothing.

DEFINING THE POPULATION WITH WHOM THE SCALE IS TO BE USED

It is important to specify this as it determines how difficult ability items should be, and how complex the vocabulary of items in personality scales and their instructions may become. If a scale is designed for use in a *very* diverse population, then it may be necessary to ensure that the items are non-verbal. For example, an ability scale might use shapes rather than words, with instructions involving animations (for example, showing that the aim of the test is to identify which piece would not fit into a jigsaw). A personality scale might ask people to show which cartoon figure best depicts how they might react or feel in a certain situation. For examples of how non-verbal personality items may be designed and used, see Paunonen et al. (1990) and Paunonen's subsequent work.

There is literature on the vocabulary and complexity of sentence structure that is typically found in personality scales (e.g., Schinka, 2012), which suggests that several of the words used in the items and the instructions of popular scales are far above the vocabulary level of the average American. However, this seems to rather miss the point; the vocabulary and sentence structure used should surely be suitable for the *least* well-educated, *least* intelligent individual who will ever be given the scale. Short, common words, short sentences and simple grammar are advisable (no double-negatives, passive voice, gerunds etc.) unless the population for whom the scale is designed is well educated and will answer the items in their first language.

Consideration should also be given to what background knowledge each person should be assumed to have. For example, items in some American personality questionnaires refer to concepts ('United Way', 'Grade Point Average') which will be unfamiliar to those outside North America. One can only assume that when these scales were being devised someone decided that their use would be confined to that continent. Having culturally inappropriate items in a scale is a problem because it will reduce the reliability of the scale, as people will need to guess what the concepts mean or respond randomly. Participants may also object to seeing culturally inappropriate items and may not take the rest of the items seriously.

Psychologists are finally starting to take the problem of generalisability of results seriously. If a scale is developed using a sample of psychology students from Queen's University, Belfast, will it show identical psychometric properties (difficulty, reliability, validity etc.) if it is administered to chemistry students at that institution? Or psychology students at Cambridge University? Or sociology students at the University of Hawaii? Or 15-year-old Parisians? No one really knows, though one would never guess this from articles in journals. All too often, authors assume that scales that work in one context for one sample of people will miraculously generalise to almost any application with almost any group of people. Simons et al. (2017) suggest that researchers should abandon this naive assumption and be forced to rigorously justify why, precisely, on theoretical or empirical grounds, the results from one sample might be expected to generalise to another.

DETERMINING THE METHOD OF ADMINISTRATION

It is obviously sensible to develop items in the same format in which they will eventually be used (only excluding time limits, for reasons discussed below). A test that is ultimately designed to be administered orally, person-to-person by a trained psychologist should also be developed by being administered orally, person-to-person. One otherwise runs the risk that items may not work properly. For example, words which sound the same but are spelled differently could easily be confused if an item was administered orally but not if they were written. So it is necessary to think about how the items will ultimately be delivered early in the development process.

Several options are available:

- One-to-one assessments are invaluable when accurate assessments are needed, when there may be issues with literacy and when support and encouragement may be needed. However, training people to administer the items in a standard way is difficult, and data collection is slow and therefore expensive.
- Group administration of conventional printed questionnaires or computerised scales has many advantages. As with one-to-one assessments, it is possible to establish who is actually answering the questions (important when using selection tests!). As one test administrator can typically look after about 20 people, test administration is cheap. The environment is standardised; it is likely to be quiet with few distractions and it will become obvious if a participant stops paying attention or carries on working after being asked to stop. It is possible to measure how long people take to answer scales, which can be very useful when designing ability scales. By providing computers, characteristics such as screen size, the input device to be used and processor speed can be standardised, and there is little risk of participants being distracted by social media devices without this being obvious to the administrator. Disadvantages include the logistics of assembling groups of people at the same time, and, if the questions deal with sensitive issues, participants may perhaps be less honest than if there were no administrator present. However, most studies with personality scales seem to show that the validity of group-administered pencil-and-paper tests and remotely administered computerised assessments are similar (Le Corff et al., 2017). One problem with administering scales to groups of people is that some people will finish earlier than others. If participants are asked to wait until the last person finishes, this is frustrating for them; if they leave, it becomes distracting for those remaining. This is one reason for imposing (generous) time limits on the final version of an ability scale.
- Internet-based assessments are easy to set up (for personality scales, at any rate) using sites such as surveymonkey.com. Large numbers of participants can be recruited using sites such as Mechanical Turk. Anonymity can perhaps lead to honest responding. However, all this comes at a price; one can never be sure whether one person or several are responding, whether or not they are taking the task seriously, whether they understand what they are being asked to do, what the characteristics of their hardware are (cell phone or large screen?) or whether they are trying to play a video game and interact with friends at the same time. If they are anxious, there is no realistic chance of discussing their concerns or fears (which raises some ethical issues if the items are in any way disturbing). Whilst simple personality questionnaires are easy to administer over the internet, ability scales which require graphics or time limits (for either individual items or entire scales) are rather more challenging to implement.

DETERMINING THE FORMAT OF THE SCALE

Paper-and-pencil scales are still popular – largely because little can go wrong when administering them and it is possible to ask participants to make responses (such as sketches) which are difficult using computers. It is also easy for participants to change their answer at any time and revisit a previously answered question – two things that are generally difficult with computerised items. Questions are printed in a booklet and answers are written on either the test booklet or a separate answer sheet. Using a separate answer sheet means that the booklets are reusable. However, the answer sheets must be carefully designed so that it is easy for the participant to see if their answers have got out of sync with the questions in the booklet – for example, by accidentally skipping a question. Thus the layout of the answers on the answer sheet should mirror the layout of the question booklet; there should be a line or gap corresponding to each page or column break in the test booklet.

The responses need to be scored as described in Chapter 3. Many students forget that it is essential to record the responses to individual items when developing scales (using templates to calculate the total score will not suffice). It is necessary to enter each person's response to each item onto a spreadsheet – a tedious job, which can be error-prone.

Another possibility involves group testing where each participant has only an answer sheet, the items being projected onto a screen. It is straightforward to produce a series of slides using standard presentation software, perhaps with a standard time limit for each slide and a warning tone to indicate how much time is left. This can allow videos etc. to be incorporated, if necessary, and professional-looking presentations can be produced very quickly. However, the display must be large enough to ensure that those seated further away are not disadvantaged, and care must be taken to ensure that the image brightness is fairly uniform. Problems can also arise if participants need to change glasses to view the screen and mark the answer sheet.

Items administered on stand-alone computers allow the greatest flexibility. Customised hardware can be used where necessary (e.g., to measure ability to track objects using a joystick or to display very brief presentations of stimuli). Commercial or in-house software can be written to record responses, along with the time taken to answer each item. This is invaluable when developing ability scales that will eventually have time limits. Several computer programs allow items which were developed using item response theory to be administered adaptively, as described in Chapter 12. Davey (2011) has produced an excellent guide to the practicalities of computerised assessments.

As mentioned earlier, internet administration of personality scales is straightforward; internet-based administration of ability scales is less easy, particularly if graphics are required or if time limits are needed, whilst internet-based adaptive testing requires specialised software, such as FastTest. Although several scales which were originally administered using printed booklets also seem to work well when administered by computer, guidelines exist for the development and use of computerised scales (Bartram, 2009); those who plan to develop adaptive tests should consult a text such as Wainer (2014) at the outset.

Some scales require hardware – anything from a (standard) toy elephant through cards with inkblots printed on them to a set of small nuts, bolts, screws and washers and a plate into which they are fixed. However, these are so specialised that they cannot be discussed here.

DETERMINING THE FORMAT OF THE ITEMS

Several options are available for self-report items which are answered using a Likert scale; 'How much do you agree with each of the following statements?', 'How well does each statement describe you?', 'How much do you like . . .?', 'I see myself as . . .', 'How much do you usually . . . ?' and there is no real rationale for preferring one to the other.

Ability scales usually just present participants with a set of problems to be solved.

We have not yet encountered situational judgement tests. These are measures which present participants with a standard situation (real or imagined) and ask them what they think, feel or would do. An example of a situational judgement test involving a real situation would be an 'in-tray' selection test; a job applicant might be given a set of typical issues which they would be expected to deal with (these could be anything relevant to the job; dealing with letters of complaint, balancing books, filleting a fish, scheduling a delivery round), and, as all applicants are given the same problems, it should be possible to compare their performance. Several computerised or paper-and-pencil tests rely on hypothetical situations. Participants might be asked how they would probably act in different situations. For example, 'If you are walking down the sidewalk (pavement) and a group of children are blocking it, would you (a) walk round them saying nothing, (b) walk round them smiling and reminding them that an elderly or disabled person would find it difficult to pass, (c) push through' etc. This example is of a forced-choice (ipsatised) scale, for each action will represent a different personality trait; it is also possible to ask people to rate how likely they would be to perform each action.

DETERMINING THE FORMAT OF THE RESPONSES

Likert scales of either five or seven items are popular for personality scales, though some use just a three-point scale and some as many as 10. It is sensible to choose an odd number of categories so that respondents have a 'neutral' answer, rather than being forced to express a preference one way or the other.

The same number of alternatives should be used for all items in the scale, otherwise participants may become confused. It is also important to ensure that a few words are used to give meaning to each level of the scale. Rather than asking people to write a number

Strongly disagree	1	2	3	4	5	6	7	Strongly agree

or tick or fill in a box or circle

Strongly disagree	O	O	O	O	O	O	O	Strongly agree

corresponding to their answer, it is better to anchor each response, to try to make sure that people use the scale in similar ways. For example,

	Strongly disagree	Disagree	Slightly disagree	Neutral/ unsure	Slightly agree	Agree	Strongly agree
I like betting	O	O	O	O	O	O	O

The problem is that social desirability might taint these responses, and of course different people might understand different things by 'like', 'strongly' or 'slightly'. For this reason, it is better still if the responses can be tied to actual behaviour:

	Never in the past year	Once or twice in the last year	3–20 times in the last year	21–50 times in the last year	More than 50 times in the past year
I have placed a bet	O	O	O	O	O

The last example asks people to say what they actually *did*, and unless they choose to deliberately lie or have forgotten, this sort of format is likely to yield far more valuable data than simply asking people what they like or dislike. If some items ask about very common behaviours ('How often do you brush your teeth?') whilst others ask about very rare ones, it is difficult to find a rating scale which suits all items. Using different scales for different items (rather than showing one header which applies to all of the items in a scale) can cause confusion, takes up a lot of space and requires a lot of reading.

Ability scales generally ask people to either write the correct answer to a problem (free response) or choose between various alternatives (multiple choice) as discussed in Chapters 2 and 3. If item response theory is to be used (see Chapter 12), then estimating the 'guessing' parameter for each multiple-choice item may be a problem; pretending that guessing does not happen in order to justify the use of the Rasch model might only be sensible if the number of distracters is large.

Writing good distracters is a difficult art to master. The objective is to produce answers which all sound plausible so that none can be eliminated as 'obviously incorrect' by the test taker who resorts to guessing. Here are a few examples:

Example 1

Tadpole is to frog as caterpillar is to (a) garden (b) toad (c) pond (d) butterfly.

My rationale for choosing (a), (b) and (c) as distracters was that caterpillars are found in gardens, so if someone thinks that this could be the rule linking tadpole and frog, they might choose this option; (b) is there because frogs and toads are somewhat similar; (c) is there because both tadpoles and frogs are found in ponds. I deliberately made sure that all of the distracters had some sort of relationship to the first three terms of the analogy; if I had chosen 'coal' I suspect that most people would recognise that this was unlikely to be the answer.

Example 2

Which shape completes the pattern?

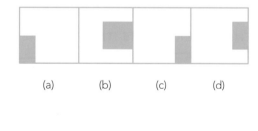

(a)   (b)   (c)   (d)

Figure 13.1 A typical spatial reasoning problem

There is less of an obvious rationale for choosing distracters for items such as this. Distracter (a) was chosen in case they did not notice the shift to the right, and (d) was chosen in case the participant did not notice the vertical shift downwards. (b) is there in case they thought they may have to combine two shapes somehow.

Example 3

Which is the odd one out: light bulb, radio, air-conditioner, cuckoo clock?

These items are really difficult to write, because it is almost impossible to ensure that there is only one correct answer. When writing this item, I originally had 'spotlight' in place of 'light bulb' but then realised that as spotlights are often found outside the home, this (rather than d – not electric) could be construed as being the odd one out. Or one could argue that (b) is correct – it contains electronic circuits whereas the others may not. Or perhaps (c) is correct – it cannot easily be lifted. There again, all make a noise apart from the light bulb . . . It may be better to avoid such items.

Example 4

What are the base 3 numbers 0121+1112 in base 3 notation? (a) 1233 (b) 2010 (c) 1200 (d) 11011

(a) is correct, (b) is the answer in decimal, (c) is the answer one would get if one forgot to carry numbers greater than 2, and (d) is a random binary number, on the assumption that such numbers may be familiar to participants who do not understand the concept of base 3.

The key to writing all such items is to try to think flexibly and have *some* sort of hypothesis about the way in which participants might be trying to approach the problem, rather than choosing words or numbers at random.

THE ORDER OF THE ITEMS AND ALTERNATIVE RESPONSES

It is usual to randomise the order of items in a personality scale or test. When items are written to measure several different facets, they should all be mixed up together rather than having several items measuring the same facet next to each other. If several similar items are adjacent to each other, participants may simply check the same answer to each of them to ensure that they are behaving consistently. Unfortunately, however, there is literature that shows that the order in which items are presented can affect the scores that people obtain – a finding which has particular implications for the use of adaptive personality scales based on item response theory (Ortner, 2008; Steinberg, 1994). So, once an arbitrary order of items has been decided, it is probably wise to keep the same rank ordering of items in the final version of the scale (i.e., after removing items which do not work).

Ability items are normally ordered in terms of difficulty, with the easiest ones at the start of the scale to give participants confidence. Whilst the difficulty of the items obviously cannot be known before any data is gathered, informal estimates (e.g., from friends or pilot studies) might be better than nothing in helping one to decide on the initial order of the items. However, once the items have been administered to a sample as part of the item-analysis procedure, subsequent versions of the scale should arrange them in their actual order of difficulty. It goes without saying that the position of the correct answer in multiple-choice items should be randomised.

THE INSTRUCTIONS

In this section we describe how a typical group-testing session might be run. In the case of computer-based assessments some (or, if the scale is being administered remotely, *all*) of this information will need to appear on screen. After making introductions, the test administrator should thank the participants for taking part and make it clear that they are welcome to leave at any time without giving any explanation as to why and that any data they have provided will then be destroyed. They should then spell out to participants what they are being asked to do (e.g., complete three personality questionnaires), what the purpose of the study is, how long it is likely to last, whether their responses are anonymous and who will have access to individual and collated data. There should always be reference to the fact that ethical approval for the study has been obtained, and it is important to give the name and contact details of someone who can be approached if the participants have any concerns after participating. Business cards are good for this. A consent form should be signed by every participant, indicating that they agree to take part in the study as described.

This preamble will vary from study to study, and it is important to consult the ethical standards of one's psychological association in case other issues need to be considered. If vulnerable people (children, patients, prisoners etc.) are participating, or if deception is to be used, a more detailed risk assessment will always be needed. This will also be necessary if the scales deal with information which is in any way personal (e.g., sexual or political behaviour, experience of violence or prejudice, attitudes to abortion or rape).

If any of the scales are believed to be valid, feedback should normally be offered on these scales if participants want it. If scales are unvalidated, the reason for not offering feedback on these scales should be explained. It is important to give all this information before gathering data so that participants can decide to withdraw should they choose to.

It is best to try to make this introduction as friendly and as relaxed as possible; rather than using a script it is better to just consult a list of bullet points to ensure that all of the above issues have been mentioned. I usually then explain (apologetically) that assessments need to be standardised so that everyone has the same experience, and so it is necessary to read a standard set of instructions for each scale. And these *should* be read verbatim.

The instructions for each scale should be drafted when the scale is being developed and should be read verbatim even when the scale is being trialled for the first time. They can then be amended if necessary for any further studies. These instructions should normally make it clear what each scale measures, how participants should indicate their responses (e.g., whether they should use an answer sheet), how quickly they should work, what to do if they are unsure about an answer, whether to turn the page, whether there is a time limit and whether/how it is possible to change their answer to a question either immediately or by returning to it if they have time at the end. When group testing, there should also be the opportunity to ask if anything is unclear. All this needs to be couched in clear, simple language.

For personality scales, it is also advisable to ask participants to give the first answer which comes naturally to mind, otherwise some people will start agonising about the precise meaning and nuance of every word in the scale. Kline (1986) argues that a well-written item should evoke an immediate response.

A typical set of instructions for a personality questionnaire might resemble the following:

> This scale measures personality. The printed sheet contains 50 statements. Please decide how well each statement describes you. To the right of each statement there are five boxes. These are labelled 'strongly disagree', 'disagree' 'neutral or unsure', 'agree' and 'strongly agree'. Please put a tick through the box which shows how well the statement describes how you usually feel or behave. Then move on to the next statement. There are 50 statements in total, 25 on the first page and 25 on the second page. Just turn the page when you reach the bottom. You can take as long as you like to answer them. However, please do not spend too long thinking about the exact meaning of the words. Just give the answer which comes naturally to mind. If you are unsure about any answer, please just give your best guess. Please give an answer for every statement. If you change your mind about an answer, cross it out and put a tick to indicate your new answer. Does anyone have any questions?

Ability scales sometimes ask people to solve quite complex problems. It may be necessary to check that participants understand what they are being asked to do by showing them an item with the correct answer marked for them and then asking them to solve a second (very easy) practice item themselves before starting the test proper, marking their answer on the answer sheet or question booklet. The test administrator can check that everyone has answered this item correctly before proceeding. Good examples of this can be seen in the instructions for Raven's Matrices (Raven et al., 2003) and Cattell's Culture Fair Tests series 3 (Cattell, 1965) – though here the instructions are so detailed that reading the instructions takes longer than answering the items!

With ability scales it is important to tell participants how fast to work, what their error-rate should be and whether they should guess if they do not know an answer. Care must be taken when developing ability scales that are designed to be used with very restricted time limits ('speeded tests'). Since some candidates may not reach the items at the end of the test, it is very difficult to estimate the difficulty of those items. It is better to administer the test with unlimited time at the development stage, and to impose time limits when putting together the final version.

A typical set of instructions for a multiple-choice ability scale might resemble the following:

> This scale measures [some ability]. The printed sheet contains 50 puzzles. To the right of each puzzle there are four possible answers. Only one of these answers is correct. Please put a tick through the box by the correct answer, then move on to the next puzzle. If you are unsure of an answer, please guess. Please work as quickly as you can. You will have 30 minutes to complete the test, though do not worry if you finish long before then. There are 50 puzzles in total, 25 on the first page and 25 on the second page. Just turn the page when you reach the bottom. If you change your mind about an answer, cross it out and put a tick to indicate your new answer. Does anyone have any questions?

WRITING ITEMS

No-one can write perfect items on their first attempt. It is possible that an item may be drafted so that almost everybody will answer it in the same way (who would ever claim that they have a below-average sense of humour?). There may be some ambiguity of meaning which has not been noticed. Sexist language may have crept in. In the case of ability scales, an item may be so easy that everyone gets it correct or so difficult that no one does – or worse still, more than one of the answers to a multiple-choice test may be correct. It is also possible that the items simply do not measure the trait or state which they are designed to assess; indeed, it might be the case that the trait or state simply does not exist! It is therefore necessary to draft the items, administer them to a sample of people similar to that with which the scale will eventually be used and perform statistical analyses to identify and remove items which do not work properly. What follows are some general guidelines, followed by more detailed guidelines for writing personality and ability items:

a) How many items should be written? This is a commonly-asked question to which there is no simple answer. Chapter 6 showed that reliability increases with test length, and so it is advisable to start with as many items as possible – 30 per scale is the suggestion given by Kline (1986) – in the hope that about 20 of them will eventually work. However, it also depends on the breadth of the concept being measured. Measuring a broad trait such as anxiety will require more items than measuring a single narrow facet such as test anxiety, where there are fewer different questions that *can* be asked.

b) Items should be short and clear, using simple words. They should be clear enough for anyone to read – which is especially important if formulae are used.

c) Items should be locally independent. In other words, the only thing which should affect a person's response is the trait which the item is supposed to measure – *not* their response to any previous item. We pointed out in Chapter 6 that items which are similar in meaning will inevitably fail this test; item writers should examine every possible pair of items in a scale and check that the way a person answers one item does not force him or her to answer any other item in a particular way, other than through the influence of the trait that the test is designed to measure.

d) Check words using a dictionary to ensure that an item does not have several possible interpretations. One personality questionnaire used to include the item 'Do you enjoy gay parties?', 'gay' then meaning 'lively'.

e) The cultural appropriateness of each item should be carefully considered. This will typically include the implicit knowledge required to understand the item or solve the problem. Would every 80-year-old know what a vegan is? Would every 18-year-old know what 'carbon copy' means?

f) Items should be written so that they only measure the trait which the scale is supposed to assess. They should not require a sophisticated vocabulary and should not be influenced by social desirability or by any other traits.

g) Decide on the response format, as discussed above. For multiple-choice ability items there should be at least four alternatives in order to reduce the effects of lucky guessing.

h) Write an equal number of items for each facet, taking care to construct good, plausible distracters (possibly based on an analysis of common errors from an earlier, free-response pilot version of the test if using a multiple-choice format). Ensure that the items in each facet appear to span a similar and appropriate range of difficulty.

i) Do not test the trivial just because it is easy to do so. When assessing students' statistical prowess, the easiest type of item to write would involve formulae and definitions, e.g. 'What is the equation for calculating the sample standard deviation from a set of data?' The problem is, of course, that the instructor probably *should* be interested in testing how well students *understand* and can *apply* the concepts – repeating definitions parrot-fashion is rarely what is wanted. The UK driving test provides another good example. I can remember learning and reciting stopping distances, although the examiners never checked that candidates knew what those distances actually looked like when they were driving, thereby missing the point entirely.

Writing items for personality tests

a) Try to write items that are clear, unambiguous and require as little self-insight as possible. Wherever possible you should refer to behaviours rather than to feelings.

b) If it is obvious what an item measures, some test takers will identify what the trait is and respond to the item in the way which matches their view of where they stand on the trait. This may not be the same as where they really stand on the trait. For example, 'Are you honest?' is an awful item, as anyone reading it can see that the scale is meant to measure honesty. Respondents will probably all decide that they *are* usually honest and answer the item accordingly. A better approach might be 'I told a lie (a) today (b) within the last week . . .', with possibly more items asking about breaking laws etc. Guilford (1959) argued that the best items will produce scores on traits which the test taker does not know, as a result of asking them questions the answers to which they do know.

c) Ensure that each item asks only one question. For example, do not use a statement such as 'I sometimes feel depressed and have attempted suicide', since extremely depressed people who have not (quite) got round to attempting suicide would have to disagree with it, which is presumably not what is intended.

d) Try to avoid negatively phrased items such as 'I dislike crowds: yes/?/no', since choosing 'no' requires the participant to interpret a double negative.

e) Try to avoid questions asking about frequency or amount. How frequently is 'often'? Different people will probably mean different things by the term. Instead, refer to specific rather than general behaviour. Instead of asking 'Do you read a lot?', try asking 'How many books have you read for pleasure in the past month?' – or better still, 'List the books that you have read for pleasure in the past month' (which may reduce socially desirable responses).

f) If possible, try to avoid items reflecting feeling, but refer to behaviours instead. 'How many parties have you been to in the last month?' rather than 'Do you enjoy parties?'

g) Try to ensure that about 50% of the items in each facet are keyed so that a 'yes/ strongly agree' response indicates a high score on the trait, and the others are keyed in the opposite direction. For example, 'I generally fall asleep at night as soon as the light is turned off' would be scored so that 'strongly disagree' indicated anxiety. However, it may be difficult to write such items without using double negatives.

h) If you *must* ask about something socially undesirable, consider phrasing the item from another person's point of view, e.g., 'Some people might describe me as mean' or, better still 'My friends have occasionally called me mean', rather than 'Are you mean?'

Writing items for ability or attainment tests

Any test measuring ability or attainment consists of a problem to be solved, some cognitive operations which are used to solve the problem and some response. This may sound banal, but it is important to recognise that the difficulty of an item, and its validity, depend on all of these factors. The modality of the problem also varies. Some problems will involve sounds, others words, shapes, behaviours (e.g., video clips of interactions between people) and there are other possibilities, too.

Tasks whose difficulty involves identifying the precise problem to be solved are common in everyday life. For example, one may have a very broad issue to address such as 'I have run out of money'. To address this issue, it is necessary to perform more detailed analyses. Are you *sure* you are penniless? Is it a temporary glitch for reasons that you understand? Have you been robbed? Can expenditure be reduced? Can income be increased? These are the sorts of questions which need to be asked to identify what the precise problem is. Most ability scales do not require such high-level thinking, but there are exceptions. For example, an item might present a picture or video, the task being to see what is wrong with it. This could be anything (inconsistent shadows, water flowing uphill, objects falling at different speeds, parts of objects missing), and so the difficult part of this task is to determine what to look for. However, most problems make the problem to be solved as unambiguous as possible; 'What is the next letter in the sequence?' etc.

The great majority of ability items depend for their difficulty on the cognitive processes needed to solve a well-defined problem. These include how well lists can be memorised whilst performing other cognitive operations on the data (working memory), memory scanning, devising novel uses for objects, solving anagrams, mental rotation, various forms of inductive and deductive reasoning or indeed any other cognitive processes, singly or in combination. Surprisingly, perhaps, it does not seem to be common practice for item writers to consult research on cognitive psychology or cognitive neuroscience to try to ensure that their items involve fundamental processes – and ideally that all items in a scale focus on just one of them. Instead, items seem to be developed on a much more ad hoc basis. This was obviously necessary in the days before cognitive psychology had a sound theoretical and experimental basis, but it might not now be so appropriate.

A few items are difficult because the response is hard to make. Tracking a moving object on a screen using a joystick, sight-reading a challenging extract of music, flying an aeroplane using a simulator or assembling a small object using tweezers would be examples. However, as most scales are designed to measure cognitive processes rather than coordination or adroitness, such scales are in a minority.

Most readers of this book will probably be graduates, with extensive vocabularies and good numerical skills. As such, it can be difficult to gauge the difficulty of items written for other groups. It is therefore important to draft some items which seem extremely easy. Otherwise, the test may be too difficult for some members of the general population.

EXAMPLES OF ABILITY ITEMS

There are several widely used types of ability items.

Analogies – such as the 'Tadpole is to frog as caterpillar is to . . .' (Example 1 above) can be used either to test knowledge (where the hard part of the item is understanding the meanings of the nouns) or reasoning (where the relationship between the terms is hard to discern). These items require participants to identify the relationship between the first two terms and apply this to the third term in order to find the answer.

Sequences ask participants to identify what comes next in some series. The series can be a list of shapes, numbers, musical notes or virtually anything else which form a logical series. As with analogies, the difficulty of these items can stem from either knowing what the elements in the sequence are or what the rule connecting them is. For example, in order to give the next term in the sequence 'Helium, Neon, Argon . . .' it is necessary to know that these are chemical elements rather than planets. And it is also necessary to recognise that these form a column in the periodic table in order to complete the sequence. That said, it is most common to use sequence items to explore how well people can identify the relationships between items – 'inductive reasoning'.

Matrices – Example 2 above shows that this is basically a mixture of two sequence problems – one sequence runs from left to right and the other from top to bottom. They can be made quite difficult.

Odd one out – this format was mentioned above. Once again it is only possible to solve these items if one knows the meaning of all the terms in the question and can think of some rationale for grouping several of them together. As mentioned above, the problem with these items is that it is possible to think of an almost unlimited number of groupings. 'Helium, Neon, Argon, Iron' looks straightforward until it is appreciated that only one of the words does not end in 'n' . . . If such items have to be used, they should be tried out on friends and colleagues before they even enter a draft ability scale. It is possible to create odd-one-out problems using shapes, too. For example, three shapes might have a dot which is inside a circle but outside a square, whilst the other has the dot outside the circle. These unfamiliar items are probably safer.

Linkages – these problems typically ask respondents to identify a word which links two others; for example back **** mat. The same thing could be done with sequences of musical notes – what four notes end one well-known tune and start another?

Mazes – a printed maze has four entrances and participants identify which one leads to the centre. (The problem here is that people will explore the entrances in different orders, which will add random error to the score, if the scale is timed.)

Embedded figures – a complex geometrical figure has one (but only one) of a list of simple figures embedded within it.

These are just some examples of commonly used item formats for ability tests, but almost anything can be used.

SPEED TESTS AND POWER TESTS

One important decision which needs to be made when developing an ability scale is whether the final form of the scale should have a time limit and, if so, what it should be. Almost all ability tests do have time limits – particularly if people are given the opportunity to go back and revise their answers. This is because a sample of people may contain some who are highly conscientious but with an unexceptional level of the ability which is being assessed. They might therefore spend a great deal of time trying to solve the items which puzzle them, and if the test is administered to a group of people this will frustrate others who might need to wait until they have finished before moving on to the next task. So it is good practice to always set some sort of time limit for an ability scale. This time limit can be very generous, in which case the scale is known as a 'power test' because it really measures *level* of performance rather than *speed* of performance. For example, the time limit could be set to the time taken for 90% of a sample drawn from the target population to complete as many items as they can. On the other hand, the time limit can be rather short, requiring participants to complete as many items as possible in the time allocated. Here it is unlikely that anyone will have time to attempt all items. These 'speeded tests' measure the speed with which people can correctly solve problems. These terms stem from Gulliksen (1950b).

Some scales must necessarily be speeded. For example, scales measuring the speed with which people can cross out every 'e' in a passage of text or substitute letters for symbols to reveal a coded message clearly need a time limit, for almost everyone could get full marks if they were given unlimited time. There are some problems with measuring the reliability of speeded scales as discussed by Gulliksen (1950a) because not everyone will reach the later items in the scale, making it hard to compute alpha etc. unless one assumes that all of the 'not-reached' items would have been guessed.

Do speeded tests and power tests measure the same things? Vernon (1961) argues that they do in fact correlate so substantially that moderate speeding is not a major issue. However, this was within the context of intelligence research, and matters may be different when measuring other abilities. Subsequent writers suggest that speeded and power tests do tend to load on rather different factors; Partchev et al. (2013) summarise this later literature and perform a rather sophisticated study which shows that for verbal analogy items, at any rate, speed and power tests have only a very modest correlation.

TIME LIMITS DURING SCALE DEVELOPMENT

It is difficult to know how long participants will take to solve the problems in ability scales (or answer personality items, for that matter) so unless a speeded scale is being developed it is advisable to allow participants plenty of time to attempt all items when developing a scale. If arbitrary time limits *are* imposed, the first problem is that these will need to be revised if and when items are dropped from the draft version of the scale as a result of the item-analysis procedure described below.

Second, if time limits are imposed, then some participants will not reach the items near the end of the scale. This makes it extremely difficult to perform any form of item analysis. In the case of personality items, the people who respond slowly (because of high conscientiousness, dyslexia or any other reason) will be dropped from the sample when analysing the psychometric properties of the later items in the scale. This makes it impossible to justify that the sample is a cross-section of the population which it is supposed to represent.

In the case of ability items, those who reach the final items are likely to be higher in ability and so calculating item difficulties based on the responses of these individuals alone will lead to inaccurate estimates. The later items will appear easier than they truly are. One 'solution' might be to assume that everyone who worked slowly would have failed the later items. However, as the items will not be ordered in terms of difficulty (as the difficulty levels cannot be known at this stage), this is not sensible.

When administering the scale (with a very generous time limit), it is important to note how long it takes people to finish. It is possible to observe the respondents' behaviour and note – for example – that roughly 50% finish after 15 minutes, 80% after 18 minutes and 90% by the end of 20 minutes. This information can be used to estimate the average time to answer or solve an item, which will be useful for estimating an appropriate time limit for the shortened version of the scale which will be created by the item-analysis procedure. Of course, computer-administered items should record the amount of time taken for each person to answer each item, which is far more accurate.

TRANSLATING ITEMS

Translating items – particularly personality items – raises a whole set of interesting issues. The problem is that the nuanced meaning of the words in the item will probably be lost in translation and may well be culturally specific. Cultural attitudes, too, will almost certainly affect the way in which people respond to items, even if they translate perfectly. For example, in some cultures it is considered impolite to say 'no'. So even if the traits being measured are the same in several different cultures, one cannot simply take a questionnaire, translate it and hope that it will yield valid results.

It is instead necessary to have the items professionally translated and then 'back translated' (by a different person or team). So, if a Japanese scale was to be used in England, one would have the items translated into English and then have each English item translated back into Japanese. If the back-translated item does not closely resemble the original, as will almost certainly be the case for some items, the two teams of translators meet to agree the best possible form of words.

The translated scale then needs to be given to a large representative sample of people from the target population and validated as if it were a new scale. Some items may need to be dropped, and this will tend to make the translated scale have rather lower reliability than the original and may also affect its validity. Its factor structure therefore needs to be checked, as does its validity. There are many examples of good practice in the literature – for example Perczek et al. (2000) – which can be used for guidance.

ITEM ANALYSIS

Having compiled a draft test, it is necessary to ensure that all of the items measure the same construct before proceeding to check that the test is reliable and valid. In order to do this, the test should be administered to a large sample of people, similar in composition to the individuals who will ultimately use the test. We have seen (Chapter 6) that the standard error of the reliability coefficient is large unless large samples are used, and so developing a scale using a small sample or one which is unrepresentative of the population with which the scale will be used is pure folly. Several hundred people are necessary.

Each person's response to each item is then entered into a spreadsheet. Before scoring multiple-choice ability items it is useful to look at the popularity of the various distracter items. If the distracters were written with sufficient cunning, someone who did not know the answer to the item would have chosen one at random. On the other hand, if some distracters were obviously incorrect, these will be less frequently chosen. Looking at the frequency with which each of the *incorrect* distracters is chosen should reveal if any of the distracters is grossly unpopular. A note should be made to redraft it if so. There is no point in performing statistical analyses – with a large sample all differences will be significant.

The responses are then scored. In the case of ability tests, this will typically involve giving one point for a correct answer and zero points for an incorrect response or an omitted item. In the case of Likert-scaled items (e.g., strongly agree/agree/neutral/disagree/strongly disagree) the response is converted to a number indicating the strength of the response, as described in Chapter 3, remembering to reverse the items where necessary. The easiest way of scoring items is to use a spreadsheet to convert the raw responses into numbers.

Missing data should be estimated as described in Chapter 3. If people are dropped from the sample because of missing data, it is advisable to check their demographic data (and scores on other scales) carefully to ensure that they form a reasonably random sample of the group. For, obviously, if all the anxious men in a sample left many items unanswered, the sample would no longer be representative of the population which the scale was designed to assess.

Table 13.1 Average total score on a scale for each alternative response

	Answer (a)	Answer (b)	Answer (c)	Answer (d)
Item 1	11.3	20.2	18.9	8.7

In the case of multiple-choice ability scales, it is advisable to check that the 'correct' answer to each item is indeed correct. The easiest way of doing so is simply to work out the average score on the scale obtained by people who chose each alternative for each item.

For a four-choice item this might show the results presented in Table 13.1.

Here it can be seen that the participants with the highest scores on that scale chose answer (b). This should be the answer that was keyed 'correct' when the scale was being designed, and this should be checked. In this case answer (c) was *also* chosen by high-ability participants, which might indicate that it too might be correct. It is important to double-check the wording of this item to ensure that item (b) is, indeed, the only correct answer and that there are no ambiguities of meaning in the item.

The next stage is to examine the mean score. In the case of an ability test (where items are scored 0 or 1) the mean score indicates the difficulty of each item. A mean score of 0.95 would indicate that 95% of the sample gave the correct response to an item. In the case of personality tests, the mean score shows the extent to which individuals tend to agree or disagree with statements. As a general rule of thumb, it would be undesirable to have *too* many very easy or very difficult items in the test, so if more than about 10% of ability items have an average score above 0.8 or below 0.2 (or if more than about 10% of Likert-scaled items have average scores at the extreme ends of the scales – between 0 and 1 or between 4.1 and 5 for a five-point scale scored 1–5), it would be prudent to consider removing some of them.

Examine the standard deviation for each item. This shows the level of individual differences found in participants' responses to it. For example, if an item has a standard deviation of zero, everyone has answered it in the same way, and the item is therefore clearly not tapping any kind of individual differences and should be removed from the scale. (When items are scored using a two-point scale, such as correct/incorrect, the standard deviation is linked directly to the mean. This step should be skipped in such cases.)

Although checking the items' means and standard deviations is a necessary first step, this cannot reveal which questions in the test are flawed in content. For example, suppose that one item in a personality test used language that was too difficult for the participants to understand, so causing them all to guess an answer. Responses to this item will look good, the mean will probably be near the middle of the scale and the standard deviation will be large. However, the item is clearly useless. We shall mention four techniques of *item analysis* for identifying items that, for whatever reason, simply do not measure the same thing as the other items in the test.

When using any of the four techniques described below to eliminate items from the test, it is important to try to ensure that the test retains approximately equal numbers of items in all of its facets. Suppose, for example, that a teacher started off by writing five items in each of seven facets of mathematical attainment; long division, long multiplication, geometry/trigonometry, solution of simultaneous equations, finding roots of quadratic equations, differentiation and integration. Item analysis will remove some of the 35 items (those that are too easy, too hard or which simply do not seem to work), but it would clearly be unfortunate if the analysis led to the removal of *all* of the long-division items and *all* of the long-multiplication items, since the teacher believes that these are two important components of the pupils' mathematical attainment. Item analysis is an art as well as a science, and, when removing items, it is important to try to ensure that approximately equal numbers are left in each of the facets.

METHOD 1: CONSTRUCTING TESTS BY CRITERION KEYING

Suppose that we are asked to construct a psychological test to select individuals who will successfully learn to pilot an aircraft. The goal is to develop a test whose total score will be able to predict the pilots' final score on their training course. Having no clear idea of what may be appropriate personality and ability characteristics for this application, we might put together 600 items that we hope will measure all of the main abilities and personality traits that can be assessed. But which ones actually predict pilot performance?

Suppose that the draft version of the scales has been administered to several hundred trainees. The most obvious way of identifying the good (i.e., predictive) items in the test is to validate each item directly against the criterion. For example, suppose that at the end of their training, each trainee-pilot is awarded a mark of between 0 and 100. Surely the item-analysis process would simply involve correlating the trainees' scores on each of the items in the test with their scores on the training course. Items that have substantial correlations would appear to be able to predict the criterion, and those that do not would be dropped from the test.

This procedure, which is known as *criterion keying*, has been used in the construction of several well-known scales, including the Minnesota Multiphasic Personality Inventory, the MMPI and MMPI-2 (Graham, 1990; Hathaway and McKinley, 1967) and the California Psychological Inventory (Gough, 1975), the scales of which can supposedly discriminate between various clinical groups. *Do not use this method of item analysis.* As Nunnally (1978) observes, it has several fatal flaws.

First, it is very likely to produce scales that have very low reliability – that is, scales containing items that measure a number of different things. For example, suppose that success in the training course depended on spatial ability, hand–eye coordination, low neuroticism and extraversion. If criterion keying were to be applied to a large sample of items, it would produce a scale that measured a mixture of all of these things rather than four distinct scales. Second, it is rarely possible to identify a *single* criterion to be used when selecting items. For example, consider the activities of a university professor. These will typically include lecturing, obtaining research funding, performing research, taking tutorials, managing other staff, marking essays and examination papers, coordinating certain laboratory activities, supervising PhD students and a host of other activities. Which one of these should be used as the criterion against which their performance should be judged? If they are to be averaged in some way, marking how many exam scripts or securing how many dollars of research grants is equivalent to supervising one PhD student, writing a scientific paper or giving a lecture? If one criterion is used, one particular set of predictive items will be identified – if another criterion is chosen, the chances are that quite a different selection of items will be indicated. The third point is a little more statistical. In order to select the 'best' items by criterion keying, one correlates responses to particular items with the criterion – if the test consists of 400 or so items (as does the MMPI), then one calculates 400 correlations. If large numbers of correlations are being calculated, we would expect several of the correlations to be appreciably larger than their true (population) values, even if there is really no relationship between the test scores and the behaviour; this is, after all, what '$p<0.05$' means – 5% of the correlations will be spuriously significant. So, if 400 items are correlated with some behaviour and 25 of these correlations are significant (rather than the 20 which one would expect) how can one tell which if any of these correlations indicate a genuine relationship? Finally, this procedure gives us no real understanding of *why* the test works – it is completely atheoretical. Without an understanding of what psychological constructs are being measured by the 'useful' items, it is impossible to tell whether the test is likely to be useful in other applications (e.g., for air-traffic controllers), and it becomes very difficult to 'fix' the test if it suddenly stops predicting performance. For all of these reasons, criterion keying should be avoided.

METHOD 2: CONSTRUCTING TESTS BY FACTOR ANALYSIS OF ITEMS

Psychologists such as Cattell advocate the use of factor analysis to construct tests, although others (e.g., Nunnally, 1978) argue that individual items are so unreliable – i.e., have so much measurement error associated with them, and hence such small factor loadings – that this is dangerous. Here the correlations between the (scored) items are factor analysed, and the factor(s) that emerge are tentatively identified on the basis of their loadings on the rotated factors. When putting together a set of items to measure one particular construct, we would of course *hope* that just one factor will emerge and that all of the variables will have large loadings (in the same direction) on that factor. In practice, there may be more than one factor, and some variables may not have loadings above 0.4 on *any* factor and so should be dropped. This method of constructing scales simply involves identifying and retaining those items that have a substantial loading on the main factor(s).

METHOD 3: CONSTRUCTING A SCALE USING ITEM RESPONSE THEORY

See Chapter 12.

METHOD 4: CONSTRUCTING TESTS USING CLASSICAL ITEM ANALYSIS

We have left the oldest and easiest method of item analysis until last. This technique *assumes* that a set of items all measure just one scale, and so it is important to perform a factor analysis first, just to check that this is the case. All one needs to do is check that parallel analysis (and possibly other methods) show that the items form just one factor. If not, it will be necessary to perform several item analyses, one for each factor.

You will recall that high reliability is generally thought to be an excellent feature of a test. It therefore seems sensible to try to estimate the extent to which each of the items in a test correlates with individuals' 'true scores', which are the scores that each individual would have obtained if he or she had been administered all of the items that could possibly have been written to measure the topic. If we somehow identify items each of which has a substantial correlation with the true score, when we add up individuals' scores on these items, the total scores on the test are bound to show a substantial correlation with the true score. This is, of course, another way of saying that the test has high internal consistency reliability. Thus, if it is possible to detect items that show appreciable correlations with the true score, it is also possible to choose those items that will produce a highly reliable test.

The problem is that we can never know individuals' true scores. However, it is possible to estimate them from their total scores on all of the items in the scale. Thus classical item analysis simply correlates the total score on the test with the scores on each of the individual items. Consider, for example, the data shown in Table 13.2, which represent the responses of six people to a five-item test (where a correct answer was scored as 1 and an incorrect answer as 0) together with each person's total score on the test. The row marked '*r* with total' simply correlates the responses to each of the items with the total scores on the test. You may wish to check one or two of these so that you can

Table 13.2 Data for item analysis

	Item 1	Item 2	Item 3	Item 4	Item 5	Total
Person 1	1	0	1	1	1	4
Person 2	0	1	1	1	0	3
Person 3	0	0	1	0	0	1
Person 4	0	0	1	0	0	1
Person 5	0	1	0	1	1	3
Person 6	1	0	1	1	0	3
r with total	0.63	0.32	−0.20	0.95	0.63	
Corrected r with total	0.11	0.22	−0.48	0.87	0.50	

see how they have been calculated. Here Item 4 appears to be the best measure (that is, it correlates well with the total score) whilst Item 3 is the worst. It is probable that dropping Item 3 will improve the reliability of the scale.

The correlations between each item and the total score are as close as we can get to estimating the correlation between each item and the true score, so it seems sensible to drop those items that have low correlations with the total score – keeping a careful eye on which facet of the trait is measured by a particular item and ensuring that the items that are left contain approximately equal numbers of items from each of the facets. Thus whilst the item-analysis procedure involves removing an item which has a low correlation with the total score at each stage, this will not always be the very lowest-correlating item.

There is one obvious problem associated with correlating items with total scores, and this is the fact that each item *contributes* to the total score, so we are to some extent correlating each item with itself. In order to circumvent this difficulty, the item analyses use 'corrected item–total correlations', also called 'Guilford-corrected item–total correlations', which are simply the correlations between each item and the sum of the *other* remaining items. In the present example, Item 1 would be correlated with the sum of Items 2, 3, 4 and 5. Item 2 would be correlated with the sum of Items 1, 3, 4 and 5 and so on. Other techniques for performing such corrections have been proposed, but they create as many problems as they solve (Cooper, 1983).

Each time an item is eliminated, the test's reliability (alpha) needs to be recalculated. As items that have low correlations with the total score are eliminated, the value of alpha will rise. As more and more items are removed, the value of alpha will eventually start to fall, since it depends on both the average correlation between the items and

EXERCISE 13.1: ITEM ANALYSIS

Resources required: Spreadsheet 13.1: Item analysis. From
www.routledge.com/9781138228894

Purpose: To perform classical item analysis by identifying items having small
corrected correlations with the total score. It can analyse data from 100 variables
and 2000 people

Contents of spreadsheet: Sample data from a five-item scale, with eight
participants. Data are in the 'Data_only' tab

Suggested activity:

- Click on the 'Data_only' tab to see/amend/replace the data to be analysed. Each
  row represents a different person.
- In the 'Item analysis' tab check that the number of cases and items is
  correct and that the minimum and maximum scores are correct – in case of
  typological errors.
- Type '1' in the green cell if an item is to be scored normally, or '−1' if it is to be
  reverse-scored.
- Note coefficient alpha, the correlation between each item and the total score,
  the corrected item–total correlation and other statistics.
- Remove an item by typing 0 into the green cell. Note how alpha and the
  statistics for the other items change. An item can be replaced at any time by
  entering −1 or 1.
- Continue removing items until the scale is sufficiently reliable and sufficiently
  short.

Points to note:

- The (scored) data are simply pasted into the 'Data_only' tab. This calculates how
  many participants and items there are.
- With the given dataset, Item 1 has a large *negative* item–total correlation,
  indicating that it probably should not have been reverse-scored.
- The corrected correlation between each item and the total score is often
  modest, showing that each item is only weakly related to the trait that it is
  designed to measure.

Learning outcomes:

Readers should now be able to

- perform an item analysis to produce a shorter, more reliable scale.

the number of items in the test. Of course, removing a 'poor' item boosts the average correlation between the remaining items – but it also shortens the test. Items are successively removed (on the basis of a consideration of their corrected item–total correlations and the facets from which they originate) until the test is short, well balanced and highly reliable.

It is not possible simply to look at the table of corrected item–total correlations and decide from this precisely which items should be eliminated. This is because each person's total score will inevitably change each time an item is dropped, and consequently each of the correlations between the remaining items and the total score will also change. Therefore, it is necessary to decide which item to drop, recompute the total scores and recompute all of the remaining item–total correlations, as well as recomputing alpha at each stage. Spreadsheet 13.1 performs such analyses.

VALIDATION AND DOCUMENTATION

The test constructor's task is far from finished once the item analysis has been completed. Instructions should be refined and time limits adjusted before the revised (shorter and more reliable) test is given to another sample of several hundred individuals so that its reliability and factor structure may be checked. It might also be possible to gather some validation data at this stage – for example, by administering the scale alongside other standard tests and correlating scores, jointly factor analysing the items etc. In the case of ability tests, the amount of time that individuals take to complete the test should be noted and a final decision taken as to what time limits (if any) should be imposed.

In the case of item response theory, the sample-independence of the parameters should also be checked – e.g., by splitting the sample into two groups (one predominantly low ability and the other mainly high ability) and ensuring that the item difficulties are similar in each. Its validity should also be established at this stage (e.g., by construct validation). A test manual should be prepared showing the results of these analyses, the administration instructions, the marking scheme and as much evidence as possible that the test is reliable and valid.

SUMMARY

This chapter has covered some basic principles of item writing for both ability tests and personality tests. It has introduced classical item analysis as a quick and straightforward way of identifying and eliminating items which perform badly. Eliminating such items will generally boost coefficient alpha. Gulliksen (1986) is still essential reading for anyone who is developing a scale measuring abilities or educational attainment, whilst Most and Zeidner (1995) and Spector (1992) are also recommended for all scale developers.

CHAPTER 14
PROBLEMS WITH
TEST SCORES

This chapter addresses some commonly encountered misconceptions and misuses of psychometric techniques. Some of them will be of particular interest to practitioners – those who use scores on psychometric tests to help them make decisions about individuals. Some of the issues raised in this chapter are quite fundamental, such as whether scores on tests which comprise several sub-scales and which have coefficients alpha in the order of 0.95 are really as accurate as many practitioners assume. The issues in this chapter mainly arose during conversations with my psychometrically inclined ex-colleagues in educational and clinical psychology, who focus more on the interpretation of individual scores than on the correlational analyses typically used by researchers in individual differences.

CONFIDENCE INTERVALS

Every time an individual person's score on a test is measured, it is usual to also report 'confidence intervals' to show what the range of scores is likely to be. For, given that every test score is affected, to some extent, by random errors of measurement, it would be naive to assume that a person would obtain exactly the same score if the test were administered on another occasion. The confidence interval uses the 'standard error of measurement' to show the likely range of scores which a person might have. For example, a practitioner might establish that someone has an IQ of 100, and, given the particular test that was used, we can estimate that if they were to be given the same test on 1000 occasions(!) they would score somewhere between 94 and 106 on 950 of those occasions. This can be deduced by knowing the standard deviation of the test and its reliability; the standard error of measurement is

$$standard\ deviation \times \sqrt{1 - reliability}$$

So if a test has a reliability of 0.9 and a standard deviation of 15, the standard error of measurement is

$$15 \times \sqrt{0.1} = 4.7$$

It is possible to use the normal distribution to allow us to decide on the width of this confidence interval; for 95% confidence this would be 1.96×4.7 on either side of the person's estimated true score. In the case of someone who scores 100 on the IQ test, this implies that there is a 95% chance that their true score lies between 100−9.2 and 100+9.2; between 91 and 109, in other words. This sort of analysis can be very important indeed, as it may be used to help make legal and other decisions about the individual (fitness to plead, suitability for gifted education etc.). Most of these applications involve assessing people whose scores are either very high or very low – and this presents particular problems, as we will see.

This will be familiar territory to most professionals, who probably wonder why I am stressing it. The reason is that there are two important issues which are not always properly addressed in test manuals.

WHAT IS THE BEST ESTIMATE OF THE PERSON'S TRUE SCORE?

Given that

- each person's score on every scale is influenced by measurement error;
- the error is normally distributed with a mean of zero;
- the amount of random error is determined by the reliability of the scale;
- each person's observed score is the sum of their true score plus random error;

it follows that someone who obtains an extremely high score on a test is (a) likely to have an above-average score, and is (b) likely to be lucky, in that the random measurement error has boosted (rather than lowered) their score. The next time that they are assessed, their error score will probably be closer to zero, and so their observed score will probably be rather lower on a second occasion. Likewise, a person with a very low score on one occasion will probably achieve a higher score if they are tested on another occasion.

So what *is* the best estimate of the person's true score on the test? A simple equation allows it to be estimated: it is mean + (observed score − mean) × reliability. It is vital to construct one's confidence intervals on either side of *this* score − not the score which is indicated by scoring the test. It is easy to see if someone has followed this advice by checking that the confidence interval is *not* symmetrical around the observed score − unless the observed score is close to the mean.

Assuming that scores on a scale or test are normally distributed, if its reliability is 0.9 the best estimate of the true score of a person who obtains a score of 80 is

100+(−20×0.9)=82. It is important that the confidence interval should be constructed around *this* value rather than the observed score of 80, which is likely to be too extreme because of the effects of random error. If the standard deviation of the scale is 15, the standard error is

$$\sqrt{(1-0.9)} \times 15$$

or 4.7. Thus there is a 95% chance that their true score lies between 82−1.96×4.7 and 82+1.96×4.7. One would report that their estimated IQ was 80, with a 95% confidence interval from 72 to 92. Had the confidence interval been constructed

EXERCISE 14.1: CONFIDENCE INTERVALS AROUND AN INDIVIDUAL'S SCORE

Resources required: Spreadsheet 14.1: Confidence intervals around an individual's score. From www.routledge.com/9781138228894

Purpose: To calculate confidence intervals around an individual's score on a scale whose scores follow a normal distribution

Contents of spreadsheet: Typical values for the reliability etc. of an IQ test

Suggested activity:

- Enter an individual's IQ score and note the estimated true score and confidence interval.
- Repeat for values close to the mean and extreme values (e.g., measured IQs of 60 or 140).
- Note that the confidence interval is symmetrical only when the IQ is equal to the mean (100).

Points to note:

- Several commercial scales do not construct confidence intervals either side of the estimated true score. They may incorrectly advise using the scale score.
- The problems with using coefficient alpha as a measure of reliability (see Chapter 6) should be carefully considered before using it to estimate confidence intervals.

Learning outcomes:

Readers should now be able to

- correctly report confidence intervals about an individual's score on a scale whose scores follow a normal distribution.

around the observed score (80) this would have misleadingly suggested that the confidence interval included the value of 70, which might have important practical consequences for the individual.

The other thing to notice from this is that, if the reliability of a scale is modest, it is patently useless for saying anything sensible about an individual. For example, if the reliability of the scale were 0.7, the confidence interval for the above example extends from 70 to 102, a massive range of over two standard deviations. So someone with a score of 80 could be either slightly above normal or two standard deviations below normal. It is difficult to see how this says anything useful about that individual – and of course explains why correlations between such imprecise measures and other things are generally woefully small.

The reliability of the test appears twice in these analyses – once in determining how much to move extreme scores closer to the mean before constructing the confidence intervals and once when determining the width of the confidence intervals themselves. It is clearly important that the reliability of the test should be as large as possible – and also that there should be no doubt about its actual value within a particular population. We shall see later that neither of these issues is clear cut.

CHANGE SCORES

Before considering how to calculate (and interpret) change scores from individuals, it is important to outline one design which occasionally creeps into journals. Change scores involve administering the same test (or two alternative forms of a test) to a sample of people on two occasions. A t-test or similar could be used to determine whether there is an overall increase or decrease in scores from one occasion to the next. However, researchers sometimes also attempt to discover which individuals' scores improve the most; this is a very dangerous procedure.

Suppose that a researcher assesses children's cognitive ability. There is then some sort of intervention – listening to Mozart every day for a week, perhaps – designed specifically to enhance the cognitive skills of the weakest children in the class. The cognitive ability scale (or an alternative form of it) is then administered a second time and a change score is calculated by subtracting each child's first score from their second score. The researcher feels that this shows how much the intervention has improved each child's cognitive ability scores. Then this difference score is correlated with the first reading score. This is supposed to show whether the intervention has its most marked effect on the lowest-ability children, which is what one might hope could happen.

Given the issues outlined in the previous session, it should be clear what is wrong with this design, which is *bound* to produce a large, significant, negative correlation between the change score and the first score. Not only does this look excitingly significant, the negative correlation suggests that the intervention is most effective for the children who showed the lowest initial levels of reading, which is exactly what the author hoped would happen.

However, a negative correlation will inevitably be found, even if the intervention is completely ineffective, as long as the scale scores are affected by some measurement error. If this is not obvious, consider Spreadsheet 14.2. This shows the true scores of 199 people. These scores follow a normal distribution with a mean of 100 and standard deviation of 15. Each person is tested twice, and their true score is exactly the same on each occasion. However, on each occasion there is some random measurement error; this mimics exactly what happens when someone is tested twice on a scale. The difference score (their 'Time 2' score minus their 'Time 1' score) is then correlated with their score at Time 1. The correlation will be negative.

This just gives a flavour of one problem with change scores; there are others too. For example, the amount of error associated with change scores is large, as each of the two scores has measurement error associated with it. Hence the change score is more inaccurate than a single measurement would be.

EXERCISE 14.2: CHANGE SCORES

Resources required: Spreadsheet 14.2: Change scores. From www.routledge.com/9781138228894

Purpose: To show why change scores should never be correlated with a baseline score

Contents of spreadsheet: Normally distributed true scores of 199 simulated people, plus two random error terms per person

Suggested activity:

* Note the correlation between the change score and the Time 1 score. Altering the standard deviation adjusts the amount of measurement error; 15 corresponds to a scale with a reliability of 0.7.
* Recalculate using f9 etc.
* Increasing the standard deviation of the error term is equivalent to reducing the reliability of the scale. Note how this affects the correlation.

Learning outcomes:

Readers should now be able to

* appreciate why change scores should not be correlated with the baseline score.

Rather than subtracting one observed score from the other, it might seem better to estimate each person's true score (as shown above) – by working out the size of the difference between each person's score and the mean, multiplying this by the reliability of the scale and adding this back to the mean. This is a step in the right direction – however it fails to recognise that the two scales are correlated . . . There is substantial literature on this issue. At the end of a still-influential paper, Cronbach and Furby (1970: 80) conclude, 'it appears that investigators who ask questions regarding gain scores would ordinarily be better advised to frame their questions in other ways'. Researchers who really need to work with change scores will find that this venerable paper gives a good discussion of methods for computing and interpreting them, though they may wish to supplement this reading with more recent work on structural equation modelling (e.g., Kline, 2011). Cascio and Kurtines (1977) give an example of how the techniques outlined by Cronbach and Furby may be applied in practice.

DIFFERENCE SCORES

Educational psychologists and others often need to decide whether one person's scores on two rather different scales are large enough to suggest that there is some underlying problem which requires further investigation. For example, if a child is found to perform better than average at cognitive scales that involve processing shapes and memory for patterns and so on but poorly at cognitive tests involving the use of language, the educational psychologist may then gather other evidence to help them decide whether dyslexia is a possible explanation.

Four things influence the size of a difference score:

- the mean of each scale;
- the standard deviation of each scale;
- the reliability of each scale;
- the correlation between the two scales.

From a psychometric (and statistical) point of view, difference scores can have several different meanings.

Is the difference between a person's scores on two scales statistically significant? In other words, can we measure these traits with sufficient precision to determine that they are different? To answer this question, we need to estimate the size of the difference score (after standardising or using percentiles to get round the problem that the scales will have different means and standard deviations) and perform some sort of statistical test to determine whether a person's difference score is significantly different from zero. This is basically an issue about the precision with which we can measure difference scores. What this analysis does *not* attempt to show is whether a large difference score is at all unusual. For if two highly reliable, well-validated scales measure very different things (Extraversion and general intelligence, for example) it will be quite common for people to have a high score on one scale and a low score on the other; after all, this is what a low correlation between the two scales implies. It might be found that 80% of people who take these two scales score significantly higher on one scale than the other; a lot of people may have difference scores which are significantly different from zero. The technical manuals of tests such as the WAIS-III include a table showing how often various difference scores are found for each level of ability, which may help a professional decide whether a particular individual's score is unusual.

Rather than testing whether two scores are significantly different, it is more common for a professional psychologist to ask whether a difference in scores is uncommon. For example, they may wish to determine whether a child's language skills are markedly lower than one would expect, given their level of nonverbal skills, or whether their educational performance is significantly worse than would be expected, given their level of general intelligence. In order to determine whether a child's difference score is so large as to be 'unusual', it is necessary to gather data on both scales from a large, representative sample and plot their joint distribution. This might show that only 2% of children who score 100 on one scale score below 80 on another scale, and so a child with a difference score this large might well have some form of language-related issue which needs to be explored further. Details of how to perform such analyses will vary from test to test, and so the test handbook should be consulted.

There are other techniques too. For example, a regression line may be used to predict scores on the language scale from scores on the nonverbal reasoning test. Figure 14.1 shows an example of such a regression line, together with one individual whose language score is far lower than would be expected on the basis of their nonverbal ability. It is a simple matter to use the equation of the regression line to estimate what this individual's language ability would be expected to be on the basis of their nonverbal reasoning. Then it is straightforward to compute the distance (the vertical distance in Figure 14.1) between that individual and the regression line. The significance of this distance can be easily calculated.

Reliable Component Analysis (RCA; Cliff and Caruso, 1998) is a more recent development which may perhaps be useful when computing difference scores between factors, each of which is measured by several scales. For example, the eight scales measuring the Perceptual Organisation and the Verbal Comprehension scales of the Wechsler Intelligence Scale for Children might be administered to a sample of people. But rather than scoring the Perceptual Organisation scale by averaging the scores on the four perceptual sub-tests, RCA weights them unequally. These weights are chosen so that each of the two factors (Perceptual Organisation and Verbal Comprehension) contain as much *reliable* variance as possible whilst being uncorrelated with each other. This, of course, maximises the reliability of the difference scores.

Figure 14.1 Regression to predict language score from nonverbal ability

The weights are available for several published tests (e.g., Caruso and Cliff, 2000) or they can be computed from data provided in the test manual given a little programming skill. The procedure leads to difference scores that are far more reliable than those which are calculated conventionally. However, these components are not identical to the 'conventional' Perceptual Organisation and Verbal Comprehension scales, and this will present problems for practitioners. In short, the technique is a neat psychometric technique but one which will affect the validity of the scores to an unknown extent.

HOW RELIABLE IS AN IQ TEST?

This may seem an odd question to ask, given that Chapter 6 considered reliability theory in some detail. But that chapter dealt with a rather simple case, where several items formed a scale, and the reliability coefficient could easily be computed from the responses of a sample of people. However, most practitioners do not use a single scale to measure IQ. Instead they use tests which comprise a dozen or so different scales – comprehension, memory for designs etc. Each of these scales consists of a number of items, and each of them is reliable (although alpha is normally the only reliability coefficient which is reported). These scales are then combined to give a measure of intelligence or possibly of other ability variables, such as perceptual reasoning or verbal comprehension. The problem is how one should estimate the reliability when combining scores on several (fairly reliable) scales in order to produce a composite measure, such as IQ.

Tests such as the Wechsler Adult Intelligence Scale or the Stanford–Binet all claim to assess the same thing (general intelligence) – and indeed it is largely a matter of chance which test a clinician will use when assessing someone; it all depends on which scales an individual is licensed to use, coupled with some personal preference. Furthermore, factor analytic evidence (Johnson et al., 2008) shows clearly that test batteries which are very different in content measure 'general intelligence' factors that are almost identical. So it should be a matter of indifference which test is used.

Knowing a test's overall reliability is enormously important for practitioners. If reliability is estimated incorrectly, then the estimates of the standard error of measurement will be inaccurate, and this will affect the size of confidence intervals, the significance of difference scores, as well as other corrections which are performed on data (e.g., for restriction of range). So what *is* the reliability of one of these tests?

I am indebted to Bob Basham and Paul Barrett who raised this issue in a now-defunct internet forum in 1994 and on whose analysis I have drawn extensively below. Bob's observation was simple. Top-quality tests such as the Wechsler scales and Stanford–Binet all claim to have extremely high reliabilities (alpha of 0.95 or over) – and we know from Chapter 6 that alpha is supposedly an underestimate of the true reliability of a measure. They each consist of a number of sub-scales, each of which measures a particular facet of general cognitive ability. Scores on these scales are weighted equally when they are combined to produce the overall estimate of a person's IQ. So how is the reliability of the IQ score calculated?

The problem is that there are several different ways of estimating the reliability of the total score, which, unfortunately, do not give the same results. The usual way of estimating the overall reliability of a test such as the WAIS is based on knowing the reliabilities of its 11 constituent sub-scales (vocabulary, Digit Span etc.) together with the correlations between them. When combined, the reliability of the sum of these sub-scales is given by

$$reliability\ of\ total = 1 - \frac{no.\ of\ variables - sum\ of\ reliability\ of\ subscales}{sum\ of\ all\ correlations\ between\ subscales}$$

which is Formula 7.13 from Nunnally (1978).

Some fairly typical data for the sum of all of the correlations in the WAIS correlation matrix (from Paul Barrett) suggest that according to this formula the reliability of the WAIS is approximately

$$1 - \frac{11 - (11 \times 0.83)}{67.45}$$

or 0.97, which is impressively large and roughly what the test manual states. Thus far there seems to be no problem.

Table 14.1 Reliability of the sum of a number of scales as a function of their average correlation and average reliability

	Sum of all correlations	Average reliability of sub-tests								
		0.10	0.30	0.50	0.60	0.70	0.80	0.85	0.90	0.95
Average off-diagonal correlation between 11 scales										
0.0	11	0.10	0.30	0.50	0.60	0.70	0.80	0.85	0.90	0.95
0.1	22	0.55	0.65	0.75	0.80	0.85	0.90	0.93	0.95	0.98
0.2	33	0.70	0.77	0.83	0.87	0.90	0.93	0.95	0.97	0.98
0.3	44	0.78	0.83	0.88	0.90	0.93	0.95	0.96	0.98	0.99
0.4	55	0.82	0.86	0.90	0.92	0.94	0.96	0.97	0.98	0.99
0.5	66	0.85	0.88	0.92	0.93	0.95	0.97	0.98	0.98	0.99
0.6	77	0.87	0.90	0.93	0.94	0.96	0.97	0.98	0.99	0.99
0.7	88	0.89	0.91	0.94	0.95	0.96	0.98	0.98	0.99	0.99
0.8	99	0.90	0.92	0.94	0.96	0.97	0.98	0.98	0.99	0.99

Table 14.1 shows some rather interesting results obtained by applying this formula to some typical values for the reliability of 11 scales and the average correlations between these scales.

It can be seen that, when calculated this way, high reliability can be achieved by combining several scales which are themselves highly reliable, regardless of their intercorrelations, or by combining scales with reasonable reliability which correlate well together. When the reliability of the constituent sub-scales is high, coefficient alpha can approach 1.0 *even if the average correlation between the sub-scales is close to zero!* In other words, adding together scores on highly reliable sub-scales which measure wildly different things produces a highly reliable score – and this can happen even if the sub-scales measure totally different traits so that the total score makes no psychological sense. Nunnally's formula simply shows the amount of measurement error in the overall score. It does *not* show how closely the score on the test (IQ) resembles the trait which the scale is supposed to measure (general intelligence). Unfortunately, it seems likely that most test users probably assume that it does.

However, let us put this aside for a moment. Given the high reliability of the total score (at least 0.95, according to the test manuals), one would expect the Wechsler Adult Intelligence Scale and the Wechsler Intelligence Scale for Children – Revised to show a correlation of 0.95. This is what reliability implies, after all, given that both tests measure the same trait. The problem is that the actual correlation (shown in the WISC test manual) is just 0.88. The correlation between the WAIS-III and the WISC-III is also 0.88 (Tulsky et al., 2000). These figures are substantially lower than one might reasonably expect given the supposed high reliability of the scale, as computed above. It also has practical implications. If the reliability of the IQ is really 0.88 rather than 0.97, the estimate of the person's true score will be too extreme, and the confidence interval will be twice as large as it is supposed to be. These two things will wreak havoc with interpretations of individuals' scores. For example, children may be wrongly identified as dyslexic because the discrepancy between their two scores is wrongly identified as being clinically significant. So what *is* the reliability of a test which combines data from several sub-tests to measure IQ or something similar? And why might such discrepancies arise?

Perhaps the problem arises because the reliabilities of the individual scales are overestimated. Can we assume that the reliabilities of the sub-scales are as large as the test manuals tell us? If they truly are, when a factor analysis is performed on the scale scores, the loadings of each scale on the appropriate factor should also be large – equal to the square root of the reliability of the scale.

The reality is very different. Basham shows that Digit Span (which has a reliability of 0.83, according to the test manual) does not have the factor loading of

$$\sqrt{0.83} = 0.91$$

Table 14.2 Reliability of 11 sub-tests from a commercial IQ test

	alpha from manual	$\sqrt{alpha}$ which should resemble the g factor loading	g factor loading from factor analysis	square of g loading: reliability?
Information	0.89	0.94	0.80	0.64
Digit Span	0.83	0.91	0.60	0.36
Vocabulary	0.96	0.98	0.85	0.72
Arithmetic	0.84	0.92	0.75	0.56
Comprehension	0.84	0.92	0.78	0.61
Similarities	0.84	0.92	0.79	0.62
Picture Completion	0.81	0.90	0.69	0.48
Picture Arrangement	0.74	0.86	0.64	0.41
Block Design	0.87	0.93	0.71	0.50
Object Assembly	0.68	0.82	0.59	0.35
Digit Symbol	0.82	0.90	0.60	0.36
Average	0.83			0.51

that would be expected; the actual loading is only 0.60. *All* of the scales have factor loadings that are much lower than would be expected, given their supposed reliability. Perhaps a better measure of the scales' reliability would be the square of their factor loadings? These are shown in the final column of Table 14.2. Using Nunnally's formula with the estimates of sub-scale reliability from the factor analysis suggests that, with an average reliability of 0.51 (from Table 14.2) and an average off-diagonal correlation of 0.51, the reliability of the total score should be 0.92.

So what *is* the reliability of this IQ test?

- The manual tells us that it is 0.97, which agrees with Nunnally's formula using the published reliabilities of the sub-scales.
- Using Nunnally's formula with a more realistic estimation of the sub-scales' reliabilities suggests that the overall reliability might be 0.92.
- The correlation with other tests suggests that the reliability is closer to 0.88.
- It is also possible to look at the correlation between two halves of the tests – rather like a split-half reliability. The correlation between the numerical sub-tests and verbal sub-tests is 0.74 (from the test manual), giving a split-half reliability of 0.85.

Nunnally's formula seems just to tell us how much random measurement error there is in the overall IQ score and *not* how closely the total score correlates with the trait which the total score is supposed to measure. Table 14.1 shows that as long as the average reliability of the sub-tests is 0.7 or more, the reliability of the total score is 0.9 or more, even if the average correlation between the scales is a feeble 0.2.

This is a general issue and not one which is specific to any particular test. It is important because the way in which professionals use tests to assess individuals frequently relies heavily on the assumption that the reliability of the composite scores – Full Scale IQ, Verbal IQ, Performance IQ, Cognitive Proficiency Index etc. – is very substantial indeed and indicates how closely scores on these tests are aligned with the trait(s) which they are designed to measure. We have shown that this last assumption may not be true.

Practitioners purchase these tests at great expense precisely because they do seem to provide highly reliable (therefore presumably accurate) measures of intelligence and other ability traits. The problem is that reliability can be calculated in many different ways. I would personally have greatest faith in estimating reliability based on the correlation between two different scales – assuming that these are equally reliable. After all, the whole purpose of reliability analysis is to predict the correlation between scores on the test and the true score – and correlating two different tests together is really the simplest way of estimating this.

I mention these issues towards the end of this book in order to inject a note of healthy scepticism. Psychometrics is an inexact science (if indeed it is a science at all). Even if one assumes that the items that we write form scales, it is always necessary to make a lot of rather unlikely assumptions about the data (for example, that the responses form a ratio scale, that we have properly sampled all of the items from the domain, that the item characteristic curve is a certain shape, that people guess alternatives at random, that we base our analyses on a random sample of the population or that it is appropriate to calculate a particular form of correlation from the data that we have collected). If these assumptions are incorrect (and they almost certainly will be), no one knows what the consequences will be for a particular analysis. Many psychometricians view the subject as a series of interesting mathematical, statistical and computational challenges rather than a set of tools that practitioners need to help them to make informed and defensible decisions which will affect the lives of real people.

SUMMARY

Practitioners frequently use scores on tests to help make decisions about individuals, and this chapter has outlined a few issues that are not always adequately addressed in test manuals etc. The importance of setting confidence limits on either side of the estimated true score (rather than the actual test score) is often not stressed in test manuals, and this could lead to erroneous decisions. We also mentioned some issues with difference scores and change scores and, finally, invited readers to worry about how, precisely, one can establish the reliability of a test that consists of multiple sub-tests. Does a test whose manual says its reliability is 0.97 actually *behave* like a test whose reliability is 0.97? And does reliability (in this context) actually mean what we assume it does? It is as well to be sceptical; having read this far, readers should have no problems turning to more statistically orientated psychometrics books to find the answers to other issues that start to worry them.

CHAPTER 15
PSYCHOMETRICS IN CONTEXT

The previous chapters have focused on the minutiae of scale development, refinement and the logical basis of psychological assessment, and so it seems appropriate to end by putting these issues into a little psychological context and suggesting how scores on psychological tests might best be used to develop theory. It seems that the way in which we view personality and ability traits has major implications for our approach to psychological assessment, so I think it is important to consider our whole rationale for trying to measure traits before reaching for a questionnaire or designing a new one.

TRAITS: BEHAVIOUR OR IMPUTATIONS?

The first issue concerns what we try to measure with scales, questionnaires or other devices. Do we try to measure how people actually behave, or do we impute some characteristic to them? The difference between these approaches becomes obvious if we consider a scale that is developed to measure a person's anxiety and another to measure their beauty. The anxiety scale has been used in several examples. It assumes that anxiety is a genuine characteristic of people that affects several aspects of their behaviour; they may report feeling nervous, sweat, be vigilant and so on, and the idea of the anxiety questionnaire is to try to measure each of those behaviours. They are all caused by something inside each person that varies. This cause can take many forms. It might be physiological (as with anxiety), psychological (as with post-traumatic stress disorder), developmental (as with theory of mind) or have other origins. The key point is that the questions try to measure some real characteristic of the person. It is easy to tell whether the theory is incorrect. If scores on an anxiety questionnaire are manifestly unconnected to any physiological or psychological variables, then it is clear that the theory is incorrect and must be abandoned or modified. It is falsifiable, hence scientific.

Strangely enough, this is not always the case. Social psychologists argue that we view people in an arbitrary way, determined by society; there is no such 'thing' as a personality trait which reflects some internal process which itself affects how people behave. Instead we can choose how we view and categorise behaviour, and we do so according to societal norms. From this perspective, it would be perfectly easy to put together a questionnaire measuring beauty. This could assess things such as body mass index, hairstyle and social poise. However, there is no hint of causality. No one would suggest that a person's beauty *causes* them to be slim, with a particular aesthetic. Indeed, the definition of beauty will change from society to society and over time; we choose to categorise certain behaviours as indicating beauty, but in a few years' time society might change its mind entirely and look for quite different characteristics. Beauty is a social construction, and we can try to measure people's beauty using whatever definition is currently fashionable.

One of the problems with social construction is that it limits the use to which test scores can be put. If general intelligence

- does not reflect something which actually occurs within the individual and
- is defined in an arbitrary way,

next year, society might decide that 'intelligence' is all about Morris dancing and gardening, rather than cognitive processes, and so it makes no sense to use intelligence test scores to try to predict behaviour. Most readers of this book will probably agree that this approach is sterile. Furthermore, it seems to be difficult to falsify and therefore unscientific. How could one ever show that one's conception of beauty was 'wrong' since it is arbitrary in the first place?

It might be more productive to measure the way in which people really behave and deduce from these measurements which personality and ability traits exist. We might *notice* that some people sweat more than others, are fearsome of heights and so on and hypothesise that this is because something about their psychological, physiological or other makeup (we call it 'anxiety') affects all of these behaviours. We then research why some people are more anxious than others.

The reason I mention this here is that it seems to impact on the way in which personality scales, in particular, are developed and used. The example of anxiety is a 'bottom-up' approach. The traits that are discovered are determined by observation; we observe that several behaviours tend to occur together and, because of this, infer the presence of a trait. It is a data-driven process, which takes place without requiring any form of theory or preconceived ideas about the structure of personality. Social constructionism is a top-down approach. Society determines what characteristics it chooses to combine (no matter how arbitrary and diverse these are) and imputes these characteristics to an individual.

Researchers such as Cattell (1946, 1971, 1973) and Costa and McCrae (1992) argue that factor analysis is capable of identifying traits using the bottom-up approach. All one needs to do is measure as many behaviours as possible, perform a factor analysis, and the factor analysis will show whether apparently different behaviours (sweating, avoiding high places) form a factor. There is no theoretical expectation at all: the data drive the theory. On the other hand, social psychologists frequently seem to use the top-down approach. A theorist decides to measure 'insecure insubordination', or some other trait that exists only in their own mind, and develops a questionnaire to measure it, without any evidence that it is related to the way in which people actually behave. This is one reason why I have been so repeatedly scathing about attempts to measure personality by inventing traits. This approach to developing a theory of personality seems analogous to trying to build a high wall by continually bringing two or three new bricks to the project and arranging them by the side of the existing structure, rather than trying to do anything useful with the materials which are already there.

The other problem with this approach to personality is that it is rare for a theorist to hypothesise that several different characteristics should be combined in a questionnaire (probably because they fear that this could not be shown to be the case). A questionnaire which paraphrases the same item over and over again will *appear* reliable but only because the items ask the same thing and so participants have to answer them in a certain way in order to be consistent. The total score on the questionnaire is a mixture of the true score plus the nuisance variables, which affect all the questions in similar ways. A questionnaire measuring Extraversion, on the other hand (a trait discovered during the 'bottom-up' analysis of data) will ask about sociability, optimism, thrill-seeking, a high activity level etc. These characteristics appear to be quite different, and so each will be affected by a different set of response biases and each will correlate with a different set of other (nuisance) variables.

To my mind, the scientific study of personality and abilities involves trying to measure how people actually behave and then trying to determine why these consistencies of behaviour (traits) occur, using the methods of experimental psychology. Inventing traits oneself (unless these are later shown to be linked to actual behaviour, as with emotional intelligence) seems to be a recipe for disaster – although it now seems to be the norm. It seems to me that the discipline is fragmenting as researchers carve out small new niches for themselves and their students to develop, rather than tackling the far more difficult job of developing and testing theories about the processes which cause some people to vary.

KEEPING IN TOUCH WITH ONE'S DATA

This book began by reminding users that psychometric tests and scales are terribly simple. They almost always just involve gathering data from questionnaires or measures of performance, making some dangerous statistical assumptions, converting the responses into numbers and adding together these numbers. However, many researchers seem to forget how simple this process is and develop grandiloquent theories in which highly abstract concepts are interrelated in complex ways. When structural equation modelling is used, there are frequently so many paths and correlations that the whole thing resembles a plate of spaghetti. This worries me. In Chapter 2 we showed that several scales, which supposedly measure quite different things, contain items that are virtually identical. This will almost invariably not be noticed by the researchers who use these scales even though it is guaranteed to affect the correlation between them. It will hence spawn all sorts of complex theories, moderation analyses, mediation analyses etc. to explain them.

I suspect (without a shred of evidence) that the problem is that researchers who design such studies are not the ones who actually administer the questionnaires; these senior figures may have long forgotten the precise content of the items and so may be unaware of the difficulties that shared items can pose. There is a lot to be said for slowly and thoughtfully reading each item in each scale that is to be administered and asking oneself whether answering one item in a particular way has to influence the answer that is made to another item. If this happens on just one occasion, there is a problem, and it needs to be recognised and addressed during the analysis of the data. Structural equation modelling makes it quite straightforward to do this at the item level.

Part of the problem is probably also having too much faith in psychological scales. After all, the only thing that any scale can do is combine several pieces of information. It cannot tell us anything that is unavailable by other means or provide deep insights into the soul; it may not even measure what it claims to measure very well. One frequently sees papers justifying the use of a test because it has a reliability of 0.7. This is a convenient misreading of Nunnally (1978: 245) who actually advocated a reliability of 0.8 for all but the most exploratory research. But the acid test for any scale is whether its score correlates substantially with behaviour (rather than scores on other scales) and this is rarely reported. It is all too easy to focus on the reliability of a scale, rather than evidence for its validity.

SCIENCE OR TECHNOLOGY?

Michell's (1997a, b, 2000) appraisals of psychological measurement make it clear that the scales that we use just count (rather than measure) responses to questionnaires and tests. Test scores therefore do not behave like weight, length and other physical measures, and so, even if a highly accurate measure were devised, it is not obvious how its scores could ever be used as the basis for quantitative laws. It is hard to see how scores on psychological scales could ever lead to the discovery of mathematically defined relationships – psychological equivalents to Newton's laws of motion in physics or the gas laws in chemistry, which state clear mathematical relationships between quantitative variables. The problem is not just that these relationships are viewed through the fog of probability; it is that the scores that are used may simply not be quantitative. Whilst it is sometimes claimed that item response theory is the panacea for all of the issues identified by Michell, it is clear from Chapter 12 that this is certainly not universally accepted.

This does not mean that psychological scales are devoid of merit. First of all, they can have practical applications; it might be rather useful to be able to say that one person is (probably) more depressed or intelligent than another or that they are more likely to succeed if appointed to a job, even if it is impossible to quantify the extent of the difference between them. Second, it is possible that scores on psychological scales could correlate so substantially with physical measurements that they could be used as a sort of proxy for the physical measurements. The only problem is that there are no such large relationships at present. Intelligence tests show an impressive correlation with 'inspection time' (the amount of time for which a shape has to be shown in order to be correctly recognised), but this correlation (circa -0.5) is not large enough to allow us to use intelligence tests as a sort of proxy for whatever neural processes go on when inspection-time tasks are solved. There is plenty of evidence that traits such as general intelligence are closely linked to the biology of the nervous system, genetic makeup and so on (Cooper, 2015), and this is important because it tells us that IQ is not a social construction and that scores on IQ tests have a roughly linear relationship with some physical variables. Despite the sophisticated mathematical underpinnings of some modern developments in psychometric theory, it seems safest to regard psychological assessments as technological rather than scientific achievements.

REFERENCES

Achenbach, T. M. & Rescorla, L. A. 2001. *Manual for the ASEBA School-Age Forms & Profiles*. Burlington, VT: University of Vermont, Research Center for Children, Youth, & Families.

Alf, E. & Abrahams, N. 1971. A Significance Test for Biserial. *Educational and Psychological Measurement*, 31, 637–640.

Angoff, W. H. & Ford, S. F. 1973. Item–Race Interaction on a Test of Scholastic Aptitude. *Journal of Educational Measurement*, 10, 95–106.

Armstrong, T. 1994. *Multiple Intelligences in the Classroom*. Alexandria, VA: Association for Supervision and Curriculum Development.

Arro, G. 2013. Peeking into Personality Test Answers: Inter- and Intraindividual Variety in Item Interpretations. *Integrative Psychological and Behavioral Science*, 47, 56–76.

Baron, H. 1996. Strengths and Limitations of Ipsative Measurement. *Journal of Occupational and Organizational Psychology*, 69, 49–56.

Barrett, P. T. 1986. Factor Comparison: An Examination of Three Methods. *Personality and Individual Differences*, 7, 327–340.

Barrett, P. T. 2007. Structural Equation Modelling: Adjudging Model Fit. *Personality and Individual Differences*, 42, 815–824.

Barrett, P. T. 2011. Invoking Arbitrary Units Is Not a Solution to the Problem of Quantification in the Social Sciences. *Measurement*, 9, 28–31.

Barrett, P. T. & Kline, P. 1980. The Location of Superfactors P, E and N within an Unexplored Factor Space. *Personality and Individual Differences*, 1, 239–247.

Barrett, P. T. & Kline, P. 1981a. The Observation to Variable Ratio in Factor Analysis. *Personality Study and Group Behavior*, 1, 23–33.

Barrett, P. T. & Kline, P. 1981b. Radial Parcel Factor Analysis. *Personality and Individual Differences*, 2, 311–318.

Bartholomew, D. J., Deary, I. J. & Lawn, M. 2009. The Origin of Factor Scores: Spearman, Thomson and Bartlett. *British Journal of Mathematical & Statistical Psychology*, 62, 569–582.

Bartlett, M. 1950. Tests of Significance in Factor Analysis. *British Journal of Psychology*, 3, 77–85.

Bartram, D. 1996. The Relationship between Ipsatized and Normative Measures of Personality. *Journal of Occupational and Organizational Psychology*, 69, 25–39.

Bartram, D. 2009. The International Test Commission Guidelines on Computer-Based and Internet-Delivered Testing. *Industrial and Organizational Psychology – Perspectives on Science and Practice*, 2, 11–13.

Beloff, H. 1992. Mother, Father and Me: Our IQ. *The Psychologist*, 5, 309–311.

Bentler, P. M., Jackson, D. N. & Messick, S. 1971. Identification of Content and Style – 2-Dimensional Interpretation of Acquiescence. *Psychological Bulletin*, 76, 186–204.

Birnbaum, M. H. 1973. The Devil Rides Again – Correlation as an Index of Fit. *Psychological Bulletin*, 79, 239–242.

Bloxom, B. A. 1968. A Note on Invariance in Three-Mode Factor Analysis. *Psychometrika*, 33, 347–350.

Bollen, K. A. & Barb, K. H. 1983. Collapsing Variables and Validity Coefficients – Reply. *American Sociological Review*, 48, 286–287.

Borsboom, D. & Scholten, A. Z. 2008. The Rasch Model and Conjoint Measurement Theory from the Perspective of Psychometrics. *Theory & Psychology*, 18, 111–117.

Borsboom, D., Mellenbergh, G. J. & Van Heerden, J. 2004. The Concept of Validity. *Psychological Review*, 111, 1061–1071.

Brogden, H. E. 1969. Pattern, Structure and the Interpretation of Factors. *Psychological Bulletin*, 72, 375–378.

Brown, R. T., Reynolds, C. R. & Whitaker, J. S. 1999. Bias in Mental Testing since Bias in Mental Testing. *School Psychology Quarterly*, 14, 208–238.

Butler, R. P. 1973. Effects of Signed and Unsigned Questionnaires for Both Sensitive and Nonsensitive Items. *Journal of Applied Psychology*, 57, 348–349.

Byrne, B. 1995. One Application of Structural Equation Modeling from Two Perspectives. *In:* R. H. Hoyle (ed.) *Structural Equation Modeling: Concepts, Issues and Applications*. Thousand Oaks, CA: Sage.

Byrne, D. 1961. The Repression-Sensitisation Scale: Rationale, Reliability and Validity. *Journal of Personality*, 29, 334–339.

Calvin, C. M., Fernandes, C., Smith, P., Visscher, P. M. & Deary, I. J. 2010. Sex, Intelligence and Educational Achievement in a National Cohort of over 175,000 11-Year-Old Schoolchildren in England. *Intelligence*, 38, 424–432.

Carroll, J. B. 1993. *Human Cognitive Abilities: A Survey of Factor-Analytic Studies*. Cambridge: Cambridge University Press.

Carroll, J. B. 2003. The Higher-Stratum Structure of Cognitive Abilities: Current Evidence Supports *g* and About Ten Broad Factors. *In:* H. Nyborg (ed.) *The Scientific Study of General Intelligence: Tribute to Arthur R. Jensen*. London: Elsevier Science.

Caruso, J. C. & Cliff, N. 2000. Increasing the Reliability of Wechsler Intelligence Scale for Children – Third Edition Difference Scores with Reliable Component Analysis. *Psychological Assessment*, 12, 89–96.

Cascio, W. F. & Kurtines, W. M. 1977. A Practical Method for Identifying Significant Change Scores. *Educational and Psychological Measurement*, 37, 889–895.

Catron, D. W. & Thompson, C. C. 1979. Test-Retest Gains in WAIS Scores after 4 Retest Intervals. *Journal of Clinical Psychology*, 35, 352–357.

Cattell, R. B. 1946. *Description and Measurement of Personality*. New York: World Book Company.

Cattell, R. B. 1965. *The IPAT Culture Fair Intelligence Scales 1, 2 and 3*. Champaign, IL: Institute for Personality and Ability Testing.

Cattell, R. B. 1966. The Scree Test for the Number of Factors. *Multivariate Behavioral Research*, 1, 140–161.

Cattell, R. B. 1971. *Abilities, Their Structure Growth and Action*. New York: Houghton Mifflin.

Cattell, R. B. 1973. *Personality and Mood by Questionnaire*. San Francisco, CA: Jossey-Bass.

Cattell, R. B. 1978. *The Scientific Use of Factor Analysis in Behavioral and Life Sciences*. New York: Plenum.

Cattell, R. B., Eber, H. W. & Tatsuoka, M. M. 1970. *Handbook for the Sixteen Personality Factor Questionnaire*. Champaign, IL: IPAT.

Cattell, R. B. & Muerle, J. L. 1960. The 'Maxplane' Program for Factor Rotation to Oblique Simple Structure. *Educational and Psychological Measurement*, 20, 569–590.

Cattell, R. B. & Vogelman, S. 1977. A Comprehensive Trial of the Scree and KG Criteria for Determining the Number of Factors. *Journal of Educational Measurement*, 14, 289–325.

Chalmers, R. P. in press. On Misconceptions and the Limited Usefulness of Ordinal Alpha. *Educational and Psychological Measurement*.

Chan, D. & Schmitt, N. 1997. Video-Based Versus Paper-and-Pencil Method of Assessment in Situational Judgment Tests: Subgroup Differences in Test Performance and Face Validity Perceptions. *Journal of Applied Psychology*, 82, 143–159.

Choi, J., Peters, M. & Mueller, R. O. 2010. Correlational Analysis of Ordinal Data: From Pearson's R to Bayesian Polychoric Correlation. *Asia Pacific Education Review*, 11, 459–466.

Clarkson, D. B. & Jennrich, R. I. 1988. Quartic Rotation Criteria and Algorithms. *Psychometrika*, 53, 251–259.

Cliff, N. & Caruso, J. C. 1998. Reliable Component Analysis through Maximizing Composite Reliability. *Psychological Methods*, 3, 291–308.

Closs, S. J. 1996. On the Factoring and Interpretation of Ipsative Data. *Journal of Occupational and Organizational Psychology*, 69, 41–47.

Collie, A., Maruff, P., Darby, D. G. & McStephen, M. 2003. The Effects of Practice on the Cognitive Test Performance of Neurologically Normal Individuals Assessed at Brief Test-Retest Intervals. *Journal of the International Neuropsychological Society*, 9, 419–428.

Comrey, A. L. & Lee, H. B. 1992. *A First Course in Factor Analysis*. Hillsdale, NJ: Lawrence Erlbaum Associates.

Conley, J. J. 1984. The Hierarchy of Consistency: A Review and Model of Longitudinal Findings on Adult Individual Differences in Intelligence, Personality and Self-Opinion. *Personality and Individual Differences*, 5, 11–25.

Cooper, C. 1983. Correlation Measures in Item Analysis. *British Journal of Mathematical and Statistical Psychology*, 32, 102–105.

Cooper, C. 2010. *Individual Differences and Personality*. London: Hodder Education.

Cooper, C. 2015. *Intelligence and Human Abilities*. London: Routledge.

Cooper, C., Kline, P. & May, J. 1986. The Measurement of Authoritarianism, Psychoticism and Other Traits by Objective Tests: A Cross-Validation. *Personality and Individual Differences*, 7, 15–21.

Cornwell, J. M. & Dunlap, W. P. 1994. On the Questionable Soundness of Factoring Ipsative Data – a Response. *Journal of Occupational and Organizational Psychology*, 67, 89–100.

Cortina, J. M. 1993. What Is Coefficient Alpha – an Examination of Theory and Applications. *Journal of Applied Psychology*, 78, 98–104.

Costa, P. T. & McCrae, R. R. 1992. 4 Ways 5 Factors Are Basic. *Personality And Individual Differences*, 13, 653–665.

Cronbach, L. J. & Furby, L. 1970. How We Should Measure 'Change': Or Should We? *Psychological Bulletin*, 74, 68–80.

Crowne, D. P. & Marlowe, D. 1960. A New Scale of Social Desirability Independent of Psychopathology. *Journal of Consulting Psychology*, 24, 349–354.

Danner, D., Aichholzer, J. & Rammstedt, B. 2015. Acquiescence in Personality Questionnaires: Relevance, Domain Specificity, and Stability. *Journal of Research in Personality*, 57, 119–130.

Davenport, E. C. 1990. Significance Testing of Congruence Coefficients – a Good Idea. *Educational and Psychological Measurement*, 50, 289–296.

Davenport, E. C. & Elsanhurry, N. A. 1991. Phi-Phimax – Review and Synthesis. *Educational and Psychological Measurement*, 51, 821–828.

Davey, T. 2011. *Practical Considerations in Computer-Based Testing*. Princeton, NJ: Educational Testing Service.

Davidson, W. & Carroll, J. 1945. Speed and Level Components in Time-Limit Scores: A Factor Analysis. *Educational and Psychological Measurement*, 5, 411–427.

Deary, I. J., Whalley, L. J., Lemmon, H., Crawford, J. R. & Starr, J. M. 2000. The Stability of Individual Differences in Mental Ability from Childhood to Old Age: Follow-up of the 1932 Scottish Mental Survey. *Intelligence*, 28, 49–55.

Der, G., Batty, G. D. & Deary, I. J. 2006. Effect of Breast Feeding on Intelligence in Children: Prospective Study, Sibling Pairs Analysis, and Meta-Analysis. *British Medical Journal*, 333, 945–948A.

Dobson, P. 1988. The Correction of Correlation Coefficients for Restriction of Range When Restriction Results from the Truncation of a Normally Distributed Variable. *British Journal of Mathematical and Statistical Psychology*, 41, 227–234.

Dombrowski, S. C. & Watkins, M. W. 2013. Exploratory and Higher Order Factor Analysis of the WJ-III Full Test Battery: A School-Aged Analysis. *Psychological Assessment*, 25, 442–455.

Donner, A. & Wells, G. 1986. A Comparison of Confidence Interval Methods for the Intraclass Correlation Coefficient. *Biometrics*, 42, 401–412.

Dziuban, C. D. & Shirkey, E. C. 1974. When Is a Correlation Matrix Appropriate for Factor-Analysis – Decision Rules. *Psychological Bulletin*, 81, 358–361.

Edwards, A. L. 1953. *Edwards Personal Preference Schedule*. New York: Psychological Corporation.

Edwards, A. L. 1959. Social Desirability and the Description of Others. *The Journal of Abnormal and Social Psychology*, 59, 434–436.

Ellingson, J. E., Sackett, P. R. & Hough, L. M. 1999. Social Desirability Corrections in Personality Measurement: Issues of Applicant Comparison and Construct Validity. *Journal of Applied Psychology*, 84, 155–166.

Elliott, C. D., Murray, D. J. & Pearson, L. S. 1996. *British Ability Scales*. 2nd ed. Windsor: NFER-Nelson.

Eysenck, H. J. & Wilson, G. D. 1976. *Know Your Own Personality*. Harmondsworth: Penguin Books.

Eysenck, S. B. G., Eysenck, H. J. & Barrett, P. 1985. A Revised Version of the Psychoticism Scale. *Personality and Individual Differences*, 6, 21–29.

Feldt, L. S., Woodruff, D. J. & Salih, F. A. 1987. Statistical-Inference for Coefficient-Alpha. *Applied Psychological Measurement*, 11, 93–103.

Ferguson, G. 1941. The Factorial Interpretation of Test Difficulty. *Psychometrika*, 6, 323–329.

Francis, L. 1981. Anonymity and Attitude Scores among 10- and 11-Year Old Children. *Journal of Experimental Education*, 49, 74–76.

Fugett, A., Thomas, S. W. & Lindberg, M. A. 2014. The Many Faces of Malingering and Participant Response Strategies: New Methodologies in the Attachment and Clinical Issues Questionnaire (ACIQ). *Journal of General Psychology*, 141, 80–97.

Gallitto, E. & Leth-Steensen, C. 2015. Autistic Traits and Adult Attachment Styles. *Personality and Individual Differences*, 79, 63–67.

Gardner, H. 1983. *Frames of Mind*. New York: Basic Books.

Giordani, P., Kiers, H., Antonietta, M. & Ferraro, D. 2014. Three-Way Component Analysis Using the R Package Threeway. *Journal of Statistical Software*, 57, 1–23.

Golino, H. F. & Demetriou, A. 2017. Estimating the Dimensionality of Intelligence-Like Data Using Exploratory Graph Analysis. *Intelligence*, 62, 54–70.

Golino, H. F. & Epskamp, S. 2017. Exploratory Graph Analysis: A New Approach for Estimating the Number of Dimensions in Psychological Research. *Plos One*, 12. DOI 10.1371/journal.pone.0174035.

Gorsuch, R. L. 1970. Comparison of Biquartimin, Maxplane, Promax, and Varimax. *Educational and Psychological Measurement*, 30, 861–872.

Gorsuch, R. L. 1983. *Factor Analysis*. Hillsdale, NJ: Lawrence Erlbaum Associates.

Gosling, S. D., Rentfrow, P. J. & Swann, W. B. 2003. A Very Brief Measure of the Big-Five Personality Domains. *Journal of Research in Personality*, 37, 504–528.

Gough, H. G. 1975. *The California Personality Inventory*. Palo Alto, CA: Consulting Psychologists Press.

Graham, J. M. 2006. Congeneric and (Essentially) Tau-Equivalent Estimates of Score Reliability – What They Are and How to Use Them. *Educational and Psychological Measurement*, 66, 930–944.

Graham, J. R. 1990. *MMPI-2: Assessing Personality and Psychopathology*. New York: Oxford University Press.

Grudnik, J. L. & Kranzler, J. H. 2001. Meta-Analysis of the Relationship between Intelligence and Inspection Time. *Intelligence*, 29, 523–535.

Guadagnoli, E. & Velicer, W. F. 1988. Relation of Sample Size to the Stability of Component Patterns. *Psychological Bulletin*, 103, 265–275.

Guilford, J. & Lyons, T. 1942. On Determining the Reliability and Significance of a Tetrachoric Coefficient of Correlation. *Psychometrika*, 7, 243–249.

Guilford, J. P. 1959. *Personality*. New York: McGraw-Hill.

Gulliksen, H. 1950a. The Reliability of Speeded Tests. *Psychometrika*, 15, 259–269.

Gulliksen, H. 1950b. *Theory of Mental Tests*. New York: Wiley.

Gulliksen, H. 1986. Perspective on Educational Measurement. *Applied Psychological Measurement*, 10, 109–132.

Guttman, L. 1954. Some Necessary and Sufficient Conditions for Common Factor Analysis. *Psychometrika*, 19, 149–161.

Hakstian, A. R. & Mueller, V. J. 1973. Some Notes on the Number of Factors Problem. *Multivariate Behavioral Research*, 8, 461–475.

Hambleton, R. K. & Cook, L. 1983. Robustness of Item Response Models. *In*: D. J. Weiss (ed.) *New Horizons in Testing*. New York: Academic Press.

Hambleton, R. K. & Traub, R. E. 1973. Analysis of Empirical Data Using Two Logistic Latent Trait Models. *British Journal of Mathematical and Statistical Psychology*, 26, 195–211.

Hambleton, R. K. & Swaminathan, H. 1985. *Item Response Theory: Principles and Applications*. Boston: Kluwer-Nijhoff.

Hambleton, R. K., Swaminathan, H. & Rogers, H. J. 1991. *Fundamentals of Item Response Theory*. Newbury Park, CA: Sage.

Hardt, J. & Rutter, M. 2004. Validity of Adult Retrospective Reports of Adverse Childhood Experiences: Review of the Evidence. *Journal of Child Psychology and Psychiatry*, 45, 260–273.

Harman, H. H. 1976. *Modern Factor Analysis*. Chicago, IL: Chicago University Press.

Harris, C. W. 1967. On Factors and Factor Scores. *Psychometrika*, 32, 363–379.

Harter, S. 1988. *Manual for the Self-Perception Profile for Adolescents*. Denver, CO: University of Denver.

Hathaway, S. & McKinley, J. 1940. A Multiphasic Personality Schedule (Minnesota): I. Construction of the Schedule. *The Journal of Psychology: Interdisciplinary and Applied*, 10, 249–254.

Hathaway, S. R. & McKinley, J. C. 1967. *The Minnesota Multiphasic Personality Inventory Manual (Revised)*. New York: Psychological Corporation.

Heim, A. W. 1967. *AH4 Group Test of Intelligence*. Windsor: National Foundation for Educational Research.

Heim, A. W., Watts, K. P. & Simmonds, V. 1970. *AH4, AH5 and AH6 Tests*. Windsor: NFER.

Hendrickson, A. E. & White, P. O. 1966. A Method for the Rotation of Higher-Order Factors. *British Journal of Mathematical and Statistical Psychology*, 19, 97–103.

Hepburn, L. & Eysenck, M. W. 1989. Personality, Average Mood and Mood Variability. *Personality and Individual Differences*, 10, 975–983.

Herriott, P. 1989. *Assessment and Selection in Organisations*. Chichester: Wiley.

Holley, J. W. 1973. The Rorschach. *In:* P. Kline (ed.) *New Approaches in Psychological Measurement*. Chichester: Wiley.

Holster, T. A. & Lake, J. 2016. Guessing and the Rasch Model. *Language Assessment Quarterly*, 13, 124–141.

Holzinger, K. J. & Swineford, F. 1937. The Bi-Factor Method. *Psychometrika*, 2, 41–54.

Horn, J. L. & Knapp, J. R. 1973. Subjective Character of Empirical Base of Guilfords Structure-of-Intellect Model. *Psychological Bulletin*, 80, 33–43.

Howell, D. C. 2012. *Statistical Methods for Psychology*. Belmont, CA: Wadsworth Publishing.

Hu, L.-T. & Bentler, P. M. 1995. Evaluating Model Fit. *In:* R. H. Hoyle (ed.) *Structural Equation Modeling*. Thousand Oaks, CA: Sage.

Hurley, J. R. & Cattell, R. B. 1962. The Procrustes Program: Producing Direct Rotation to Test a Hypothesized Factor Structure. *Behavioral Science*, 7, 258–262.

Jackson, D. N. & Messick, S. 1958. Content and Style in Personality Assessment. *Psychological Bulletin*, 55, 243–252.

Jacobs, N., Gestel, S. V., Derom, C., Thiery, E., Vernon, P., Derom, R. & Vlietinck, R. 2001. Heritability Estimates of Intelligence in Twins: Effect of Chorion Type. *Behavior Genetics*, 31, 209–217.

Jennrich, R. I. & Bentler, P. M. 2011. Exploratory Bi-Factor Analysis. *Psychometrika*, 76, 537–549.

Jennrich, R. I. & Bentler, P. M. 2012. Exploratory Bi-Factor Analysis: The Oblique Case. *Psychometrika*, 77, 442–454.

Jennrich, R. I. & Sampson, P. F. 1966. Rotation for Simple Loadings. *Psychometrika*, 31, 313–323.

Jensen, A. R. 1980. *Bias in Mental Testing*. New York: The Free Press.

Johnson, C. E., Wood, R. & Blinkhorn, S. F. 1988. Spuriouser and Spuriouser – the Use of Ipsative Personality Tests. *Journal of Occupational Psychology*, 61, 153–162.

Johnson, W., Te Nijenhuis, J. & Bouchard, T. J. 2008. Still Just 1 g: Consistent Results from Five Test Batteries. *Intelligence*, 36, 81–95.

Judge, T. A., Rodell, J. B., Klinger, R. L., Simon, L. S. & Crawford, E. R. 2013. Hierarchical Representations of the Five-Factor Model of Personality in Predicting Job Performance: Integrating Three Organizing Frameworks with Two Theoretical Perspectives. *Journal of Applied Psychology*, 98, 875–925.

Kaiser, H. F. 1958. The VARIMAX Criterion for Analytic Rotation in Factor Analysis. *Psychometrika*, 23, 187–200.

Kaiser, H. F. 1960. The Application of Electronic Computers in Factor Analysis. *Educational and Psychological Measurement*, 20, 141–151.

Kaiser, H. F. 1970. A Second Generation Little Jiffy. *Psychometrika*, 35, 401–415.

Kaiser, H. F. 1981. A Revised Measure of Sampling Adequacy for Factor-Analytic Data Matrices. *Educational and Psychological Measurement*, 41, 379–381.

Kaiser, H. F. 1990. On Guttman's Proof That Squared Multiple Correlations Are Lower Bounds for Communalities. *Psychological Reports*, 67, 1004–1006.

Kaiser, H. F., Hunka, S. & Bianchini, J. C. 1971. Relating Factors between Studies Based Upon Different Individuals. *Multivariate Behavioral Research*, 6, 409–422.

Kampen, J. & Swyngedouw, M. 2000. The Ordinal Controversy Revisited. *Quality & Quantity*, 34, 87–102.

Kanfer, P. L., Ackerman, Y. M. & Goff, M. 1995. Personality and Intelligence in Industrial and Organizational Psychology. *In:* D. H. Saklofske & M. Zeidner (eds.) *International Handbook of Personality and Intelligence.* New York: Plenum.

Kass, F., Spitzer, R. L. & Williams, J. B. W. 1983. An Empirical-Study of the Issue of Sex Bias in the Diagnostic-Criteria of DSM-III Axis II Personality Disorders. *American Psychologist*, 38, 799–801.

Katz, J. O. & Rohlf, F. J. 1974. Functionplane – New Approach to Simple Structure Rotation. *Psychometrika*, 39, 37–51.

Kline, P. 1986. *A Handbook of Test Construction.* London: Methuen.

Kline, P. 1994. *An Easy Guide to Factor Analysis.* London: Routledge.

Kline, P. 2000a. *The Handbook of Psychological Testing.* 2nd ed. London; New York: Routledge.

Kline, P. 2000b. *A Psychometrics Primer.* London: Free Association Books.

Kline, R. B. 2011. *Principles and Practice of Structural Equation Modeling.* New York; London: Guilford Press.

Knol, D. L. & Tenberge, J. M. F. 1989. Least-Squares Approximation of an Improper Correlation Matrix by a Proper One. *Psychometrika*, 54, 53–61.

Kolen, M. J. & Brennan, R. L. 2014. *Test Equating, Scaling, and Linking: Methods and Practices.* 3rd ed. New York: Springer.

Konstabel, K., Lonnqvist, J. E., Walkowitz, G. & Verkasalo, M. 2012. The Short Five (S5): Measuring Personality Traits Using Comprehensive Single Items. *European Journal of Personality*, 26, 13–29.

Kyngdon, A. 2008. The Rasch Model from the Perspective of the Representational Theory of Measurement. *Theory & Psychology*, 18, 89–109.

Lalla, M. 2017. Fundamental Characteristics and Statistical Analysis of Ordinal Variables: A Review. *Quality & Quantity*, 51, 435–458.

Le Corff, Y., Gingras, V. & Busque-Carrier, M. 2017. Equivalence of Unproctored Internet Testing and Proctored Paper-and-Pencil Testing of the Big Five. *International Journal of Selection and Assessment*, 25, 154–160.

Levene, H. 1960. Robust Tests for Equality of Variances. *In:* I. Olkin (ed.) *Contributions to Probability and Statistics: Essays in Honor of Harold Hotelling.* Palo Alto, CA: Stanford University Press.

Linacre, J. M. & Wright, B. D. 1995. How Do Rasch and 3P Differ? An Example from the National Adult Literacy Study. *Memo 81.* Chicago: MESA Laboratory.

Little, T. D., Cunningham, W. A., Shahar, G. & Widaman, K. F. 2002. To Parcel or Not to Parcel: Exploring the Question, Weighing the Merits. *Structural Equation Modeling*, 9, 151–173.

Loehlin, J. C. 2004. *Latent Variable Models: An Introduction to Factor, Path, and Structural Equation Analysis.* 4th ed. Mahwah, NJ: Lawrence Erlbaum Associates Publishers.

Loevinger, J. 1948. The Technic of Homogeneous Tests Compared with Some Aspects of 'Scale Analysis' and Factor Analysis. *Psychological Bulletin*, 45, 507–529.

Lord, F. M. 1980. *Applications of Item Response Theory to Practical Testing Problems.* Hillsdale, NJ: L. Erlbaum Associates.

Lorenzo-Seva, U. & Ferrando, P. J. 2006. Factor: A Computer Program to Fit the Exploratory Factor Analysis Model. *Behavior Research Methods*, 38, 88–91.

Lorenzo-Seva, U. & ten Berge, J. M. F. 2006. Tucker's Congruence Coefficient as a Meaningful Index of Factor Similarity. *Methodology*, 2, 57–64.

Luce, R. & Tukey, J. W. 1964. Simultaneous Conjoint Measurement: A New Type of Fundamental Measurement. *Journal of Mathematical Psychology*, 1, 1–27.

MacCallum, R. C., Widaman, K. F., Zhang, S. B. & Hong, S. H. 1999. Sample Size in Factor Analysis. *Psychological Methods*, 4, 84–99.

MacCann, C. 2013. Instructed Faking of the Hexaco Reduces Facet Reliability and Involves More Gc Than Gf. *Personality and Individual Differences*, 55, 828–833.

Mansolf, M. & Reise, S. P. 2016. Exploratory Bifactor Analysis: The Schmid-Leiman Orthogonalization and Jennrich-Bentler Analytic Rotations. *Multivariate Behavioral Research*, 51, 698–717.

Maraun, M. D. 1998. Measurement as a Normative Practice – Implications of Wittgenstein's Philosophy for Measurement in Psychology. *Theory & Psychology*, 8, 435–461.

McCall, W. A. 1939. *Measurement*. Oxford: Macmillan.

McConville, C. & Cooper, C. 1992. Mood Variability and Personality. *Personality and Individual Differences*, 13, 1213–1221.

McCrae, R. R. & Costa, P. T. 1983. Social Desirability Scales – More Substance Than Style. *Journal of Consulting and Clinical Psychology*, 51, 882–888.

McCrae, R. R. & John, O. P. 1992. An Introduction to the 5-Factor Model and Its Applications. *Journal of Personality*, 60, 175–215.

McCrae, R. R., Zonderman, A. B., Bond, M. H., Costa, P. T. & Paunonen, S. V. 1996. Evaluating Replicability of Factors in the Revised NEO Personality Inventory: Confirmatory Factor Analysis Versus Procrustes Rotation. *Journal of Personality and Social Psychology*, 70, 552–566.

McDonald, R. P. & Burr, E. J. 1967. A Comparison of Four Methods of Constructing Factor Scores. *Psychometrika*, 32, 381–401.

McFarland, L. A. 2003. Warning against Faking on a Personality Test: Effects on Applicant Reactions and Personality Test Scores. *International Journal of Selection and Assessment*, 11, 265–276.

McFarland, L. A. & Ryan, A. M. 2000. Variance in Faking across Noncognitive Measures. *Journal of Applied Psychology*, 85, 812–821.

McGrath, R. E., Mitchell, M., Kim, B. H. & Hough, L. 2010. Evidence for Response Bias as a Source of Error Variance in Applied Assessment. *Psychological Bulletin*, 136, 450–470.

Meade, A. W. 2004. Psychometric Problems and Issues Involved with Creating and Using Ipsative Measures for Selection. *Journal of Occupational & Organizational Psychology*, 77, 531–551.

Meade, A. W. & Craig, S. B. 2012. Identifying Careless Responses in Survey Data. *Psychological Methods*, 17, 437–455.

Michell, J. 1997a. Quantitative Science and the Definition of Measurement in Psychology. *British Journal of Psychology*, 88, 355–383.

Michell, J. 1997b. Quantitative Science and the Definition of Measurement in Psychology – Reply. *British Journal of Psychology*, 88, 401–406.

Michell, J. 2000. Normal Science, Pathological Science and Psychometrics. *Theory & Psychology*, 10, 639–667.

Michell, J. 2004. Item Response Models, Pathological Science and the Shape of Error – Reply to Borsboom and Mellenbergh. *Theory & Psychology*, 14, 121–129.

Michell, J. 2014. The Rasch Paradox, Conjoint Measurement, and Psychometrics: Response to Humphry and Sijtsma. *Theory & Psychology*, 24, 111–123.

Michell, J. & Ernst, C. 1997. The Axioms of Quantity and the Theory of Measurement. *Journal of Mathematical Psychology*, 41, 345–356.

Miller, G. A. 1956. The Magical Number Seven, Plus or Minus Two: Some Limits on Our Capacity for Processing Information. *Psychological Review*, 63, 81–97.

Millsap, R. E. & Everson, H. T. 1993. Methodology Review – Statistical Approaches for Assessing Measurement Bias. *Applied Psychological Measurement*, 17, 297–334.

Mischel, W. 1968. *Personality and Assessment*. New York: Wiley.

Mokken, R. J. 1971. *A Theory and Procedure of Scale Analysis with Applications in Political Research*. New York: Mouton.

Mokken, R. J. & Lewis, C. 1982. A Nonparametric Approach to the Analysis of Dichotomous Item Responses. *Applied Psychological Measurement*, 6, 417–430.

Most, R. B. & Zeidner, M. 1995. Constructing Personality and Intelligence Instruments: Methods and Issues. *In:* D. H. Saklofske & M. Zeidner (eds.) *International Handbook of Personality and Intelligence*. New York: Plenum.

Narayan, S. & Krosnick, J. A. 1996. Education Moderates Some Response Effects in Attitude Measurement. *Public Opinion Quarterly*, 60, 58–88.

Newman, D. A. 2014. Missing Data: Five Practical Guidelines. *Organizational Research Methods*, 17, 372–411.

Nunnally, J. C. 1978. *Psychometric Theory*. New York: McGraw-Hill.

Olkin, I. & Finn, J. D. 1995. Correlations Redux. *Psychological Bulletin*, 118, 155–164.

Olsson, U. 1979. Maximum Likelihood Estimation of the Polychloric Correlation Coefficient. *Psychometrika*, 44, 443–460.

Ones, D. S., Viswesvaran, C. & Reiss, A. D. 1996. Role of Social Desirability in Personality Testing for Personnel Selection: The Red Herring. *Journal of Applied Psychology*, 81, 660–679.

Ortner, T. M. 2008. Effects of Changed Item Order: A Cautionary Note to Practitioners on Jumping to Computerized Adaptive Testing for Personality Assessment. *International Journal of Selection and Assessment*, 16, 249–257.

Osterlind, S. J. 1983. *Test Item Bias*. Beverly Hills, CA: Sage Publications.

Partchev, I., De Boeck, P. & Steyer, R. 2013. How Much Power and Speed Is Measured in This Test? *Assessment*, 20, 242–252.

Paulhus, D. L. 1984. 2-Component Models of Socially Desirable Responding. *Journal of Personality and Social Psychology*, 46, 598–609.

Paulhus, D. L. 1998. *Paulhus Deception Scales (PDS): The Balanced Inventory of Desirable Responding – User's Manual*. North Tanawanda, NY: Multi-Health Systems.

Paulhus, D. L. 2002. Social Desirable Responding: The Evolution of a Construct. *In:* H. I. Brown, D. N. Jackson & D. E. Wiley (eds.) *The Role of Constructs in Psychological and Educational Measurement*. Mahwah, NJ: Erlbaum.

Paunonen, S. V. 1997. On Chance and Factor Congruence Following Orthogonal Procrustes Rotation. *Educational and Psychological Measurement*, 57, 33–59.

Paunonen, S. V. & Lebel, E. P. 2012. Socially Desirable Responding and Its Elusive Effects on the Validity of Personality Assessments. *Journal of Personality and Social Psychology*, 103, 158–175.

Paunonen, S. V., Jackson, D. N. & Keinonen, M. 1990. The Structured Nonverbal Assessment of Personality. *Journal of Personality*, 58, 481–502.

Payne, W. L. (1983). A Study of Emotion: Developing Emotional Intelligence; Self Integration; Relating to Fear, Pain and Desire. Department of Psychology. Cincinnati, Ohio, Union Graduate School. PhD.

Pedregon, C. A., Farley, R. L., Davis, A., Wood, J. M. & Clark, R. D. 2012. Social Desirability, Personality Questionnaires, and the 'Better Than Average' Effect. *Personality and Individual Differences*, 52, 213–217.

Perczek, R., Carver, C. S., Price, A. A. & Pozo-Kaderman, C. 2000. Coping, Mood, and Aspects of Personality in Spanish Translation and Evidence of Convergence with English Versions. *Journal of Personality Assessment*, 74, 63–87.

Perline, R., Wright, B. D. & Wainer, H. 1979. The Rasch Model as Additive Conjoint Measurement. *Applied Psychological Measurement*, 3, 237–255.

Pettigrew, T. F. & Meertens, R. W. 1995. Subtle and Blatant Prejudice in Western Europe. *European Journal of Social Psychology*, 25, 57–75.

Plomin, R. & Bergeman, C. S. 1991. The Nature of Nurture – Genetic Influence on Environmental Measures. *Behavioral and Brain Sciences*, 14, 373–385.

Podsakoff, P. M., Mackenzie, S. B., Lee, J. Y. & Podsakoff, N. P. 2003. Common Method Biases in Behavioral Research: A Critical Review of the Literature and Recommended Remedies. *Journal of Applied Psychology*, 88, 879–903.

Polit, D. F. 2014. Getting Serious About Test–Retest Reliability: A Critique of Retest Research and Some Recommendations. *Quality of Life Research*, 23, 1713–1720.

Press, W. H., Teukolsky, S. A., Yetterling, W. T. & Flannery, B. P. 1993. *Numerical Recipes in Fortran*. Cambridge: Cambridge University Press.

R Core Team. 2013. *R: A Language and Environment for Statistical Computing*. Vienna: R Foundation for Statistical Computing.

Rammstedt, B., Danner, D. & Bosnjak, M. 2017. Acquiescence Response Styles: A Multilevel Model Explaining Individual-Level and Country-Level Differences. *Personality and Individual Differences*, 107, 190–194.

Rasch, G. 1960. *Probabilistic Models for Some Intelligence and Attainment Tests*. Copenhagen: Danmarks Paedogogiske Institut.

Raven, J., Raven, J. C. & Court, J. H. 2003. *Manual for Raven's Progressive Matrices and Vocabulary Scales*. Oxford: Oxford Psychologists Press.

Raykov, T. 1997. Estimation of Composite Reliability for Congeneric Measures. *Applied Psychological Measurement*, 21, 173–184.

Raykov, T. 2004. Point and Interval Estimation of Reliability for Multiple-Component Measuring Instruments Via Linear Constraint Covariance Structure Modeling. *Structural Equation Modeling: A Multidisciplinary Journal*, 11, 342–356.

Reise, S. P. 2012. The Rediscovery of Bifactor Measurement Models. *Multivariate Behavioral Research*, 47, 667–696.

Revelle, W. 2017a. *Apply the Kaiser Normalization When Rotating Factors*. Evanston, IL: Personality Project, North Western University.

Revelle, W. 2017b. *Determining the Optimal Number of Interpretable Factors by Using Very Simple Structure*. Evanston, IL: Personality Project, North Western University.

Revelle, W. 2017c. *Psych: Procedures for Personality and Psychological Research*. Evanston, IL: Personality Project, North Western University.

Revelle, W. & Rocklin, T. 1979. Very Simple Structure: An Alternative Procedure for Estimating the Optimal Number of Interpretable Factors. *Multivariate Behavioral Research*, 14, 403–414.

Reynolds, C. R. & Suzuki, L. A. 2013. Bias in Psychological Assessment: An Empirical Review and Recommendations. *In:* I. B. Weiner, J. R. Graham & J. A. Naglieri (eds.) *Handbook of Psychology: Assessment Psychology*, Vol 10. 2nd ed. Hoboken, NJ: John Wiley & Sons.

Robins, R. W., Hendin, H. M. & Trzesniewski, K. H. 2001. Measuring Global Self-Esteem: Construct Validation of a Single-Item Measure and the Rosenberg Self-Esteem Scale. *Personality and Social Psychology Bulletin*, 27, 151–161.

Robinson, E. V. & Rogers, R. 2015. Empathy Faking in Psychopathic Offenders: The Vulnerability of Empathy Measures. *Journal of Psychopathology and Behavioral Assessment*, 37, 545–552.

Roddy, S., Stewart, I. & Barnes-Holmes, D. 2010. Anti-Fat, Pro-Slim, or Both? Using Two Reaction-Time Based Measures to Assess Implicit Attitudes to the Slim and Overweight. *Journal of Health Psychology*, 15, 416–425.

Rosenbaum, P. J. & Valsiner, J. 2011. The Un-Making of a Method: From Rating Scales to the Study of Psychological Processes. *Theory & Psychology*, 21, 47–65.

Rosenberg, M. 1965. *Society and the Adolescent Self-Image*. Princeton, NJ: Princeton University Press.

Roskam, E. E., Vandenwollenberg, A. L. & Jansen, P. G. W. 1986. The Mokken Scale: A Critical Discussion. *Applied Psychological Measurement*, 10, 265–277.

Rudner, L. M. 1974. A Closer Look at Latent Trait Parameter Invariance. *Annual Meeting of the New England Educational Research Organization, May 4–7, 1974*. Manchester, NH.

Rupp, A. A. & Zumbo, B. D. 2006. Understanding Parameter Invariance in Unidimensional IRT Models. *Educational and Psychological Measurement*, 66, 63–84.

Ryan, A. M. & Ployhart, R. E. 2000. Applicants' Perceptions of Selection Procedures and Decisions: A Critical Review and Agenda for the Future. *Journal of Management*, 26, 565–606.

Sackett, P. R. & Yang, H. 2000. Correction for Range Restriction: An Expanded Typology. *Journal of Applied Psychology*, 85, 112–118.

Salzberger, T. 2010. Does the Rasch Model Convert an Ordinal Scale into an Interval Scale? *Rasch Measurement*, 24, 1273–1275.

Sass, D. A. & Schmitt, T. A. 2010. A Comparative Investigation of Rotation Criteria within Exploratory Factor Analysis. *Multivariate Behavioral Research*, 45, 73–103.

Schinka, J. A. 2012. Further Issues in Determining the Readability of Self-Report Items: Comment on McHugh and Behar (2009). *Journal of Consulting and Clinical Psychology*, 80, 952–955.

Schmid, J. & Leiman, J. M. 1957. The Development of Hierarchical Factor Solutions. *Psychometrika*, 22, 53–61.

Shearer, C. B. 2007. *The MIDAS: A Professional Manual*. Dayton, OH: Greyden Press.

Shrout, P. E. & Fleiss, J. L. 1979. Intraclass Correlations: Uses in Assessing Rater Reliability. *Psychological Bulletin*, 86, 420–428.

Sijtsma, K. 1998. Methodology Review: Nonparametric IRT Approaches to the Analysis of Dichotomous Item Scores. *Applied Psychological Measurement*, 22, 3–31.

Sijtsma, K. I. & Van Der Ark, L. A. 2017. A Tutorial on How to Do a Mokken Scale Analysis on Your Test and Questionnaire Data. *British Journal of Mathematical & Statistical Psychology*, 70, 137–158.

Simons, D. J., Shoda, Y. & Lindsay, D. S. 2017. Constraints on Generality: A Proposed Addition to All Empirical Papers. *Perspectives on Psychological Science*, 12, 1123–1128.

Sjoberg, L. 2015. Correction for Faking in Self-Report Personality Tests. *Scandinavian Journal of Psychology*, 56, 582–591.

Slough, N., Kleinknecht, R. A. & Thorndike, R. M. 1984. Relationship of the Repression-Sensitization Scales to Anxiety. *Journal of Personality Assessment*, 48, 378–379.

Spector, P. E. 1992. *Summated Rating Scale Construction*. Newbury Park, CA: Sage.

Steinberg, L. 1994. Context and Serial-Order Effects in Personality Measurement – Limits on the Generality of Measuring Changes the Measure. *Journal of Personality and Social Psychology*, 66, 341–349.

Stephenson, W. 1953. *The Study of Behavior*. Chicago, IL: University of Chicago Press.

Sternberg, R. J. 2004. Culture and Intelligence. *American Psychologist*, 59, 325–338.

Stevens, S. S. 1946. On the Theory of Scales of Measurement. *Science*, 103, 677–680.

Swaminathan, H. & Gifford, J. A. 1983. Estimation of Parameters in the Three-Parameter Latent Trait Model. *In:* D. Weiss (ed.) *New Horizons in Testing*. New York: Academic Press.

Tabachnick, B. G. & Fidell, L. S. 2007. *Using Multivariate Statistics*. Boston, MA: Allyn & Bacon.

Thorndike, R. L. 1985. The Central Role of General Ability in Prediction. *Multivariate Behavioral Research*, 1985, 241–254.

Thurstone, L. L. 1947. *Multiple Factor Analysis: A Development and Expansion of the Vectors of Mind*. Chicago, IL: University of Chicago Press.

Tran, U. S. & Formann, A. K. 2009. Performance of Parallel Analysis in Retrieving Unidimensionality in the Presence of Binary Data. *Educational and Psychological Measurement*, 69, 50–61.

Traub, R. E. 1983. A Priori Considerations in Choosing an Item Response Model. *In:* R. K. Hambleton (ed.) *Applications of Item Response Theory*. Vancouver: Educational Research Institute of British Columbia.

Trott, D. & Jackson, D. N. 1967. An Experimental Analysis of Acquiescence. *Journal of Experimental Research in Personality*, 2, 278–288.

Tucker, L. R. 1966. Some Mathematical Notes on Three-Mode Factor Analysis. *Psychometrika*, 31, 279–311.

Tulsky, D. S., Zhu, J. & Prifitera, A. 2000. Assessment of Adult Intelligence with the Wais-III. *In:* G. Goldstein & M. Hersen (eds.) *Handbook of Psychological Assessment*. 3rd ed. Amsterdam; Oxford: Pergamon.

Uziel, L. 2010. Rethinking Social Desirability Scales: From Impression Management to Interpersonally Oriented Self-Control. *Perspectives on Psychological Science*, 5, 243–262.

Van Schuur, W. H. 2003. Mokken Scale Analysis: Between the Guttman Scale and Parametric Item Response Theory. *Political Analysis*, 11, 139–163.

Vaz, S., Falkmer, T., Passmore, A. E., Parsons, R. & Andreou, P. 2013. The Case for Using the Repeatability Coefficient When Calculating Test-Retest Reliability. *Plos One*, 8. DOI 10.1371/journal.pone.0073990.

Vegelius, J. 1973. *Correlation Coefficients as Scalar Products in Euclidean Spaces* (Report 145). Uppsala: University of Uppsala, Department of Psychology.

Velicer, W. F. 1976. Determining the Number of Components from the Matrix of Partial Correlations. *Psychometrika*, 41, 321–327.

Velicer, W. F. & Jackson, D. N. 1990. Component Analysis Versus Common Factor Analysis: Some Issues in Selecting an Appropriate Procedure. *Multivariate Behavioral Research*, 25, 1–28.

Velicer, W. F., Eaton, C. A. & Fava, J. L. 2000. Construct Explication through Factor or Component Analysis: A Review and Evaluation of Alternative Procedures for Determining the Number of Factors or Components. *In:* R. D. Goffin & E. Helmes (eds.) *Problems and Solutions in Human Assessment: Honoring Douglas N. Jackson at Seventy*. Boston, MA: Kluwer Academic Publishers.

Vernon, P. E. 1961. *Intelligence and Attainment Tests*. New York: Philosophical Library.

Wainer, H. 1978. Sensitivity of Regression and Regressors. *Psychological Bulletin*, 85, 267–273.

Wainer, H. 2014. *Computerized Adaptive Testing: A Primer*. New York: Routledge.

Weirich, S., Hecht, M., Penk, C., Roppelt, A. & Bohme, K. 2017. Item Position Effects Are Moderated by Changes in Test-Taking Effort. *Applied Psychological Measurement*, 41, 115–129.

Wind, S. A. 2017. An Instructional Module on Mokken Scale Analysis. *Educational Measurement: Issues and Practice*, 36, 50–66.

Wright, B. D. 1984. Despair and Hope for Educational Measurement. *Research Memorandum 41*. Chicago: MESA Laboratory.

Wright, B. D. 1985. Additivity in Psychological Measurement. *In:* E. Roskam (ed.) *Measurement and Personality Assessment*. Amsterdam: North Holland.

Wright, B. D. & Linacre, J. 1989. Observations Are Always Ordinal; Measurements, However, Must Be Interval. *Archives of Physical Medicine and Rehabilitation*, 70, 857–860.

Yu, P. L. H., Lam, K. F. & Lo, S. M. 2005. Factor Analysis for Ranked Data with Application to a Job Selection Attitude Survey. *Journal of the Royal Statistical Society Series A – Statistics in Society*, 168, 583–597.

Zumbo, B. D., Gadermann, A. M. & Zeisser, C. 2007. Ordinal Versions of Coefficients Alpha and Theta for Likert Rating Scales. *Journal of Modern Applied Statistical Methods*, 6, 21–29.

Zwick, W. R. & Velicer, W. F. 1986. Comparison of Five Rules for Determining the Number of Components to Retain. *Psychological Bulletin*, 99, 432–442.

INDEX